Ford Esc

Mexico and RS

Owners

Workshop

Manual

I M Coomber

Models covered:
All Ford Escort Mk II Mexico and RS models 1593 cc, 1834 cc and
1993 cc; sohc and dohc

ISBN 0 85696 735 1

ABCDE
FGHIJ
KLMNO
PQRST

Printed in England

THE
BOOK

HAYNES PUBLISHING GROUP
SPARKFORD YEOVIL SOMERSET BA22 7JJ ENGLAND
distributed in the USA by
HAYNES PUBLICATIONS INC
861 LAWRENCE DRIVE
NEWBURY PARK
CALIFORNIA 91320
USA

Acknowledgements

Thanks are due to the Ford Motor Company Limited for the supply of certain illustrations and technical material, to Castrol Limited who provided lubrication data and to the Champion Sparking Plug Company Limited who provided the colour illustrations showing the various spark plug conditions.

Thanks are also due to City Speed of Gloucester (a Rallye Sport dealer) for their help in providing information on the RS 1800. Peter Vallis kindly loaned his RS2000 for part of the workshop project.

Last, but not least, thanks are due to all those people at Sparkford who assisted in the production of this manual.

About this manual

Its aim

The aim of this manual is to help you get the best value from your vehicle. It can do so in several ways. It can help you decide what work must be done (even should you choose to get it done by a garage), provide information on routine maintenance and servicing, and give a logical course of action and diagnosis when random faults occur. However, it is hoped that you will use the manual by tackling the work yourself. On simpler jobs it may even be quicker than booking the car into a garage and going there twice, to leave and collect it. Perhaps most important, a lot of money can be saved by avoiding the costs a garage must charge to cover its labour and overheads.

The manual has drawings and descriptions to show the function of the various components so that their layout can be understood. Then the tasks are described and photographed in a step-by-step sequence so that even a novice can do the work.

Its arrangement

The manual is divided into twelve Chapters, each covering a logical sub-division of the vehicle. The Chapters are each divided into Sections, numbered with single figures, eg 5; and the Sections into paragraphs (or sub-sections), with decimal numbers following on from the Section they are in, eg 5.1, 5.2, 5.3 etc.

It is freely illustrated, especially in those parts where there is a detailed sequence of operations to be carried out. There are two forms of illustration: figures and photographs. The figures are numbered in sequence with decimal numbers, according to their position in the Chapter – eg Fig. 6.4 is the fourth drawing/illustration in Chapter 6. Photographs carry the same number (either individually or in related groups) as the Section or sub-section to which they relate.

There is an alphabetical index at the back of the manual as well as a contents list at the front. Each Chapter is also preceded by its own individual contents list.

References to the 'left' or 'right' of the vehicle are in the sense of a person in the driver's seat facing forwards.

Unless otherwise stated, nuts and bolts are removed by turning anti-clockwise, and tightened by turning clockwise.

Vehicle manufacturers continually make changes to specifications and recommendations, and these, when notified, are incorporated into our manuals at the earliest opportunity.

Whilst every care is taken to ensure that the information in this manual is correct, no liability can be accepted by the authors or publishers for loss, damage or injury caused by any errors in, or omissions from, the information given.

Introduction to the Ford Escort Mexico and RS models

This manual covers the three Ford Rallye Sport Escort models produced between 1975 and 1980 in the Mk II Escort bodyshell.

The RS 1800, designated the ATS Series, was the first to be introduced in March 1975. Fitted with the enlarged Cosworth designed BDA engine, it has a simpler carburation system than its predecessor, the MK I RS 1600, a single twin venturi Weber being fitted. As with the RS 1600, the RS 1800 engine is somewhat unusual for a road car in having four valves per cylinder (two inlet and two exhaust). The valves are operated by twin overhead camshafts which are belt-driven from the crankshaft. Both the engine and the cylinder block are manufactured in aluminium alloy.

The Mk II Escort Mexico and RS 2000 variants were first introduced in January 1976 and were produced in Ford's German factory in Saarlouis. The RS 1800 was also produced in the German factory from that time.

Both the 1.6 litre Mexico and the RS 2000 model are fitted with the single OHC 'Pinto' engine, similar to that fitted to other Ford models such as the Cortina and Capri.

All models are fitted with the Ford type 'B' gearbox, but the ratios differ in the RS 1800.

The rear axle is also the same type for all models, this being the Ford type 'C' axle (semi-floating hypoid).

Brakes, steering and suspension systems are the same on all three models (in standard trim).

Of the three models, the RS 2000 is the most easily recognised, being distinguished by the four headlights set in the distinctive wedge-shaped front panel, which is a single piece design manufactured in polyurethane. The wheels of the RS 2000 also differ, being alloy with a cross-pattern design, whereas the other two models are fitted with silver painted steel wheels. Other features applicable only to the RS 2000 are the twin high-backed front seats and also some facia and trim differences.

All models are fitted with a boot mounted spoiler. As for all Ford models, a wide variety of optional extras is available for these Escort models, in particular items to improve performance for the sporting motorist. In this manual, however, we have confined the details given to the models produced in their standard guise.

Contents

Ford Escort Mexico

Ford Escort RS 1800

Ford Escort RS 2000

General dimensions, weights and capacities

Dimensions

Overall length:	
Mexico and RS 1800	155.2 in (3.94 m)
RS 2000	161.8 in (4.11 m)
Overall width	61.6 in (1.57 m)
Overall height	55.0 in (1.40 m)
Wheelbase	94.0 in (2.39 m)
Track - front wheels	50.3 in (1.28 m)
Track - rear wheels	51.1 in (1.30 m)
Turning circle (kerb to kerb)	32.8 ft (10.0 m)

Kerb weight

Mexico	1991 lb (904 kg)
RS 1800	1984 lb (901 kg)
RS 2000	2035 lb (924 kg)

Capacities

	RS 2000 and Mexico	RS 1800
Engine:		
Oil change - with filter	6.6 pints (3.75 litres)	7.5 pints (4.25 litres)
Oil change - less filter	5.7 pints (3.25 litres)	6.8 pints (3.87 litres)
Oil cooler capacity		0.75 pints (0.43 litres)
Gearbox	2.4 pints (1.35 litres)	
Rear axle	1.6 pints (0.9 litres)	
Cooling system (including heater):		
Mexico	10.2 pints (5.76 litres)	
RS 2000	10.8 pints (6.13 litres)	
RS 1800	12 pints (6.8 litres)	
Fuel tank capacity	9 gallons (41 litres)	
Effective luggage capacity	10.3 cu ft (0.3 cu m)	

Buying spare parts
and vehicle identification numbers

Buying spare parts

Spare parts are available from many sources, for example: Ford garages, other garages and accessory shops, and motor factors. Our advice regarding spare part sources is as follows:

Officially appointed Ford garages and Ford Rallye Sport dealers: These will be the best source of parts which are peculiar to your car and are otherwise not generally available (eg complete cylinder heads, internal gearbox components, badges, interior trim etc). To be sure of obtaining the correct parts it will always be necessary to give the storeman your car's vehicle identification number, and if possible, to take the 'old' part along for positive identification. This is particularly applicable to the Mexico and RS Series Escorts where special tuning or other modifications may have been made. Remember that many parts are available on a factory exchange scheme — any parts returned should always be clean! It obviously makes good sense to go straight to the specialists on your car for this type of part for they are best equipped to supply you.

Other garages and accessory shops: These are often very good places to buy materials and components needed for the maintenance of your car (eg oil filters, spark plugs, bulbs, fan belts, oils and greases, touch-up paint, filler paste etc). They also sell general accessories, usually have convenient opening hours, charge lower prices and can often be found not far from home.

Motor factors: Good factors will stock all of the more important components which wear out relatively quickly (eg clutch components, pistons, valves, exhaust systems, brake cylinders/-pipes/hoses/seals/shoes and pads etc). Motor factors will often provide new or reconditioned components on a part exchange basis — this can save a considerable amount of money.

Vehicle identification numbers

Although many individual parts, and in some cases sub-assemblies, fit a number of different models it is dangerous to assume that just because they look the same, they are the same. Differences are not always easy to detect except by serial numbers. Make sure therefore, that the appropriate identity number for the model or sub-assembly is known and quoted when a spare part is ordered.

The vehicle identification plate is mounted on the right-hand side of the front body panel (RS 1800 and Mexico), or on the inner right-hand wing panel (RS 2000), and may be seen once the bonnet is opened.

Tools and working facilities

Introduction

A selection of good tools is a fundamental requirement for anyone contemplating the maintenance and repair of a motor vehicle. For the owner who does not possess any, their purchase will prove a considerable expense, offsetting some of the savings made by doing-it-yourself. However, provided that the tools purchased are of good quality, they will last for many years and prove an extremely worthwhile investment.

To help the average owner to decide which tools are needed to carry out the various tasks detailed in this manual, we have compiled three lists of tools under the following headings: *Maintenance and minor repair*, *Repair and overhaul*, and *Special*. The newcomer to practical mechanics should start off with the *Maintenance and minor repair* tool kit and confine himself to the simpler jobs around the vehicle. Then, as his confidence and experience grow, he can undertake more difficult tasks, buying extra tools as, and when, they are needed. In this way, a *Maintenance and minor repair* tool kit can be built-up into a *Repair and overhaul* tool kit over a considerable period of time without any major cash outlays. The experienced do-it-yourselfer will have a tool kit good enough for most repair and overhaul procedures and will add tools from the *Special* category when he feels the expense is justified by the amount of use to which these tools will be put.

It is obviously not possible to cover the subject of tools fully here. For those who wish to learn more about tools and their use there is a book entitled *How to Choose and Use Car Tools* available from the publishers of this manual.

Maintenance and minor repair tool kit

The tools given in this list should be considered as a minimum requirement if routine maintenance, servicing and minor repair operations are to be undertaken. We recommend the purchase of combination spanners (ring one end, open-ended the other); although more expensive than open-ended ones, they do give the advantages of both types of spanner.

> Combination spanners - $\frac{7}{16}$, $\frac{1}{2}$, $\frac{9}{16}$, $\frac{5}{8}$, $\frac{11}{16}$, $\frac{3}{4}$ in AF
> Combination spanners - 10, 11, 12, 13, 14 & 17 mm
> Adjustable spanner - 9 inch
> Gearbox/rear axle filler plug key
> Spark plug spanner (with rubber insert)
> Spark plug gap adjustment tool
> Set of feeler gauges
> Brake bleed nipple spanner
> Screwdriver - 4 in long x $\frac{1}{4}$ in dia (flat blade)
> Screwdriver - 4 in long x $\frac{1}{4}$ in dia (cross blade)
> Combination pliers - 6 inch
> Hacksaw (junior)
> Tyre pump
> Tyre pressure gauge
> Grease gun
> Oil can
> Fine emery cloth (1 sheet)
> Wire brush (small)
> Funnel (medium size)

Repair and overhaul tool kit

These tools are virtually essential for anyone undertaking any major repairs to a motor vehicle, and are additional to those given in the *Maintenance and minor repair* list. Included in this list is a comprehensive set of sockets. Although these are expensive they will be found invaluable as they are so versatile - particularly if various drives are included in the set. We recommend the $\frac{1}{2}$ in square-drive type, as this can be used with most proprietary torque wrenches. If you cannot afford a socket set, even bought piecemeal, then inexpensive tubular box spanners are a useful alternative.

The tools in this list will occasionally need to be supplemented by tools from the *Special* list.

> Sockets (or box spanners) to cover range in previous list
> Reversible ratchet drive (for use with sockets)
> Extension piece, 10 inch (for use with sockets)
> Universal joint (for use with sockets)
> Torque wrench (for use with sockets)
> 'Mole' wrench - 8 inch
> Ball pein hammer
> Soft-faced hammer, plastic or rubber
> Screwdriver - 6 in long x $\frac{5}{16}$ in dia (flat blade)
> Screwdriver - 2 in long x $\frac{5}{16}$ in dia (flat blade)
> Screwdriver - 1$\frac{1}{2}$ in long x $\frac{1}{4}$ in square (flat blade)
> Screwdriver - 3 in long x $\frac{1}{8}$ in dia (electricians)
> Pliers - electricians side cutters
> Pliers - needle nosed
> Pliers - circlip (internal and external)
> Cold chisel - $\frac{1}{2}$ inch
> Scriber
> Scraper
> Centre punch
> Pin punch
> Hacksaw
> Valve grinding tool
> Steel rule/straight-edge
> Allen keys and splined bolt keys
> Selection of files
> Wire brush (large)
> Axle-stands
> Jack (strong scissor or hydraulic type)

Special tools

The tools in this list are those which are not used regularly, are expensive to buy, or which need to be used in accordance with their manufacturers' instructions. Unless relatively difficult mechanical jobs are undertaken frequently, it will not be economic to buy many of these tools. Where this is the case, you could consider clubbing together with friends (or joining a motorists' club) to make a joint purchase, or borrowing the tools against a deposit from a local garage or tool hire specialist.

The following list contains only those tools and instruments freely available to the public, and not those special tools produced by the vehicle manufacturer specifically for its dealer network. You will find occasional references to these manufacturers' special tools in the text of this manual. Generally, an alternative method of doing the job without the vehicle manufacturers' special tool is given. However, sometimes, there is no alternative to using them. Where this is the case and the relevant tool cannot be bought or borrowed, you will have to entrust the work to a franchised garage.

> Valve spring compressor
> Piston ring compressor
> Balljoint separator
> Universal hub/bearing puller
> Impact screwdriver
> Micrometer and/or vernier gauge
> Dial gauge
> Stroboscopic timing light
> Dwell angle meter/tachometer
> Universal electrical multi-meter
> Cylinder compression gauge
> Lifting tackle (photo)
> Trolley jack
> Light with extension lead

Buying tools

For practically all tools, a tool factor is the best source since he will have a very comprehensive range compared with the average garage or accessory shop. Having said that, accessory shops often offer excellent quality tools at discount prices, so it pays to shop around.

Remember, you don't have to buy the most expensive items on the shelf, but it is always advisable to steer clear of the very cheap tools. There are plenty of good tools around at reasonable prices, so ask the proprietor or manager of the shop for advice before making a purchase.

Care and maintenance of tools

Having purchased a reasonable tool kit, it is necessary to keep the tools in a clean serviceable condition. After use, always wipe off any dirt, grease and metal particles using a clean, dry cloth, before putting the tools away. Never leave them lying around after they have been used. A simple tool rack on the garage or workshop wall, for items such as screwdrivers and pliers is a good idea. Store all normal wrenches and sockets in a metal box. Any measuring instruments, gauges, meters, etc, must be carefully stored where they cannot be damaged or become rusty.

Take a little care when tools are used. Hammer heads inevitably become marked and screwdrivers lose the keen edge on their blades from time to time. A little timely attention with emery cloth or a file will soon restore items like this to a good serviceable finish.

Working facilities

Not to be forgotten when discussing tools, is the workshop itself. If anything more than routine maintenance is to be carried out, some form of suitable working area becomes essential.

It is appreciated that many an owner mechanic is forced by circumstances to remove an engine or similar item, without the benefit of a garage or workshop. Having done this, any repairs should always be done under the cover of a roof.

Wherever possible, any dismantling should be done on a clean, flat workbench or table at a suitable working height.

Any workbench needs a vice: one with a jaw opening of 4 in (100 mm) is suitable for most jobs. As mentioned previously, some clean dry storage space is also required for tools, as well as for lubricants, cleaning fluids, touch-up paints and so on, which become necessary.

Another item which may be required, and which has a much more general usage, is an electric drill with a chuck capacity of at least $\frac{5}{16}$ in (8 mm). This, together with a good range of twist drills, is virtually essential for fitting accessories such as mirrors and reversing lights.

Last, but not least, always keep a supply of old newspapers and clean, lint-free rags available, and try to keep any working area as clean as possible.

Spanner jaw gap comparison table

Jaw gap (in)	Spanner size
0.250	$\frac{1}{4}$ in AF
0.276	7 mm
0.313	$\frac{5}{16}$ in AF
0.315	8 mm
0.344	$\frac{11}{32}$ in AF; $\frac{1}{8}$ in Whitworth
0.354	9 mm
0.375	$\frac{3}{8}$ in AF
0.394	10 mm
0.433	11 mm
0.438	$\frac{7}{16}$ in AF
0.445	$\frac{3}{16}$ in Whitworth; $\frac{1}{4}$ in BSF
0.472	12 mm
0.500	$\frac{1}{2}$ in AF
0.512	13 mm
0.525	$\frac{1}{4}$ in Whitworth; $\frac{5}{16}$ in BSF
0.551	14 mm
0.563	$\frac{9}{16}$ in AF
0.591	15 mm
0.600	$\frac{5}{16}$ in Whitworth; $\frac{3}{8}$ in BSF
0.625	$\frac{5}{8}$ in AF
0.630	16 mm
0.669	17 mm
0.686	$\frac{11}{16}$ in AF
0.709	18 mm
0.710	$\frac{3}{8}$ in Whitworth; $\frac{7}{16}$ in BSF
0.748	19 mm
0.750	$\frac{3}{4}$ in AF
0.813	$\frac{13}{16}$ in AF
0.820	$\frac{7}{16}$ in Whitworth; $\frac{1}{2}$ in BSF
0.866	22 mm
0.875	$\frac{7}{8}$ in AF
0.920	$\frac{1}{2}$ in Whitworth; $\frac{9}{16}$ in BSF
0.938	$\frac{15}{16}$ in AF
0.945	24 mm
1.000	1 in AF
1.010	$\frac{9}{16}$ in Whitworth; $\frac{5}{8}$ in BSF
1.024	26 mm
1.063	$1\frac{1}{16}$ in AF; 27 mm
1.100	$\frac{5}{8}$ in Whitworth; $\frac{11}{16}$ in BSF
1.125	$1\frac{1}{8}$ in AF
1.181	30 mm
1.200	$\frac{11}{16}$ in Whitworth; $\frac{3}{4}$ in BSF
1.250	$1\frac{1}{4}$ in AF
1.260	32 mm
1.300	$\frac{3}{4}$ in Whitworth; $\frac{7}{8}$ in BSF
1.313	$1\frac{5}{16}$ in AF
1.390	$\frac{13}{16}$ in Whitworth; $\frac{15}{16}$ in BSF
1.417	36 mm
1.438	$1\frac{7}{16}$ in AF
1.480	$\frac{7}{8}$ in Whitworth; 1 in BSF
1.500	$1\frac{1}{2}$ in AF
1.575	40 mm; $\frac{15}{16}$ in Whitworth
1.614	41 mm
1.625	$1\frac{5}{8}$ in AF
1.670	1 in Whitworth; $1\frac{1}{8}$ in BSF
1.688	$1\frac{11}{16}$ in AF
1.811	46 mm
1.813	$1\frac{13}{16}$ in AF
1.860	$1\frac{1}{8}$ in Whitworth; $1\frac{1}{4}$ in BSF
1.875	$1\frac{7}{8}$ in AF
1.969	50 mm
2.000	2 in AF
2.050	$1\frac{1}{4}$ in Whitworth; $1\frac{3}{8}$ in BSF
2.165	55 mm
2.362	60 mm

A Haltrac hoist and gantry in use during a typical engine removal sequence

Jacking and Towing

Jacking points

To change a wheel in an emergency, use the jack supplied with the vehicle, standing it on firm level ground. Fully apply the handbrake and chock the diagonally opposite wheel. Loosen the roadwheel nuts then push the jack arm into the sleeve below the side sill panel. Position the jack vertically and turn the handle to raise the wheel off the ground (photo).

Where maintenance or repairs are being carried out, use a hydraulic or screw-type jack located beneath the front crossmember, bodyframe side-members or rear axle casing. Always supplement the jack with axle stands or block before crawling beneath the car.

Towing points

If your vehicle is being towed, attach the tow-rope to the front crossmember or towing eye (where fitted). If you are towing another vehicle, attach the tow-rope to the left-hand side spring seat or towing eye (where fitted). Note that the ignition key must be in position II when being towed so that the steering lock is released. Remember also that brake servo assistance will not be available if the engine is not running.

The Ford jack in position – ensure that it is fully located in its sleeve before raising the car

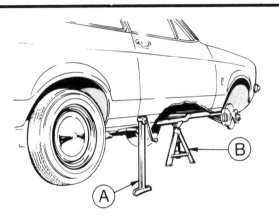

Always supplement a jack (A) with an axle stand (B) when working under the car

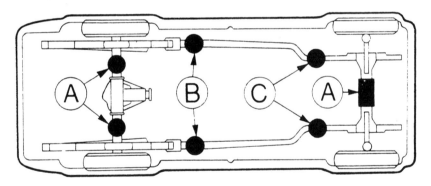

Under-vehicle jack and support points used when undertaking maintenance and repairs

A   Trolley jack lift points
B   Axle stand location points (rear)

C   Axle stand location points (front)

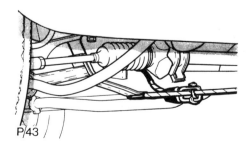

Front tow-rope position – looped around the suspension crossmember (do not loop it round the stabiliser bar)

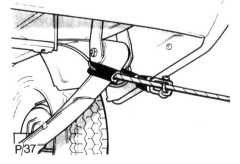

Rear tow-rope position – looped around the right-hand spring, as shown, and not to the shackle itself

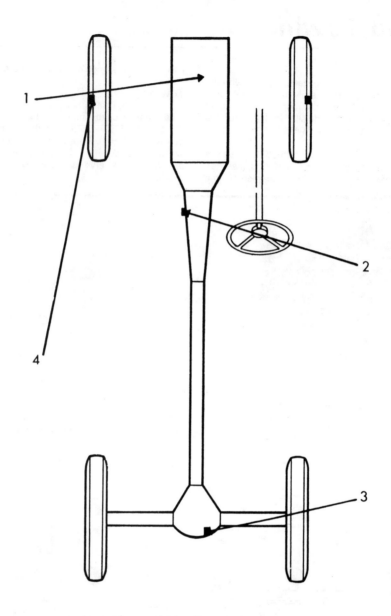

Recommended lubricants and fluids

Component or system	Lubricant type or specification	Castrol product
1 Engine oil	Multigrade engine oil SAE 20W/40, 20W/50	**GTX**
2 Gearbox (all models)	SAE 80 EP	**Hypoy Light**
3 Rear axle (all models)	SAE 90	**Hypoy B EP90**
4 Front wheel bearings	Multi-purpose lithium based grease	**LM Grease**

Note: *The above recommendations are general and are intended for guidance only. Lubrication requirements vary from territory to territory and depend upon vehicle usage. If in doubt, consult the operator's handbook supplied with the vehicle.*

Safety first!

Professional motor mechanics are trained in safe working procedures. However enthusiastic you may be about getting on with the job in hand, do take the time to ensure that your safety is not put at risk. A moment's lack of attention can result in an accident, as can failure to observe certain elementary precautions.

There will always be new ways of having accidents, and the following points do not pretend to be a comprehensive list of all dangers; they are intended rather to make you aware of the risks and to encourage a safety-conscious approach to all work you carry out on your vehicle.

Essential DOs and DON'Ts

DON'T rely on a single jack when working underneath the vehicle. Always use reliable additional means of support, such as axle stands, securely placed under a part of the vehicle that you know will not give way.

DON'T attempt to loosen or tighten high-torque nuts (e.g. wheel hub nuts) while the vehicle is on a jack; it may be pulled off.

DON'T start the engine without first ascertaining that the transmission is in neutral and the parking brake applied.

DON'T suddenly remove the filler cap from a hot cooling system — cover it with a cloth and release the pressure gradually first, or you may get scalded by escaping coolant.

DON'T attempt to drain oil until you are sure it has cooled sufficiently to avoid scalding you.

DON'T grasp any part of the engine or exhaust without first ascertaining that it is sufficiently cool to avoid burning you.

DON'T syphon toxic liquids such as fuel, brake fluid or antifreeze by mouth, or allow them to remain on your skin.

DON'T inhale brake lining dust — it is injurious to health.

DON'T allow any spilt oil or grease to remain on the floor — wipe it up straight away, before someone slips on it.

DON'T use ill-fitting spanners or other tools which may slip and cause injury.

DON'T attempt to lift a heavy component which may be beyond your capability — get assistance.

DON'T rush to finish a job, or take unverified short cuts.

DON'T allow children or animals in or around an unattended vehicle.

DO wear eye protection when using power tools such as drill, sander, bench grinder etc, and when working under the vehicle.

DO use a barrier cream on your hands prior to undertaking dirty jobs — it will protect your skin from infection as well as making the dirt easier to remove afterwards; but make sure your hands aren't left slippery.

DO keep loose clothing (cuffs, tie etc) and long hair well out of the way of moving mechanical parts.

DO remove rings, wristwatch etc, before working on the vehicle — especially the electrical system.

DO ensure that any lifting tackle used has a safe working load rating adequate for the job.

DO keep your work area tidy — it is only too easy to fall over articles left lying around.

DO get someone to check periodically that all is well, when working alone on the vehicle.

DO carry out work in a logical sequence and check that everything is correctly assembled and tightened afterwards.

DO remember that your vehicle's safety affects that of yourself and others. If in doubt on any point, get specialist advice.

IF, in spite of following these precautions, you are unfortunate enough to injure yourself, seek medical attention as soon as possible.

Fire

Remember at all times that petrol (gasoline) is highly flammable. Never smoke, or have any kind of naked flame around, when working on the vehicle. But the risk does not end there — a spark caused by an electrical short-circuit, by two metal surfaces contacting each other, or even by static electricity built up in your body under certain conditions, can ignite petrol vapour, which in a confined space is highly explosive.

Always disconnect the battery earth (ground) terminal before working on any part of the fuel system, and never risk spilling fuel on to a hot engine or exhaust.

It is recommended that a fire extinguisher of a type suitable for fuel and electrical fires is kept handy in the garage or workplace at all times. Never try to extinguish a fuel or electrical fire with water.

Fumes

Certain fumes are highly toxic and can quickly cause unconsciousness and even death if inhaled to any extent. Petrol (gasoline) vapour comes into this category, as do the vapours from certain solvents such as trichloroethylene. Any draining or pouring of such volatile fluids should be done in a well ventilated area.

When using cleaning fluids and solvents, read the instructions carefully. Never use materials from unmarked containers — they may give off poisonous vapours.

Never run the engine of a motor vehicle in an enclosed space such as a garage. Exhaust fumes contain carbon monoxide which is extremely poisonous; if you need to run the engine, always do so in the open air or at least have the rear of the vehicle outside the workplace.

If you are fortunate enough to have the use of an inspection pit, never drain or pour petrol, and never run the engine, while the vehicle is standing over it; the fumes, being heavier than air, will concentrate in the pit with possibly lethal results.

The battery

Never cause a spark, or allow a naked light, near the vehicle's battery. It will normally be giving off a certain amount of hydrogen gas, which is highly explosive.

Always disconnect the battery earth (ground) terminal before working on the fuel or electrical systems.

If possible, loosen the filler plugs or cover when charging the battery from an external source. Do not charge at an excessive rate or the battery may burst.

Take care when topping up and when carrying the battery. The acid electrolyte, even when diluted, is very corrosive and should not be allowed to contact the eyes or skin.

If you ever need to prepare electrolyte yourself, always add the acid slowly to the water, and never the other way round. Protect against splashes by wearing rubber gloves and goggles.

Mains electricity

When using an electric power tool, inspection light etc, which works from the mains, always ensure that the appliance is correctly connected to its plug and that, where necessary, it is properly earthed (grounded). Do not use such appliances in damp conditions and, again, beware of creating a spark or applying excessive heat in the vicinity of fuel or fuel vapour.

Ignition HT voltage

A severe electric shock can result from touching certain parts of the ignition system, such as the HT leads, when the engine is running or being cranked, particularly if components are damp or the insulation is defective. Where an electronic ignition system is fitted, the HT voltage is much higher and could prove fatal.

Routine maintenance

Maintenance is essential for ensuring safety and desirable for the purpose of getting the best in terms of performance and economy from the vehicle. Over the years the need for periodic lubrication – oiling, greasing and so on – has been drastically reduced, if not totally eliminated. This has unfortunately tended to lead some owners to think that because no such action is required the items either no longer exist or will last for ever. This is a serious delusion. It follows therefore that the largest initial element of maintenance is visual examination. This may lead to repairs or renewals. In 1979 the intervals between routine maintenance tasks were increased by the manufacturer, but we have not included these revised schedules as they cannot be recommended for the home mechanic.

Weekly or every 250 miles (400 km), whichever occurs first

Check the engine oil level and top up if necessary (photos)
Check the coolant level in the expansion tank or radiator and top up if necessary (photo)
Check the battery electrolyte level and top up if necessary
Top up the fluid level in the washer reservoir (photo)
Check brake fluid level (photo), investigate any sudden fall in level
Check the operation of all lights
Check the operation of the horn
Check the operation of washers and wipers
Check tyre pressures, including the spare (photo)

Six monthly or every 6000 miles (10 000 km), whichever occurs first

---

Renew the engine oil and oil filter. With car parked on level ground and the engine switched off, but at its normal operating temperature, remove the sump drain plug (photo) and drain the engine oil into a suitable container. While the engine oil is draining, unscrew and remove the oil filter cartridge using a strap wrench, if necessary (Chapter 1, Section 25). Fit the new oil filter, refit and tighten the sump drain plug and refill with the specified grade and quantity of engine oil
Check and adjust if necessary, the engine valve clearances with the engine cold (photo). For the details on the Mexico and RS 2000 models refer to Chapter 1, Section 59, whilst for the RS 1800 reference should be made to Section 76 of Chapter 1
Check all cooling system hoses for security and signs of deterioration. Renew if necessary (Chapter 2)
Check and, if necessary, adjust the drivebelt tension (Chapter 2, Section 10). Also check the alternator mountings
Check the battery terminals for tightness and clean any corrosion from the terminal posts and lead connectors. Lubricate the terminals with petroleum jelly
Remove each spark plug and compare its condition and colour with those illustrated in Chapter 4. Clean and reset the electrolyte gap. As each plug is refitted check the condition of its connector and

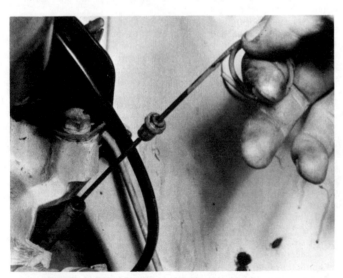

Check engine oil level weekly

Top up engine oil level, but do not exceed the maximum level mark on the oil level gauge

Check radiator coolant level

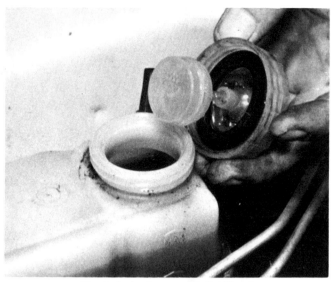

Check the brake reservoir fluid level

Check the windscreen washer reservoir fluid level

Check the tyre pressures

Sump drain plug on the Mexico/RS 2000 engine (arrowed)

Check and, if necessary, adjust the valve clearances (Mexico shown)

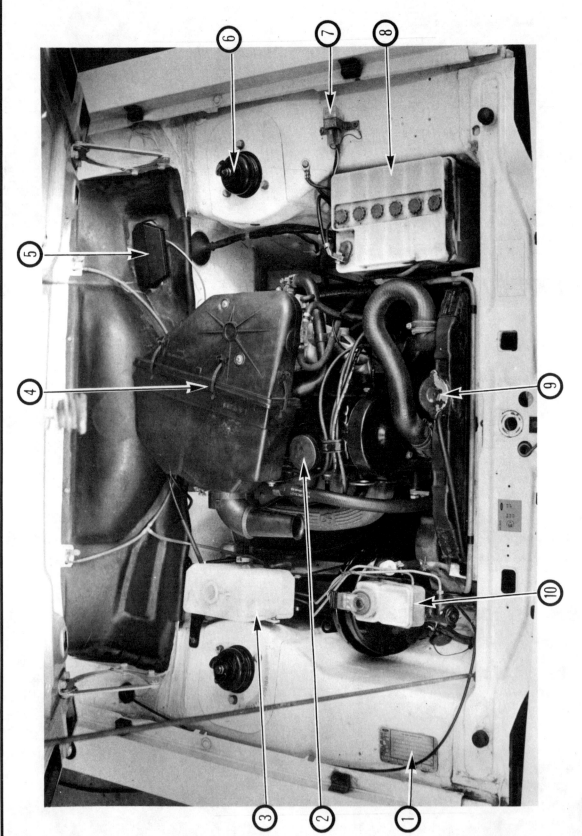

Under-bonnet view – RS 2000

1 Vehicle identification plate
2 Oil filler cap
3 Windscreen washer reservoir

4 Air cleaner
5 Fuse box
6 Suspension strut upper end

7 Auxiliary lamp relay
8 Battery

9 Coolant filler cap
10 Brake master cylinder

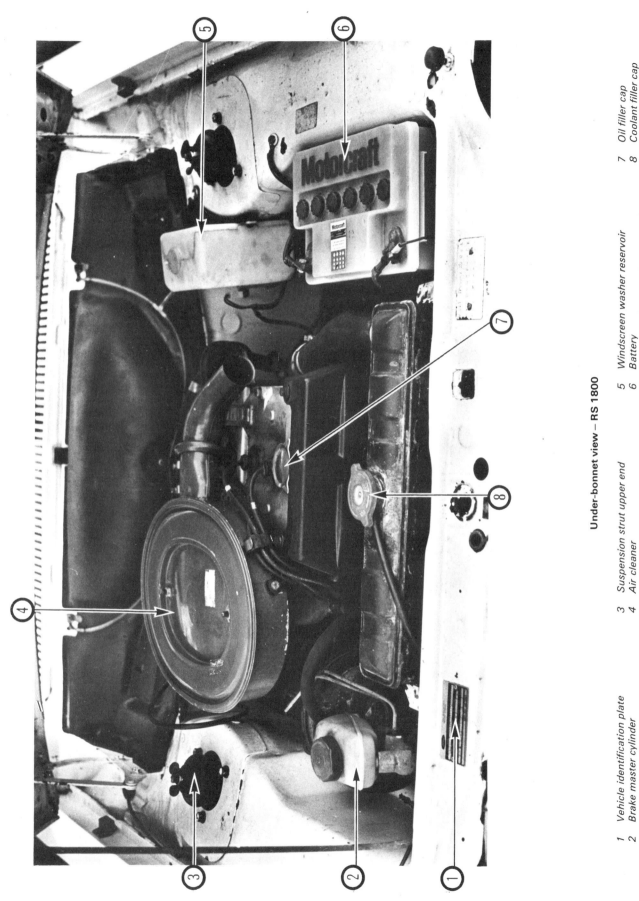

Under-bonnet view – RS 1800

1	Vehicle identification plate	5	Windscreen washer reservoir
2	Brake master cylinder	6	Battery
3	Suspension strut upper end	7	Oil filler cap
4	Air cleaner	8	Coolant filler cap

lead. Also check the HT lead between the coil and the distributor, and the LT leads for condition and security

Check, clean and adjust or renew the distributor contact points (Chapter 4). Clean inside the distributor cap, check the rotor arm for any signs of tracking or cracks, lubricate the distributor centrifugal weights and the felt wick in the spindle. Refit the rotor arm and cap, then check the ignition timing (Chapter 4) and adjust, if necessary

Check the carburettor idle setting and, if the colour of the spark plugs was not correct when removed, adjust the carburettor mixture as necessary (Chapter 3). Apply a small amount of light oil to the carburettor linkages; if necessary adjust the throttle cable

Clean the air filter element (Chapter 3)

Remove the plug on the side of the gearbox casing (photo) and inject oil of the recommended grade until it begins to run out. Refit the plug. Draining of the gearbox is not specified by Ford and no drain plug is provided

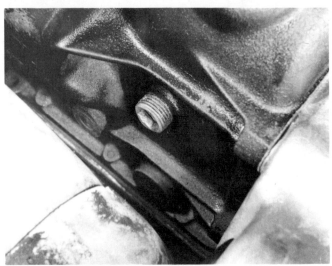

Gearbox oil level/filler plug location

Remove the plug from the rear of the axle casing (photo) and inject the specified oil until it begins to run out. Refit the plug. Draining of the rear axle is not specified by Ford and no drain plug is provided

Check the exhaust system for security and excessive corrosion or damage. Repair and renew as necessary (Chapter 3)

Check the wear of the front disc brake pads and the lining wear of the rear drum brakes (Chapter 9)

Inspect the brake lines for signs of excessive deterioration and renew as necessary

Check that the handbrake operates satisfactorily, lubricate the cable linkages and adjust if necessary

Inspect the steering and suspension components for signs of wear and deterioration (Chapter 11, Section 2)

Check the clutch free movement and, if necessary, adjust (Chapter 5)

Check the operation of all lights, the windscreen wipers (also inspect the wiper blades for excessive wear), and the windscreen washers. Repair or renew as necessary

Check the condition and operation of the seat belts and the security of their anchorage points

Lubricate the door, bonnet and boot lid hinges and locks

Check the tyres for any signs of damage and ensure that the tread depths comply with the regulations (photo). If the tyres are wearing unevenly, have the steering and suspension geometry checked

On RS 2000 models, check the security of the front panel surround fixings

---

Eighteen monthly or every 18 000 miles (30 000 km), whichever occurs first

---

In addition to the work specified above
  Renew the air filter element (Chapter 3, Section 2)
  Remove and clean the PCV valve (Chapter 1, Section 23) and the oil filler cap
  Check that the rear spring U-bolt nuts are tightened to the specified torque

---

Every two years or 24 000 miles (40 000 km), whichever occurs first

---

In addition to the work specified for the 6000 mile service
  Dismantle and inspect the front wheel bearings. Renew or repack with lubricant, reassemble and adjust (Chapter 11, Section 3)
  Drain and flush the engine cooling system and top up, using new antifreeze (Chapter 2)

Every three years or 36 000 miles (60 000 km), whichever occurs first

---

Drain and renew the brake fluid (Chapter 9, Section 3). Renew the flexible brake hoses at the same time

Rear axle oil level/filler plug location

Maintenance check points underneath at the rear

1 Brake hydraulic lines
2 Handbrake cable and linkages
3 Shock absorbers
4 Spring-to-axle casing mountings

Check the tyres for uneven wear, damage and tread depths

Fault diagnosis

Introduction

The vehicle owner who does his or her own maintenance according to the recommended schedules should not have to use this section of the manual very often. Modern component reliability is such that, provided those items subject to wear or deterioration are inspected or renewed at the specified intervals, sudden failure is comparatively rare. Faults do not usually just happen as a result of sudden failure, but develop over a period of time. Major mechanical failures in particular are usually preceded by characteristic symptoms over hundreds or even thousands of miles. Those components which do occasionally fail without warning are often small and easily carried in the vehicle.

With any fault finding, the first step is to decide where to begin investigations. Sometimes this is obvious, but on other occasions a little detective work will be necessary. The owner who makes half a dozen haphazard adjustments or replacements may be successful in curing a fault (or its symptoms), but he will be none the wiser if the fault recurs and he may well have spent more time and money than was necessary. A calm and logical approach will be found to be more satisfactory in the long run. Always take into account any warning signs or abnormalities that may have been noticed in the period preceding the fault – power loss, high or low gauge readings, unusual noises or smells, etc – and remember that failure of components such as fuses or spark plugs may only be pointers to some underlying fault.

The pages which follow here are intended to help in cases of failure to start or breakdown on the road. There is also a Fault Diagnosis Section at the end of each Chapter which should be consulted if the preliminary checks prove unfruitful. Whatever the fault, certain basic principles apply. These are as follows:

Verify the fault. This is simply a matter of being sure that you know what the symptoms are before starting work. This is particularly important if you are investigating a fault for someone else who may not have described it very accurately.

Don't overlook the obvious. For example, if the vehicle won't start, is there petrol in the tank? (Don't take anyone else's word on this particular point, and don't trust the fuel gauge either!) If an electrical fault is indicated, look for loose or broken wires before digging out the test gear.

Cure the disease, not the symptom. Substituting a flat battery with a fully charged one will get you off the hard shoulder, but if the underlying cause is not attended to, the new battery will go the same way. Similarly, changing oil-fouled spark plugs for a new set will get you moving again, but remember that the reason for the fouling (if it wasn't simply an incorrect grade of plug) will have to be established and corrected.

Don't take anything for granted. Particularly, don't forget that a 'new' component may itself be defective (especially if it's been rattling round in the boot for months), and don't leave components out of a fault diagnosis sequence just because they are new or recently fitted. When you do finally diagnose a difficult fault, you'll probably realise that all the evidence was there from the start.

Electrical faults

Electrical faults can be more puzzling than straightforward mechanical failures, but they are no less susceptible to logical analysis if the basic principles of operation are understood. Vehicle electrical wiring exists in extremely unfavourable conditions – heat, vibration and chemical attack – and the first things to look for are loose or corroded connections and broken or chafed wires, especially where the wires pass through holes in the bodywork or are subject to vibration.

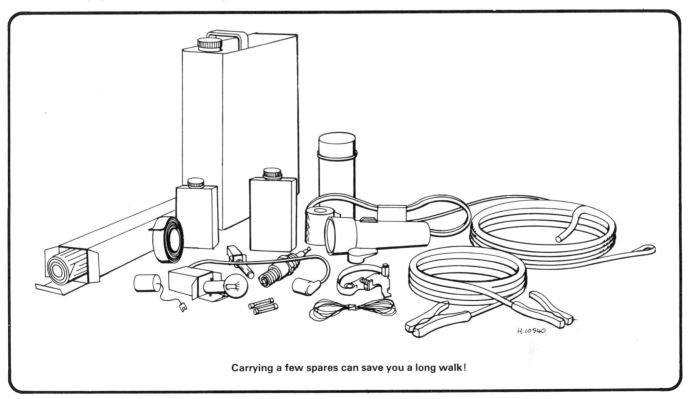

Carrying a few spares can save you a long walk!

All metal-bodied vehicles in current production have one pole of the battery 'earthed', ie connected to the vehicle bodywork, and in nearly all modern vehicles it is the negative (–) terminal. The various electrical components – motors, bulb holders etc – are also connected to earth, either by means of a lead or directly by their mountings. Electric current flows through the component and then back to the battery via the bodywork. If the component mounting is loose or corroded, or if a good path back to the battery is not available, the circuit will be incomplete and malfunction will result. The engine and/or gearbox are also earthed by means of flexible metal straps to the body or subframe; if these straps are loose or missing, starter motor, generator and ignition trouble may result.

Assuming the earth return to be satisfactory, electrical faults will be due either to component malfunction or to defects in the current supply. Individual components are dealt with in Chapter 10. If supply wires are broken or cracked internally this results in an open-circuit, and the easiest way to check for this is to bypass the suspect wire temporarily with a length of wire having a crocodile clip or suitable connector at each end. Alternatively, a 12V test lamp can be used to verify the presence of supply voltage at various points along the wire and the break can be thus isolated.

If a bare portion of a live wire touches the bodywork or other earthed metal part, the electricity will take the low-resistance path thus formed back to the battery: this is known as a short-circuit. Hopefully a short-circuit will blow a fuse, but otherwise it may cause burning of the insulation (and possibly further short-circuits) or even a fire. This is why it is inadvisable to bypass persistently blowing fuses with silver foil or wire.

Spares and tool kit

Most vehicles are supplied only with sufficient tools for wheel changing; the *Maintenance and minor repair* tool kit detailed in *Tools and working facilities*, with the addition of a hammer, is probably sufficient for those repairs that most motorists would consider attempting at the roadside. In addition a few items which can be fitted without too much trouble in the event of a breakdown should be carried. Experience and available space will modify the list below, but the following may save having to call on professional assistance:

Spark plugs, clean and correctly gapped
HT lead and plug cap – long enough to reach the plug furthest from the distributor
Distributor rotor, condenser and contact breaker points
Drivebelt(s) – emergency type may suffice
Spare fuses
Set of principal light bulbs
Tin of radiator sealer and hose bandage
Exhaust bandage
Roll of insulating tape
Length of soft iron wire
Length of electrical flex
Torch or inspection lamp (can double as test lamp)
Battery jump leads
Tow-rope
Ignition waterproofing aerosol
Litre of engine oil
Sealed can of hydraulic fluid
Emergency windscreen
Worm drive clips
Tube of filler paste

If spare fuel is carried, a can designed for the purpose should be used to minimise risks of leakage and collision damage. A first aid kit and a warning triangle, whilst not at present compulsory in the UK, are obviously sensible items to carry in addition to the above.

When touring abroad it may be advisable to carry additional spares which, even if you cannot fit them yourself, could save having to wait while parts are obtained. The items below may be worth considering:

Clutch and throttle cables
Cylinder head gasket
Alternator brushes
Fuel pump repair kit and length of flexible fuel line hose
Tyre valve core

One of the motoring organisations will be able to advise on availability of fuel etc in foreign countries.

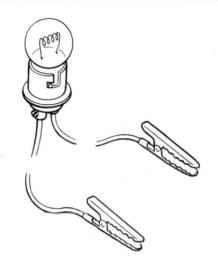

A simple test lamp is useful for tracing electrical faults

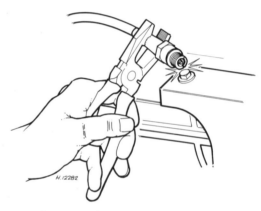

Crank engine (ignition on) and check for a spark. Use an insulated tool to hold the spark plug or HT lead

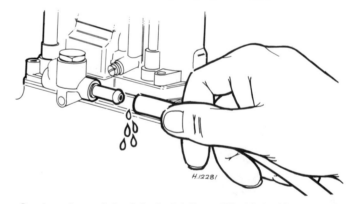

Crank engine and check for fuel delivery. Disable ignition system and take precautions against fire

Engine will not start

Engine fails to turn when starter operated
Flat battery (recharge, use jump leads, or push start)
Battery terminals loose or corroded
Battery earth to body defective
Engine earth strap loose or broken
Starter motor (or solenoid) wiring loose or broken
Ignition/starter switch faulty
Major mechanical failure (seizure)
Starter or solenoid internal fault (see Chapter 10)

Starter motor turns engine slowly
Partially discharged battery (recharge, use jump leads, or push start)
Battery terminals loose or corroded
Battery earth to body defective
Engine earth strap loose
Starter motor (or solenoid) wiring loose
Starter motor internal fault (see Chapter 10)

Starter motor spins without turning engine
Flat battery
Starter motor pinion sticking on sleeve
Flywheel gear teeth damaged or worn
Starter motor mounting bolts loose

Engine turns normally but fails to start
Damp or dirty HT leads and distributor cap (crank engine and check for spark)
Dirty or incorrectly gapped distributor points
No fuel in tank (check for delivery at carburettor)
Excessive choke (hot engine) or insufficient choke (cold engine)
Fouled or incorrectly gapped spark plugs (remove, clean and regap)
Other ignition system fault (see Chapter 4)
Other fuel system fault (see Chapter 3)
Poor compression
Major mechanical failure (eg camshaft drive)

Engine fires but will not run
Insufficient choke (cold engine)
Air leaks at carburettor or inlet manifold
Fuel starvation (see Chapter 3)
Ballast resistor defective, or other ignition fault (see Chapter 4)

Engine cuts out and will not restart

Engine cuts out suddenly – ignition fault
Loose or disconnected LT wires
Wet HT leads or distributor cap (after traversing water splash)
Coil or condenser failure (check for spark)
Other ignition fault (see Chapter 4)

Engine misfires before cutting out – fuel fault
Fuel tank empty
Fuel pump defective or filter blocked (check for delivery)
Fuel tank filler vent blocked (suction will be evident on releasing cap)
Carburettor needle valve sticking
Carburettor jets blocked (fuel contaminated)
Other fuel system fault (see Chapter 3)

Engine cuts out – other causes
Serious overheating
Major mechanical failure (eg camshaft drive)

Engine overheats

Ignition (no-charge) warning light illuminated
Slack or broken drivebelt – retension or renew (Chapter 2)

Ignition warning light not illuminated
Coolant loss due to internal or external leakage (see Chapter 2)
Thermostat defective
Low oil level
Brakes binding
Radiator clogged externally or internally
Engine waterways clogged
Ignition timing incorrect or automatic advance malfunctioning
Mixture too weak

Note: *Do not add cold water to an overheated engine or damage may result*

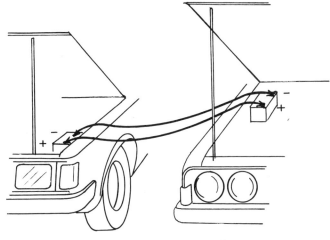

H.10541

Correct way to connect jump leads. Do not allow car bodies to touch!

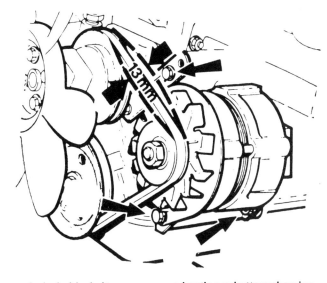

A slack drivebelt can cause overheating or battery charging problems. Slacken bolts (arrowed) to adjust

Low engine oil pressure

Gauge reads low or warning light illuminated with engine running
Oil level low or incorrect grade
Defective gauge or sender unit
Engine overheating
Oil filter clogged or bypass valve defective
Oil pressure relief valve defective
Oil pick-up strainer clogged
Oil pump worn or mountings loose
Worn main or big-end bearings

Note: *Low oil pressure in a high-mileage engine at tickover is not necessarily a cause for concern. Sudden pressure loss at speed is far more significant. In any event, check the gauge or warning light sender before condemning the engine.*

Engine noises

Pre-ignition (pinking) on acceleration
Incorrect grade of fuel
Ignition timing incorrect

Distributor faulty or worn
Worn or maladjusted carburettor
Excessive carbon build-up in engine

Whistling or wheezing noises
Leaking vacuum hose
Leaking carburettor or manifold gasket
Blowing head gasket

Tapping or rattling
Incorrect valve clearances
Worn valve gear

Worn timing belt
Broken piston ring (ticking noise)

Knocking or thumping
Unintentional mechanical contact (eg fan blades)
Worn fanbelt
Peripheral component fault (generator, water pump etc)
Worn big-end bearings (regular heavy knocking, perhaps less under load)
Worn main bearings (rumbling and knocking, perhaps worsening under load)
Piston slap (most noticeable when cold)

Chapter 1 Engine

Contents

Specifications

Part A – Mexico and RS 2000
General

	LEC (Mexico)	NEE (RS 2000)
Engine type	four-cylinder, SOHC, in line, water cooled	
Engine identity marking	LEC (Mexico)	NEE (RS 2000)
Bore (nominal)	3.451 in (87.65 mm)	3.575 in (90.8 mm)
Stroke	2.600 in (66.0 mm)	3.030 in (76.95 mm)
Cubic capacity	97.2 cu in (1593 cc)	121.6 cu in (1993 cc)
Compression ratio	9.2:1	9.2:1
Compression pressure (at starter motor speed)	142 to 170 lbf/in^2 (10 to 12 kgf/cm^2)	142 to 170 lbf/in^2 (10 to 12 kgf/cm^2)
Mean working pressure	142 lbf/in^2 (10 kgf/cm^2)	138 lbf/in^2 (9.7 kgf/cm^2)
Maximum brake horsepower	93 HP (95 PS) at 5750 rpm	108 HP (110 PS) at 5500 rpm
Maximum torque	92 lbf ft (12.7 kgf m) at 4000 rpm	124 lbf ft (16.4 kgf m) at 4000 rpm
Maximum continuous engine speed	6300 rpm	5850 rpm
Idle speed	800 ± 20 rpm	825 ± 25 rpm
Firing order	1-3-4-2 (No 1 at the front)	1-3-4-2 (No 1 at the front)

Cylinder block

Cast identification marks	16	20
Number of main bearings	5	5
Cylinder bore diameter (standard):		
Mexico	3.4520 to 3.4524 in (87.680 to 87.690 mm)	
RS 2000	3.5760 to 3.5764 in (90.830 to 90.840 mm)	
Oversizes available	+0.019 in (0.5 mm), +0.039 in (1.0 mm)	

Main bearings

Centre main bearing width .... 1.069 to 1.071 in (27.17 to 27.22 mm)

Main bearing shells (fitted) – vertical inside diameter:
    Standard .... 2.244 to 2.245 in (57.000 to 57.033 mm)
    Undersizes available .... −0.009 in (0.25 mm), −0.019 in (0.50 mm), − 0.029 in (0.75 mm), − 0.039 in (1.00 mm)

Main bearing basic bore diameter:
    Standard .... 2.3866 to 2.3874 in (60.620 to 60.640 mm)
    Oversize available .... + 0.015 in (0.4 mm)

Crankshaft

Endfloat .... 0.003 to 0.011 in (0.080 to 0.280 mm)

Thrust washer thickness:
    Standard .... 0.090 to 0.092 in (2.30 to 2.35 mm)
    Oversize available .... +0.008 in (0.2 mm)

Main bearing journal diameter:
    Standard .... 2.2429 to 2.2437 in (56.970 to 56.990 mm)
    Undersizes available .... −0.009 in (0.25 mm), −0.019 in (0.40 mm), −0.029 in (0.75 mm), −0.039 in (1.00 mm)

Main bearing shell-to-journal clearance:
    Aluminium .... 0.0004 to 0.0025 in (0.010 to 0.064 mm)
    Compound .... 0.0004 to 0.0027 in (0.010 to 0.068 mm)

Crankpin diameter:
    Standard .... 2.0465 to 2.0472 in (51.980 to 52.000 mm)
    Undersizes available .... −0.009 in (0.25 mm), −0.019 in (0.50 mm), − 0.029 in (0.75 mm), −0.039 in (1.00 mm)

Camshaft

Drive .... Toothed belt
Endfloat .... 0.003 to 0.006 in (0.09 to 0.17 mm)

Colour code:
    Mexico .... White
    RS 2000 .... Yellow

Lift of cams:
    Mexico .... 0.2349 in (5.9639 mm)
    RS 2000 .... 0.2494 in (6.3323 mm)

Cam heel-to-toe dimension:
    Mexico .... 1.412 to 1.429 in (35.86 to 36.27 mm)
    RS 2000 .... 1.427 to 1.443 in (36.23 to 36.64 mm)

Bearing diameter:
    Front .... 1.654 to 1.655 in (41.99 to 42.01 mm)
    Centre .... 1.757 to 1.758 in (44.61 to 44.63 mm)
    Rear .... 1.772 to 1.773 in (44.99 to 45.01 mm)

Pistons

Diameter (standard):
Mexico .... 3.450 to 3.451 in (87.630 to 87.655 mm)
RS 2000 .... 3.574 to 3.575 in (90.780 to 90.805 mm)
Oversizes available .... +0.019 in (0.50 mm), +0.039 in (1.00 mm)
Piston-to-bore clearance .... 0.0009 to 0.0020 in (0.025 to 0.060 mm)
Ring gap *(in situ)*
Top .... 0.015 to 0.023 in (0.38 to 0.58 mm)
Centre .... 0.015 to 0.023 in (0.38 to 0.58 mm)
Bottom .... 0.0157 to 0.055 in (0.4 to 1.4 mm)
Ring gap position:
Top .... 150° to side of expander gap
Centre .... 150° to opposite side of expander gap
Bottom .... Expander opposite the 'front' mark on the piston crown with intermediate rings 1 in (25 mm) each side of the expander gap

Gudgeon pin

Length .... 2.83 to 2.87 in (72.0 to 72.8 mm)
Diameter:
Red .... 0.94465 to 0.94476 in (23.994 to 23.997 mm)
Blue .... 0.94476 to 0.94488 in (23.997 to 24.000 mm)
Yellow .... 0.94488 to 0.94500 in (24.000 to 24.003 mm)
Clearance in piston .... 0.0003 to 0.0005 in (0.008 to 0.014 mm)
Interference in small-end bush .... 0.0007 to 0.0015 in (0.018 to 0.039 mm)

Connecting rods and big-end bearings

Big-end bore diameter .... 2.1653 to 2.1657 in (55.00 to 55.02 mm)
Small-end bore diameter .... 0.9434 to 0.9439 in (23.964 to 23.976 mm)
Big-end shell (fitted) – vertical inside diameter:
Standard .... 2.0475 to 2.0489 in (52.006 to 52.044 mm)
Undersize available .... −0.009 in (0.25 mm), −0.019 in (0.50 mm). −0.029 in (0.75 mm), −0.039 in (1.00 mm)

Crankpin-to-bearing shell clearance:
Aluminium shells .... 0.00023 to 0.0027 in (0.006 to 0.069 mm)
Compound shells .... 0.00055 to 0.0020 in (0.014 to 0.052 mm)

Cylinder head

Cast identification number:
Mexico 6
RS 2000 0
Valve seat angle (in head) .... 44°30' to 45°
Inlet and exhaust guide bore:
Standard .... 0.317 to 0.318 in (8.063 to 8.088 mm)
Oversizes available .... +0.007 in (0.2 mm), +0.015 in (0.4 mm)
Camshaft bearing bush bore:
Front .... 1.6549 to 1.6557 in (42.035 to 42.055 mm)
Centre .... 1.758 to 1.759 in (44.655 to 44.675 mm)
Rear .... 1.773 to 1.774 in (45.035 to 45.055 mm)

Valves

Valve clearances (cold):
Inlet .... 0.008 in (0.20 mm)
Exhaust .... 0.010 in (0.25 mm)

	Mexico	RS 2000
Valve timing:		
Inlet opens	22° BTDC	24° BTDC
Inlet closes	54° ABDC	64° ABDC
Exhaust opens	64° BBDC	70° BBDC
Exhaust closes	12° ATDC	18° ATDC
Valve length (inlet and exhaust)	4.455 ± 0.019 in (113.15 ± 0.5 mm)	4.376 ± 0.019 in (111.15 ± 0.5 mm)
Valve head diameter:		
Inlet	1.516 ± 0.008 in (38.5 ± 0.2 mm)	1.654 ± 0.008 in (42.0 ± 0.2 mm)
Exhaust	1.347 ± 0.008 in (34.2 ± 0.2 mm)	1.418 ± 0.008 in (36.0 ± 0.2 mm)

Stem diameter – inlet:
Standard .... 0.3159 to 0.3167 in (8.025 to 8.043 mm)
Oversizes available .... +0.007 in (0.2 mm), +0.015 in (0.4 mm)
Stem diameter – exhaust:
Standard .... 0.3151 to 0.3158 in (7.999 to 8.017 mm)
Oversizes available .... +0.007 in (0.2 mm), +0.015 in (0.4 mm)
Valve stem-to-guide clearance:
Inlet .... 0.0008 to 0.0025 in (0.020 to 0.063 mm)
Exhaust .... 0.0018 to 0.0035 in (0.046 to 0.089 mm)

Valve lift:
    Inlet:
        Mexico .... 0.373 in (9.474 mm)
        RS 2000 .... 0.399 in (10.142 mm)
    Exhaust:
        Mexico .... 0.374 in (9.5034 mm)
        RS 2000 .... 0.398 in (10.1211 mm)
Valve spring length – compressed:
    Inlet .... 0.945 (24.0 mm)
    Exhaust:
        Mexico .... 1.037 in (26.33 mm)
        RS 2000 .... 1.020 in (25.9 mm)
Valve spring free length (inlet and exhaust) .... 1.733 in (44.0 mm)

Engine lubrication data

Oil type .... See Recommended Lubricants and Fluids chart
Oil capacity:
    Initial filling (with filter) .... 6.6 Imp pints (3.75 litres)
Oil change (with filter change) .... 6.6 Imp pints (3.75 litres)
Oil change (without filter change) .... 5.7 Imp pints (3.25 litres)
Oil pressure (minimum):
    At 700 rpm .... 16 lbf/in^2 (1.1 kgf/cm^2)
    At 1500 rpm .... 35 lbf/in^2 (2.5 kgf/cm^2)
Relief valve opening pressure .... 57 to 67 lbf/in^2 (4.0 to 4.7 kgf/cm^2)
Oil pressure warning light operating pressure .... 4 to 9 lbf/in^2 (0.3 to 06 kgf/cm^2)
Oil pump outer rotor and housing clearance .... 0.006 to 0.012 in (0.15 to 0.30 mm)
Inner and outer rotor clearance .... 0.002 to 0.008 in (0.05 to 0.20 mm)
Inner and outer rotor endfloat .... 0.0012 to 0.004 in (0.03 to 0.10 mm)

Torque wrench settings (Mexico and RS 2000)

	lbf ft	kgf m
Main bearing caps	65 to 75	8.8 to 10.2
Connecting rod nuts	30 to 35	4.1 to 4.8
Crankshaft pulley bolt	41 to 44	5.5 to 6.0
Cylinder head:		
1st stage	29 to 41	4.0 to 5.5
2nd stage	44 to 51	6.0 to 7.0
3rd stage (after waiting 10 to 20 minutes)	66 to 81	9.0 to 11.0
4th stage (after running engine for 15 minutes at 1000 rpm)	66 to 81	9.0 to 11.0
Top cover:		
1st to 6th bolts	4 to 5	0.5 to 0.7
7th and 8th bolts (Stage 1)	1.5 to 1.8	0.2 to 0.25
9th and 10th bolts	4 to 5	0.5 to 0.7
7th and 8th bolts (Stage 2)	4 to 5	0.5 to 0.7
Front cover	10 to 13	1.3 to 1.7
Camshaft sprocket bolt	33 to 37	4.5 to 5.0
Oil pump	13 to 15	1.7 to 2.1
Oil pump cover	7 to 10	1.0 to 1.3
Oil pan (sump):		
Stage 1	0.7 to 1.5	0.1 to 0.2
Stage 2	4 to 6	0.5 to 0.8
Stage 3 (after engine has run for 20 minutes)	6 to 7	0.8 to 1.0
Drain plug	15 to 21	2.1 to 2.8
Oil pressure switch	9 to 11	1.2 to 1.5
Ball-pins – valve adjustment	33 to 37	4.5 to 5.0
Flywheel bolts	48 to 52	6.5 to 7.1
Inlet manifold	13 to 15	1.7 to 2.1
Exhaust manifold	15 to 18	2.1 to 2.5
Sparking plugs	15 to 21	2.1 to 2.8
Engine mounting bracket-to-block bolts (with flat washers)	19 to 23	2.6 to 3.1
Thermostat housing	12 to 15	1.6 to 2.1

Part B – RS 1800
General

Engine type .... four-cylinder, in-line, twin OHC, water cooled
Bore .... 3.415 in (86.75 mm)
Stroke .... 3.056 in (77.62 mm)
Cubic capacity .... 111.9 cu in (1834 cc)
Compression ratio 10:1
Maximum brake horsepower at 6000 rpm .... 113 HP (115 PS)
Maximum torque at 3750 rpm .... 126 lbf ft (17.39 kgf m)
Maximum continuous engine speed .... 6500 rpm
Idle speed .... 800 rpm
Firing order .... 1-3-4-2 (No 1 at the front)

Crankshaft and main bearings
Number of main bearings 5

Main bearing journal diameter .... 2.1255 to 2.1261 in (53.988 to 54.003 mm)
Reground diameters:
    0.254 mm .... 2.1152 to 2.1157 in (53.721 to 53.734 mm)
    0.508 mm .... 2.1055 to 2.1060 in (53.480 to 53.492 mm)
    0.762 mm .... 2.0955 to 2.0960 in (52.718 to 52.730 mm)
Undersize bearings available .... −0.010 in (0.25 mm), −0.020 in (0.51 mm), −0.030 in (0.76 mm) on inside diameter
Oversize bearings available .... −0.015 in (0.37 mm) on outside diameter (each size)
Crankpin journal diameter .... 1.9368 to 1.9376 in (49.195 to 49.215 mm)
Crankshaft endfloat .... 0.003 to 0.011 in (0.08 to 0.28 mm)
Thrust washer thickness .... 0.091 to 0.093 in (2.31 to 2.36 mm)
Oversize washers available .... +0.0025 in (0.064 mm), +0.0050 in (0.127 mm), +0.0075 in (0.191 mm), +0.0100 in (0.254 mm)
Spigot bearing bore .... 0.826 to 0.827 in (20.98 to 21.01 mm)

Cylinder block
Standard cylinder bore diameter .... Graded − nominally 3.415 in (86.75 mm)
Grade point .... Across block, 2.34 in (59.44 mm) down from head face

Camshafts
Rubber toothed drivebelt − pitch x width .... 0.375 x 1.00 (9.53 x 25.4 mm)
Belt length .... 54.75 in (1.39 m)
Number of teeth 146
Belt tension adjustment .... Provided by eccentric mounted idler sprocket
Belt tension − with the engine cold .... 0.38 in (9.5 mm) deflection, using spring balance method at 10.1 lbf (4.5 kgf) or 85 to 95 Burroughs Units
Endfloat .... 0.002 to 0.008 in (0.051 to 0.203 mm)
Journal diameter .... 1.8735 to 1.8740 in (47.587 to 47.599 mm)
Cam lift (inlet and exhaust) .... 0.35 in (8.76 mm)
Cam heel-to-nose dimension .... 1.504 to 1.506 in (38.20 to 38.35 mm)

Cam carrier and tappets
Camshaft bearing journal inside diameter .... 1.8760 to 1.8770 in (47.649 to 47.676 mm)
Tappet bore diameter .... 1.2000 to 1.2005 in (30.480 to 30.493 mm)
Tappet outside diameter .... 1.1985 to 1.1990 in (30.442 to 30.455 mm)
Tappet shim thickness .... 0.040 to 0.090 in (1.106 to 2.286 mm) in steps of 0.001 in (0.025 mm)

Cylinder head
Inlet/exhaust valve guide inside diameter .... 0.2812 to 0.2819 in (7.142 to 7.160 mm)
Valve guide length:
    Inlet .... 1.700 to 1.720 in (33.18 to 33.69 mm)
    Exhaust .... 1.660 to 1.680 in (42.16 to 42.67 mm)
Inlet and exhaust seat angle .... 45°
Inlet and exhaust valve seat width .... 0.154 in (3.91 mm)
Inlet seat insert outside diameter .... 1.303 to 1.304 in (33.09 to 33.12 mm)
Exhaust seat insert outside diameter .... 1.088 to 1.089 in (27.64 to 27.66 mm)
Head recess inside diameter:
    Inlet seat .... 1.300 to 1.301 in (33.02 to 33.05 mm)
    Exhaust seat .... 1.085 to 1.086 in (27.56 to 27.58 mm)

Valves
Valve stem diameter:
    Inlet .... 0.2792 to 0.2800 in (7.092 to 7.112 mm)
    Exhaust .... 0.2787 to 0.2795 in (7.079 to 7.099 mm)
Valve stem-to-guide clearance:
    Inlet .... 0.0012 to 0.0027 in (0.030 to 0.069 mm)
    Exhaust .... 0.0017 to 0.0032 in (0.043 to 0.081 mm)
Valve face angle .... 45°
Valve head diameter:
    Inlet .... 1.218 to 1.222 in (30.90 to 30.91 mm)
    Exhaust .... 0.998 to 1.002 in (27.35 to 27.45 mm)
Valve springs:
    Free length .... 1.48 in (37.59 mm)
    Wire diameter .... 0.151 to 0.153 in (3.84 to 3.89 mm)
    Fitted length (valve closed) .... 1.259 to 1.277 in (31.98 to 32.44 mm)
Valve timing and clearances:
    Inlet valve at full lift .... 107° to 113° ATDC
    Exhaust valve at full lift .... 107° to 113° BTDC
Valve clearances (cold):
    Inlet .... 0.005 to 0.007 in (0.13 to 0.18 mm)
    Exhaust .... 0.006 to 0.008 in (0.15 to 0.20 mm)

Pistons
Type .... Solid skirt with valve clearance recess in crown

Weight	0.845 lb (0.383 kg)
Piston diameter (standard)	3.415 in (86.75 mm)
Oversize piston available	3.420 in (86.88 mm)
Piston-to-cylinder bore clearance	0.0030 to 0.0036 in (0.076 to 0.091 mm)
Piston ring gap in cylinder bore	0.016 to 0.021 in (0.41 to 0.53 mm)

Gudgeon pins

Length	2.795 to 2.810 in (70.99 to 71.37 mm)
Outside diameter	0.8119 to 0.8123 in (20.622 to 20.632 mm)
Clearance in piston (selected)	0.0001 in (0.003 mm)
Clearance in small-end bush	0.0002 to 0.00045 in (0.005 to 0.013 mm)
Weight	0.265 lb (0.129 kg)

Connecting rods and big-end bearings

Type	'H' section steel forging
Weight:	
Small end	0.592 to 0.601 lb (269 to 273 g)
Big-end	0.847 to 0.856 lb (385 to 389 g)
Total	1.439 to 1.457 lb (654 to 662 g)
Big-end bore	2.0825 to 2.0830 in (52.896 to 52.908 mm)
Undersize bearings available	0.002 in (0.051 mm), 0.010 in (0.254 mm), 0.020 in (0.508 mm), 0.030 in (0.762 mm), 0.040 in (1.016 mm)
Crankpin-to-bearing clearance	0.0004 to 0.0024 in (0.010 to 0.061 mm)
Small-end bush inside diameter	0.8122 to 0.8126 in (20.629 to 20.640 mm)

Auxiliary shaft

Journal diameter	1.5597 to 1.5605 in (39.606 to 39.627 mm)
Bearing inside diameter	1.5615 to 1.5620 in (39.881 to 39.893 mm)
Bearing clearance	0.001 to 0.0023 in (0.025 to 0.058 mm)
Endfloat	0.0025 to 0.0075 in (0.064 to 0.191 mm)

Flywheel and ring gear

Tyoe	Ring gear shrunk on
Ring gear fitting temperature	316°C (600°F)
Maximum run-out	0.005 in (0.13 mm)
Clutch pilot spigot bearing	Sintered bronze
Flywheel weight	15.5 lb (7.04 kg)

Lubrication system

Type	Wet sump, pressure feed system with full-flow filter. External oil pump with oil cooler flow and return pipe connections
Oil pressure	55 to 65 lbf/in^2 (3.87 to 4.57 kgf/cm^2)
Sump capacity (including filter)	7.46 Imp pints (4.25 litres)
Oil filter capacity	0.67 Imp pints (0.38 litres)
Oil cooler capacity	0.75 Imp pints (0.43 litres)
Oil pump:	
Type	Eccentric bi-rotor or rotary vane
Driveshaft-to-body clearance	0.0015 to 0.003 in (0.038 to 0.076 mm)
Inner and outer rotor clearance	0.006 in (0.15 mm) maximum
Outer rotor and housing clearance	0.010 in (0.25 mm) maximum
Inner and outer rotor endfloat	0.005 in (0.13 mm) maximum
Grade of oil	See Recommended Lubricants and Fluids chart

Torque wrench settings

	lbf ft	kgf m
Cylinder head	60 to 65	8.3 to 9.0
Main bearing	65 to 70	9.0 to 9.7
Connecting rod	30 to 35	4.1 to 4.8
Flywheel to crankshaft	50 to 55	6.9 to 7.6
Camshaft sprocket	20 to 25	2.8 to 3.5
Auxiliary shaft sprocket	15 to 20	2.1 to 2.8
Crankshaft sprocket	24 to 28	3.2 to 3.9
Cam carrier to hand	8 to 10	1.1 to 1.3
Idler sprocket nut	30 to 35	4.1 to 4.8
Sump	7 to 9	1.0 to 1.2
Alternator to bracket	15 to 18	2.1 to 2.5
Cam cover	1.5 to 2.7	0.2 to 0.3
Auxiliary shaft thrust plate bolts	2.9 to 3.6	0.4 to 0.5
Sump drain plug	20 to 25	2.70 to 3.40
Front cover bolts	5 to 7	0.70 to 2.10
Oil pump bolts	13 to 15	1.70 to 2.10
Bolts not listed above:		
6 mm ($\frac{1}{4}$ in)	5 to 7	0.7 to 1.0
8 mmm ($\frac{5}{16}$ in)	10 to 15	1.4 to 2.1
10 mm ($\frac{3}{8}$ in)	20 to 25	2.8 to 3.5

* Mountings to be tightened with car free standing (weight resting on wheels).

PART A: MEXICO AND RS 2000

1 General description

The engines fitted to the two models covered in this part of Chapter 1 have four cylinders and a single overhead camshaft. Both the 1600 cc engine fitted to the Mexico and the 2000 cc engine fitted to the RS 2000 are of the same design (Ford 'B') and an exploded view illustrating the main components is shown in Figure 1.1.

The cylinder head is of crossflow design with the inlet manifold one side and the exhaust manifold on the other. As flat top pistons are used the combustion chambers are contained in the cylinder head.

The combined crankcase and cylinder block is made of cast iron and houses the pistons and crankshaft. Attached to the underside of the crankcase is a pressed steel sump which acts as a reservoir for the engine oil. Full information on the lubricating system will be found in Section 23.

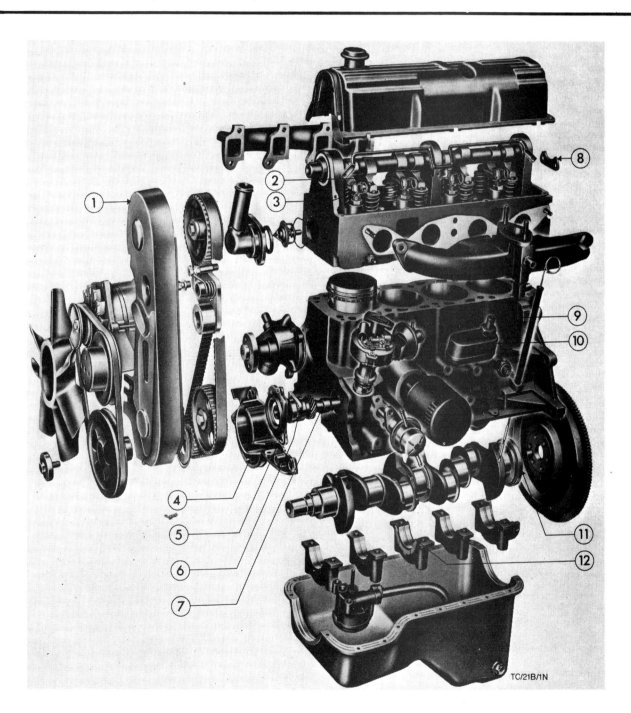

TC/21B/1N

Fig. 1.1 The Ford 'B' type engine — exploded view of the main components (Sec 1)

1 Toothed belt guard	4 Crankshaft timing cover	7 Auxiliary shaft	10 Oil separator
2 Cam follower	5 Auxiliary shaft front cover	8 Camshaft thrust plate	11 Crankshaft oil seal
3 Cam follower spring	6 Auxiliary shaft thrust plate	9 PCV valve	12 Thrust washer

The cast iron cylinder head is mounted on top of the cylinder block and acts as a support for the overhead camshaft. The slightly angled valves operate directly in the cylinder head and are controlled by the camshaft, via cam followers. The camshaft is operated by a toothed reinforced composite rubber belt from the crankshaft. To eliminate backlash and prevent slackness of the belt a spring loaded tensioner in the form of a jockey wheel is in contact with the back of the belt. It serves two further functions, to keep the belt away from the water pump and also to increase the contact area of the camshaft and crankshaft sprocket.

The drivebelt also operates the auxiliary shaft sprocket and it is from this shaft that the oil pump, distributor and fuel pump operate.

The inlet manifold is mounted on the left-hand side of the cylinder head and to this the carburettor is fitted. A water jacket is incorporated in the inlet manifold so that the petrol/air charge may be correctly prepared before entering the combustion chambers.

The exhaust manifold is mounted on the right-hand side of the cylinder head and connects to a single downpipe and silencer system.

Aluminium alloy pistons are connected to the crankshaft by 'H' section forged steel connecting rods and gudgeon pins. The gudgeon pin is a press fit in the small end of the connecting rod but a floating fit in the piston boss. Two compression rings and one scraper ring, all located above the gudgeon pin, are fitted.

The forged crankshaft runs in five main bearings and endfloat is accommodated by fitting thrust washers either side of the centre main bearing.

Before commencing any overhaul work on the engine refer to Section 8 where information is given about special tools that are required to remove the cylinder head, drive belt tensioner and oil pump.

2   Major operations possible with the engine in position

The following major operations can be carried out to the engine when it is in position in the car. It should be noted that where operations 5, 6, 7 and 8 are concerned, they can only be achieved by disconnecting the steering column from the steering rack-and-pinion assembly and lowering the crossmember to which this is attached, in order to allow sufficient clearance for sump removal.

1   Removal and refitting of cylinder head
2   Removal and refitting of camshaft (only with cylinder head removed)
3   Removal and refitting of camshaft drivebelt
4   Removal and refitting of the engine mountings
5   Removal and refitting of the sump
6   Removal and refitting of the oil pump
7   Removal and refitting of the big-end bearings
8   Removal and refitting of the connecting rods and piston

3   Major operations requiring engine removal

The following major operations can be carried out with the engine out of the body frame on the bench or floor:

1   Removal and refitting of the main bearings
2   Removal and refitting of the crankshaft
3   Removal and refitting of the flywheel (unless gearbox is removed – see Chapter 6)
4   Removal and refitting of the crankshaft rear oil seal

4   Method of engine removal

The engine complete with gearbox can be lifted as a unit from the engine compartment. Alternatively, the engine and gearbox can be split at the front of the bellhousing, a stand or jack placed under the gearbox to provide additional support, and the engine lifted out. The easiest method of engine removal is to remove the engine leaving the gearbox in place in the car. If the engine and gearbox are removed as a unit they have to be lifted out at a very steep angle which can be difficult, especially if the lifting height is limited.

5   Engine – removal (without gearbox)

1   Before commencing operations it is essential to have a good hoist, a pair of axle stands (if an inspection pit is not available) and four 3 inch long $\frac{3}{8}$ inch UNF bolts. During the engine removal you will need the help of an assistant to steady the engine and guide it clear of surrounding components in the engine compartment.

2   Open the bonnet and get an assistant to support it, then mark an outline of the hinge-to-bonnet position each side (for correct realignment when refitting). Unscrew and remove the hinge-to-bonnet securing bolts and washers each side, then lift the bonnet clear and place it safely out of the way.

3   Drain the cooling system, as given in Chapter 2.

4   Disconnect the battery earth lead then the positive lead, and remove the battery from its tray. Also disconnect the low tension and high tension leads between the coil and the distributor (at the coil) and the water temperature sender unit wire.

5   Disconnect and remove the servo vacuum hose.

6   Remove the air cleaner unit from the carburettor, referring to Chapter 3 if necessary (photo).

7   Disconnect the throttle cable by prising it free from the support bracket and disengage the cable balljoint connection to the throttle link rod.

8   Disconnect the radiator top hose from the radiator and the thermostat housing (photo), and remove the hose.

5.6 Remove the air cleaner unit

5.8 Disconnect the radiator top hose

9 Unbolt and remove the radiator side-mounting bolts and then carefully lift the radiator out of the engine compartment. Where fitted, place the oil cooler unit to one side out of the way.

10 Unbolt and remove the cooling fan.

11 Remove the alternator (see Chapter 10). Detach the engine earth strap.

12 Disconnect the fuel line-to-fuel pump connection and plug the end of the line to prevent leakage.

13 Disconnect the oil pressure line connection to the cylinder block and unclip it from the throttle cable location bracket then secure it out of the way.

14 Unscrew and remove the three exhaust pipe-to-manifold retaining nuts and separate the pipe from the manifold (photo).

15 The steering column-to-rack flexible joint must now be separated. To ensure correct realignment on assembly make a mating mark between the two, then unscrew the retaining nut and withdraw the clamp bolt (photo). To withdraw the column you will need to detach it from the dash panel and floorpan inside the car, and disconnect the multi-connectors. Withdraw and lower the column to disconnect it from the rack. Further details are given in Chapter 11.

16 Before raising the car to work underneath the front end it is advisable to remove the engine oil drain plug and drain the oil into a suitable container for disposal, then refit the drain plug.

17 Raise the front of the vehicle and support it with axle stands at a suitable working height, but also bear in mind the amount of lift height at your disposal. If your hoist is suspended from a fixed point you will need to lower the car later before lifting out the engine to enable the car to be pushed back out of the way when the engine is lifted clear.

18 Locate a jack under the engine front crossmember to support it, then remove each of the four crossmember securing bolts in turn and replace them with 3 inch long UNF bolts. When all the bolts have been replaced, lower the jack under the crossmember so that it is supported by the 3 inch bolts.

19 Disconnect the clutch cable from the clutch release arm, as given in Chapter 5.

20 Disconnect the starter motor leads (photo), then unscrew the starter motor securing bolts and withdraw the starter motor.

21 Unscrew and remove the lower engine-to-gearbox housing bolts

each side, then position a jack under the gearbox to support it.

22 The car can now be lowered from the axle stands, the lifting sling fitted to the special lift eyes on the cylinder head, one on the rear left-hand side and one on the front right-hand side. Take up the slack in the sling, but do not lift the engine yet.

23 Remove the remaining engine-to-transmission housing securing bolts.

24 Unbolt and detach the engine mountings on each side, four bolts to each (photo).

25 Make a check to ensure that all fittings are clear and disconnected, then slowly lift the engine whilst pulling it forwards away from the transmission). Get an assistant to simultaneously raise the jack under the gearbox until the top of the gearbox bellhousing is almost touching the underside of the body floor. Now pull the engine forward until the clutch unit is clear of the gearbox input (1st motion) shaft. On no account allow the weight of the engine to hang on this shaft. Once the engine is clear tilt the engine up at the front and, with the aid of an assistant, guide it upwards and clear of the engine compartment (photo). You may find it necessary to remove the crankshaft pulley to enable it to clear the front upper crossmember.

26 Check that no loose nuts and bolts have been left in the empty engine compartment. Lightly screw any nuts or bolts back from where they were removed or place them where they will not become lost.

27 If you are going to move the car back out of the way to lower the engine you will need to support the gearbox in the raised position using suitable rope or similar so that the jack can be lowered before pushing the car back.

6 Engine and gearbox – removal

1 Referring to the previous Section complete the operations given in paragraphs 1 to 20, but note that the starter motor can be left in position, although its leads will have to be disconnected. Refer to Chapter 6 for further details of gearbox detachment.

2 Remove the propeller shaft, as described in Chapter 7. You will need to position a suitable container under the rear end of the gearbox to catch the oil which will leak out of the rear extension housing. To

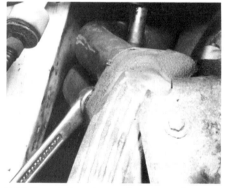
5.14 Detach the exhaust pipe-to-manifold connection

5.15 Steering column clamp bolt (arrowed)

Fig. 1.2 Fit longer bolts and lower the crossmember (Sec 5)

5.20 Disconnect the starter motor leads

5.24 Unscrew and remove the engine mounting bolts

5.25 Lifting the engine clear

prevent further gearbox oil leakage when removing the engine and gearbox, plug or seal off the extension housing aperture.

3   From inside the car lift up the gearlever gaiter and then remove the circlip on the spring.

4   Bend back the locktab and, with a pair of mole grips or similar across the flats, undo the plastic dome nut and lift out the gearlever from the car.

5   Free the speedometer cable from the gearbox extension housing by extracting the circlip which holds the cable in place. Detach the reversing light leads.

6   From under the car, detach the crossmember which supports the gearbox. To do this first place a jack (preferably of the trolley type) under the gearbox and undo the two bolts at each end of the gearbox crossmember (see photo 2.19 in Chapter 6).

7   Lower and remove the jack, and then remove the stands from the front of the car to lower the front to its normal height.

8   Attach the engine lifting sling to the lift eyes, one on the rear left-hand side of the cylinder head, the other on the front right-hand side of the cylinder head. When securing the sling, bear in mind that the engine and gearbox will have to be tilted upwards to a considerable angle at the front during the lifting operation. When the sling is in position take the weight of the engine, but do not lift it just yet.

9   Unscrew and remove the four engine mounting-to-cylinder block retaining bolts from each side.

10   Undo the nut on each side which holds the front engine mounting in place.

11   If a trolley jack is available it is helpful to position it under the gearbox so the gearbox rolls forward with the jack. Pull the power unit forward, at the same time lifting it on the hoist. As the gearbox tilts oil will run out of the rear of the gearbox extension, unless it was sealed off.

12   As the combined units are being removed get an assistant to guide them past the surrounding components within the engine bay, in particular taking care not to snag the rear of the engine or gearbox on the brake pipe which runs across the bulkhead. You may find it necessary to remove the crankshaft pulley to clear the front upper crossmember. Once the gearbox is clear of the transmission tunnel the power unit can be lifted clear.

13   With the combined units lifted clear they can be moved to a suitable area for cleaning prior to separating them.

14   To separate the gearbox from the engine, remove the starter motor and the engine-to-clutch housing retaining bolts (photo).

15   Pull the gearbox away from the engine whilst simultaneously keeping it supported, to prevent any strain being put onto the gearbox input shaft (photo).

16   You may initially have to pull the two units apart until free of the location dowels (photo).

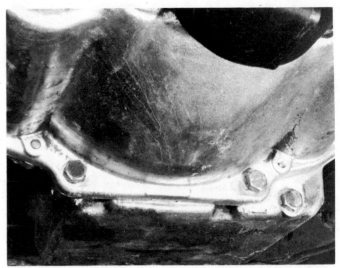

6.14 Remove the gearbox-to-engine retaining bolts – the lower ones are shown here

6.15 Pull the gearbox free from the engine

---

7   Dismantling the engine – general

1   It is best to mount the engine on a dismantling stand, but if one is not available, then stand the engine on a strong bench so it is at a comfortable working height.

2   During the dismantling process the greatest care should be taken to keep the exposed parts free from dirt. As an aid to achieving this, it is a sound scheme to thoroughly clean the outside of the engine, removing all traces of oil and congealed dirt.

3   Use paraffin or a good grease solvent. The latter compound will make the job much easier, as, after the solvent has been applied and allowed to stand for a time, a vigorous jet of water will wash off the solvent and all the grease and filth. If the dirt is thick and deeply embedded, work the solvent into it with a stiff paintbrush.

4   Finally wipe down the exterior of the engine with a rag and only then, when it is quite clean, should the dismantling process begin. As the engine is stripped, clean each part in a bath of paraffin or petrol.

5   Never immerse parts with oilways eg the crankshaft, in paraffin, but wipe down carefully with a petrol dampened rag. Oilways can be cleaned out with wire. If an air line is present all parts can be blown dry and the oilways blown through as an added precaution.

6   Re-use of old engine gaskets is a false economy and can give rise to oil and water leaks, if nothing worse. To avoid the possibility of trouble after the engine has been reassembled always use new gaskets.

7   Do not throw away the old gaskets, as it sometimes happens that an immediate replacement cannot be found and the old gasket is then

6.16 Engine-to-gearbox location dowel

very useful as a template. Hang up the old gaskets, as they are removed, on a suitable hook or nail.

8 To strip the engine it is best to work from the top down. The sump provides a firm base on which the engine can be supported in an upright position. When the stage where the sump must be removed is reached, the engine can be turned on its side and all other work carried out with it in this position.

9 Wherever possible, refit nuts, bolts and washers finger tight from wherever they were removed. This helps avoid later loss and muddle. If they cannot be refitted, then lay them out in such a fashion that it is clear where they came from.

8 Removing ancillary engine components

1 Before basic engine dismantling begins the engine should be stripped of its ancillary components, depending upon the extent of the work necessary. All of the following items should be removed if an exchange reconditioned unit is to be purchased:

    (a) *Fuel system components:*
        Carburettor and manifold assembly
        Exhaust manifold
        Fuel pump
        Fuel line
    (b) *Ignition system components:*
        Spark plugs
        Distributor
    (c) *Cooling system components:*
        Water pump
        Thermostat housing and thermostat
        Water temperature indicator sender unit
    (d) *Engine:*
        Oil filter
        Oil pressure sender unit
        Oil level dipstick
        Oil filler cap and top cover
        Engine mountings
        Crankcase ventilation valve and oil separator
    (e) *Clutch:*
        Clutch pressure plate assembly
        Clutch friction plate assembly

Some of those items have to be removed for individual servicing or renewal periodically and details can be found in the appropriate Chapter.

2 Before dismantling begins, it is important that three special tools are obtained, otherwise certain work cannot be carried out. The special tools are shown in the photo, and will enable the cylinder head bolts, the oil pump bolts and the valve springs to be removed. These tools are:

Cylinder head bolt wrench	Ford No. 21-002 (or equivalent)
Oil pump bolt wrench	Ford No 21-012 (or equivalent)
Valve spring compressor	Ford No 21-005 (or equivalent, see Section 18)

9 Cylinder head – removal (engine in car)

1 Before any attempt is made to remove the cylinder head you will need to have, or be able to hire or borrow, Ford special tools 21-002 (cylinder head bolt removal tool) and 21-005 (valve spring compressor), or their equivalents, the latter being for cylinder head dismantling.

2 You will probably find it to be advantageous if the bonnet is removed and placed out of the way. To do this, open the bonnet and, using a soft pencil, mark the outline of both the hinges at the bonnet to act as a datum for refitting.

3 With the help of a second person to take the weight of the bonnet, undo and remove the hinge-to-bonnet securing bolts with plain and spring washers. There are two bolts to each hinge. Lift away the bonnet and put in a safe place where it will not be scratched.

4 Refer to Chapter 10, Section 4, and remove the battery.

5 Unbolt and remove the air cleaner unit from the carburettor, referring to Chapter 3 if necessary.

6 Note their locations, then disconnect the HT leads from the spark plugs and their securing clips on the side of the rocker cover.

7 Drain the cooling system, as given in Chapter 2.

8 The cylinder head can be removed with or without the carburettor, inlet manifold and exhaust mnaifold in position, as required. If the cylinder head is being removed for overhaul, then the carburettor and inlet manifold are best removed now (see Chapter 3). The exhaust manifold can either be disconnected at the downpipe connection and removed with the cylinder head, or disconnected from the cylinder head and left connected to the downpipe. If disconnecting the manifolds from the cylinder head at this stage, note the locations of the engine lifting eyes, the carburettor, fuel and coolant (auto choke) pipe connection and the vacuum (servo unit and distributor advance) connections, all of which must be detached. Plug the fuel line to prevent leakage and the ingress of dirt.

9 New manifold gaskets must be fitted on reassembly, but if the old ones can be removed intact, keep them to check that the correct replacements have been supplied.

10 Detach the temperature transmitter electric cable from the inlet manifold side of the cylinder head (photo).

11 Slacken the radiator top hose clips and completely remove the hose.

12 Undo and remove the bolts, spring and plain washers that secure the top cover to the cylinder head.

13 Lift away the top cover (photo).

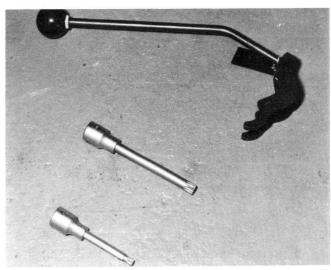

8.2 Three special tools necessary for engine dismantling

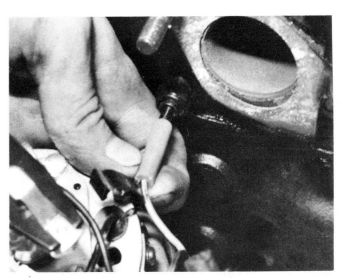

9.10 Temperature transmitter cable detachment

9.13 Lift away the top cover

9.14 Remove the belt guard securing bolts ...

9.15 ... and lift away the guard

9.17 Remove the drivebelt

9.18 Loosen the cylinder head securing bolts

9.19 Cylinder head removal

14 Undo and remove the bolts, spring and plain washers that secure the toothed drivebelt guard (photo).

15 Lift away the guard (photo).

16 Release the tension from the drivebelt by slackening the spring-loaded roller mounting plate securing bolt.

17 Ease the toothed drivebelt from the camshaft sprocket (photo).

18 Using the special tool (21-002) together with a socket wrench (photo), slacken the cylinder head securing bolts in a diagonal and progressive manner until all are free from tension (Fig. 1.3). Remove the ten bolts, noting that because of the special shape of the bolt head no washers are used. Unfortunately there is no other tool suitable to slot into the bolt head, so do not attempt to improvise as it will only cause damage to the bolt.

19 The cylinder head may now be removed by lifting upwards (photo). If the head is stuck, try to rock it or break the seal. Under no circumstances try to prise it apart from the cylinder block with a screwdriver or cold chisel, as damage may be done to the faces of the cylinder head and block. If the head will not free readily, temporarily refit the battery and turn the engine using the starter motor, as the compression in the cylinders will often break the cylinder head joint. If this fails to work, strike the head sharply with a plastic headed or wooden hammer, or with a metal hammer with an interposed piece of wood to cushion the blow. Under no circumstances hit the head directly with a metal hammer as this may cause the casting to fracture. Several sharp taps with the hammer, at the same time pulling upwards, should free the head. Lift the head off and place to one side.

10 Cylinder head – removal (engine on bench)

The procedure for removing the cylinder head with the engine on the bench is similar to that for removal when the engine is in the car, with the exception of disconnecting the controls and services. Refer to Section 9 and follow the sequence given in paragraphs 8 and 9 and 12 to 19 inclusive.

11 Auxiliary shaft – removal

1 Using a metal bar lock the shaft sprocket and, with an open-ended spanner, undo and remove the bolt and washer that secure the sprocket to the shaft (photo).

2 Undo and remove the three bolts and spring washers that secure the shaft timing cover to the cylinder block (photo).

3 Lift away the timing cover (photo).

4 Undo and remove the two cross-head screws that secure the shaft thrust plate to the cylinder block (photo).

5 Lift away the thrust plate (photo).

6 The shaft may now be drawn forwards and then lifted away (photo).

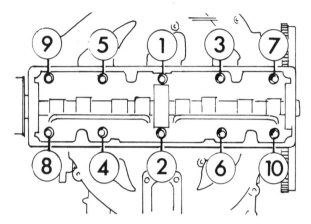

Fig. 1.3 Correct order for tightening the cylinder head bolts (slacken them in the reverse order) (Secs 9, 10 and 56)

11.1 Auxiliary shaft sprocket securing bolt removal

11.2 Remove the auxiliary shaft timing cover securing bolts

11.3 Remove the auxiliary shaft timing cover

11.4 Remove the auxiliary shaft thrust plate screws ...

11.5 ... and withdraw the thrust plate

11.6 Withdraw the auxiliary shaft

12.1 Remove the flywheel securing bolts ...

12.2 ... then lift the flywheel clear

13.2 Remove the oil pump securing bolts

13.4 Remove the oil pump driveshaft

14.3 Remove the crankshaft sprocket

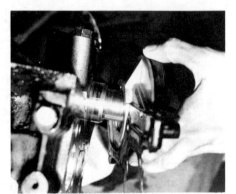

14.5 Remove timing cover and gasket

12 Flywheel and sump – removal

1   With the clutch removed, as described in Chapter 5, lock the flywheel using a screwdriver in mesh with the starter ring gear and undo the six bolts that secure the flywheel to the crankshaft in a diagonal and progressive manner (photo). Lift away the bolts.
2   Mark the relative position of the flywheel and crankshaft and then lift away the flywheel (photo).
3   Undo and remove the bolts that secure the sump to the underside of the crankcase.
4   Lift away the sump and its gasket.
5   Unbolt and remove the rear oil seal carrier.

13 Oil pump and strainer – removal

1   Undo and remove the screw and spring washer that secure the oil pump pick-up pipe support bracket to the crankcase.
2   Using special tool (21-012) undo the two special bolts that secure the oil pump to the underside of the crankcase (photo). Unfortunately there is no other tool suitable to slot into the bolt head so do not attempt to improvise, as it will only cause damage to the bolt.
3   Lift away the oil pump and strainer assembly.
4   Carefully lift away the oil pump drive making a special note of which way round it is fitted (photo).

14 Crankshaft pulley, sprocket and timing cover – removal

1   Lock the crankshaft using a block of soft wood placed between a crankshaft web and the crankcase then using a socket and suitable extension, undo the bolt that secures the crankshaft pulley. Recover the large diameter plain washer.
2   Using a large screwdriver ease the pulley from the crankshaft. Recover the large diameter thrust washer.
3   Again, using the screwdriver, ease the sprocket from the crankshaft (photo).

4   Undo and remove the bolts and spring washers that secure the timing cover to the front of the crankcase.
5   Lift away the timing cover and gasket (photo).

15 Pistons, connecting rods and big-end bearings – removal

1   Note that the pistons have an arrow marked on the crown showing the forward direction (photo). Inspect the big-end bearing caps and connecting rods to make sure identification marks are visible. This is to ensure that the correct end caps are fitted to the correct connecting rods and the connecting rods placed in their respective bores (Fig. 1.4).
2   Undo the big-end nuts and place to one side in the order in which they were removed.

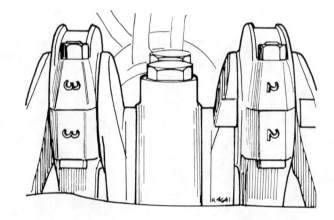

Fig. 1.4 Big-end bearing cap and connecting rod identification marks (Sec 15)

15.1 The piston identification marks are on the piston crowns

15.3 Withdraw the big-end caps

16.2 Main bearing cap – identification marks

16.4 Withdrawing the No 2 main bearing cap

16.9 Remove the crankshaft rear oil seal

17.6 Lift away the crankshaft pulley

3   Remove the big-end caps (photo), taking care to keep them in the right order and the correct way round. If the big-end caps are difficult to remove, they may be gently tapped with a soft hammer.
4   To remove the shell bearings, press the bearing opposite the groove in both the connecting rod and its cap, and the bearing will slide out easily. Ensure that the shell bearings are kept with their correct connecting rods, unless they are to be renewed.
5   Withdraw the pistons and connecting rods upwards and ensure they are kept in order for refitting in the same bore as they were originally fitted.

16 Crankshaft and main bearings – removal

1   With the engine removed from the car and separated from the gearbox, and the drivebelt, crankshaft pulley and sprocket, flywheel and backplate, oil pump, big-end bearings and pistons all dismantled, proceed to remove the crankshaft and main bearings.
2   Make sure that identification marks are visible on the main bearing end caps (photo), so that they may be refitted in their original positions and also the correct way round.
3   Undo the bolts which hold the five bearing caps by one turn at a time.
4   Lift away each main bearing cap and the bottom half of each bearing shell (photo), taking care to keep the bearing shell in the right caps.
5   When removing the rear main bearing end cap note that this also retains the crankshaft rear oil seal.
6   When removing the centre main bearing, note the bottom semi-circular halves of the thrust washers, one half lying on either side of the main bearing. Place them with the centre main bearing along the correct side.
7   As the centre and rear bearing end caps are accurately located by dowels it may be necessary to gently tap the end caps to release them.
8   Slightly rotate the crankshaft to free the upper halves of the bearing shells and thrust washers which can be extracted and placed over the correct bearing cap.
9   Carefully lift away the crankshaft rear oil seal (photo).

10 Remove the crankshaft by lifting it away from the crankcase.

17 Camshaft drivebelt – removal (engine in car)

It is possible to remove the camshaft drivebelt with the engine in situ, but experience shows that this type of belt is very reliable and unlikely to break or stretch considerably. However, during a major engine overhaul it is recommended that a new belt is fitted.
1   Refer to Chapter 2, Section 2, and drain the cooling system. Slacken the top hose securing clips and remove the top hose.
2   Slacken the alternator mounting bolts and push the unit towards the engine. Lift away the fanbelt.
3   Undo and remove the bolts that secure the drivebelt guard to the front of the engine. Lift away the guard.
4   Slacken the bent tensioner mounting plate securing bolt and release the tension on the belt.
5   Place the car in gear, and apply the brakes firmly. Undo and remove the bolt and plain washer that secure the crankshaft pulley to the nose of the crankshaft.
6   Using a screwdriver carefully ease off the pulley (photo).
7   Recover the plain large diameter thrust washer.
8   The drivebelt may now be eased away (photo).

18 Valves – removal

1   To enable the valve to be removed, a special valve spring compressor is required. This has a part number of '21-005'. However, it was found that it was just possible to use a universal valve spring compressor, provided extreme caution was taken.
2   Make a special note of how the cam follower springs are fitted and, using a screwdriver, remove these from the cam followers (photo).
3   Back off the cam follower adjustment fully and remove the cam followers. Keep these in their respective order so that they can be refitted in their original positions.
4   Using the valve spring compressor, compress the valve springs and lift out the collets (photo).

17.8 Remove the drivebelt

18.2 Removing a cam follower spring

18.4 Compressing a valve spring

5   Remove the spring cap and spring and use a screwdriver to prise the oil retainer caps out of their seats. Remove each valve and keep in its respective order unless they are so badly worn that they are to be renewed. If they are going to be used again, place them in a sheet of card having eight numbered holes corresponding with the relative positions of the valves when fitted. Also keep the valve springs, cups etc in the correct order.
6   If necessary unscrew the ball-head bolts.

19 Camshaft – removal

It is not necessary to remove the engine from the car in order to remove the camshaft. However, it will be necessary to remove the cylinder head first (Section 9) as the camshaft has to be withdrawn from the rear.
1   Undo and remove the bolts, spring washers and bracket that secure the camshaft lubrication pipe (photo). Lift away the pipe.
2   Carefully inspect the fine oil drillings in the pipe to make sure that none are blocked (photo).
3   Using a metal bar lock the camshaft drive sprocket, then undo and remove the sprocket securing bolt and washer (photo).
4   Using a soft-faced hammer, or screwdriver, ease the sprocket from the camshaft (photo).
5   Undo and remove the two bolts and spring washers that secure the camshaft thrust plate to the rear bearing support (photo).

6   Lift away the thrust plate, noting which way round it is fitted.
7   Remove the cam follower springs and then the cam followers, as detailed in Section 18, paragraphs 2 and 3.
8   The camshaft may now be removed by using a soft-faced hammer and tapping rearwards. Take care not to cut the fingers when the camshaft is being handled as the sides of the lobes can be sharp.
9   Lift the camshaft through the bearing inserts as the lobes can damage the soft metal bearing surfaces (photo).
10 If the oil seal has hardened or become damaged, it may be removed by prising it out with a screwdriver (photo).

20 Thermostat housing and belt tensioner – removal

1   Removal of these parts will usually only be necessary if the cylinder head to be completely dismantled.
2   Undo and remove the two bolts and spring washers that secure the thermostat housing to the front face of the cylinder head.
3   Lift away the thermostat housing and recover its gasket (photo).
4   Undo and remove the bolt and spring washer that secure the belt tensioner to the cylinder head. It will be necessary to override the tension using a screwdriver as a lever (photos).
5   Using tool number '21-012' (the tool for removal of the oil pump securing bolts) unscrew the tensioner mounting plate spring bolt and lift away the tensioner assembly.

19.1 Remove the camshaft lubrication pipe

19.2 Note oil holes in camshaft lubrication pipe

19.3 Use a metal rod to lock the camshaft sprocket

19.4 Removing the camshaft sprocket

19.5 Remove the camshaft thrust plate bolts

19.9 Withdraw the camshaft

19.10 Camshaft oil seal removal

20.3 Thermostat housing removal

20.4a Removal of belt tensioner mounting plate securing bolt

20.4b Ease off the belt spring tension with a screwdriver

23.0 Disconnecting the PCV hose

21 Gudgeon pin – removal

Interference fit type gudgeon pins are used and it is important that no damage is caused during removal and refitting. Because of this, should it be necessary to renew pistons or connecting rods, take the parts along to the local Ford garage who will have the special equipment to do this job.

22 Piston rings – removal

1   To remove the piston rings, slide them carefully over the top of the piston, taking care not to scratch the aluminium alloy; never slide them off the bottom of the piston skirt. it is very easy to break the cast iron piston rings if they are pulled off roughly, so this operation should be done with extreme care. It is helpful to make use of an old 0.020 inch (0.5 mm) feeler gauge.

2   Lift one end of the piston ring to be removed out of its groove and insert under it the end of the feeler gauge.

3   Turn the feeler gauge slowly round the piston and, as the ring comes out of its groove, apply slight upward pressure so that it rests on the piston above the groove. It can be then be eased off the piston with the feeler gauge stopping it from slipping into an empty groove if it is any but the top piston ring that is being removed.

23 Lubrication and crankcase ventilation system (PCV) – description

The oil sump is attached to the underside of the crankcase and acts as a reservoir for the engine oil. The oil pump draws oil through a strainer located under the oil surface, passes it along a short passage and into the full-flow oil filter. The freshly filtered oil flows from the centre of the filter element and enters the main gallery. Five small drillings connect the main gallery to the five main bearings. The big-end bearings are supplied with oil by the front and rear main bearings, via skew oil bores.

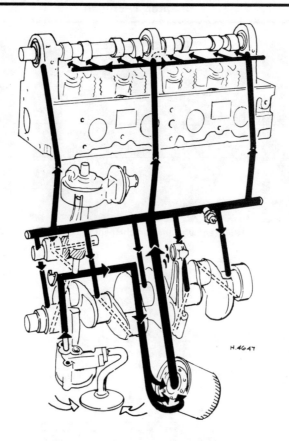

H.4647

Fig. 1.5 Engine lubrication circuit (Sec 23)

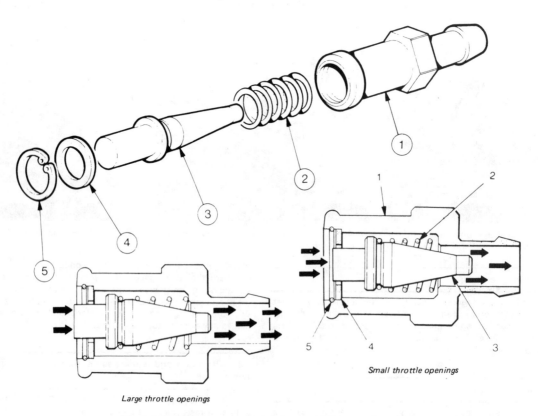

Small throttle openings

Large throttle openings

Fig. 1.6 Exploded and sectional views of PCV valve (Sec 23)

1	Valve body	3	Piston	5	Circlip
2	Spring	4	Washer		

When the crankshaft is rotating, oil is thrown from the oil in each big-end bearing and splashes the thrust side of the piston and bore.

The auxiliary shaft is lubricated directly from the main oil gallery. The distributor shaft is supplied with oil passing along a drilling inside the auxiliary shaft.

A further three drillings connect the main oil gallery to the overhead camshaft. The centre camshaft bearing has a semi-circular groove from which oil is passed along a pipe running parallel with the camshaft. The pipe is drilled opposite to each cam and cam follower so providing lubrication to the cams and cam followers. Oil then passes back to the sump, via large drillings in the cylinder head and cylinder block.

A semi-enclosed engine ventilation system is used to control crankcase vapour. It is controlled by the amount of air drawn in by the engine when running and the throughput of the regulator valve.

The system is known as the PCV system (Positive Crankcase Ventilation) and the advantage of the PCV system is that should the 'blow-by' exceed the capacity of the PCV valve, excess fumes are fed into the engine through the air cleaner. This is caused by the rise in crankcase pressure which creates a reverse flow in the air intake pipe.

Periodically, pull the valve and hose from the rubber grommet of the oil separator (photo) and inspect the valve for free movement. If it is sticky in action or is choked with sludge, dismantle it and clean the components by washing in paraffin and then blowing dry with compressed air.

Occasionally check the security and condition of the system connecting hoses.

---

24 Oil pump – dismantling, inspection and reassembly

1   If oil pump wear is suspected it is possible to obtain a repair kit.

Check for wear first, as described later in this Section, and if confirmed, obtain an overhaul kit or a new pump. The two rotors are a matched pair and form a single replacement unit. Where the rotor assembly is to be re-used the outer rotor, prior to dismantling, must be marked on its front face in order to ensure correct reassembly.

2   Undo and remove the two bolts and spring washers that secure the intake cowl to the oil pump body. Lift away the cowl and its gasket.

3   Note the relative position of the oil pump cover and body and then undo and remove the three bolts and spring washers. Lift away the cover.

4   Carefully remove the rotors from the housing.

5   Using a centre punch tap a hole in the centre of the pressure relief valve sealing plug (make a note to obtain a new one).

6   Screw in a self-tapping screw and, using an open-ended spanner, withdraw the sealing plug, as shown in Fig. 1.8.

7   Thoroughly clean all parts in petrol or paraffin and wipe dry using a lint-free rag. The necessary clearances may now be checked using a machined straight-edge (a good steel rule) and a set of feeler gauges. The critical clearances are between the lobes of the centre rotor and convex faces of the outer rotor; between the rotor and the pump body (Fig. 1.9); and between both rotors and the end cover plate (Fig. 1.19). All these clearances are given in the Specifications.

8   If the only excessive clearance is endfloat it is possible to reduce it by removing the rotors and lapping the face of the body on a flat bed until the necessary clearance is obtained. It must be emphasised, however, that the face of the body must remain perfectly flat and square to the axis of the rotor spindle otherwise the clearance will not be equal over the whole area and the end cover will not be a pressure tight fit to the body. It is worth trying, of course, if the pump is in need of renewal anyway, but unless done properly, it could seriously jeopardise the rest of the overhaul. Any excessive variations in the other two clearances should be overcome with a new unit.

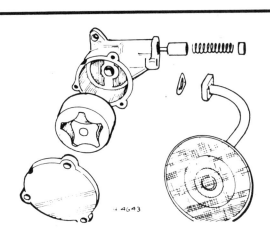

Fig. 1.7 Oil pump components (Sec 24)

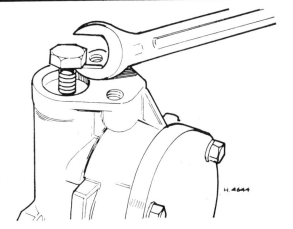

Fig. 1.8 Removal of sealing plug from oil pump pressure relief valve (Sec 24)

Fig. 1.9 Check the oil pump outer rotor-to-body clearance (Sec 24)

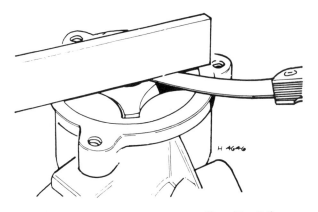

Fig. 1.10 Check the oil pump endfloat (Sec 24)

9 With all parts scrupulously clean first refit the relief valve and spring, and lightly lubricate with engine oil.

10 Using a suitable diameter drift drive in a new sealing plug, flat side outwards, until it is flush with the intake cowl bearing face.

11 Well lubricate both rotors with engine oil; and insert into the body. Fit the oil pump cover and secure with the three bolts in a diagonal and progressive manner to the final torque wrench setting stated in the Specifications.

12 Fit the intermediate shaft into the rotor driveshaft and make sure that the rotor turns freely.

13 Fit the cowl to the pump body, using a new gasket and secure with the two bolts.

25 Oil filter – removal and refitting

1 The oil filter is a complete throwaway cartridge screwed into the left-hand side of the cylinder block.

2 To remove the old cartridge, wipe its external surfaces dry and, gripping it firmly, unscrew it. When renewing the filter during routine maintenance, allow for a certain amount of oil spillage as it is unscrewed. You may find that it is too tight to unscrew by hand, in which case you will need to use a proprietary tool as shown (photo), or drive a screwdriver through the filter casing to enable extra leverage to be applied when unscrewing it.

3 Clean the filter seating on the block face and lubricate with engine oil, then screw the new filter into position, taking care not to cross the thread. Continue until the sealing ring just touches the block face then tighten one half turn, using the hands only. Always run the engine and check for signs of leaks after installation.

26 Engine components – examination for wear

When the engine has been stripped down and all parts properly cleaned, decisions have to be made as to what needs renewal, and the following sections tell the examiner what to look for. In any borderline case it is always best to decide in favour of a new part. Even if a part is still serviceable, its life will have been reduced by wear, and the degree of trouble needed to replace it in the future must be taken into consideration. However, these things are relative and it depends on whether a quick 'survival' job is being done or whether the car as a whole is being regarded as having many thousands of miles of useful and economical life remaining.

Ford advocate the use of 'Plastigage' for assessing bearing and journal wear. This product may not be generally available to the home mechanic, but the traditional measuring instruments such as a micrometer or vernier gauge will suffice.

27 Crankshaft – examination and renovation

1 Look at the main bearing journals and the crankpins, and if there are any scratches or score marks then the shaft will need regrinding. Such conditions will nearly always be accompanied by similar deterioration in the matching bearing shells.

2 Each bearing journal should also be round and can be checked with a micrometer or caliper gauge around the periphery at several points. If there is more than 0.001 in of ovality regrinding is necessary.

3 A main Ford agent or motor engineering specialist will be able to decide to what extent regrinding is necessary, and also supply the special undersize shell bearing to match whatever needs grinding off.

4 Before taking the crankshaft for regrinding check also the cylinder bore and pistons as it may be advantageous to have the whole engine done at the same time.

5 Note that oversize main bearing parent bores, and/or undersize main and big-end bearing journals, may be found even in an engine which has not been previously overhauled. See Figs. 1.11 to 1.14 for details.

28 Main and big-end bearings – examination and renovation

1 With careful servicing and regular oil and filter changes bearings will last for a very long time, but they can still fail for unforeseen reasons. With big-end bearings an indication is a regular rhythmic loud

25.2 Using a proprietary tool (arrowed) to remove the oil filter

Fig. 1.11 White paint marks (arrowed) denote main bearing bore 0.015 in (0.38 mm) oversize (Sec 27)

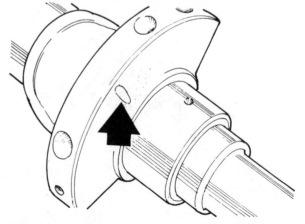

Fig. 1.12 Green stripes on crankshaft web (arrowed) denotes main bearing journals 0.010 in (0.25 mm) undersize (Sec 27)

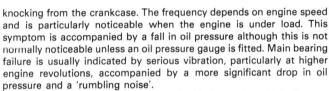

Fig. 1.13 Green spot on crankcase web denotes big-end bearing journals 0.010 in (0.25 mm) undersize (Sec 27)

Fig. 1.14 A crankshaft with both main and big-end journals undersize is marked as shown (Sec 27)

knocking from the crankcase. The frequency depends on engine speed and is particularly noticeable when the engine is under load. This symptom is accompanied by a fall in oil pressure although this is not normally noticeable unless an oil pressure gauge is fitted. Main bearing failure is usually indicated by serious vibration, particularly at higher engine revolutions, accompanied by a more significant drop in oil pressure and a 'rumbling noise'.

2 Big-end bearings can be removed with the engine still in the car. If the failure is sudden and the engine has a low mileage since new or overhaul this is possibly worth doing. Bearing shells in good condition have bearing surfaces with a smooth, even matt silver/grey colour all over. Worn bearings will show patches of a different colour when the bearing metal has worn away and exposed the underlay. Damaged bearings will be pitted or scored. It is always well worthwhile fitting new shells as their cost is relatively low. If the crankshaft is in good condition, it is merely a question of obtaining another set of the appropriate size shells. A reground crankshaft will need new bearing shells as a matter of course.

3 Undersize bearing shells are colour-coded on the back and/or side.

29 Cylinder bore – examination and renovation

1 A new cylinder is perfectly round and the walls parallel throughout its length. The action of the piston tends to wear the walls at right-angles to the gudgeon pin due to side thrust. This wear takes place principally on that section of the cylinder swept by the piston rings.

2 It is possible to get an indication of bore wear by removing the cylinder head with the engine still in the car. With the piston down in the bore first signs of wear can be seen and felt just below the top of the bore where the top piston ring reaches and where there will be a noticeable lip. If there is no lip it is fairly reasonable to expect that bore wear is not severe and any lack of compression or excessive oil consumption is due to worn or broken piston rings or pistons (see Section 30).

3 If it is possible to obtain a bore measuring micrometer, measure the bore in the thrust plane below the lip and again at the bottom of the cylinder in the same plane. If the difference is more than 0.003 in (0.076 mm) then a rebore is necessary. Similarly, a difference of 0.003 in (0.076 mm) or more between two measurements of the bore diameter taken at right-angles to each other is a sign of ovality, again calling for a rebore.

4 Any bore which is significantly scratched or scored will need reboring. This symptom usually indicates that the piston or rings are damaged also. In the event of only one cylinder being in need or reboring it will still be necessary for all four to be bored and fitted with new oversize pistons and rings. Your Ford agent or local motor engineering specialist will be able to rebore and obtain the necessary matched pistons. If the crankshaft is undergoing regrinding also, it is a good idea to let the same firm renovate and reassemble the crankshaft and pistons to the block. A reputable firm normally gives a

guarantee for such work. In cases where engines have been rebored already to their maximum, new cylinder liners are available which may be fitted. In such cases, the same reboring processes have to be followed and the services of a specialist engineering firm are required.

30 Pistons and piston rings – inspection and testing

1 Worn pistons and rings can usually be diagnosed when the symptoms of excessive oil consumption and lower compression occur and are sometimes, though not always, associated with worn cylinder bores. Compression testers that fit into the spark plug hole are available and these can indicate where low compression is occurring. Wear usually accelerates the more it is left so when the symptoms occur, early action can possibly save the expense of a rebore.

2 Another symptom of piston wear is piston slap – a knocking noise from the crankcase not to be confused with big-end bearing failure. It can be heard clearly at low engine speed when the engine is cold and there is no load (idling for example) and is much less audible when the engine speed increases. Piston wear usually occurs in the skirt or lower end of the piston and is indicated by vertical streaks in the worn area which is always on the thrust side. It can also be seen where the skirt thickness is different.

3 Piston ring wear can be checked by first removing the rings from the pistons as described in Section 22. Then place the rings in the cylinder bores from the top, pushing them down about $1\frac{1}{2}$ in (38 mm) with the head of a piston (from which the rings have been removed) so that they rest square in the cylinder. Then measure the gap at the ends of the ring with a feeler gauge. If it exceeds the value given in the Specifications the rings need renewal.

4 The grooves in which the rings locate in the piston can also become enlarged in use. The clearance between ring and piston, in the groove, should not exceed 0.004 in (0.102 mm) for the top two compression rings and 0.003 in (0.076 mm) for the lower oil control ring.

5 However, it is rare that a piston is only worn in the ring grooves and the need to renew them for this fault alone is hardly ever encountered. Wherever pistons are renewed the weight of the four piston/connecting rod assemblies should be kept within the limit variations of 10 gm to maintain engine balance.

6 If piston rings are renewed without reboring, the top piston rings must be stepped ('ridge dodger' type ring) as unstepped top rings may hit the wear ridge at the top of the bore and break.

31 Connecting rods and gudgeon pins – examination and renovation

1 Gudgeon pins are a shrink fit into the connecting rods. Neither of these would normally need renewal unless the pistons were being changed, in which case the new pistons would automatically be

supplied with new gudgeon pins.

2   Connecting rods are not subject to wear, but in extreme circumstances such as engine seizure they could be distorted. Such conditions may be visually apparent but where doubt exists they must be checked for alignment and straightened, or renewed, if necessary. Entrust this task to a qualified automotive engineer.

3   The bearing caps should also be examined for indications of filing down which may have been attempted in the mistaken belief that bearing slackness should be remedied in this way. If there are such signs then the connecting rods should be renewed.

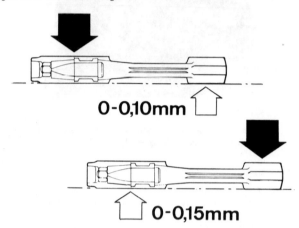

Fig. 1.15 Check connecting rods for misalignment on a flat surface – the maximum acceptable deviations are shown (Sec 31)

32 Camshaft and camshaft bearings – examination and renovation

1   The camshaft bearing bushes should be examined for signs of scoring and pitting. If they need renewal they will have to be dealt with professionally as, although it may be relatively easy to remove the old bushes, the correct fitting of new ones requires special tools. If they are not fitted evenly and squarely from the very start they can be distorted, thus causing localised wear in a very short time. See your Ford dealer or local engineering specialist for this work.

2   The camshaft itself may show signs of wear on the bearing journals, or cam lobes. The main decision to take is what degree of wear justifies renewal, which is costly. Any signs of scoring or damage to the bearing journals cannot be removed by regrinding. Renewal of the whole camshaft is the only solution. When overhauling the valve gear, check that oil is being ejected from the nozzles onto the cam followers. Turn the engine on the starter to observe this.

3   The cam lobes themselves may show signs of ridging or pitting on the high points. If ridging is light then it may be possible to smooth it out with fine emery. The cam lobes, however, are surface hardened, and once this is penetrated wear will be very rapid thereafter.

33 Cam followers – examination

The faces of the cam followers which bear on the camshaft should show no signs of pitting, scoring or other forms of wear. They should not be a loose sloppy fit on the ball-headed bolt.

Inspect the face which bears onto the valve stem and, if pitted, the cam follower must be renewed.

34 Cylinder head and piston crowns – decarbonization

1   When the cylinder head is removed, either in the course of an overhaul, or for inspection of bores or valve condition when the engine is in the car, it is normal to remove all carbon deposits from the piston crowns and heads.

2   This is best done with a cup-shaped wire brush and an electric drill, and is fairly straightforward when the engine is dismantled and the pistons removed. Sometimes hard spots of carbon are not easily removed except by a scraper. When cleaning the pistons with a

scraper, take care not to damage the surface of the piston in any way.

3   When the engine is in the car certain precautions must be taken when decarbonising the piston crowns in order to prevent dislodged pieces of carbon falling into the interior of the engine which could cause damage to cylinder bores, piston and rings, or if allowed into the water passages, damage to the water pump. Turn the engine so that the piston being worked on is at the top of its stroke and then mask off the adjacent cylinder bores and all surrounding water jacket orifices with paper and adhesive tape. Press grease into the gap all round the piston to keep carbon particles out and then scrape all carbon away by hand carefully. Do not use a power drill and wire brush when the engine is in the car as it will virtually be impossible to keep all the carbon dust clear of the engine. When completed, carefully clear out the grease around the rim of the piston with a matchstick or something similar – bringing any carbon particles with it. Repeat the process on the other piston crowns. It is not recommended that a ring of carbon is left round the edge of the piston on the theory that it will aid oil consumption. This was valid in the earlier days of long stroke low revving engines but modern engines, fuels and lubricants cause less carbon deposit anyway and any left behind tends merely to cause hot spots.

35 Valve guides – inspection

Examine the valve guides internally for wear. If the valves are a very loose fit in the guides and there is the slightest suspicion of lateral rocking using a new valve, then the guides will have to be reamed and oversize valves fitted. This is a job best left to the local Ford garage.

36 Valves and valve seats – examination and renovation

1   With the valves removed from the cylinder head examine the heads for signs of cracking, burning away and pitting of the edges where they seat in the ports. The valve seats in the cylinder head should also be examined for the same signs. Usually it is the valve that deteriorates first, but if a bad valve is not rectified the seat will suffer and this is more difficult to repair.

2   Provided there are no obvious signs of serious pitting the valve should be ground into its seat. This may be done by placing a smear of carborundum paste on the edge of the valve and, using a suction type valve holder, grinding the valve in situ. This is done with a semi-rotary action, rotating the handle of the valve holder backwards and forwards between the hands, and lifting it occasionally to redistribute the traces of paste. Use a coarse paste to start with. As soon as a matt grey unbroken line appears on both the valve and seat the valve is 'ground in'. All traces of carbon should also be cleaned from the head and neck of the valve stem. A wire brush mounted in a power drill is a quick and effective way of doing this.

3   If the valve requires renewal, the new valve should be ground into the seat in the same way as the old valve.

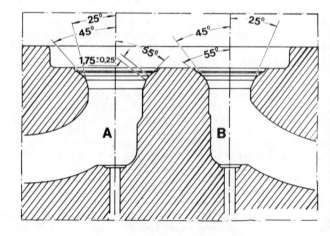

Fig. 1.16 Valve seat angles (Sec 36)

A   Inlet   B   Exhaust

4 Another form of valve wear can occur on the stem where it runs in the guide in the cylinder head. This can be detected by trying to rock the valve from side to side. If there is any movement at all it is an indication that the valve stem or guide is worn. Check the stem first with a micrometer at points along and around its length and if it is not within the specified size new valves will probably solve the problem. If the guides are worn, however, they will need reboring for oversize valves or for fitting guide inserts. The valve seats will also need recutting to ensure they are concentric with the stems. This work should be given to your Ford dealer or local engineering works.
5 When valve seats are badly burnt or pitted, requiring renewal, inserts may be fitted – or renewed if already fitted once before – and once again this is a specialist task to be carried out by a suitable engineering firm.
6 When all valve grinding is completed it is essential that every trace of grinding paste is removed from the valves and ports in the cylinder head. This should be done by thorough washing in petrol or paraffin and blowing out with a jet of air. If particles of carborundum should work their way into the engine they would cause havoc with bearings or cylinder walls.

37 Timing gears and belt – examination and renovation

1 Any wear which takes place in the timing mechanism will be on the teeth of the drivebelt or due to stretch of the fabric. Whenever the engine is to be stripped for major overhaul a new belt should be fitted.
2 It is very unusual for the timing gears (sprockets) to wear at the teeth. If the securing bolt/nuts have been loose it is possible for the keyway or hub bore to wear. Check these two points and, if damage or wear is evident, a new sprocket must be obtained.

38 Flywheel ring gear – examination and renovation

1 If the ring gear is badly worn or has missing teeth it should be renewed. The old ring can be removed from the flywheel by cutting a notch between two teeth with a hacksaw and then splitting it with a cold chisel.
2 To fit a new ring gear requires heating the ring to 400°F (204°C). This can be done by polishing four equal spaced sections of the gear, placing it on a suitable heat resistant surface (such as fire bricks) and heating it evenly with a blow lamp or torch until the polished areas turn a light yellow tinge. Do not overheat or the hard-wearing properties will be lost. The gear has a chamfered inner edge which should go against the shoulder when put on the flywheel. When hot enough place the gear in position quickly, tapping it home if necessary and let it cool naturally without quenching in any way.

39 Sump – examination and renovation

Wash out the sump in petrol and wipe dry. Inspect the exterior for signs of damage or excessive rust. If evident, a new sump must be obtained. To ensure an oiltight joint scrape away all traces of the old gasket from the cylinder block mating face.

40 Engine reassembly – general

All components of the engine must be cleaned of oil, sludge and old gaskets, and the working area should also be cleared and clean. In addition to the normal range of good quality socket spanners and general tools which are essential, the following must be available before reassembling begins:

(a) Complete set of new gaskets
(b) Supply of clean rags
(c) Oil can full of clean engine oil
(d) Torque wrench
(e) All new spare parts, as necessary

41 Crankshaft – refitting

Ensure that the crankcase is thoroughly clean and that all oilways are clear. A thin twist drill or a piece of wire is useful for cleaning them out. If possible blow them out with compressed air.
Treat the crankshaft in the same fashion, and then inject engine oil into the crankshaft oilways.
1 Wipe the bearing shell locations in the crankcase with a soft, lint-free rag.
2 Wipe the crankshaft journals with a soft, lint-free rag.
3 If the old main bearing shells are to be renewed (not to do so is a false economy, unless they are virtually new) fit the five upper halves of the main bearing shells to their location in the crankcase (photo).
4 Identify each main bearing cap and place them in order. The number is cast onto the cap and with intermediate caps an arrow is also marked which should point to the front of the engine (photo).
5 Wipe the end cap bearing shell location with a soft lint-free rag.
6 Fit the bearing half shell onto each main bearing cap (photo).
7 Apply a little grease to each side of the centre main bearing so as to retain the thrust washers (photo).
8 Fit the upper halves of the thrust washers into their grooves either side of the main bearing. The slots must face outwards (photo).
9 Lubricate the crankshaft journals and the upper and lower main bearing shells with engine oil (photo).
10 Carefully lower the crankshaft into the crankcase (photo).
11 Lubricate the crankshaft main bearing journals again and then fit No 1 bearing cap (photo). Fit the two securing bolts but do not tighten yet.
12 Apply a little gasket cement to the crankshaft rear main bearing end cap location (photo).
13 Next fit No 5 end cap (photo). Fit the two securing bolts, but, as before, do not tighten yet.
14 Apply a little grease to either side of the centre main bearing end cap so as to retain the thrust washers. Fit the thrust washers with the tag located in the groove and the slots facing outwards (photo).
15 Fit the centre main bearing end cap and the two securing bolts. Then refit the intermediate main bearing end caps (photo). Make sure that the arrows point towards the front of the engine (photo).
16 Lightly tighten all main cap securing bolts and then fully tighten in a progressive manner to the specified torque (photo).
17 Using a screwdriver ease the crankshaft fully forwards and, with

41.3 Inserting bearing shells into the crankcase

41.4 Main bearing cap identification marks

41.6 Fitting bearing shells to main bearing caps

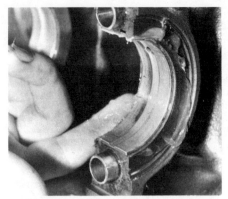

41.7 Apply grease to each side of the centre main bearing ...

41.8 ... and then fit the thrust washers to the centre main bearing

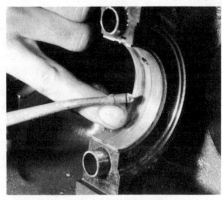

41.9 Lubricate the bearing shells ...

41.10 ... then fit the crankshaft into position

41.11 Refit the No 1 main bearing cap (note identification mark)

41.12 Apply gasket cement to the rear main bearing cap location

41.13 Refit the rear main bearing cap

41.14 Fit the thrust washers to the centre main bearing cap

41.15 With main bearing caps fitted ...

41.16 ... tighten their securing bolts to the specified torque

41.17 Use feeler gauges to check endfloat

feeler gauges, check the clearance between the crankshaft journal side and the thrust washers (photo) to ensure that the endfloat does not exceed that specified. Oversize thrust washers are available.

18 Test the crankshaft for freedom of rotation. Should it be very stiff to turn or possess high spots, a most careful inspection must be made with a micrometer, preferably by a qualified mechanic, to get to the root of the trouble. It is very seldom that any trouble of this nature will be experienced when fitting the crankshaft.

42 Pistons and connecting rods – reassembly

As an interference fit type gudgeon pin is used (see Section 21), this operation must be carried out by the local Ford garage. Make sure that the correct relationship is maintained between the piston and the connecting rod (Fig 1.17).

Fig. 1.17 The piston front marking relative to the connecting rod oil hole gives correct fitting (Sec 42)

43 Piston rings – fitting

1 Check that the piston ring grooves and oilways are thoroughly clean and unblocked. Piston rings must always be fitted over the head of the piston and never from the bottom.
2 The easiest method is to use a feeler gauge in a similar way to that for ring removal (Section 22).
3 Refit the rings one at a time, starting with the bottom oil control ring.
4 An alternative method is to fit the rings by holding them slightly open with the thumbs and both of the index fingers. This method requires a steady hand and great care, as it is easy to open the ring too much and break it.

44 Pistons – fitting

The pistons, complete with connecting rods, can be fitted to the cylinder bores in the following sequence:
1 With a wad of clean rag wipe the cylinder bores clean.
2 The pistons, complete with connecting rods, are fitted to their bores from the top of the block.
3 Locate the piston ring gaps in the following manner (photo):

Top: 150° from one side of the helical expander gap
Centre: 150° from the opposite side of the helical expander gap
Bottom: Helical expander: opposite the marked piston front side
Intermediate rings: 1 in (25 mm) each side of the helical expander gap

4 Lubricate well the piston and rings with engine oil (photo).
5 Fit a universal piston ring compressor and prepare to insert the first piston into the bore. Make sure it is the correct piston/connecting rod assembly for that particular bore, that the connecting rod is the correct way round and that the arrow on the piston points towards the front of the bore, ie towards the front of the engine (see photo 15.1).
6 Again lubricate the piston skirt and insert into the bore up to the bottom of the piston ring compressor (photos).

44.3 Position the ring gaps, as specified

44.4 Lubricate the pistons and rings before fitting

44.6a Insert the connecting rod into the cylinder bore ...

44.6b ... then fit the piston ring compressor ...

44.7 ... and push the piston down the bores

45.6 Refit the big-end cap nuts ...

45.7 ... and tighten them to the specified torque

46.3 Tighten the oil pump retaining bolts

48.1 Refit the auxiliary shaft

48.2 Locate the auxiliary shaft thrust plate ...

48.3 ... and tighten the thrust plate securing screws

48.4 Position a new gasket on the cylinder block front face

48.6a Refit the crankshaft timing cover and ...

48.6b ... tighten the securing bolts

48.8 Tighten the auxiliary shaft timing cover securing bolts

7   Gently, but firmly, tap the piston through the piston ring compressor and into the cylinder bore with a wooden or plastic faced hammer (photo).

45 Connecting rods to crankshaft – reassembly

1   Wipe clean the connecting rod half of the big-end bearing cap and the underside of the shell bearing, and fit the shell bearing in position with its locating tongue engaged with the corresponding cut-out in the rod.
2   If the old bearings are nearly new and are being refitted ensure they are replaced in their correct locations on the correct rods.
3   Generously lubricate the crankpin journals with engine oil and turn the crankshaft so that the crankpin is in the most advantageous position for the connecting rod to be drawn onto it.
4   Wipe clean the connecting rod bearing cap and back of the shell bearing, and fit the shell bearing in position ensuring that the locating tongue at the back of the bearing engages with the locating groove in the connecting rod cap.
5   Generously lubricate the shell bearing and offer up the connecting rod bearing cap to the connecting rod, Make sure it is the right way round.
6   Refit the connecting rod nuts (photo).
7   Tighten the nuts with a torque wrench to the specified setting (photo).
8   When all the connecting rods have been fitted, rotate the crankshaft to check that everything is free, and that there are no high spots causing binding. The bottom half of the engine is now nearly built up.

46 Oil pump – refitting

1   Wipe the mating faces of the oil pump and underside of the cylinder block.

2   Insert the hexagonal driveshaft into the end of the oil pump.
3   Before fitting the oil pump, lubricate it with engine oil to prime it, then offer it up and refit the two special bolts. Using the special tool (21-012) and a torque wrench, tighten the two bolts to the specified torque (photo).
4   Refit the one bolt and spring washer that secure the oil pump pick-up pipe support bracket to the crankcase.

47 Crankshaft rear oil seal – refitting

1   Lubricate the sealing lip of the oil seal, and then insert it into the carrier.
2   Refit the carrier and seal, driving it into position using a suitable tube drift, then fit and tighten the four securing bolts.

48 Auxiliary shaft and timing cover – refitting

1   Carefully insert the auxiliary shaft into the front face of the cylinder block (photo).
2   Position the thrust plate into its groove in the auxiliary shaft – countersunk faces of the holes facing outwards – and refit the two cross-head screws (photo).
3   Tighten the two cross-head screws using a cross-head screwdriver and an open-ended spanner (photo).
4   Smear some grease on the cylinder block side of a new gasket and carefully fit into position (photo).
5   Apply some gasket cement to the slot in the underside of the crankshaft timing cover. Insert the shaped seal.
6   Offer up the timing cover and secure with the bolts and spring washers (photos).
7   Smear some grease onto the seal located in the shaft timing cover over the end of the auxiliary shaft.
8   Secure the auxiliary shaft timing cover with the four bolts and spring washers (photo).

49 Sump – refitting

1   Locate the rubber gasket into the front and rear main bearing caps and the timing cover.
2   Wipe the mating faces of the crankcase and sump and smear some sealing compound over the block-to-timing cover joints.
3   Smear some grease on the underside of the crankcase.
4   Fit the sump gasket making sure that the bolt holes line up.
5   Offer the sump up to the gasket, taking care not to dislodge the gasket and secure in position with the bolts.
6   Tighten the sump bolts in a progressive manner to the specified torque.

50 Crankshaft sprocket, pulley and auxiliary shaft sprocket – refitting

1   Check that the keyways in the end of the crankshaft are clean and that the keys are free from burrs. Fit the keys into the keyways (photo).
2   Slide the sprocket into position on the crankshaft. This sprocket is the small diameter one (photo).
3   Ease the drivebelt into mesh with the crankshaft sprocket (photo).
4   Slide the large diameter plain washer onto the crankshaft (photo).
5   Check that the keyway in the end of the auxiliary shaft is clean and the key is free of burrs. Fit the key to the keyway.
6   Slide the sprocket onto the end of the auxiliary shaft (photo).
7   Slide the pulley onto the end of the crankshaft (photo).
8   Refit the bolt and thick plain washer to the end of the crankshaft (photo).
9   Lock the crankshaft pulley with a metal bar and using a socket wrench fully tighten the bolt to the specified torque (photo).

51 Water pump – refitting

1   Make sure that all traces of the old gasket are removed, and then smear some grease on the gasket face of the cylinder block.
2   Fit a new gasket to the cylinder block.
3   Offer up the water pump and secure in position with the four bolts and spring washers (photo).

52 Flywheel and clutch – refitting

1   Remove all traces of any protective coating from the flywheel if a new one is to be fitted, then offer up the flywheel to the crankshaft and align any previously made marks.
2   Fit the six crankshaft securing bolts and lightly tighten.
3   Lock the flywheel using a screwdriver engaged in the starter ring gear and tighten the securing bolts in a diagonal and progressive manner to the specified torque (photo).
4   Refit the clutch disc and pressure plate assembly to the flywheel making sure the disc is the right way round.
5   Secure the pressure plate assembly with the six retaining bolts and spring washers.
6   Centralise the clutch disc using an old input shaft or piece of wooden dowel and fully tighten the retaining bolts. See Chapter 5 for further details.

53 Valve – refitting

1   With the valves suitably ground in (see Section 36) and kept in their correct order, start with No 1 cylinder and insert the valve into its guide (photo).
2   Lubricate the valve stem with engine oil and slide on a new oil seal. The spring must be uppermost, as shown in the photo.
3   Fit the valve spring and cap (photo).
4   Use either the special valve spring compressor, part number 21-005, or carefully use a universal valve spring compressor. Compress the valve spring until the split collets can be slid into position (photo). Note these collets have serrations which engage in slots in the valve stem. Release the valve spring compressor.
5   Repeat this procedure until all eight valves and valve springs are fitted.

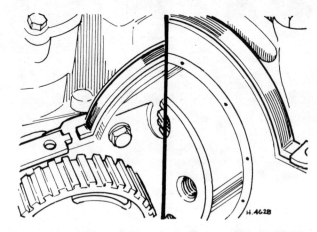

Fig. 1.18 Correct fitment of sump gasket at front and rear main bearing caps (Sec 49)

50.1 Locate the crankshaft Woodruff keys and ...

50.2 ... then slide the crankshaft sprocket into position

50.3 Locate the drivebelt over the crankshaft sprocket

50.4 Fit the large diameter plain washer

50.6 Fit the auxiliary shaft sprocket

50.7 Fit the crankshaft pulley and ...

50.8 ... then the securing bolt with large washer

50.9 Lock the pulley and tighten the securing bolt

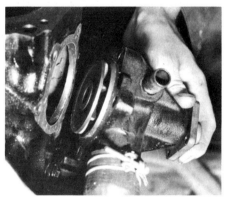

51.3 Refit the water pump with new gasket

52.3 Tighten the flywheel retaining bolts

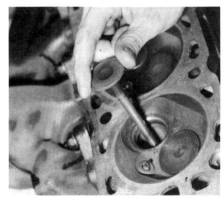

53.1 Insert valve into guide, then locate ...

53.2 ... the seal over the stem

53.3 Fit the valve spring and cap

53.4 Compress the spring to refit the collets

54 Camshaft – refitting

1   If the oil seal was removed (Section 19) a new one should be fitted, taking care that it is fitted the correct way round. Gently tap it into position so that it does not tilt (photo).
2   Apply some grease to the lip of the oil seal. Wipe the three bearing surfaces with a clean lint-free rag.
3   Lift the camshaft through the bearing taking care not to damage the bearing surfaces with the sharp edges of the cam lobes (photo). Also take care not to cut the fingers.
4   When the journals are ready to be inserted into the bearings, lubricate the bearings with engine oil (photo).
5   Push the camshaft through the bearings until the locating groove in the rear of the camshaft is just rearwards of the bearing carrier.
6   Slide the thrust plate into engagement with the camshaft taking care to fit it the correct way round, as previously noted (photo).
7   Secure the thrust plate with the two bolts and spring washers.
8   Check that the keyway in the end of the camshaft is clean and the key is free of burrs. Fit the key into the keyway (photo).
9   Fit the camshaft sprocket backplate, tag facing outwards (photo).
10 Fit the camshaft sprocket to the end of the camshaft and with a soft-faced hammer make sure it is fully home (photo).
11 Refit the sprocket securing bolt and thick plain washer and tighten to the specified torque (photo).

55 Cam followers – refitting

1   Undo the ball-headed bolt locknut (photo) and screw down the bolt fully. This will facilitate refitting the cam followers.
2   Rotate the camshaft until the cam lobe is away from the top of the cylinder head. Pass the cam follower under the back of the cam until the cup is over the ball-headed bolt (photo).
3   Engage the cup with the ball-headed bolt (photo).
4   Refit the cam follower spring by engaging the ends of the spring with the anchor on the ball-headed bolt (photo).
5   Using the fingers pull the spring up and then over the top of the cam follower (photos).
6   Repeat the above sequence for the remaining seven cam followers.
7   Check that the jet holes in the camshaft lubrication pipe are clear, and offer up the pipe to the camshaft bearing pedestals (photo).
8   Refit the pipe securing bolts and spring washers.

56 Cylinder head – refitting

1   Wipe clean the mating faces of the cylinder head and cylinder block.
2   Carefully place a new gasket on the cylinder block (photo) making

54.1 Locate the camshaft oil seal

54.3 Insert the camshaft through the bearings

54.4 Lubricate the camshaft bearings

54.6 Fit the camshaft thrust plate

54.8 Refit the Woodruff key

54.9 With the backplate refitted ...

54.10 ... refit the sprocket

54.11 Tighten the bolt to the specified torque

55.1 Slackening the ball-headed bolt locknut

55.2 Pass cam follower under camshaft

55.3 Cup located over ball-headed bolt

55.4 Cam follower spring engaged with the anchor

55.5a Cam follower spring being lifted over the cam follower

55.5b Cam follower springs correctly fitted

55.7 Refit the lubrication pipe

56.2 Positioning the cylinder head gasket on top of the cylinder block

56.4a Refit the cylinder head bolts and ...

56.4b ... tighten them using the special tool ...

56.5 ... to the specified torque

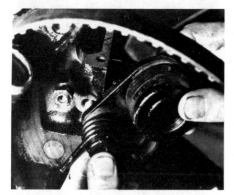

57.1 Refit the drivebelt tensioner

57.3 Use a screwdriver to relieve the spring tension for bolt fitting

58.2 Line up the camshaft timing marks

sure that it is the correct way up and the right way round.

3 Gently lower the cylinder head into place being as accurate as possible first time, so that the gasket is not dislodged.

4 Refit the cylinder head bolts (photo) ensuring that the threads are cleaned and lightly oiled before doing so. Using the special tool (21-0002) (photo) lightly tighten all the bolts.

5 Progressively tighten the cylinder head bolts in the sequence shown in Fig. 1.3. Tighten the bolts in three stages to the torque settings given in the Specifications (photo).

6 After the engine has been run for 15 minutes at a fast idle, slacken the cylinder head bolts half a turn, one at a time, in the correct sequence and then retighten them to the final fourth stage torque setting.

57 Camshaft drivebelt tensioner and thermostat housing – refitting

1 Thread the bolt through the spring and tensioner plate and screw the bolt into the cylinder head (photo).

2 Tighten the bolt securely using the special tool (21-012 also used on the oil pump).

3 Using a screwdriver to overcome the tension of the spring, position the plate and screw its securing bolt into the cylinder head (photo).

4 Clean the mating faces of the cylinder head and thermostat housing and fit a new gasket.

5 Offer up the thermostat housing and secure it in position with the two bolts and spring washers.

6 Tighten the bolts to the specified torque.

58 Camshaft drivebelt – refitting and timing

1 Rotate the crankshaft until No 1 piston is at its TDC position. This is indicated by the crankshaft sprocket keyway being uppermost. If the pulley is fitted, position by means of the timing marks to give TDC (see Chapter 4). If the distributor is fitted, also check that the rotor arm is pointing to No 1 spark plug electrode.

2 Rotate the camshaft until the pointer is in alignment with the for mark on the front bearing pedestal (photo). To achieve this always rotate the camshaft in the direction shown in Fig. 1.19.

3 Engage the drivebelt with the crankshaft sprocket and auxiliary shaft sprocket. Pass the back of the belt over the tensioner jockey wheel and then slide it into mesh with the camshaft sprocket.

4 Slacken the tensioner plate securing bolt and allow the tensioner to settle by rotating the crankshaft twice. Retighten the tensioner plate securing bolt.

5 Line up the timing marks and check that these are correct, indicating the belt has been correctly refitted.

6 Refit the drivebelt guard, easing the guard into engagement with the bolt and large plain washer located under the water pump (photos).

7 Refit the guard secureing bolts and tighten fully.

59 Valve clearances – checking and adjustment

1 With the engine top cover removed, turn the crankshaft until the two cams of one cylinder point upwards to form a 'V'. This will ensure that the cam follower is at the back of the cam.

2 Using feeler gauges as shown in the photo check the clearance, which will be found in the Specifications.

3 If adjustment is necessary, using open-ended spanners slacken the ball-headed bolt securing locknut (photo).

4 Screw the ball-headed bolt up or down, as necessary, until the required clearance is obtained. Retighten the locknut.

5 An alternative method of adjustment is to work to the following table:

Valves open	Valves to adjust
1 ex and 4 in	6 in and 7 ex
6 in and 7 ex	1 ex and 4 in
2 in and 5 ex	3 ex and 8 in
3 ex and 8 in	2 in and 5 ex

6 On completion refit the top cover (photo) and tighten the bolts in the sequence shown in Fig. 1.21 in the stages indicated in the Specifications.

58.6a Refit the drivebelt guard

58.6b Guard location between washer and pedestal

59.2 Checking a cam follower clearance

59.3 Slacken the ball-headed bolt locknut to make adjustment

59.6 Refit the top cover

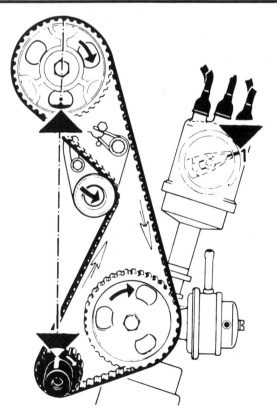

Fig. 1.19 Camshaft, crankshaft and distributor timing marks (triangular arrows) with No 1 piston at TDC on its firing stroke (Sec 58)

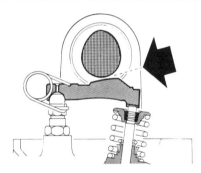

Fig. 1.20 Cam follower and camshaft clearances (Sec 59)

Fig. 1.21 Tightening order for the engine top cover securing bolts (Sec 59)

60 Engine and gearbox – reconnection

If the engine was removed in unit with the gearbox they may be re-attached in the following manner:

1   With the engine on the floor and a wooden block under the front of the sump, lift up the gearbox and insert the gearbox input shaft into the centre of the clutch and push, so that the input shaft splines pass through the internal splines of the clutch disc.
2   If difficulty is experienced in engaging the splines, try turning the gearbox slightly, but on no account allow the weight of the gearbox to rest on the input shaft, as it is easily bent.
3   With the gearbox correctly positioned on the engine backplate support its weight using a wooden block.
4   Secure the gearbox to the engine and backplate with the bolts and spring washers.
5   Refit the starter motor to its aperture in the backplate and secure with the bolts and spring washers.

61 Final reassembly (engine)

1   Reconnect the ancillary components to the engine in the reverse order to which they were removed.
2   It should be noted that in all cases it is best to reassemble the engine as far as possible before refitting it to the car. This means that the inlet and exhaust manifolds (photos), carburettor, alternator, water thermostat, oil filter, distributor and engine mounting brackets, should all be in position.

62 Engine refitting – general

1   Although the engine can be installed by one person with a suitable winch, it is easier if two are present, one to lower the engine into the engine compartment and the other to guide the engine into position and to ensure that it does not foul anything.
2   At this stage one or two tips may come in useful. Ensure all the loose leads, cables, etc are tucked out of the way. If not, it is easy to trap one and so cause much additional work after the engine is replaced. Smear grease on the top of the gearbox input shaft before fitting the gearbox.
3   Always fit a new fan drivebelt, new cooling hoses and new worm drive clips, as this will help eliminate the possibility of failure while on the road.

63 Engine – refitting (without gearbox)

1   Attach the lifting sling to the engine and secure it to the hoist. Raise the power unit to the required height, then push the car into position (or move the hoist, as applicable).
3   Before lowering the engine, check that all cables, controls and attachments within the engine compartment are tucked out of the way. Get an assistant to steady and guide the engine into position as it is lowered.
3   If it has been moved, reposition the jack under the gearbox to raise and support it. Now lower the engine into the engine compartment, ensuring that nothing is fouling. Align the height of the engine with the gearbox.
4   Move the engine rearward until the splines of the gearbox first motion shaft enter the splined hub of the clutch driven plate (friction disc). The clutch driven plate will have already been aligned, as described in Chapter 5. The engine may need turning fractionally to obtain engagement. If so, turn the crankshaft pulley using a spanner applied to its centre bolt.
5   Move the engine fully to the rear to mate the faces of the clutch bellhousing and the engine crankcase. Insert and tighten the securing bolts; fit the starter.
6   Locate the engine mounting on each side. You will need to raise or lower the engine to align the mounting bolt holes.
7   Position a jack under the crossmember and raise it so that it meets the main frame. Now unscrew and remove each 3 inch bolt in turn and refit the original mounting bolts. The engine lifting sling can now be removed.
8   Reconnect the steering column-to-rack pinion lower joint, aligning

61.2a Locate a new gasket before ...

61.2b ... fitting the manifold and carburettor

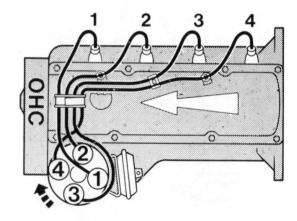
Fig. 1.22 Correct fitment of the HT leads is essential (Sec 63)

the mating marks made on removal. Refit the clamp bolt.
9 Reconnect the starter motor cable and engine earth strap.
10 Unplug the fuel line and connect it to the fuel pump.
11 Reconnect the coil, distributor and spark plug leads.
12 Reconnect the exhaust downpipe to the manifold or the manifold to the cylinder head (in which case use a new gasket).
13 Reconnect the throttle cable to its location bracket and to the throttle control rod.
14 Reconnect the oil pressure line to the cylinder block (left-hand side at rear) and locate the pipe in the throttle bracket.
15 Refit the temperature gauge transmitter unit lead.
16 If necessary, adjust the alternator drivebelt tension (Chapter 10) and reconnect its leads.
17 Refit the cooling fan followed by the radiator and, where applicable, the oil cooler. Reconnect the hoses.
18 Reconnect the heater hoses and the carburettor auto choke hoses.
19 Connect the vacuum hose to the servo unit at one end and to the inlet manifold at the other.
20 Refit the air cleaner unit.
21 Working inside the car, reconnect the steering column and the associated fittings that were detached during removal.
22 Refit and reconnect the battery, then check the steering column and associated switches and controls for satisfactory operation.
23 Refit the bonnet and check its alignment before fully tightening the hinge bolts. An assistant will be necessary here.
24 Refill the cooling system (Chapter 2).
25 Refill the engine with the correct grade and quantity of oil (an extra pint will be required for absorption by the new filter element).
26 Check around the engine to ensure that there are no signs of leaks and that all fittings have been reconnected and are secure before attempting to start the engine.

64 Engine and gearbox – refitting

The procedures for fitting the combined engine and gearbox into the car are, in general, the same as those given in the previous Section, but the following differences apply:
1 When attaching the lift sling, allow for the considerable tilt necessary when refitting the two units.
2 Once the units are lowered into the car and the gearbox has passed under the transmission tunnel, jack up the gearbox whilst simultaneously lowering the engine. Then locate the gearbox mounting plate bolts to secure it in position.
3 If not already done, refit the starter motor before raising the crossmember and reconnecting the engine mountings and steering column joint, as given in Section 63, paragraphs 7 and 8.
4 When the engine and gearbox are both located and their mountings fully tightened, remove the lifting sling and then reconnect the various engine fittings as given in Section 63, paragraphs 9 to 26 inclusive.
5 In addition you will also need to:

(1) Reconnect the clutch cable, and adjust it as given in Chapter 5
(b) Remove the plug or temporary seal from the gearbox rear extension and refit the propeller shaft, as given in Chapter 7
(c) Reconnect the speedometer drive cable and the reversing light switch wires
(d) Refit the gear lever
(e) Top up the gearbox oil level, as necessary
(f) When the battery is reconnected, check the functions of the steering column switches and controls to ensure that they operate. If not, recheck the appropriate connections.

65 Engine – initial start-up after major overhaul or repair

1 Make sure that the battery is fully charged and that all lubricants, coolant and fuel are replenished.
2 If the fuel system has been dismantled it will require several revolutions of the engine on the starter motor to pump the petrol up to the carburettor.
3 As soon as the engine fires and runs, keep it going at a fast tick-over only (no faster) and bring it up to normal working temperature.
4 As the engine warms up there will be odd smells and some smoke from parts getting hot and burning off oil deposits. The signs to look for are serious leaks of water or oil which will be obvious. Check also the exhaust pipe and manifold connections, as these do not always find their exact gastight position until the warmth and vibration have acted on them, and it is almost certain that they will need tightening further. This should be done, of course, with the engine stopped.
5 When normal running temperature has been reached, adjust the engine idle speed as described in Chapter 3.
6 Stop the engine and wait a few minutes to see if any lubricant or coolant is dripping out when the engine is stationary.
7 Recheck the engine oil level since it is likely that a small amount of topping-up will be required due to oil circulation through the system.
8 Run the engine for a further 15 minutes and then remove the engine top cover and tighten the cylinder head bolts (see Section 56). Also check the tightness of the sump bolts.
9 Road test the car to check that the timing is correct and that the engine is giving the necessary smoothness and power. Do not race the engine – if new bearings and/or pistons have been fitted it should be treated as a new engine and run in at a reduced speed for the first 1000 miles (2000 km). After this mileage it will be beneficial to change the engine oil and renew the oil filter.

PART B: RS 1800

66 General description

The RS 1800 engine, sometimes referred to as the BDA or belt drive engine, is a four-cylinder, twin overhead camshaft unit with a capacity of 1834 cc (111.9 cu in).
Dry liners are pressed into bores machined in the aluminium cylinder block, which is cast integrally with the upper half of the crankcase. The bores are provided with full length water jacketing.
The cylinder head is an aluminium casting, with fully machined wedge-shaped combustion chambers. There are two inlet and two exhaust valves for each cylinder. The ports for each pair of valves are siamesed. Both the inlet and the exhaust valves are inclined at 20° from the vertical, and the valve guides are renewable.
The two overhead camshafts are mounted in a separate carrier and operate the valves by acting directly on piston-type tappets. The camshafts are driven at half engine speed by a single row toothed belt from a sprocket on the crankshaft via a sprocket on an auxiliary shaft and a tension adjusting idler. A second idler mounted on the front cover provides the necessary belt wrap-around for the crankshaft sprocket. The camshafts each run in six bearings machined directly in the aluminium casting of the carrier. A 'half-moon' thrust washer locates each shaft axially in the carrier and controls endfloat. An oil

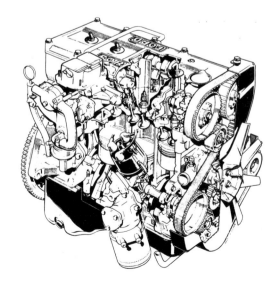

Fig. 1.23 Cutaway view of the RS 1800 engine (Sec 66)

seal at the front of the carrier and a sealing plug (located by a pin) at the rear prevent oil leakage from the carrier.

The auxiliary shaft is a modification of the camshaft normally used in the pushrod overhead valve unit and is retained to drive the oil pump, distributor and fuel pump. The front journal of the auxiliary shaft has a groove machined in its periphery to regulate the supply of oil to the camshafts and valve gear. The sump is a steel fabrication and has a rear well for the lubricating oil. The engine lubrication system is the force feed type incorporating a full-flow oil filter. The oil pump, which is mounted externally on the engine, is of the eccentric bi-rotor type incorporating a non-adjustable plunger type relief valve. An oil cooler is fitted as standard to all vehicles. The oil take-off is from an adaptor assembled with the oil filter bowl.

An oil filler is located on the camshaft cover. Crankcase ventilation is by a closed system, crankcase fumes being discharged directly into the carburettor air intake.

67 Variations from Mexico and RS 2000 engine

In the preparation of this part of Chapter 1 we have worked on the principle that, apart from three sub-assemblies on the RS 1800 engine, the design of the cylinder block is almost identical with that of the Mexico and RS 2000 engines covered in Part A. The main difference concerning the cylinder block itself is that it is manufactured in aluminium alloy rather than cast iron. This means, of course, that greater care must be taken when handling the block and when tightening its fastenings. Apart from this, the three main sub-asemblies which differ on the RS 1800 engine are:

(a) *The overhead camshaft mechanism*
(b) *The cylinder head*
(c) *The timing belt and its associated driven components*

To avoid duplication, we therefore make references in this part of Chapter 1 to Part A for those operations which are the same for the single overhead camshaft engine, but reference should be made to Part B of the Specifications for the figures relevant to the RS 1800 engine.

68 Major operations possible with the engine in place

The following major operations can be carried out on the engine with it in place in the bodyframe:

1 *Removal and refitting of the cam cover, carrier and camshafts*
2 *Removal and refitting of the cylinder head assembly*
3 *Removal and refitting of the sump (see below)*
4 *Removal and refitting of the big-end bearings*
5 *Removal and refitting of the pistons and connecting rods*
6 *Removal and refitting of the timing belt and pulleys*
7 *Removal and refitting of the oil pump*
8 *Removal and refitting of the engine front mountings*
9 *Removal and refitting of the engine/gearbox rear mounting*
10 *Removal and refitting of the engine front cover*

Before removing the sump with the engine in position in the car, you will need to support the engine from above by means of a sling.

The steering column must then be disconnected at the lower joint and the engine mounting crossmember lowered to allow the sump sufficient clearance for removal. Because of this it is often preferable to remove the engine from the car, which allows greater accessibility for working within the crankcase and on any other items on the engine.

69 Major operations requiring engine removal

The following major operations can only be carried out with engine out of the bodyframe and on the bench or floor:

1 *Removal and refitting of the main bearings*
2 *Removal and refitting of the crankshaft*
3 *Removal and refitting of the flywheel*
4 *Removal and refitting of the crankshaft rear bearing oil seal*
5 *Removal and refitting of the auxiliary shaft*

70 Method of engine removal

The engine complete with gearbox can be lifted as a unit from the engine compartment. Alternatively the engine and gearbox can be split at the front of the bellhousing, a stand or jack placed under the gearbox to provide additional support, and the engine lifted out. The easiest method of engine removal is to remove just the engine, leaving the gearbox in place in the car. If the engine and gearbox are removed as a unit they have to be lifted out at a very steep angle which can be difficult.

71 Engine – removal (without gearbox)

1   In order to carry out the removal efficiently, it is desirable that a pair of stands, lifting tackle and a portable hydraulic jack are available. Other equipment can be used, such as blocks and a fixed screw jack, but it does tend to make the operation a bit more difficult.
2   Start by disconnecting the battery earth lead. To protect the paintwork on the wing panels during the following operations, cover them with old newspapers or similar.
3   Detach the bonnet light from the fuse block connection, then unbolt and remove the bonnet (photo), as described in Chapter 12.
4   Remove the air cleaner unit, referring to Chapter 3 if necessary, then disconnect the throttle cable from its bracket connection.
5   Disconnect the oil pressure gauge pipe at the engine adaptor (photo), and the water temperature sender unit lead. Remove the exhaust manifold retaining nuts, pull the manifold to one side and tie it back out of the way.
6   Unscrew the sump drain plug and drain the engine oil into a suitable container.
7   Referring to Chapter 2, drain the cooling system and remove the radiator. Disconnect the heater hoses at their bulkhead connections (photo). Remove the engine cooling fan.
8   Disconnect the fuel pump and plug the open end of the supply line.
9   Disconnect the brake servo hose at the induction manifold and the oil cooler hoses at the oil filter bowl connections.
10 Disconnect the high tension lead and distributor lead from the coil,

71.3 Remove the bonnet

71.5 Disconnect the oil pressure gauge pipe (arrowed)

71.7 Disconnect the bottom hose

and disconnect the lead from the solenoid at the starter motor. Disconnect the engine earth strap.

11 The steering column must now be detached at the flexible joint, so first make an alignment mark across the shaft and joint to ensure correct realignment during assembly. Unscrew and remove the clamping bolt.

12 From inside the driving compartment, unscrew the two bolts securing the lower end of the steering column to the floorpan. Then unscrew the two cross-head screws securing the top end of the column to the facia panel, disconnect the two multi-plug connectors and withdraw the assembly.

13 Jack up the front of the car and fit stands, but not under the crossmember.

14 Support the engine front crossmember with a jack and remove the four mounting bolts, exchanging each one in turn with a 3 in (8.00 cm) long bolt and washer. Unscrew the four bolts securing the stabilizer bar to the chassis, after bending the locking tabs. Then lower the crossmember until it is supported on the long bolts (see Figs. 1.2).

15 Attach a sling to the engine and support its weight using suitable lifting tackle.

16 Now detach the left-hand engine mounting bracket from its block and the rubber insulator from the crossmember. Withdraw the bracket together with the insulator.

17 Remove the rubber insulator from the right-hand side crossmember and engine mounting brackets.

18 Remove the two top bellhousing bolts and the dipstick tube. Then, from underneath the car, remove the three bolts securing the flywheel dust cover to the bellhousing, and disconnect the clutch cable.

19 Remove the two bolts securing the starter motor and move it forwards to disengage the starter pinion. Remove the remainder of the bellhousing-to-engine bolts.

20 Support the gearbox with a jack, and pull the engine carefully forwards and upwards with the crane until it is free of the engine compartment. Place the engine on blocks on the floor, or on a carefully prepared bench, or trestles. The bench, or trestles, must be substantial enough to bear the engine, and the whole area should be clean and large enough so that the whole engine is accessible for stripping.

72 Engine and gearbox – removal

1 Disconnect the appropriate attachments as detailed in the previous Section, up to and including paragraph 17. Also disconnect the clutch and speedometer cables.

2 Continue, as described in Section 6 of this Chapter, to disconnect the gearbox from the propeller shaft and remove the engine/gearbox unit from the car.

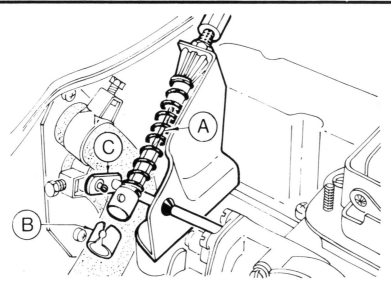

Fig. 1.24 Throttle cable connection (Sec 71)

A   Cable   B   Securing clip   C   Linkage

Fig. 1.25 Steering shaft flexible joint – remove arrowed bolt (Sec 71)

Fig. 1.26 Removing the RS 1800 engine (Sec 71)

73 Engine dismantling – general

Refer to Part A of this Chapter, Section 7.

74 Ancillary engine components – removal

1   The ancillary engine components to be removed before dismantling begins are given in Section 8 of this Chapter.
2   It is suggested that reference is made to the relevant Chapters for removal instructions of units such as the cooling system components (Chapter 2), the fuel system components (Chapter 3) and the clutch (Chapter 5).
3   In order to remove the alternator drivebelt and water pump it is necessary to remove the timing cover. Refer to Section 75, paragraphs 4, 6 and 7.

75 Timing belt – adjustment and renewal

1   In order to adjust or renew the timing belt it is first necessary to remove the cooling fan.
2   Disconnect the battery negative lead then drain the cooling system and disconnect the radiator hoses.
3   Remove the radiator bolts and lift the radiator out of the car, then remove the cooling fan. Refer to Chapter 2 for details, if necessary.
4   Remove the two front (top) cam cover bolts (photo), two idler stud nuts, bottom retaining bolt and ease off the timing belt cover (photo).
5   To check the tension in the timing belt, turn the exhaust camshaft sprocket so that all slack is along the section between the exhaust sprocket and the idler sprocket (the belt's longest run). Check the tension using a Burroughs gauge between the two sprockets, the tension should be as given in the Specifications. Alternatively the tension can be checked by pulling the belt to one side with a spring balance and measuring the deflection. The recommended pulling force and total deflection are given in the Specifications.
6   To correct the tension in the timing belt, slacken the adjuster locknut (photo) and adjust as necessary. Tighten the locknut, recheck the tension and adjust again if necessary.
7   If the timing belt is to be removed rotate the engine forwards until No 1 piston is at TDC on its compression stroke. At this point the timing marks on the sprockets will align. Remove the fanbelt together with the water pump pulley. Then remove the crankshaft fanbelt pulley and the idler retaining nut. Slacken the adjuster pulley and pull it off the stud. The belt can now be removed with the idler pulley (photos).
8   Inspect the belt for cracks, frayed edges or other evidence of deterioration and obtain a new belt if necessary.
9   Before replacing the belt, degrease the sprockets thoroughly, and then spray them with a pure molybdenum disulphide air drying bonding resin.
10 Ensure that all the sprocket timing marks are correctly aligned

Fig. 1.27 Checking the timing belt tension using a Burroughs gauge (Sec 75)

Fig. 1.28 Checking the timing belt tension using a spring balance (Sec 75)

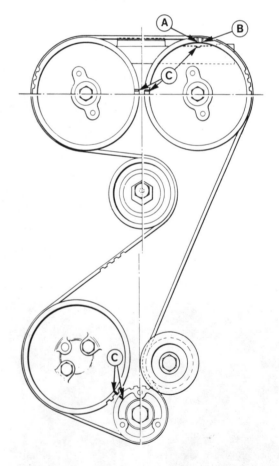

Fig. 1.29 Timing belt and sprockets with timing marks set in alignment (Sec 75)

A   TDC mark   C   Sprocket timing marks
B   Ignition timing mark

75.4a Removing the timing cover upper bolts

75.4b Easing off the timing cover. Note the timing mark on the cam cover immediately behind the belt (arrowed)

75.6 Slackening adjuster pulley locknut

75.7a Remove the water pump pulley bolts ...

5.7b ... the crankshaft pulley ...

75.7c ... and the adjuster pulley

75.7d Ease off the belt with the idler

75.10a Camshaft sprocket timing marks aligned

75.10b Crankshaft and auxiliary shaft timing marks aligned

76.1 Removing the cam cover

76.2 Checking a valve clearance

77.1 Removing cam carrier bolts

with No 1 piston at TDC on the compression stroke (photos), and then refit the belt and idler with the large bearing shoulder to the rear. With the belt in position refit the adjuster pulley and retension the belt as described in paragraphs 5 and 6.

11 Reassembly is the reverse of the removal procedure.

76 Valve clearances – adjustment

1 If the engine is in the car you will need to remove the air cleaner unit (Chapter 3), the spark plugs (to reduce the compression when turning the engine), and the cam cover, which is secured by ten bolts (photo).

2 To check the valve clearances, turn the engine so that the top of each cam in turn is 180° away from the tappet to be checked. Then select a feeler blade or blades that can just be inserted between the tappet and the heel of the cam to measure the clearance (photo). Note the clearance and repeat the procedure for the other valves. Refer to the Specifications for details of the clearances. If the clearances require adjusting, the camshaft carrier must be removed according to Section 77 when the engine is out of the car, and according to Section 78 when it is in the car.

3 When the camshaft carrier is removed, the correct valve clearance is obtained by fitting a different size shim in the recess in the valve spring retainer. A thinner shim will be needed to increase the clearance, and a thicker one to reduce the clearance. The shim's thickness should be measured accurately with a micrometer. The correct thickness needed in each case can be calculated from the following formula.

Shim thickness require = A + B - C
where A is the actual valve clearance
B is the existing shim thickness
and C is the correct valve clearance

On no account use more than one shim for each valve.

4 If it was found necessary to adjust the valve clearances, refit the

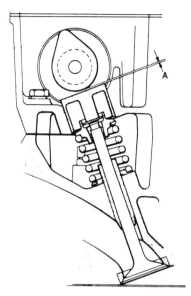

Fig. 1.30 Valve clearance check – measure clearance (A) between the cam heel and the tappet with feeler gauge (Sec 76)

cam carrier (Section 77 or 78) and then recheck the valve clearances before refitting the cam cover.

77 Cam carrier – removal and refitting (engine out of car)

1 Having removed the cam cover and its gasket, unscrew and remove all of the cam carrier bolts (photo), except the centre row end bolts. Now invert the engine, remove the two end bolts and lower the

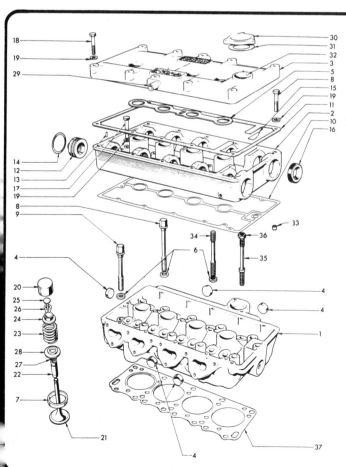

Fig. 1.31 The cam carrier and cylinder head assembly components (Sec 77)

1	Cylinder head	18	Bolt
2	Cam carrier	19	Lockwasher
3	Cam cover	20	Tappets
4	Plug	21	Valve
5	Gasket – plug bosses	22	Valve guide
6	Washer	23	Valve spring
7	Valve seat insert	24	Valve spring retainer
8	Bolt	25	Tappet shim (selected)
9	Bolt	26	Collets
10	Gasket – head to cam carrier	27	Valve guide circlips
11	Gasket – cam carrier to cover	28	Valve spring platform
12	Cam carrier plug	29	Tube
13	Pin – cam carrier plug	30	Oil filler cap assembly
14	O-ring – cam carrier plug	31	Gasket
15	Key	32	Rivet
16	Oil seal	33	Dowel
17	Bolt	34	Cylinder head stud
		35	Cylinder head stud
		36	Nut
		37	Gasket

carrier from the engine carefully to avoid losing any of the valve shims. Try not to damage the gasket, and renew it if necessary.

2   If for any reason you are not able to invert the engine for carrier removal you will need to proceed as described in Section 78, paragraphs 6 to 9 inclusive.

3   Refitting is the reverse of removal, but the operations detailed in paragraphs 11 to 18 in the following Section should be adhered to, especially if the valve clearances have been adjusted.

78 Cam carrier – removal and refitting (engine in car)

1   This operation is normally carried out during a complete strip of the engine, or when the valve clearances are adjusted. In any event, the valve clearances, Section 76, must be checked first.

2   Drain the cooling system and disconnect the radiator hoses. Next, remove the radiator and cooling fan as described in Chapter 2. Pull the HT leads off the spark plugs.

3   Remove the timing belt cover, the fanbelt and the water pump pulley, also as described in Chapter 2.

4   Remove the crankshaft fanbelt pulley and the idler retaining nut. Rotate the engine to align the timing marks.

5   Slacken the adjuster sprocket and pull it off the stud. The belt can now be removed together with the idler.

6   Slacken the fifteen cam carrier bolts evenly until all the valves have closed. Carefully clean the area around the tappets and the heads of the tappets themselves, to get rid of surplus oil.

7   Position eight bar magnets (as in Fig. 1.32), one to each of the exhaust valve tappets, turning the camshaft as necessary to ensure that the magnets pick up on the tappets. Remove the cam carrier bolts, evenly; lift the exhaust side of the cam carrier clear of the cylinder head, at the same time push down the inlet valve tappets so that the shims do not become displaced. Completely invert the cam carrier and refit any shims that have become dislodged into the correct seat. Ensure that any displaced tappets are also returned to the correct bores. In our experience, if bar magnets are not used, it is almost certain that the tappets and shims will be displaced. Obviously, there are other methods of ensuring that the shims are not displaced, but this is not the place to list them. Suffice it to say that it was found that the bar magnet method was very satisfactory, but any other method that serves the primary function of retaining the shims in their seats would be satisfactory.

8   If, during the operations described in para 7, any of the shims become displaced, they should be put back in any order and the cam carrier, sprockets, belt etc refitted so that the valve clearances can be measured again (Section 76). Then repeat paragraphs 4 to 8 and carry on as in paragraph 9. If the shims were not displaced then proceed with paragraph 9 anyway.

9   Remove the incorrect shim(s), select shims of the correct thickness, and fit them, along with the correct old shims in their respective seats. Lightly grease each shim to ensure it 'sticks' on the valve stem. Do not use more than one shim for each valve.

10   Remove the tappets and magnets from the cam carrier.

11   Before refitting the cam carrier, thoroughly clean the tappets and the cam carrier in a proprietary degreasing agent, lightly grease the tappets and refit them in their respective positions in the carrier. Locate the magnets on top of the tappets. Position a gasket on the cylinder head using a suitable sealant (ensure that the gasket is correctly fitted and that the two locating dowels are in the cylinder head).

12   Locate the cam carrier on the cylinder head, remove the magnets and rotate the camshaft so that the timing marks are approximately aligned.

13   Tighten the carrier bolts evenly to the specified torque, then degrease the sprockets thoroughly and spray them with a pure molybdenum disulphide air drying bonding resin.

14   Ensure that all the sprocket timing marks are correctly aligned and then refit the belt and idler with the large bearing shoulder to the rear. Roughly tension the belt. Until this rough tensioning is carried out the aligning mark on the auxiliary shaft sprocket may be slightly higher than the corresponding mark on the crankshaft sprocket; as the belt is tensioned the two marks should come into line.

15   Check the valve clearances, as detailed in Section 76. If they are incorrect the complete series of operations from paragraph 4 will need to be repeated. If correct, carry on with paragraph 16.

16   Secure the idler nut, tightening it to the specified torque, and then

refit the crankshaft pulley, securing it with three bolts.

17   Rotate the engine through one revolution, until the sprocket timing marks are all aligned. The tension can be checked, as described in Section 75.

18   If the belt tension is incorrect, slacken the adjuster locknut and adjust as necessary. Repeat paragraph 17 (and 18 if necessary).

19   Refit the fanbelt and position the water pump pulley on its boss. Then locate the timing belt cover on the idler studs and refit the nuts and bottom bracket bolt. Refit the cooling fan and tighten the bolts to the specified torque.

20   Check the fanbelt tension and adjust, if necessary (see Chapter 2, Section 10).

21   Refit the radiator and connect the top and bottom hoses. Reconnect the rear heater hose, then refill the cooling system.

22   Reconnect the battery.

79 Camshaft – removal and refitting

1   Before a camshaft can be removed, it is obviously necessary to remove the cam cover and carrier. These operations are detailed in Section 77 or 78 as applicable.

2   Remove the camshaft sprocket centre bolt and washer (photo),

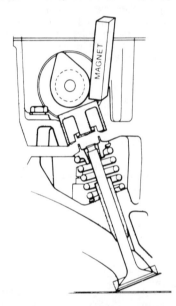

Fig. 1.32 Use magnets to retain the tappets when removing the cam carrier (Sec 78)

79.2 Camshaft sprocket bolt removal

79.3 Woodruff key on the camshaft taper

79.4a Remove the pin from the rear sealing plug ...

79.4b ... the crescent-shaped thrust washer ...

79.4c ... and the rear sealing plug ...

79.4d ... then withdraw the camshaft

79.6 Lubricate the camshaft bearings before reassembling

80.2 Detaching an oil drain tube

80.4a Removing the cylinder head bolts

80.4b Remove the cylinder head

then, using a puller, ease the sprocket off its taper. If a puller is not available it is possible to lever the sprocket off the taper using two tyre levers, but this needs to be done with care.

3   Remove the key from the slot in the taper and store in a safe place (photo).

4   Extract the pin locating the rear sealing plug (photo), then remove the crescent-shaped thrust washer from near the front of the cam carrier (photo) and ease out the camshaft rearwards: this will push out the sealing plug in the process, which should be retained in a safe place (photos).

5   Using a piece of wood or some other blunt tool, push the front oil seal out of the carrier.

6   Before fitting the camshaft, first lightly oil the bearings (photo), then relocate the camshaft in the carrier. Next, fit a new oil seal. Push it too far into its housing, and tap it forwards gently with the camshaft until the front face of the seal is flush with the bottom of the chamfer in the carrier.

7   Refit the crescent-shaped thrust washer. Refit the sealing plug, with a new O-ring, in the rear of the carrier and locate with the small pin.

8   Refit the sprocket locating key in its slot in the camshaft nose and fit the sprocket, tightening the centre bolt to the specified torque.

80 Cylinder head – removal and refitting (engine removed)

1   The cam cover and carrier will need to be removed before the cylinder head; these operations are described in Section 77 or 78, as applicable.

2   First, disconnect the oil drain tubes from the head to the front cover (photo).

3   Remove the dipstick tube support bracket from the inlet manifold.

4   Slacken the cylinder head bolts evenly, ie in the reverse sequence to that shown in Fig. 1.33 (photo). Remove the cylinder head, manifold and carburettor assembly complete with gaskets (photo).

5   If the head is jammed, try to rock it to break the seal. Under no circumstances try to prise it apart from the block with a screwdriver or cold chisel, as damage may be done to the faces of the head or block. If the head will not free readily, turn the engine with the flywheel as the compression in the cylinders will often break the cylinder head

joint. If this fails to work, strike the head sharply with a plastic-headed hammer, or with a wooden hammer, or with a metal hammer with an interposed piece of wood to cushion the blows. Under no circumstances hit the head directly with a metal hammer as this may cause irreparable damage. Several sharp taps with the hammer, at the same time pulling upwards, should free the head. Lift the head off and place on one side.

6   Before refitting the cylinder head, position the cylinder head gasket, copper side uppermost, on the block face. To assist in keeping it in position put a smear of grease on the underside of the gasket. Gently lower the head into position, ensuring that the crankcase breather pipe is in position in the head (photo).

7   Refit the cylinder head bolts, remembering that the shorter bolts must be positioned at the right-hand rear end of the cylinder head. Tighten the bolts in the sequence shown (Fig. 1.33) to the specified torque, taking care not to damage any valve assembly. Finally, reconnect the oil drain tubes and dipstick tube support bracket.

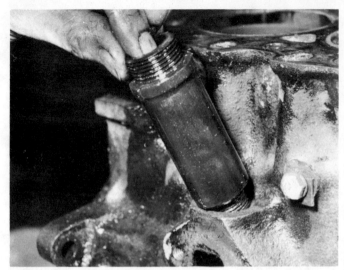

80.6 Locate the crankcase breather pipe

81 Cylinder head – removal (engine in car)

To remove the cylinder head with the engine still in the car the following additional procedure to that above must be followed. This procedure should be carried out before that listed in Section 80.

1   Disconnect the battery by removing the lead from the negative terminal.

2   Drain half the engine coolant, as described in Chapter 2.

3   Remove the air cleaner unit from the carburettor (see Chapter 3).

4   Disconnect the carburettor auto choke hoses, fuel line connections, the vacuum advance tube, the breather hose and the throttle linkage. The carburettor can be left in position and removed with the inlet manifold and cylinder head.

5   On the left-hand side of the cylinder head, undo the worm drive clip that holds the thermostat hose in place. Remove the thermostat hose and tie it back out of the way.

6   Pull the cable away from the temperature gauge sender unit.

7   Undo the nuts and washers which hold the exhaust manifold to the cylinder head. Tie the exhaust manifold back, away from the engine.

8   Pull free each spark plug lead and fold them back out of the way.

9   The procedure is now the same as for removing the cylinder head when on the bench. One tip worth noting is that should the cylinder head refuse to free easily, the battery can be reconnected and the engine turned with the starter. Ensure the fuel pipe is disconnected from the fuel pump (at the carburettor end) and plugged.

Fig. 1.33 Cylinder head bolt tightening sequence (Sec 80)

82 Valves and valve guides – removal and refitting

There is no particular problem raised when considering valve removal and installation in the RS 1800 engine. Assuming the cylinder head is removed, proceed as follows:

1   Compress each spring in turn with a valve spring compressor until the two halves of the collets can be removed. Release the compressor and remove the spring and spring retainers (photos).

2   If, when the valve spring compressor is screwed down, the valve spring retaining cap refuses to free to expose the split collet, do not continue to screw down on the compressor as there is a likelihood of damaging it.

3   Gently tap the top of the tool directly over the cap with a light hammer. This will free the cap. To avoid the compressor jumping off the valve spring retaining cap when it is tapped, hold the compressor firmly in position with one hand.

4   Extract each valve through the combustion chamber (photo).

5   It is essential that the valves are kept in their correct sequence unless they are so badly worn that they are to be renewed. If they are going to be kept and used again place them in a sheet of card having holes numbered 1 to 16 corresponding to the positions the valves were in when fitted (photo). Also keep the valve springs, washers etc in the correct order.

6   The valve guides can be removed from the cylinder head by using a suitable drift and driving them from their housings (photo).

7   When fitting new valve guides, first locate a circlip on the guide, then heat the cylinder head to 100 to 150°C (212 to 302°F) in an oil bath and press the new guide into the cylinder head up to the circlip

82.1a Compressing the valve springs

82.1b Extracting the collets

82.1c Remove the spring and retainer

82.1d Remove the spring platform

82.4 Remove the valve

82.5 Retain valves in cylinder order on a suitably marked sheet of card

82.6 Driving out a valve guide

(photos). If the special Ford tool (No 6180/2) is available, use that to drive in the valve guides.

8   Refitting the valves is the reverse of the removal. Do not attempt to ream the valve guide bore, or its lubricating properties will be lost. If necessary the valves can be ground to mate with their respective seats in the same manner as described for the Mexico and RS 2000 engines in Part A of this Chapter.

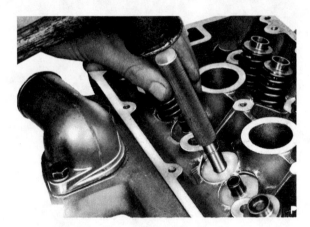

Fig. 1.34 Driving a new valve guide into position using the Ford special service tool (No 6180/2) (Sec 82)

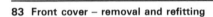

83   Front cover – removal and refitting

If it is necessary to remove the front cover, for example to renew the crankshaft or auxiliary shaft oil seals, it is possible to do this with the engine still in the vehicle, but the four sump bolts that locate in the front cover must be removed.

1   Remove the cooling fan and radiator as described in Chapter 2. Then remove the timing belt cover and timing belt as described in Section 75.

2   Remove the central bolt and washer that secure the crankshaft sprocket and pull it off with the Woodruff key that locates it on the crankshaft (photos). Store the Woodruff key in a safe place. Then remove the two bolts and washers that retain the auxiliary shaft sprocket and ease it off the locating dowel (photos).

3   Disconnect the cam carrier oil drain tubes by slackening the worm drive clips that secure them.

4   Remove the bolts that retain the front cover, noting their positions in relation to their various lengths. Then pull off the cover and its associated gasket (photo). The auxiliary shaft seal can now be pushed out of the front cover by hand. The crankshaft seal will need more pressure to remove it, and before this is applied the cover should be supported either side of the seal. A piece of wood or pipe will often suffice to drive out the seal.

5   At this stage it is just as well to remove the water pump assembly by releasing the three retaining bolts (photo). If the heater hose has not been previously disconnected, this must be removed first.

6   Before refitting the front cover, clean the front face of the cylinder block and locate a new front cover gasket, with a light smear of sealant on the block face (photo). Fit the water pump assembly and secure with the three bolts. Note that one of the bolts also secures the front cover so it is better not to tighten this bolt too much at this stage.

7   Carefully hand fit a new auxiliary shaft oil seal in the front cover, ensuring that the front faces of the seal and cover are flush. The lip of the seal should be towards the engine. The crankshaft oil seal can be pressed into the front cover by very careful use of a vice. Put two flat pieces of wood on the vice shoulder faces to avoid damaging the seal. Again, the lip should be innermost and the faces of the seal and cover should be flush. Smear a little silicone grease on the bearing face of each seal.

8   Refit the front cover, ensuring the lower face of the cover is flush with the lower face of the crankcase. Insert the bolts and do up finger tight only. Locate the crankshaft sprocket on the crankshaft Woodruff key and the auxiliary shaft sprocket on the shaft dowel, and tighten their locating bolts; the front cover may have to be moved very slightly

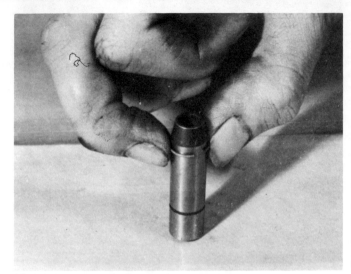

82.7a Locate a new circlip onto the valve guide ...

82.7b ... before locating it into position in the cylinder head

83.2a Remove the crankshaft sprocket bolt and washer ...

83.2b ... then withdraw the sprocket

83.2c Unscrew and remove the auxiliary shaft sprocket bolts ...

83.2d ... then withdraw the auxiliary sprocket

83.4 Withdraw the front cover

83.5 Removing the water pump

83.6 New gasket in position

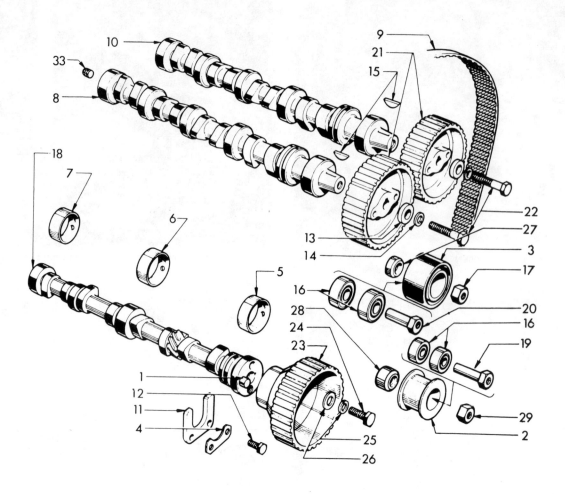

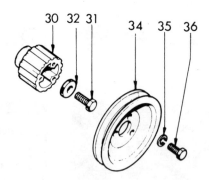

Fig. 1.35 Camshaft auxiliary shaft and sprocket details (Sec 83)

1 Dowel	11 Auxiliary shaft thrust plate	20 Hub – adjustable idler sprocket	28 Spacer
2 Fixed idler	12 Bolt	21 Camshaft sprockets	29 Nut
3 Adjustable idler	13 Washer	22 Bolts	30 Sprocket
4 Retainer plate	14 Lockwasher	23 Auxiliary shaft sprocket	31 Bolt
5 Auxiliary shaft bearing	15 Woodruff key	24 Bolt	32 Washer
6 Auxiliary shaft bearing	16 Ball-race	25 Lockwasher	33 Plug
7 Auxiliary shaft bearing	17 Nut	26 Washer	34 Crankshaft pulley
8 Inlet camshaft	18 Auxiliary shaft	27 Spacer	35 Washer
9 Timing belt	19 Hub – fixed idler sprocket		36 Bolt
10 Exhaust camshaft			

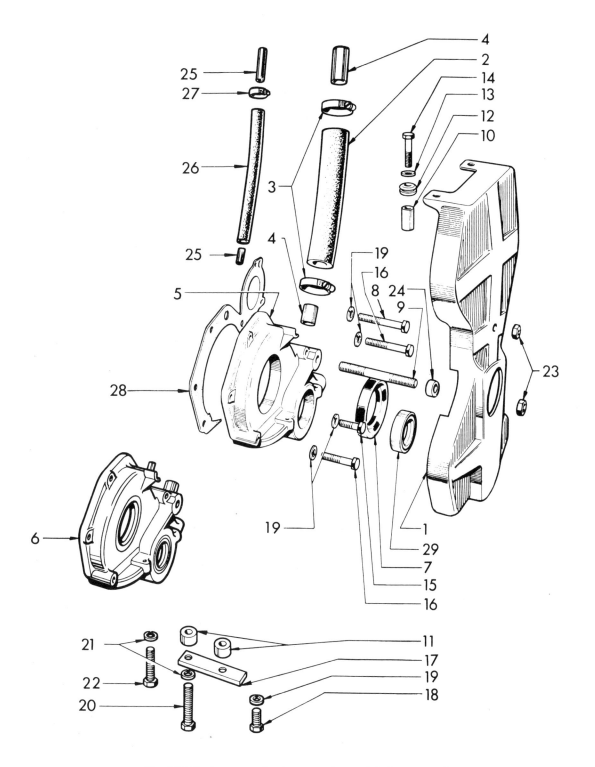

Fig. 1.36 Timing cover, front cover and associated components
(Sec 83)

1	Timing belt cover	9	Stud	16	Bolt	23	Nuts
2	Oil drain hose	10	Spacer	17	Bracket	24	Camshaft sprocket
3	Hose clips	11	Spacers	18	Bolt (timing cover)	25	Tubular inserts
4	Tubular insert	12	Grommet	19	Lockwasher	26	Hose
5	Front cover	13	Lockwasher	20	Bolt (sump)	27	Clip
6	Front cover assembly	14	Bolt	21	Lockwasher	28	Gasket
7	Oil seal	15	Bolt	22	Bolt (sump)	29	Seal
8	Bolt						

during this operation, in order to centralise the cover and seals on the shafts. Finally, tighten the front cover retaining bolts.
9   Refit the cylinder head-to-front cover oil drain tubes and tighten the water pump bolts.
10 Where the engine is still in the car, refit the four sump bolts. Where the sump itself was removed refit it as described in Section 85.

84 Auxiliary shaft – removal and installation

After the auxiliary shaft sprocket has been removed the auxiliary shaft can be extracted as follows:
1   Ease back the turned-up edges of the retainer plate and remove the two bolts that hold the thrust plate in position (photo).
2   Lift the thrust plate up and out of the retaining groove in the auxiliary shaft (photo).
3   The shaft can now be pulled forward, out of its housing (photo). Take care that the cam lobe peaks do not damage the bearings as the shaft is pulled forward.
4   Before refitting the auxiliary shaft, oil the bearings, then insert the shaft into the block.
5   Make sure the shaft turns freely and then fit the thrust plate behind the shaft flange as shown. Measure the endfloat with a feeler gauge – it should be between the values stated in the Specifications. If this is not so then renew the plate.
6   Fit the two auxiliary shaft flange bolts into their retainer plate and screw down the bolts securely.
7   Turn up the tab under the head of each bolt to lock it in place.

85 Sump – removal and refitting

1   The sump can be removed with the engine in or out of the car. If out of the car it is only necessary to follow the instructions in paragraph 8. If the engine is in the car it is necessary to disconnect the lower end of the steering column and lower the front engine crossmember. The additional instructions in paragraphs 2 to 7 apply.
2   Disconnect the battery and drain the engine oil.
3   Apply the handbrake firmly, jack up the front of the car and fit stands under the frame rails at each side. Remove the jack and place it to take the weight of the gearbox at the front of the bellhousing.
4   If fitted, remove the sump shield, and then undo the bolts/nuts which retain the dust cover and the sump-to-clutch housing support bracket.
5   Undo the two bolts which hold the starter motor in place and remove the motor.
6   Refer to Section 7 and proceed as described in paragraphs 11 to 15 inclusive.
7   With the crossmember lowered away from the engine there should be sufficient clearance to remove the sump.
8   Undo all the sump retaining bolts in the reverse order to that given in Fig. 1.37, and remove the sump. Note that two of the front sump bolts are longer, and have spacers beneath them. This is because they are utilised to carry a bracket that supports the bottom of the timing cover.

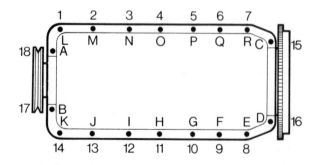

Fig. 1.37 Sump bolts tightening sequence (Sec 85)

A to R 1st tightening   1 to 18 2nd tightening

84.1 Remove the auxiliary shaft retaining bolts and retainer plate

84.2 Withdraw the thrust plate

84.3 Extract the auxiliary shaft

9   Before refitting the sump make quite sure that all big-end bearing cap nuts and main bearing cap bolts are tight. Fit a new sump gasket to the mating face on the base of the cylinder block, having first made sure that the face has been thoroughly cleaned of all remnants of old gasket and jointing compound.

10   If you have removed the sump baffle plate for cleaning, make sure it is relocated before putting the sump back on the block.

11   Clean off all traces of gasket and jointing compound from the mating face of the sump itself. The sump gasket comes in four pieces: two semi-circular cork seals which engage in the grooves of the housings at each end of the engine and two side gaskets which fit the flanges of the sump pan. Fit the side gaskets to the crankcase first. It is not essential to use a jointing compound although many people prefer to do so as a precaution. However, when fitting the cork seals into the grooves of the housings the ends of the seals should be treated with a quick setting jointing compound where they bear on to the ends of the side gaskets. Carefully place the sump in position over the gaskets and locate all the sump holding bolts into position before tightening them in the two stages shown in Fig. 1.37.

12   Where the engine is in the car, refit the crossmember and the steering column connection as described in Section 63, paragraphs 7 and 8; also reconnect the stabiliser bar and brackets.

86 Cylinder block and associated components – dismantling

At this stage of engine overhaul, most of the components that are unique to the RS 1800 have been dismantled. Since the heart of the engine is essentially the same as the Mexico RS 2000 engines, we give below a list of these common components and a cross reference to the removal techniques given in Part A.

Component	Section reference
Piston, con-rod and big-end bearing	*15*
Gudgeon pin	*21*
Piston rings	*22*
Flywheel	*12*
Main bearing and crankshaft	*16*
Oil filter	*25*

87 Oil pump unit – removal and inspection

1   The oil pump unit is fitted externally on the right-hand side of the cylinder block. It can be removed for inspection, with the engine in position in the car. The oil pump unit has the oil filter screwed into its underside and, if required, this can be removed seperately, but allow for a certain amount of oil spillage.

2   The oil pump is secured to the cylinder block by three bolts (with spring washers). Unscrew these bolts and withdraw the oil pump unit.

3   To dismantle the oil pump for inspection, remove the end cover retaining bolts and withdraw the cover. Prise free the O-ring seal from the groove in the cover face of the main body.

4   If the pump is known to have operated over a high mileage or is found to be worn, it is best to purchase an exchange reconditioned unit, as a good oil pump is at the very heart of long engine life.

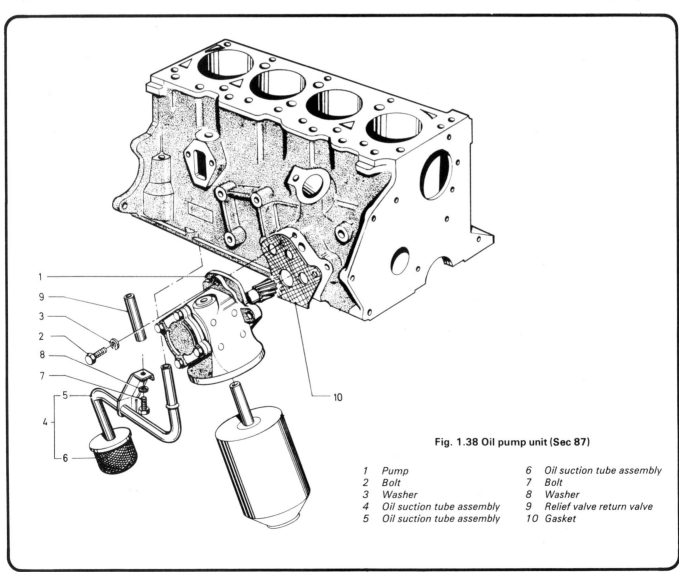

Fig. 1.38 Oil pump unit (Sec 87)

1	*Pump*	*6*	*Oil suction tube assembly*
2	*Bolt*	*7*	*Bolt*
3	*Washer*	*8*	*Washer*
4	*Oil suction tube assembly*	*9*	*Relief valve return valve*
5	*Oil suction tube assembly*	*10*	*Gasket*

Generally speaking, an exchange or overhauled pump should be fitted at a major engine reconditioning.

5   The oil pump fitted will be either an eccentric bi-rotor type or a rotary vane type. The inspection method of both types is dealt with below.

Eccentric bi-rotor type pumps

6   Check the clearance between the inner and outer rotors with a feeler gauge (Fig. 1.39). This should not exceed the specified maximum.

7   Check the clearance between the outer rotor and the pump body (Fig. 1.40). This should not exceed the specified maximum.

Rotary vane type pump

8   Check the clearances as indicated (Fig. 1.41).

All pumps

9   Check the endfloat of both types of pump by placing a straightedge across the open face of the pump casing and measuring the gap between its lower edge and the face of the rotor. This should not exceed the specified maximum.

10   Replacement rotors are only supplied as a matched pair so that if the clearance is excessive, a new rotor assembly must be fitted. When it is necessary to renew the rotors, drive out the pin securing the skew gear and pull the gear from the shaft. Remove the inner rotor and driveshaft and withdraw the outer rotor. Install the outer rotor with the chamfered end towards the pump body.

11   Fit the inner rotor and driveshaft assembly, position the skew gear and install the pin. Tap over each end of the pin to prevent it loosening in service. Position a new O-ring in the groove in the pump body, fit the endplate in position and secure with the four bolts and lockwashers.

12   Prime the pump with oil and then refit the oil pump assembly, together with a new gasket, and secure in place with three bolts and lockwashers.

88 Examination and renovation – general

With the engine stripped down and all parts thoroughly cleaned, it is now time to examine everything for wear. The following items should be checked and, where necessary, renewed or renovated as described in the following Sections. Where components are similar to those in the Mexico RS 2000 engine, we shall merely list them and give a cross-reference to Part A.

It should be noted that whilst the examination and renovation procedures for the following items are similar to their counterparts listed in Part A of this Chapter, in some instances there are differences in the inspection tolerances. Reference should therefore be made to the Specifications for the RS 1800 during the inspection and renovation of each of the following.

Component	Section reference
Crankshaft	27
Big-end and main bearings	28
Cylinder bores	29
Pistons and piston rings auxiliary shaft (as for the camshaft in the Mexico/ RS 2000)	30
	32
Valves and valve seats	36
Connecting rods	31
Flywheel starter ring	38
Cylinder head	34

89 Cam cover, carrier and camshafts – examination and renovation

1   Wash the cover and carrier in petrol until all the oily deposits are

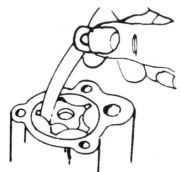

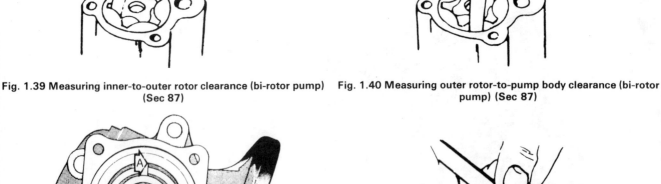

Fig. 1.39 Measuring inner-to-outer rotor clearance (bi-rotor pump) (Sec 87)

Fig. 1.40 Measuring outer rotor-to-pump body clearance (bi-rotor pump) (Sec 87)

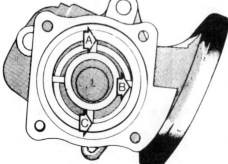

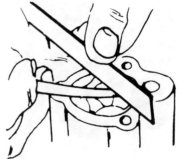

Fig. 1.41 The rotary vane type oil pump clearances (Sec 87)

A = 0.010 in (0.25 mm)   B = 0.005 in (0.13 mm)
C = 0.005 in (0.13 mm)

Fig. 1.42 Measuring the pump endfloat (Sec 87)

removed, then carefully inspect both components for cracks or other evidence of deterioration. Look particularly at the bearings machined directly in the cam carrier for evidence of cracking, scratches or other signs of wear: all the bearing surfaces should be unmarked.

2   The camshafts should show no signs of wear. If scoring on the cams is noticed, the only permanently satisfactory cure is to fit a new camshaft. A temporary cure can be effected by removing the score marks by very gentle rubbing down with fine emery cloth. This latter course is likely to break through the case hardening.

3   Measure the camshaft endfloat. If the endfloat measured is beyond that given in the Specifications, renew the crescent-shaped thrust plate in the groove of the cam carrier.

4   Measure the camshaft journal diameters and check against the specified tolerances. If a camshaft is found to be excessively worn it must be renewed.

5   Fit the camshafts into the carrier and check the bearing clearances. If the specified tolerance is exceeded, but the camshaft journals are within their specified tolerance, the cam carrier must be renewed.

6   Check that the tappet bore diameters are within the specified tolerance limits.

---

90 Timing belt and sprockets – examination and renovation

1   Inspect the belt for general condition, and renew if necessary. The total length of the belt should be as stated in the Specifications if it has stretched much in excess of this it will be difficult to achieve the correct adjustment, and it should therefore be renewed.

2   Check all of the sprockets for broken or chipped teeth, or any other evidence of cracks or deterioration; if a sprocket is not renewed, this could lead to the belt breaking.

3   Inspect the idler wheels for any serrations or cracks that could damage the belt. Also check the idler wheels for excessive play on their centre shaft and bearings. Renew if necessary.

---

91 Engine – reassembly (general)

Refer to Part A, Section 40.

---

92 Engine – reassembly

Since the engine cylinder block and its associated components are, in general, the same as the Mexico and RS 2000 engines, reference is made to the sections in Part A of this Chapter which also apply to the RS 1800 engine. Proceed with the engine cylinder block reassembly in the following order, but note that where the instructions for the RS 1800 engine differ from those for the Mexico/RS 2000 models, they are given accordingly.

1   Refit the crankshaft (Section 41).

2   Press the new crankshaft rear oil seal into position in its carrier, then, having lightly lubricated the seal lip, refit the rear oil seal carrier and gasket against the engine rear face and secure it with its retaining bolts and spring washers. When fitting the carrier into position tap it lightly with a tube drift and take care not to damage the oil seal.

3   Reassemble the pistons and connecting rods (Section 42).

4   Refit the piston rings (Section 43).

5   Refit the pistons (Section 44).

6   Reassemble the connecting rods to the crankshaft (Section 45).

7   Refit the auxiliary shaft (Section 84, paragraphs 4 to 7 inclusive).

8   Refit the front cover (Section 83, paragraphs 6 to 8 inclusive).

9   Apply some sealing compound to the mating face of the oil suction pipe before refitting it into position and tightening its retaining bolt.

10 Refit the sump (Section 85, paragraphs 9 to 11 inclusive).

11 Refit the oil separator, inserting it up to the stop, and tighten its securing bolt. Then refit the oil feed pipe.

12 Refit the oil pressure sender unit.

13 Refit the water pump unit, securing it with the three retaining bolts. The alternator bracket bolt should only be hand tightened at this stage.

14 Locate the rear cover, refit the flywheel and tighten the retaining bolts to the specified torque.

15 Refit the clutch unit (Chapter 5).

16 Rotate the crankshaft and position it so that the No 1 piston is at

top dead centre (TDC) then, referring to Chapter 4, insert the distributor.

17 Refit the oil pump unit (using a new gasket) and secure with the three bolts and lockwashers. It should be noted that a new or reconditioned pump needs to be filled with engine oil and the pump turned through 360° to prime it prior to fitting. The new oil filter can be fitted to the pump at this stage also (refer to Section 25).

18 Refit the cylinder head (Section 80, paragraphs 6 and 7). If the valve clearances were found to be correct when dismantling, then refit the original shims in the same seats from which they were removed. If the valve clearances needed adjusting, then the shim sizes required should also have been determined when dismantling took place; these new shims should now be placed in position in their seats.

19 Refit the camshafts into the carrier (Section 79, paragraphs 6 to 8 inclusive).

20 Refit the cam carrier as described in Section 78, paragraphs 11 to 18 inclusive. Locate the alternator and adjust the fanbelt tension, as described in Chapter 2, Section 10. Check on completion that the fan does not foul the timing cover when it is rotated.

21 Refit the fuel pump, the thermostat and spark plugs. The inlet and exhaust manifolds can also be refitted at this stage. If the carburettor is fitted on the inlet manifold, special care will be needed not to damage it during the refitting of the engine.

---

93 Engine and gearbox – reconnecting

Refer to Section 60.

Fig. 1.43 Refitting the rear oil seal carrier (Sec 92)

Fig. 1.44 Refitting a piston (with arrow pointing to the front) using a ring compressor (Sec 92)

94 Engine – refitting (without gearbox)

1   First refer to the general notes given for engine refitting in Section 62.

2   Now refer to Section 63 for the engine refitting details which are almost identical. Because of its close proximity to the bulkhead, particular care must be taken when lowering and manoeuvring the engine into position not to damage the bulkhead and the brake pipe and associated fittings attached to the bulkhead.

3   Once the crossmember is relocated you will need to refit the stabiliser bar and brackets, but do not fully tighten the securing bolts until after the engine is fully fitted and the lifting sling and jacks are removed. When these bolts are tightened to the specified torque, bend up the locking tabs to secure them.

4   When the engine is fully fitted make a final check to ensure that you have not forgotten to connect anything, and that all fittings are secure.

5   Top up the engine oil and the cooling system and make an initial check for any signs of leaks.

6   The engine is now ready for restarting. Some useful details are given in Section 65.

95 Engine and gearbox – refitting

1   With the engine and the gearbox units reconnected, locate the lifting sling. Arrange it in such a manner as to allow for the steep angle required when lowering into the engine compartment.

2   Refer to Section 64 and proceed as given in paragraphs 2 to 5 inclusive. When tightening the fastenings, refer to the Specifications for the necessary torque settings.

3   With the engine and gearbox located, the refitting of the associated components can be completed as in Section 63, paragraphs 9 to 26 inclusive.

96 Engine – initial start-up afte major overhaul or repair

Refer to Section 65 and proceed as described.

PART C: ALL ENGINES

97 Fault diagnosis – engine

The following chart refers to all engine types covered in this manual

Symptom	Reason(s)
Engine turns but will not start	Ignition damp or wet
	Ignition leads to spark plugs loose
	Shorted or disconnected low tension leads
	Dirty, incorrectly set or pitted contact breaker points
	Faulty condenser
	Defective ignition switch
	Ignition LT leads connected wrong way round
	Faulty coil
	Contact breaker point spring earthed or broken
	No petrol in petrol tank
	Vapout lock in fuel line (in hot conditions or at high altitude)
	Blocked float chamber needle valve
	Fuel pump filter blocked
	Choked or blocked carburettor jets
	Faulty fuel pump
	Too much choke allowing too rich a mixture to wet plugs
	Float damaged or leaking or needle not seating
	Float lever incorrectly adjusted
Engine stalls and will not start	Ignition failure – see Chapter 4
	No petrol in petrol tank
	Petrol tank breather choked
	Other fuel failure – see Chapter 3
Engine misfires or idles unevenly	Ignition leads loose
	Battery leads loose on terminals
	Battery earth strap loose on body attachment point
	Engine earth lead loose
	Low tension leads to terminals on coil loose
	Low tension lead from coil to distributor loose
	Dirty or incorrectly gapped spark plugs
	Dirty, or incorrectly set or pitted contact breaker points
	Tracking across distributor cap
	Ignition timing incorrect
	Faulty coil
	Mixture too weak
	Air leak in carburettor
	Air leak at inlet manifold to cylinder head, or inlet manifold to carburettor
	Incorrect valve clearances
	Burnt out exhaust valves
	Sticking or leaking valves
	Worn or broken valve springs
	Worn valve guides or stems
	Worn pistons and piston rings

Symptom	Reason(s)
Poor compression	Burnt out exhaust valves Sticking or leaking valves Worn valve guides and stems Weak or broken valve springs Blown cylinder head gasket (accompanied by increase in noise) Worn pistons and piston rings Worn or scored cylinder bores Ignition timing wrongly set
Lack of power	Contact breaker points incorrectly gapped Incorrect valve clearances Incorrectly set spark plugs Carburettor mixture too rich or too weak Dirty contact breaker points Fuel filter blocked causing top end fuel starvation Distributor automatic balance weights or vacuum advance and retard mechanism not functioning correctly Faulty fuel pump giving top end fuel starvation Faulty PCV system
Excessive oil consumption	Badly worn, perished or missing valve stem oil seals Excessively worn valve stems and valve guides Worn piston rings Worn piston and cylinder bores Excessive piston ring gap allowing blow-by Piston oil return holes choked
Oil being lost due to leaks	Leaking oil filter gasket Leaking top cover gasket Leaking timing case gasket Leaking sump gasket Loose sump plug
Unusual noises from engine	Worn valve gear (noisy tapping from top cover) Worn big-end bearing (regular heavy knocking) Worn main bearings (rumbling and vibration) Worn crankshaft (knocking, rumbling and vibration
Engine fails to turn when starter button operated	Discharged or defective battery Dirty or loose battery leads Defective starter solenoid or switch Engine earth strap disconnected Defective starter motor

Chapter 2 Cooling system

Contents

Specifications

Type of system .... Pressurised fluid circulation

Coolant
Type .... Mixture of water and an ethylene glycol based antifreeze
Concentration .... Varied according to weather conditions
System capacity (including heater):
    Mexico .... 10.15 Imp pts (5.76 litres)
    RS 2000 .... 10.79 Imp pts (6.13 litres)
    RS 1800 .... 11.97 Imp pts (6.80 litres)

Radiator
Type .... Tube and fin
Cap pressure rating .... 13 lbf/in^2 (0.91 kgf/cm^2)

Thermostat
Type .... Wax capsule
Opening temperature .... 180° to 198° F (82° to 92°C)
Fully open temperature* .... 210° to 216°F (99 to 102°C)
* New thermostat quoted – for used thermostat add + 5°F (3°C)

Water pump
Type .... Centrifugal
Drive .... V-belt
Drivebelt free play .... 0.5 in (13 mm) measured midway along belt's longest run

Torque wrench settings

	lbf ft	kgf m
Thermostat housing	12 to 15	1.6 to 2.0
Water pump	5 to 7	0.7 to 1.0
Fan bolts (standard type)	5 to 7	0.7 to 1.0
Fan bolts (viscous type)	6 to 9	0.8 to 1.2

1 General description

The engine coolant is circulated by a water pump assisted system, and the whole system is pressurised. This is both to prevent the loss of water down the overflow pipe with the radiator cap in position, and to prevent premature boiling in adverse conditions. The radiator cap is pressurised to 13 lbf/in². This has the effect of considerably increasing the boiling point of the coolant. If the temperature goes above this increased boiling point the extra pressure in the system forces the internal part of the cap off its seat, thus exposing the overflow pipe down which the steam from the boiling fluid escapes, thereby relieving the pressure. It is therefore important to check that the radiator cap is in good condition and that the spring behind the sealing washer has not weakened. Most garages have a special machine in which radiator caps can be tested. The cooling system comprises the radiator, top and bottom hoses, heater hoses, the impeller water pump (mounted on the front of the engine, it carries the fan blades, and is driven by the drivebelt), the thermostat and the cylinder block drain plug. The inlet manifold is heated by warm coolant, as is the automatic choke.

The system functions in the following fashion. Cold fluid in the bottom of the radiator circulates up the lower radiator hose to the water pump where it is pushed round the passages in the cylinder block, helping to keep the cylinder bores and pistons cool.

The coolant then travels up into the cylinder head and circulates round the combustion spaces and valve seats absorbing more heat, and then, when the engine is at its proper operating temperature, travels out of the cylinder head, past the open thermostat into the upper radiator hose and so into the radiator header tank.

The fluid travels down the radiator where it is rapidly cooled by the in-rush of cold air through the radiator core, which is created by both the fan and the motion of the car. The cooling fluid now cold, reaches the bottom of the radiator, when the cycle is repeated.

When the engine is cold the thermostat (which is a valve which opens and closes according to the temperature of the coolant) maintains the circulation of the same coolant in the engine. Only when the correct minimum operating temperature has been reached, as shown in the Specifications, does the thermostat begin to open, allowing coolant to return to the radiator.

As from April 1979, all models are fitted with viscous-coupled fans. The coupling operates in a similar manner to a torque converter in that the drive is transmitted through fluid under the influence of centrifugal force. This unit also incorporates limited torque output which, in effect, limits the maximum speed, thereby reducing fan noise and excessive power absorption. As the unit is sealed, there are no repair or maintenance procedures and, if a fault develops, a replacement item must be obtained. The removal and refitting procedures are similar to those for the conventional fan.

The cooling system of the RS 1800 model is basically the same, but there are slight variations in the water pump and radiator patterns, and the thermostat is located on the left-hand side of the cylinder head.

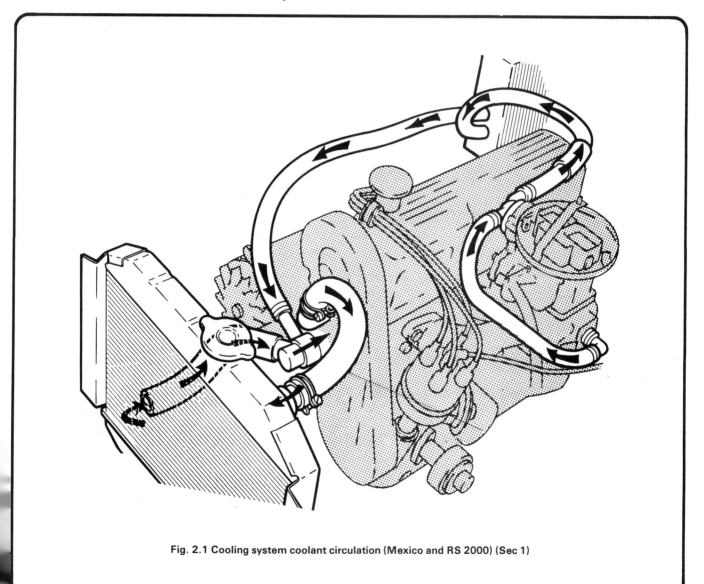

Fig. 2.1 Cooling system coolant circulation (Mexico and RS 2000) (Sec 1)

2 Cooling system – draining

1   With the car on level ground drain the system as follows:
2   If the engine is cold remove the filler cap from the radiator by turning the cap anti-clockwise. If the engine is hot, having just been run, then turn the filler cap very slightly until the pressure in the system has dissipated. Use a rag over the cap to protect your hand from escaping steam. If the cap is released suddenly, the drop in pressure can result in the coolant boiling. With the pressure released the cap can be removed. Turn the heater controls on.
3   If antifreeze is in the radiator drain it into a clean bucket or bowl for re-use, unless it has completed its working life (see Section 4).
4   Remove the cylinder block drain plug, located on the rear right-hand side of the block, using a suitably sized spanner (photo).
5   As there is no radiator drain plug fitted to the Escort radiator, the system must be further drained by slackening the radiator bottom hose clip and pulling the hose off the radiator outlet (photo).

3 Cooling system – flushing

1   Provided the coolant is kept to its recommended concentration with antifreeze and it is renewed at the recommended intervals, flushing will not usually be required. However, due to neglect, or gas or oil entering the system because of a faulty gasket, the radiator may become choked with rust scales, deposits from the water and other sediment.
2   To flush the radiator it must first be removed, as described in Section 5.
3   Ensure that the radiator cap is in place, then turn the radiator upside-down, insert a hose in the lower hose stub and force water from a high pressure supply through the radiator and out of the upper hose stub.
4   Similarly insert the hose in the thermostat housing (after first removing the thermostat) and force water through the engine and out of the lower hose.
5   Continue flushing both radiator and engine until the emerging water runs clean.

4 Cooling system – filling

1   Ensure that the cylinder block drain plug is securely tightened and that the radiator bottom hose is connected.
2   Fill the system slowly to ensure that no airlocks develop. Check that the valve to the heater unit is open, otherwise an airlock may form in the heater. The best type of water to use in the cooling system is rainwater, so use this whenever possible. See Section 14 about the use of antifreeze.
3   Do not fill the system higher than within 1 inch (25 mm) of the filler orifice. Overfilling will merely result in wastage, which is especially to be avoided when antifreeze is in use.
4   Refit the filler cap and turn it firmly clockwise to lock it in position.

5 Radiator – removal, inspection, cleaning and refitting

1   To remove the radiator first drain the cooling system, as described in Section 2.
2   Slacken the clip securing the radiator top hose to the radiator or water pump connection, and detach the hose.
3   Remove the bottom hose which will have been partly detached when draining the radiator.
4   Detach and remove the servo unit vacuum hose which passes over the top of the radiator.
5   Undo and remove the two bolts and washers on each side of the radiator which hold it in place, then lift the radiator out of the engine compartment (photo). Where necessary detach the engine oil cooler and place it out of the way.
6   With the radiator out of the car any leaks can be soldered or repaired. Clean out the inside of the radiator by flushing, as detailed in Section 3. When the radiator is out of the car, it is advantageous to turn it upside down for reverse flushing. Clean the exterior of the radiator by hosing down the radiator matrix with a strong jet of water to clear away road dirt, dead flies etc.

2.4 Cylinder block drain plug location – Mexico and RS 2000 engine

2.5 Detach radiator bottom hose to drain the radiator

5.5 Lifting out the radiator

7   Inspect the radiator hoses for cracks, internal or external perishing and damage caused by overtightening of the securing clips. Renew the hoses as necessary. Examine the radiator hose securing clips and renew them if they are rusted or distorted.

8   Refitting is the reversal of removal. After refilling the system, run the engine up to its normal operating temperature and check for leaks of coolant.

6   Thermostat – removal, testing and refitting

1   Partially drain the cooling system by detaching the radiator bottom hose, but take note of the precautionary notes in Section 2 if the engine coolant is still hot when removing the radiator cap.

2   Loosen the top radiator hose at its connection to the thermostat housing and detach the hose (photo).

3   Unscrew the thermostat housing securing bolts and then carefully pull the unit away from the engine.

4   Remove the retaining clip and extract the thermostat from its housing (photo). Also remove the sealing ring from the housing (photo). Note which way round the thermostat is fitted as it is removed.

5   Test the thermostat for correct functioning by suspending it on a string in a saucepan of cold water. Heat the water and note the temperature at which the thermostat begins to open. This should be within the temperature range given in the Specifications. It is advantageous in winter to fit a thermostat that does not open too early. Continue heating the water until the thermostat is fully open. Then let it cool down naturally.

6   If the thermostat does not fully open in boiling water, or does not close down as the water cools, then it must be discarded and a new one fitted. Should the thermostat be stuck open when cold this will usually be apparent when removing it from the housing.

7   Refitting the thermostat is the reverse sequence to removal. Always ensure that the thermostat housing and cylinder head mating faces are clean and flat. If the thermostat housing is badly corroded fit a new housing. Always use a new paper gasket. Tighten the two securing bolts to the specified torque.

8   When the engine coolant level has been topped up, run the engine up to its normal operating temperature to ensure that the new thermostat is operating correctly, and also to check for any signs of coolant leaks around the housing or hoses.

7   Water pump (Mexico and RS 2000) – removal and refitting

1   Drain the cooling system, as described in Section 2.

2   Refer to Section 5 and remove the radiator.

3   Slacken the alternator mounting bolts and push the alternator towards the cylinder block. Lift away the drivebelt.

4   Undo and remove the four bolts and washers that secure the fan assembly to the water pump spindle hub. Lift away the fan and pulley.

5   Slacken the clip that secures the heater hose to the water pump. Pull the hose from its union on the water pump.

6   Slacken the clamp that secures the lower hose to the water pump. Pull the hose from the pump.

7   Remove the three bolts and take off the timing belt cover.

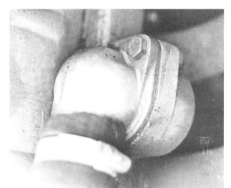

6.2 The thermostat housing and hose connection on the RS 1800

6.4a Removal of the thermostat retaining clip

6.4b Removal of the sealing ring from the thermostat housing

Fig. 2.2 Thermostat housing removal (arrowed) (Mexico and RS 2000) (Sec 6)

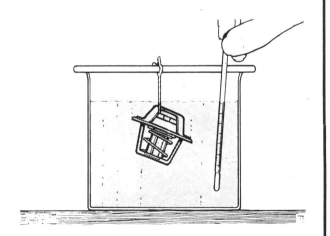

Fig. 2.3 Testing the thermostat (Mexico and RS 2000) (Sec 6)

8   Undo and remove the four bolts and spring washers that secure
the water pump to the cylinder block. Lift away the water pump and
recover the gasket.
9   Refitting the water pump is the reverse sequence to removal. The
following additional points should, however, be noted:

(a) Make sure the mating faces of the cylinder block and water
     pump are clean. Always use a new gasket
(b) Tighten the water pump securing bolts to the specified torque
(c) Tighten the water pump fan and pulley bolts to the specified
     torque
(d) On completion, run the engine up to its normal operating
     temperature and check for any sign of coolant leaks

8 Water pump (RS 1800) – removal and refitting

1   Drain the cooling system, as described in Section 2.
2   Refer to Section 5, and remove the radiator.
3   Unscrew and remove the four fan blade retaining bolts and
remove the fan.
4   Unscrew and remove the two upper bolts from the timing cover,
place the earth strap aside, then remove the lower bolt and detach the
timing cover.
5   Loosen the alternator mounting bolts, pivot the alternator towards
the engine and remove its drivebelt.
6   Withdraw the fan pulley.
7   Detach the coolant and heater hoses from the water pump unit.
8   Unscrew and remove the three retaining bolts and remove the
water pump.
9   Refitting of the pump unit is a direct reversal of the removal
procedure, but refer to the previous Section, paragraph 9, for
cautionary notes which also apply for this water pump type. For
drivebelt adjustment refer to Section 10.

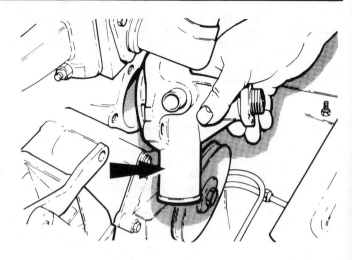

Fig. 2.4 Water pump removal (Mexico and RS 2000) (Sec 7)

9 Water pump – dismantling and overhaul

1   Before undertaking the dismantling of a water pump to effect a
repair, check that all parts are available. It may be quicker and more
economical to renew the complete unit.
2   The water pump shown in Fig. 2.5 is typical of the type fitted to
all models, although small variations may occur.
3   Using a universal three leg puller and a suitable thrust block, draw
the pulley hub from the shaft.

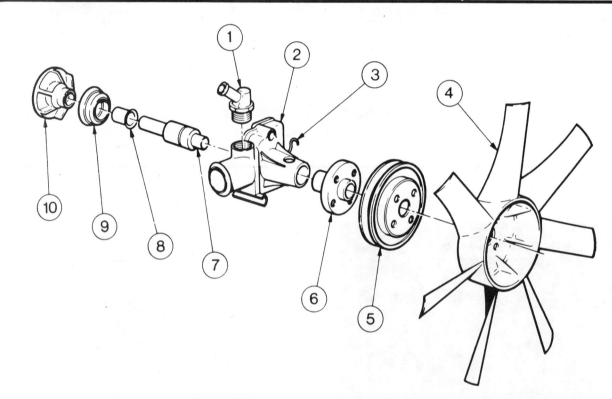

Fig. 2.5 Water pump components (typical) (Sec 9)

1 Heater connection	4 Cooling fan	7 Shaft and bearing assembly	9 Seal assembly
2 Pump body	5 Fan pulley	8 Slinger	10 Impeller
3 Bearing retainer	6 Pulley hub		

4 Carefully pull out the bearing retaining clip from the slot in the water pump housing. On some water pumps this clip is not fitted.

5 Using a soft-faced hammer drive the shaft and bearing assembly out towards the rear of the pump body.

6 The impeller vane is removed from the spindle by using a universal three leg puller and suitable thrust block.

7 Remove the seal and the slinger by splitting the latter with the aid of a sharp cold chisel.

8 Carefully inspect the condition of the shaft and bearing assembly, and if it shows signs of wear or corrosion, new parts should be obtained. If it was found that coolant was leaking from the pump, a new seal should be obtained. If it was evident that the pulley hub or impeller were a loose fit they must be renewed. The repair kit available comprises a new shaft and bearing assembly, a slinger seal, bush, clip and gasket.

9 To reassemble the water pump first fit the shaft and bearing assembly to the housing with the larger end of the shaft to the front of the housing, and press the assembly into the housing until the front of the bearing is flush with the pump housing.

10 Refit the bearing locating wire (if applicable).

11 Next press the pump pulley onto the front end of the shaft until the end of the shaft projects 0.06 in (1.5 mm) from the hub.

12 Press the new slinger (flanged end first) onto the shaft until the non-flanged end is approximately 0.5 in (13 mm) from the shaft end. To act as a rough guide the flanged end of the slinger will be just in line with the impeller side of the window in the water pump body.

13 Refit the pump seal with the thrust face towards the impeller.

14 Press the impeller onto the shaft until a clearance of 0.03 in (0.76 mm) is obtained between the impeller blades and the housing face (Fig. 2.6). Whilst this is being carried out the slinger will be pushed into its final position by the impeller.

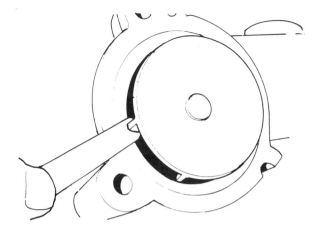

Fig. 2.6 Checking the impeller clearances with feeler gauges (Sec 9)

---

10 Drivebelt – adjustment

1 It is important to keep the drivebelt correctly adjusted and it is considered that this should be a regular task (see Routine Maintenance). If the belt is loose it will slip, wear rapidly and cause the alternator and water pump to malfunction. If the belt is too tight the alternator and water pump bearings will wear rapidly causing premature failure of these components.

2 The drivebelt tension is correct when there is the specified movement at the mid-point position of the belt run between the alternator pulley and the water pump (Fig. 2.7).

3 To adjust the drivebelt, slacken the alternator securing bolts and move the alternator in or out until the correct tension is obtained. It is easier if the alternator bolts are only slackened a little so it requires some effort to move the alternator. In this way the tension of the belt can be arrived at more quickly than by making frequent adjustment.

4 When the correct adjustment has been obtained fully tighten the alternator mounting bolts.

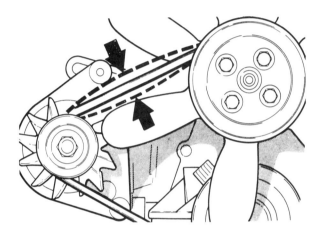

Fig. 2.7 Drivebelt tension adjustment check point (Sec 10)

---

11 Drivebelt – removal and refitting

If the drivebelt is worn or has stretched unduly, it should be renewed. The most usual reason for replacement is that the belt has broken in service. It is recommended that a spare belt be always carried in the car. Proceed as follows, according to model.

Mexico and RS 2000

1 Loosen the alternator mounting bolts and move the alternator towards the engine.

2 Slip the old belt over the crankshaft, alternator and water pump pulley wheels and lift it off over the fan blades.

3 Put a new belt onto the three pulleys and adjust it as described in Section 10. Note that after fitting a new belt it will require a further tension check, and possible adjustment, after approximately 250 miles (400 km).

RS 1800

4 Drain the cooling system, disconnect the radiator hoses and remove the radiator – refer to Sections 2 and 5 for details.

5 Unbolt and remove the cooling fan, then remove the two front cam cover bolts, the two idler stud nuts and the bottom bracket bolt; then lift away the timing belt cover.

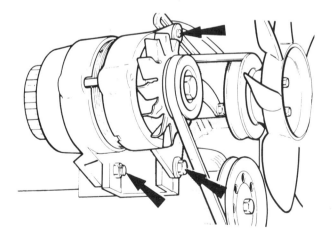

Fig. 2.8 Alternator mounting bolts (Sec 10)

6 Loosen the alternator bolts, pivot the alternator inwards towards the engine and remove the drivebelt.

7 Locate the new drivebelt over the pulleys and adjust it as given in Section 10.

8 Reassemble the cam cover, fan and radiator and top up the

cooling system. Note that after fitting a new belt it will require a further adjustment due to its initial stretch after about 250 miles (400 km).

12 Temperature gauge – fault diagnosis

1 If the temperature gauge fails to work, either the gauge, the sender unit, the wiring or the connections are at fault.
2 It is not possible to repair the gauge or the sender unit and they must be renewed if at fault.
3 First check the wiring connections are sound. Check the wiring for breaks using an ohmmeter. The sender unit and gauge should be tested by substitution.

13 Temperature gauge and sender unit – removal and refitting

1 Information on the removal of the gauge will be found in Chapter 10.
2 Drain the cooling system, referring to Section 2, if it is wished to remove the sender unit.
3 Disconnect the wires leading into the unit at its connector and unscrew the unit with a spanner. The unit is located in the cylinder head just below the manifold on the left-hand side (Mexico and RS

2000) and between the thermostat and heater hose on RS 1800 models.
4 Refitting is a direct reversal of the removal procedure.

14 Antifreeze – use and precautions

1 The cooling system contains parts which are particularly prone to corrosion, if filled with just water, so it is recommended that a mixture of water and antifreeze with a corrosion inhibiting additive is used throughout the year.
2 It is important that the antifreeze concentration should be suitable for the outside temperature range in which it is used. Information about such mixtures is usually printed on the antifreeze bottle.
3 Any ethylene glycol based antifreeze which conforms with the specifications of BS3151 or BS3152 can be used, as long as it contains an anti-corrosion additive. Never use an antifreeze with an alcohol base, as the evaporation rate is too high. Do not use engine antifreeze in the windscreen washer, as it will cause damage to the paintwork.
4 Topping-up of the system should be done with a water/antifreeze mixture with the same concentration as the coolant already in the system. The entire system should be drained and refilled with new coolant at the intervals stated in Routine Maintenance.

15 Fault diagnosis – cooling system

Symptom	Reason(s)
Overheating	Insufficient water in cooling system Drivebelt slipping (accompanied by a shrieking noise on rapid engine acceleration), or broken Radiator core blocked or radiator grille restricted Bottom water hose collapsed, impeding flow Thermostat not opening properly Ignition advance and retard incorrectly set (accompanied by loss of power, and perhaps misfiring) Carburettor incorrectly adjusted (mixture too weak) Exhaust system partially blocked Oil level in sump too low Blown cylinder head gasket (water/steam being forced down the radiator overflow pipe under pressure) Brakes binding
Cool running	Thermostat jammed open Incorrect thermostat fitted, allowing premature opening of valve Thermostat missing
Loss of cooling water	Loose clips on water hose Top, bottom or by-pass water hoses perished and leaking Radiator core leaking Thermostat gasket leaking Radiator pressure cap spring worn, or seal ineffective Blown cylinder head gasket (pressure in system forcing water/steam down overflow pipe) Cylinder wall or head cracked

Chapter 3 Fuel system and carburation

Contents

Specifications

General

Fuel tank capacity (all models)	9 gallons (41 litres)
Fuel filters	Nylon mesh – one in the fuel pump and one in the carburettor inlet.
Air cleaner	Paper element – disposable

Fuel pump

Type	Mechanical diaphragm, driven by an eccentric on the auxiliary shaft
Delivery pressure:	
RS 2000 and Mexico	4.0 to 5.5 lbf/in^2 (0.28 to 0.39 kgf/cm^2)
RS 1800	3.0 to 5.0 lbf/in^2 (0.21 to 0.35 kgf/cm^2)

Carburettor

Mexico:

Type	Single Weber (DGAV 1D) dual venturi
Throttle barrel diameter	1.26/1.42 in (32/36 mm)
Venturi diameter	1.02/1.06 in (26/27 mm)
Main jet	130/120
Float level	1.38 ± 0.01 in (35.0 ± 0.3 mm)
Float travel	0.64 in (16.25 mm)
Choke plate pull-down	0.16 ± 0.01 in (4.0 ± 0.25 mm)
Choke phasing	0.08 in (2.0 mm)
Idle speed	800 ± 20 rpm
Fast idle speed	2000 ± 100 rpm
Exhaust emission (% CO)	1.5 ± 0.25

RS 1800:

Type	Single Weber (DGAV), dual venturi
Throttle barrel diameter	1.26/1.42 in (32/36 mm)
Venturi diameter	1.02/1.06 in (26/27 mm)
Main jet	135/155
Float level	1.61 ± 0.01 mm (41.00 ± 0.25 mm)
Float travel	0.45 in (11.5 mm)
Choke plate pull-down	0.16 ± 0.01 in (4.0 ± 0.25 mm)
Choke phasing	0.08 in (2.0 mm)
Idle speed	800 rpm
Fast idle speed	2100 ± 100 rpm
Exhaust emission (% CO)	1.5 ± 0.25

RS 2000:

Type	Single weber (DGAV), dual venturi
Throttle barrel diameter	1.26/1.42 in (32/36 mm)
Venturi diameter	1.02/1.06 in (26/27 mm)
Main jet	127/137
Float level	1.61 ± 0.01 in (41.0 ± 0.25 mm)
Float travel	0.37 in (9.5 mm)
Choke plate pull-down	0.16 ± 0.01 in (4.0 ± 0.25 mm)
Choke phasing	0.08 in (2.0 mm)
Idle speed	825 ± 25 rpm
Fast idle speed	2000 ± 100 rpm
Exhaust emission (% CO)	1.5 ± 0.25

Torque wrench settings

	lbf ft	kgf m
Fuel pump bolts	12 to 15	1.6 to 2.1
Exhaust manifold to downpipe	15 to 20	2.1 to 2.8
Exhaust U-bolts and clamps	28 to 33	3.9 to 4.6

1 General description

The fuel system comprises a rear mounted fuel tank, a mechanically operated fuel pump and a Weber carburettor (the type depending on model – see Specifications).

The fuel tank is located within the luggage compartment on the right-hand side of the vehicle, with the filler neck protruding through the right-hand quarter panel. The fuel outlet pipe is located in the bottom of the tank and can be easily removed if the tank needs to be drained. The sender unit is located in the front face of the tank and can be removed with the tank in place. Fuel tank ventilation is achieved via a breather pipe clipped to the tank and protruding through the quarter panel.

The fuel pump is mounted on the side of the engine, on the right side for the RS 1800, on the left for the Mexico and RS 2000 models. The pump unit has a nylon mesh filter located within the top housing and this can be removed for inspection and cleaning when necessary. The pump is operated by means of an eccentric on the engine ancillary shaft.

The air cleaner unit fitted to all models is of the renewable paper element type. The air intake spout is manually adjustable for direction to suit winter or summer operation.

For a description of the carburettor refer to Section 9.

2 Air cleaner – removal, servicing and refitting

1 The renewable paper element air cleaner is fitted on to the top of the carburettor installation. Servicing is confined to cleaning, or renewal, of the element at the specified service intervals (see Routine Maintenance).

2 Tap the element on a hard surface or use compressed air from a tyre pump to remove surface dust. Never attempt to clean it in solvent or petrol. Renew the element regularly.

3 Always check the condition of the rubber sealing rings and renew them if they are perished or deformed.

Element removal – Mexico and RS 2000

4 To remove the element, the complete air cleaner unit must be removed and then the two casing halves separated. To do this unscrew and remove the single retaining nut or two screws (depending on model) from the top face of the container (photo). Then unscrew and remove the two bolts securing the container support brackets on the right-hand side (photo).

5 Lift the air cleaner unit container from the carburettor (photo).

6 Release the retaining clips to separate the two halves of the container and lift the element out (photo).

7 Refitting is the reversal of the removal procedure, but ensure that any dust within the air cleaner body is carefully wiped out. Do not allow dust to enter the carburettor.

Element renewal – RS 1800

8 Unscrew and remove the two container lid retaining screws from the top face (photo), then remove the lid and lift out the old element.

9 Refit in the reverse order to removal, ensuring that the container is wiped clean before inserting the new element.

10 Should you wish to remove the filter container from the carburettor, first remove the lid and then detach the spark plug HT lead location block from the clamp on the front face of the filter container. Unscrew and remove the adjacent bracket bolt (see photo 2.8).

11 The container is secured to the top of the carburettor by means of four nuts which are locked in position by means of locktabs (photo). Bend the tabs from the nuts, unscrew and remove the nuts and then lift the cleaner unit clear. Do not lose the nuts or the locktabs.

12 Now disconnect the hose from the base of the unit to remove it completely (photo).

13 Reassembly is a reversal of the removal process. Bend up the locktabs to secure the four container retaining nuts once they are tightened.

3 Fuel pump – servicing

1 Remove the single screw securing the fuel pump cover to the

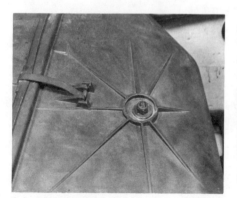
2.4a Air cleaner top securing nut (Mexico)

2.4b Removing the air cleaner unit top securing screws on the RS 2000. The side retaining bolts are arrowed

2.5 Lift the cleaner unit from the carburettor

2.6 Separate the container to remove the element

2.8 The air cleaner unit fitted to the RS 1800 engine showing the lid retaining nuts and support bracket bolt

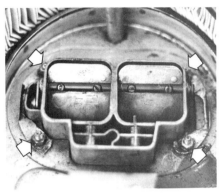

2.11 Remove the four securing nuts (arrowed) to enable cleaner container to be lifted clear ...

2.12 ... then detach the hose from the base of the unit

3.1a Withdraw the cap, filter and seal from the fuel pump

3.1b Removal of filter from fuel pump cap

pump body and lift off the cover, then detach the cover seal and withdraw the 'top hat' filter from the pump body (photos).

2   Thoroughly clean the cover, filter and pump body, using a paintbrush and clean petrol to remove any sediment.

3   Reassemble the pump and carry out the test detailed in Section 4. Should the pump prove to be in need of attention it will have to be renewed as a complete unit, as it is not possible to dismantle it, or obtain spare parts.

4   Fuel pump – testing

1   To test the pump fitted in position on the crankcase, detach the fuel inlet pipe at the carburettor and disconnect the HT lead from the ignition coil.

2   Operate the starter switch, and well defined spurts of petrol should be ejected from the disconnect end of the pipe. Catch the ejected petrol in a rag, or suitable container.

3   If the pump is removed from the engine, place a finger over the inlet port and work the rocker arm several times. Remove the finger – a distinct suction noise should be heard.

4   Now place a finger over the outlet port, immerse the pump in paraffin and depress the rocker arm to its fullest extent. Watch for air bubbles which would indicate leakage at the pump flanges.

5   If the fuel pump is defective, no repairs are possible and it must therefore be renewed.

5   Fuel pump – removal and refitting

1   Disconnect the fuel inlet and outlet pipes. Where crimped hose clips are fitted these should be discarded and replaced by screw type hose clamps.

2   Unscrew and remove the two securing bolts from the pump flange and remove the pump with gasket from the crankcase.

3   Refitting is a reversal of removal, but use a new gasket and make sure that the pump rocker arm is correctly positioned on top of the auxiliary shaft eccentric.

6   Fuel tank – removal and refitting

1   The fuel tank is positioned in the right-hand rear wing. Remove the filler cap and from under the car, disconnect the flexible fuel pipe from the metal pipe and allow the contents of the tank to drain into a suitable container, taking great care to reduce all risks of fire.

2   Disconnect the battery and then open the boot lid. Pull off the wire from the fuel gauge sender unit, unclip and remove the vent pipe (photo).

3   Unscrew and remove the three screws securing the filler pipe neck to the quarter panel.

4   From underneath the vehicle undo and remove the two bolts securing the lower edge of the tank to the body.

6.2 The sender unit wire and vent pipe location at the forward end of the fuel tank

6.5 The fuel tank upper retaining bolts (arrowed)

9.0 The Weber carburettor fitted on the RS 2000 engine. Note that the anti-stall device (arrowed) is not fitted to all models

5   From inside the boot, undo and remove the two upper securing bolts (photo) and lift the tank from the vehicle.
6   Refitting is quite straightforward and is a reversal of the removal sequence. Ensure that the grommet at the filler neck aperture in the body is in good condition and renew it if it is split or otherwise suspect. Make certain that the fuel pipe grommet is in place and ensure the spacers and washers are correctly positioned. Finally check for leaks.

7   Fuel tank – cleaning and repair

1   With time it is likely that sediment will collect in the bottom of the fuel tank. Condensation, resulting in rust and other impurities, will usually be found in the fuel tank of any car more than three or four years old.
2   When the tank is removed (see Section 6), it should be swilled out using several changes of paraffin and finally rinsed out with clean petrol. Remember that the float mechanism is delicate and the tank should not be shaken violently or turned upside down quickly in case damage to the sender unit is incurred.
3   If the tank is leaking, it should be renewed or taken to a specialist firm for repair. **Do not** attempt to solder, braze or weld it yourself, it can be lethal. A temporary repair may be made with a suitable proprietary product, but a new tank should be fitted as quickly as possible.

8   Fuel gauge sender unit – removal and refitting

1   The fuel gauge sender unit can be removed with the tank in position in the car, but the tank must be empty. Store any drained fuel in a suitable sealed container in a safe place. In view of the highly inflammable nature of both the fuel and its fumes, particular care must be taken to guard against fire risk during the removal and refitting of the sender unit.
2   Disconnect the battery earth lead.
3   Detach the lead wire and the vent pipe connection from the sender unit (see photo 6.2).
4   Now unscrew the sender unit retaining ring using a suitably modified C-spanner or tapping the projections carefully with a hammer and cold chisel. Remove the sealing ring.
5   If found to be defective, or damaged in any way, the sender unit must be renewed.
6   Refitting is a reversal of the removal procedure. Always use a new sealing ring during assembly.

9   Carburettor – general description

A Weber dual venturi (twin choke) carburettor is fitted to all

models, but the carburettor type for each model differs, although they are all of similar construction.
    The carburettor body comprises two castings which form the upper and lower bodies. The upper incorporates the float chamber cover, float pivot brackets, fuel inlet and return unions, gauze filter, spring-loaded needle valve, twin air intakes, choke plates and the section of the power valve controlled by vacuum.
    Incorporated in the lower body is the float chamber, accelerator pump, two throttle barrels and integral main venturis, throttle plates, spindles, levers, jets and the petrol power valve.
    The throttle plate opening is in a preset sequence so that the primary starts to open first and is then followed by the secondary, in such a manner that both plates reach full throttle position at the same time. The primary barrel, throttle plate and venturi are smaller than the secondary, whereas the auxiliary venturi size is identical in both the primary and secondary barrels.
    All the carburation systems are located in the lower body and the main progression systems operate in both barrels, whilst the idling and the power valve systems operate in the primary barrel only and the full load enrichment system in the secondary barrel.
    The accelerator pump discharges fuel into the primary barrel.
    A connection for the vacuum required to control the distributor advance/retard vacuum unit is located on the lower body.
    In addition, the idle mixture adjustment and basic idle adjustment screws are tamperproof. (Refer to Section 10).
    A fully automatic strangler type choke is used to ensure any starting when the engine is cold, and will automatically and progressively release as the engine warms up.
    Some models have an anti-stall device fitted, and this is shown in the accompanying photo.

10   Slow running adjustment – general

1   In view of the increasing awareness of the dangers of exhaust pollution, and the very low levels of carbon monoxide (CO) emission for which these carburettors are designed, the slow running mixture setting, and the basic idle setting, *should not be adjusted without the use of a proper CO meter (exhaust gas analyser)*.
2   Even if such equipment is available, the plastic tamperproof plugs can only be removed by destroying them. Satisfy yourself that you are not contravening local or national anti-pollution regulations by doing so.

11   Slow running adjustment

1   Warm up the engine to its normal operating temperature.
2   Connect a CO meter, according to the manufacturer's instructions.
3   Clear the engine exhaust gases by running the engine at 3000 rpm

for approximately 30 seconds and allow the engine to idle.

4   Wait for the meter to stabilise and compare the CO and idle speed readings against those given in the Specifications at the beginning of this Chapter.

5   Adjust the idle speed screw (or bypass idle speed screw on carburettors so equipped) to give the correct rpm (see Fig. 3.1). If the correct rpm cannot be achieved using the bypass idle screw (when fitted), the tamperproof plug will have to be removed from the idle speed adjustment screw and adjustment made there.

6   During normal routine maintenance servicing, normally no adjustment of the mixture (CO level) will be required. If however the CO level is found to be incorrect the following procedure should be adopted.

7   Remove the air cleaner assembly, as described in Section 2.

8   Using a small screwdriver, prise out the tamperproof plug covering the mixture adjusting screw.

9   Loosely refit the air cleaner; it is not necessary to bolt it in position.

10   Clear the engine exhaust gases by running the engine at 3000 rpm for approximately 30 seconds and allow the engine to idle.

11   Adjust the mixture screw and the idle screw until the correct idle speed and CO reading are obtained. If the correct readings are not obtained within 10 to 30 seconds, clear the engine exhaust gases as described in paragraph 10 and repeat the adjustment procedure until correct readings are obtained.

12   Refit the air cleaner and fit a new tamperproof plug.

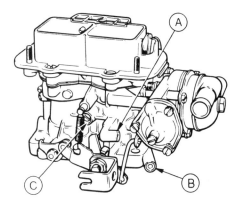

Fig. 3.1 Weber carburettor slow running adjustments (Sec 11)

   A   Idle speed adjustment screw
   B   Idle mixture adjustment screw
   C   Bypass idle speed screw (where fitted)

12 Carburettor – removal and refitting

1   Disconnect the battery earth lead.

2   Remove the air cleaner, as described in Section 2.

3   Bend back the locktabs, then remove the four nuts and take off the air cleaner mounting plate.

4   Clamp the coolant hoses on each side of the auto choke and then unscrew the hose clips (photo). Disconnect the inlet and outlet hoses from the auto choke housing. If no clamps are available partially drain the cooling system, before detaching the hoses, to prevent coolant spillage.

5   Disconnect and plug the fuel supply line at the carburettor.

6   Detach the vacuum hose which runs to the distributor.

7   Unclip the throttle connecting rod (photo).

8   Remove the retaining nuts and lift off the carburettor. Remove the gasket and spacer, if fitted.

9   Refitting is the reversal of the removal procedure, but note the following:

   (a)   Ensure that all mating surfaces are clean and that new gaskets are used
   (b)   Where a spacer is used, position a gasket on each side of it
   (c)   Screw-type hose clips should be used as replacements for crimped-type clips
   (d)   Top up the cooling system before running the engine
   (e)   Check for any signs of fuel or cooling system leaks on completion, and then adjust the carburettor as given in Section 11.

13 Carburettor – overhaul (general)

1   With time, the component parts of the carburettor will wear and petrol consumption increase. The diameter of drillings and jets may alter, and air and fuel leaks may develop around spindles and other moving parts. Because of the high degree of precision involved it is best to purchase an exchange carburettor. This is one of the few instances where it is better to take the latter course rather than to rebuild the component oneself.

2   It may be necessary to partially dismantle the carburettor to clear a blocked jet. The accelerator pump itself may need attention and gaskets may need renewal. Providing care is taken, there is no reason why the carburettor may not be completely reconditioned at home, but ensure a full repair kit can be obtained before you strip the carburettor down. Never poke out jets with wire or similar to clean them, but blow them out with compressed air or air from a car tyre pump.

14 Carburettor – dismantling, assembly and float level adjustment

1   Initially remove the carburettor from the car, as described in Section 12, then clean the exterior with a water soluble cleaner.

12.4 Detach the hoses from the auto choke

12.7 Unclip the throttle rod. Also shown is the throttle cable connection to the rod and support bracket

2   Carefully prise out the U-circlip with a screwdriver and disconnect the choke plate operating link (Fig. 3.2).

3   Remove the six screws and detach the carburettor upper body.

4   Unscrew the brass nut located at the fuel intake and detach the fuel filter.

5   Tap out the float retaining pin, and detach the float and needle valve (Fig. 3.4).

6   Remove the three screws and detach the power valve diaphragm assembly.

7   Unscrew the needle valve housing.

8   Unscrew the jets and jet plugs from the carburettor body, noting the positions in which they are fitted (photos).

9   From the carburettor body, remove the two primary diffuser tubes (Fig. 3.5).

10 Remove four screws and detach the accelerator pump diaphragm, taking care that the spring is not lost (Fig. 3.6).

11 Before attempting to remove the mixture screw, refer to Section 11.

12 Remove four screws and detach the anti-stall diaphragm, taking care that the spring is not lost (Fig. 3.7). Note that this is only fitted on certain variants.

13 Clean the jets and passageways using clean, dry compressed air. Check the float assembly for signs of damage or leaking. Inspect the power valve and pump diaphragms and gaskets for splits or deterioration. Examine the mixture screw, needle valve seat and throttle spindle for signs of wear. Renew parts as necessary,

14 When reassembling, refit the accelerator pump diaphragm assembly (Fig. 3.8).

15 Fit the mixture screw and spring in the same position as originally fitted.

Fig. 3.2 Remove the choke link circlip (arrowed) (Sec 14)

16 Slide the two diffuser tubes into position, then refit the jets and jet plugs.

17 Refit the anti-stall diaphragm assembly, if applicable (Fig. 3.9).

18 Loosely fit the three screws to retain the power valve diaphragm assembly, then compress the return spring so that the diaphragm is not twisted or distorted. Lock the retaining screws and release the return spring.

Fig. 3.3 Lift the upper body clear (Sec 14)

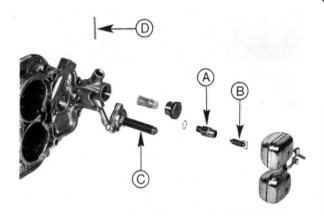

Fig. 3.4 Float chamber components (Sec 14)

A   Valve housing   C   Power valve diaphragm
B   Needle valve   D   Float retaining pin

Fig. 3.5 Jets and diffuser tubes (Y) removed for cleaning (Sec 14)

Fig. 3.6 Carefully withdraw the accelerator pump diaphragm (arrowed) (Sec 14)

Fig. 3.7 Withdraw the anti-stall diaphragm (where fitted) (Sec 14)

A   Spring   B   Cover

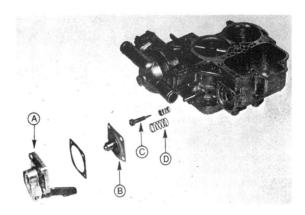

Fig. 3.8 Assemble the accelerator pump components (Sec 14)

A   Housing   C   Mixture screw
B   Diaphragm   D   Pump return spring

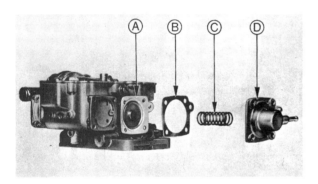

Fig. 3.9 Anti-stall device components (Sec 14)

A   Diaphragm   C   Return spring
B   Gasket   D   Housing

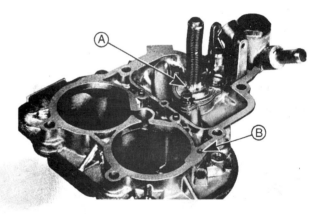

Fig. 3.10 The power valve assembly (Sec 14)

A   Valve   B   Diaphragm bleed hole

14.8a Remove the jets (arrowed) for cleaning, but do not intermix or damage them

14.8b Removing an idle jet and its retaining screw. There is one on each side of the carburettor, one being for the primary and the other for the secondary venturi

14.8c An idle jet and screw separated for inspection

14.21 Float level check method. To adjust, bend the tag (arrowed)

19 Hold the diaphragm down, block the air bleed with a finger then release the diaphragm. If the diaphragm stays down it has correctly sealed to the housing.
20 Refit the needle valve housing, needle valve and float assembly to the upper body.

21 To check the float level, hold the upper body vertically so that the needle valve is closed by the float, then measure the dimension from the face of the upper body to the base of the float (photo). Adjust to the specified figure by bending the tag.
22 Refit the fuel inlet filter and brass nut.
23 Position a new gasket and refit the carburettor upper body to the main body. Ensure that the choke link locates correctly through the upper body.
24 Reconnect the choke link and refit the U-circlip.

15 Carburettor automatic choke – removal, overhaul and refitting

1   Disconnect the battery earth lead.
2   Remove the air cleaner, as described in Section 2.
3   Remove the three screws, detach the cover and move it clear of the carburettor. For access to the lower screw it will be necessary to make up a suitably cranked screwdriver.
4   Detach the internal heat shield.
5   Remove the single U-circlip and disconnect the choke plate operating link
6   Remove the three screws, disconnect the choke link at the operating lever and detach the choke assembly. For access to the lower screw the cranked screwdriver will again be required.
7   Remove the three screws and detach the vacuum diaphragm assembly.
8   Dismantle the remaining parts of the choke mechanism.
9   Clean all the components, inspect them for wear and damage and wipe them dry with a lint-free cloth. Do not use any lubricants during reassembly.

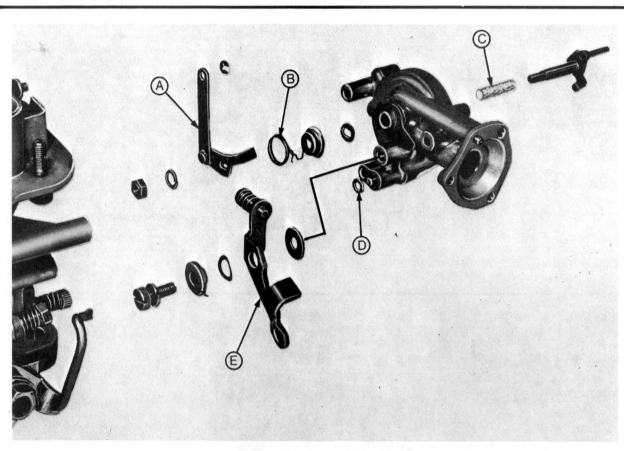

Fig. 3.11 The Weber carburettor automatic choke assembly
component parts (Sec 15)

A   Operating link (upper choke)   C   Spindle sleeve   E   Choke link and adjuster screw
B   Fast idle cam return spring   D   Sealing ring

10 Reassemble the choke mechanism, after checking the diaphragm and sealing ring for splits.

11 Refit the vacuum diaphragm and housing, ensuring that the diaphragm is flat before the housing is fitted.

12 Ensure that the O-ring is correctly located in the choke housing then reconnect the lower choke link. Position the assembly and secure it with the three screws; ensure that the upper choke link locates correctly through the carburettor body.

13 Reconnect the upper choke link to the choke spindle.

14 Check the vacuum pull-down and choke phasing, as described in Section 16.

15 Refit the internal heat shield ensuring that the hole in the cover locates correctly onto the peg cast in the housing (Fig. 3.14).

16 Connect the bi-metal spring to the choke lever, position the choke cover and loosely fit the three retaining screws.

17 Rotate the cover until the marks are aligned (Fig. 3.15), then tighten the three screws.

18 Reconnect the battery, run the engine and adjust the fast idle speed, as described in Section 16.

19 Refit the air cleaner (Section 2).

16 Carburettor automatic choke – adjustment

The procedure is described for a carburettor which is fitted in the car, but with the exception of fast idle speed adjustment, can be carried out on the bench if required where the carburettor has been removed.

1 Disconnect the battery earth lead.

2 Remove the air cleaner, as described in Section 2.

3 Remove the three screws, detach the choke cover and move it clear of the carburettor. For access to the lower screw it will be necessary to make up a suitable cranked screwdriver.

4 Detach the internal heat shield.

Vacuum pull-down

5 Fit an elastic band to the choke plate lever and position it so that the choke plates are held closed. Open, then release, the throttle to ensure that the choke plates close fully. Unscrew the plug from the diaphragm unit then manually push open the diaphragm up to its stop from inside the choke housing. Do not push on the rod as it is spring

Fig. 3.12 Automatic choke securing screws (Sec 15)

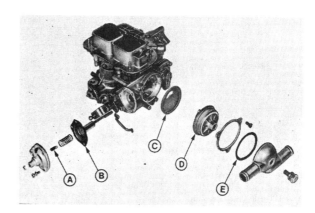

Fig. 3.13 The vacuum diaphragm and outer housing components
(Sec 15)

A   Adjusting screw (diaphragm)   D   Bi-metal spring and housing
B   Diaphragm   E   Outer gasket
C   Heat shield

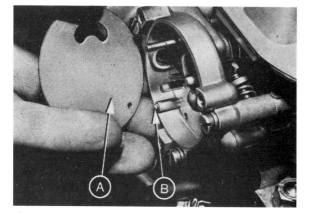

Fig. 3.14 Locate heat shield (A) onto location peg (B) (Sec 15)

Fig. 3.15 Align the choke housing marks when reassembling
(Sec 15)

Fig. 3.16 Withdraw the choke housing and bi-metal spring assembly (A) and then detach the internal heat shield (B) (Sec 16)

Fig. 3.17 Hold vacuum diaphragm fully open when checking its vacuum pull-down (Sec 16)

Fig. 3.18 Vacuum pull-down adjustment (note elastic band holding choke plates closed) (Sec 16)

Fig. 3.19 Choke phasing check showing the screw to cam position (Sec 16)

loaded, but push on the diaphragm plug body. The choke plate pull-down should now be measured, using an unmarked twist drill shank between the edge of the choke plate and the air horn wall, and compared with the specified figure. Adjust, if necessary, by screwing the adjusting screw in or out, using a short bladed screwdriver. Refit the end plug and detach the elastic band on completion.

Choke phasing

6   Hold the throttle partly open and position the fast idle cam so that the fast idle adjusting screw locates on the upper section of the cam. Release the throttle to hold the cam in this position, then push the choke plates down until the step on the cam jams against the adjusting screw (Fig. 3.19). Measure the clearance between the edge of the choke plate and the air horn wall using a specified sized drill. Adjust, if necessary, by bending the tag (Fig. 3.20).
7   Refit the internal heat shield ensuring that the hole in the cover locates correctly onto the peg cast in the housing.
8   Connect the bi-metal spring to the choke lever, position the choke cover and loosely fit the three retaining screws.
9   Rotate the cover until the marks are aligned then tighten the three screws.
10 Reconnect the battery, run the engine and adjust the fast idle speed as described in the following paragraph.

Fast idle speed adjustment

11 Run the engine up to normal operating temperature, then switch off and, if fitted, remove the air cleaner. Open the throttle partially, hold the choke plates fully closed then release the throttle so that the choke mechanism is held in the fast idle position. Release the choke plates, checking that they remain fully open (if they are not open, the

assembly is faulty or the engine is not at operating temperature). Without touching the accelerator pedal, start the engine and adjust the fast idle screw as necessary to obtain the correct fast idle rpm (Fig. 3.21).
12 Finally refit the air cleaner (Sec 2).

17 Exhaust system – inspection, removal and refitting

1   At regular intervals the system should be checked for corrosion, joint leakage, condition and security of the flexible mountings and the tightness of the joints. Exhaust systems do not normally last for more than two or three years. Provision has therefore been made for easy removal and replacement of the exhaust system components on the Escort.
2   The exhaust system is secured by means of brackets and suspended O-rings, allowing it a certain amount of flexibility and sound insulation (photo).
3   At regular intervals the exhaust system should be checked for excessive corrosion, damage and joint leakage, and the condition of the mountings and joints inspected for security.
4   Inspection and repairs to the system are obviously best carried out with the car raised on suitable ramps, or placed over an inspection pit. Alternatively jack up the car and support it on axle stands to obtain the maximum amount of working room underneath.
5   Before trying to remove a leaking and badly rusted exhaust system squirt a de-rusting and lubricating agent over the fixings to be disconnected.
6   Unscrew and remove the nuts securing the system to the exhaust manifold, then unhook the O-rings which secure the system in place

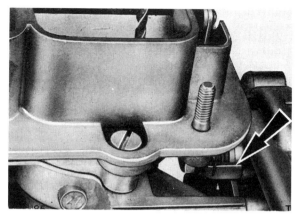

Fig. 3.20 Bend tag (arrowed) to adjust choke phasing (Sec 16)

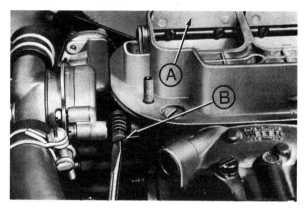

Fig. 3.21 Fast idle adjustment (B) with choke plates open (A)
(Sec 16)

and lower the complete system for removal and repair, or possibly complete renewal.

7   If renewing a section of the system, remove the U-clamp at the joint and separate the pipe connections. If badly rusted in position you may have to cut through the outer pipe at the joint to enable the joints to be prised apart, but care must be taken not to damage the section of pipe being re-used. The application of heat will also assist in separating a joint (but take care when working under the car).

8   When connecting a replacement section to the exhaust system, apply some exhaust sealant to the joint surfaces and fit the U-clamp loosely, so that when the system is refitted under the car, any alterations and adjustments to the fitted angles can be made.

9   Refitting is otherwise a reversal of the removal procedure. Ensure on completion that the system is securely located and does not chafe against any surrounding components. When the car is restarted check the system for any signs of leaks.

17.2 Exhaust system O-rings are used to suspend it. A system joint and U-clamp can be seen beyond

18 Fault diagnosis – fuel system and carburation

Symptom	Reason(s)
Fuel consumption excessive	Air cleaner choked and dirty giving rich mixture Fuel leaking from carburettor, fuel pumps, or fuel lines Float chamber flooding Generally worn carburettor Distributor condenser faulty Balance weights or vacuum advance mechanism in distributor faulty Carburettor incorrectly adjusted, mixture too rich Idling speed too high Contact breaker gap incorrect Valve clearances incorrect Auto choke mechanism defective Positive crankcase ventilation (PCV) valve defective (see Chapter 1) Incorrectly set spark plugs Tyres under-inflated Wrong spark plugs fitted Brakes dragging
Insufficient fuel delivery or weak mixture	Petrol tank air vent restricted Partially clogged filters in pump and carburettor Incorrectly seating valves in fuel pump Fuel pump diaphragm leaking or damaged Gasket in fuel pump damaged Fuel pump valve sticking due to petrol gumming Too little fuel in fuel tank (prevalent when climbing steep hills) Union joints on pipe connections loose Split in fuel pipe on suction side of fuel pump Inlet manifold to block or inlet manifold to carburettor gasket leaking Positive crankcase ventilation (PCV) valve defective (see Chapter 1)

Chapter 4 Ignition system

Contents

Specifications

General

System type	12 volt, contact breaker and coil
Firing order	1-3-4-2
Location of No 1 cylinder	Front of engine

Coil

Make	Motorcraft or Bosch
Type	Low voltage, used with 1.5 ohm ballast resistor
Primary resistance:	
Motorcraft	0.95 to 1.2 ohms
Bosch	1.2 to 1.3 ohms
Secondary resistance:	
Motorcraft	5900 to 6900 ohms
Bosch	7000 to 9300 ohms

Distributor

Make	Motorcraft or Bosch
Type	Single contact breaker, mechanical and vacuum advance mechanisms
Drive rotation (viewed from top):	
Mexico and RS 2000	Clockwise
RS 1800	Anti-clockwise
Contact breaker gap:	
Motorcraft	0.025 in (0.64 mm)
Bosch	0.018 in (0.45 mm)
Dwell angle (all distributors)	48° to 52°
Distributor shaft endfloat	
Bosch	0.021 to 0.051 in (0.53 to 1.31 mm)
Motorcraft (except RS 1800)	0.024 to 0.041 in (0.61 to 1.04 mm)
Motorcraft (RS 1800)	0.025 to 0.033 in (0.64 to 0.84 mm)
Distributor shaft lubricant	Castrol Perfecto heavy, Shell Turbo 41 or similar

Ignition timing

Static or at idle:	
Mexico and RS 2000	8° BTDC
RS 1800	4° BTDC
At 2000 rpm (vacuum connected):	
Mexico	31° to 39° BTDC
RS 1800	22° to 32° BTDC
RS 2000	27° to 35° BTDC

Spark plugs

Type:	
Mexico	Motorcraft BF22, Champion F7Y, or equivalent
RS 1800	Motorcraft AGR 12, Champion N6Y or equivalent
RS 2000	Motorcraft BF/32/BRF32 Champion F7Y, or equivalent
Electrode gap	0.023 in (0.6 mm)

Torque wrench settings

	lbf ft	kgf m
Spark plugs:		
Mexico and RS 2000	15 to 21	2.0 to 2.8
RS 1800	10 to 12	1.4 to 1.7

1 General description

In order that the engine can run correctly it is necessary for an electrical spark to ignite the fuel/air mixture in the combustion chamber at exactly the right moment in relation to engine speed and load. The ignition system is based on feeding low tension voltage from the battery to the coil where it is converted to high tension voltage. The high tension voltage is powerful enough to jump the spark plug gap in the cylinders many times a second under high compression, providing that the system is in good condition and that all adjustments are correct.

The ignition system is divided into two circuits, the low tension circuit and the high tension circuit. The low tension (sometimes known as the primary) circuit consists of the battery, lead to the control box, lead to the ignition switch, lead from the ignition switch to the low tension or primary coil windings (terminal + or SW), and the lead from the low tension coil windings (coil terminal - or CB) to the contact breaker points and condenser in the distributor. The high tension circuit consists of the high tension or secondary coil windings, the heavy ignition lead from the centre of the coil to the centre of the distributor cap, the rotor arm, and the spark plug leads and spark plugs.

A schematic diagram of the ignition circuit is shown in Fig. 4.1 which is applicable to the Mexico and RS 2000 models. The RS 1800 variant is similar in layout, but the distributor rotation when viewed from above is anti-clockwise. The firing order for all models is the same.

The system functions in the following manner. Low tension voltage is changed in the coil into high tension voltage by the opening and closing of the contact breaker points in the low tension circuit. High tension voltage is then fed via the carbon brush in the centre of

the distributor cap to the rotor arm of the distributor cap, and each time it comes in line with one of the four metal segments in the cap, which are connected to the spark plug leads, the opening and closing of the contact breaker points causes the high tension voltage to build up, jump the gap from the rotor arm to the appropriate metal segment and so via the spark plug lead to the spark plug, where it finally jumps the spark plug gap to earth.

The ignition is advanced and retarded automatically, to ensure that the spark occurs at just the right instant for the particular load at the prevailing engine speed. The ignition advance is controlled both mechanically and by a vacuum operated system. The mechanical governor mechanism comprises two weights, which move out from the distributor shaft due to centrifugal force as the engine speed rises. As they move outwards they rotate the cam relative to the distributor shaft, and so advance the spark. The weights are held in position by two light springs and it is the tension of the springs which is largely responsible for correct spark advancement. The vacuum control consists of a diaphragm, one side of which is connected via a small bore tube to the carburettor, and the other side to the contact breaker plate. Depression in the inlet manifold and carburettor, which varies with engine speed and throttle opening, causes the diaphragm to move, so moving the contact breaker plate, and advancing or retarding the spark.

2 Contact breaker – adjustment

1 To adjust the contact breaker points to the correct gap, first pull off the two clips securing the distributor cap to the distributor body, and lift away the cap. Clean the cap inside and out with a dry cloth. It is unlikely that the segments will be badly burned or scored, but if they are the cap will have to be renewed.

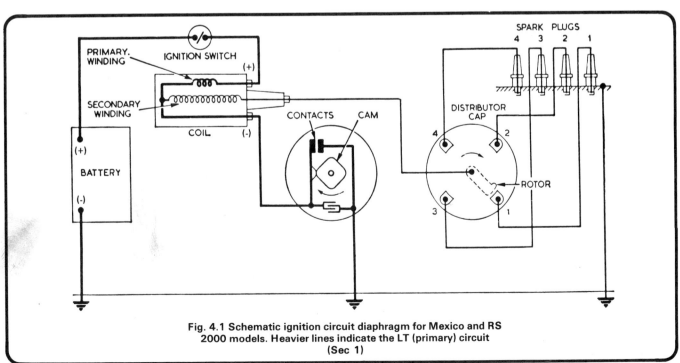

Fig. 4.1 Schematic ignition circuit diaphragm for Mexico and RS 2000 models. Heavier lines indicate the LT (primary) circuit
(Sec 1)

2 Inspect the carbon brush contact located in the top of the cap –
see that it is unbroken and stands proud of the plastic surface.
3 Check the contact spring on the top of the rotor arm. It must be
clean and have adequate tension to ensure good contact.
4 Gently prise the contact breaker points open to examine the
condition of their faces. If they are rough, pitted or dirty, it will be
necessary to remove them for new points to be fitted.
5 Assuming the points are satisfactory, or that new ones have been
fitted, measure the gap between the points by turning the engine until
the heel of the breaker arm is on the highest point of the cam.
6 A feeler gauge corresponding to the specified contact breaker gap
(depending upon distributor type) should now be inserted between the
points (photo). If the points clearance is correct, the feeler gauge will
be offered a slight resistance to movement.
7 If the gap is too wide (gauge is a slack fit) or too small (gauge is
a tight fit) the points are in need of adjustment.
8 To adjust the clearance, slacken the contact plate securing
screw(s). The Bosch distributor has one screw (Fig. 4.2), the
Motorcraft distributor has two (photo). Move the contact breaker plate
until the gap is correct, retighten the securing screw(s) and then check
the gap again, as the plate will sometimes move slightly when
tightening the securing screw(s).
9 On completion, refit the rotor arm and the distributor cap,
fastening it in position with the two clips.
10 On modern engines, setting the contact breaker gap in the
distributor using feeler gauges must be regarded as a basic adjustment
only. For optimum engine performance, the dwell angle must be
checked. The dwell angle is the number of degrees through which the
distributor cam turns during the period between the instants of closure
and opening of the contact breaker points. Checking the dwell angle
not only gives a more accurate setting of the contact breaker gap but
also evens out any variations in the gap which could be caused by
wear in the distributor shaft or its bushes, or difference in height of any
of the cam peaks.
11 The angle should be checked with a dwell meter connected in
accordance with the maker's instructions. Refer to the Specifications
for the correct dwell angle. If the dwell angle is too large, increase the
points gap; if too small, reduce the points gap.
12 The dwell angle should always be adjusted before checking and
adjusting the ignition timing.

3 Contact breaker – removal and refitting

1 Disconnect the battery earth terminal.
2 Unplug the spark plug leads, unclip the distributor cap and lift it
clear.
3 Remove the rotor arm by pulling it straight up from the top of the
cam spindle.
4 If the contact breaker points are burned, pitted or badly worn, they
must be renewed, since attempting to file or grind them will destroy
the special facing.
5 Detach the LT lead at the contact breaker by either pulling off the
lead (Bosch), or by slackening the screw and sliding out the forked
ends (Motorcraft) (photo).
6 Remove the securing screw(s) and lift out the contact breaker.
7 To refit the points is the reverse sequence to removal. Smear a

trace onto the cam to lubricate the moving heel, then reset the gap, as
described in Section 2.
8 Push the rotor arm onto the cam spindle, ensuring that the
locating boss is aligned with the slot.
9 Place the distributor cap squarely on the distributor and retain in
position with the two clips.
10 Push the leads onto the plugs, in the correct order, and reconnect
the battery.

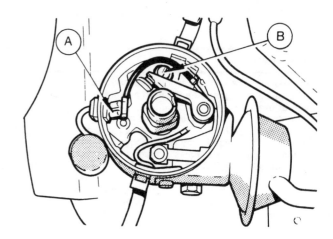

Fig. 4.2 Low tension lead connection (A) and contact breaker
screw (B) in Bosch distributor (Sec 2)

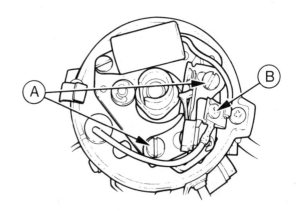

Fig. 4.3 Contact breaker screws (A) and low tension lead
connection (B) in Motorcraft distributor (Sec 3)

2.6 Checking the distributor contact breaker
points gap (Motorcraft shown)

2.8 Contact breaker adjustment screws
(arrowed) – Motorcraft distributor

3.5 Detaching Motorcraft LT leads

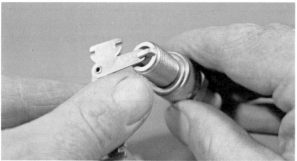

Measuring plug gap. A feeler gauge of the correct size (see ignition system specifications) should have a slight 'drag' when slid between the electrodes. Adjust gap if necessary

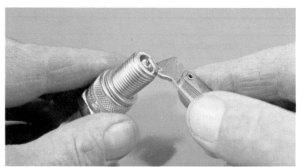

Adjusting plug gap. The plug gap is adjusted by bending the earth electrode inwards, or outwards, as necessary until the correct clearance is obtained. Note the use of the correct tool

Normal. Grey-brown deposits, lightly coated core nose. Gap increasing by around 0.001 in (0.025 mm) per 1000 miles (1600 km). Plugs ideally suited to engine, and engine in good condition

Carbon fouling. Dry, black, sooty deposits. Will cause weak spark and eventually misfire. Fault: over-rich fuel mixture. Check: carburettor mixture settings, float level and jet sizes; choke operation and cleanliness of air filter. Plugs can be re-used after cleaning

Oil fouling. Wet, oily deposits. Will cause weak spark and eventually misfire. Fault: worn bores/piston rings or valve guides; sometimes occurs (temporarily) during running-in period. Plugs can be re-used after thorough cleaning

Overheating. Electrodes have glazed appearance, core nose very white – few deposits. Fault: plug overheating. Check: plug value, ignition timing, fuel octane rating (too low) and fuel mixture (too weak). Discard plugs and cure fault immediately

Electrode damage. Electrodes burned away; core nose has burned, glazed appearance. Fault: pre-ignition. Check: as for 'Overheating' but may be more severe. Discard plugs and remedy fault before piston or valve damage occurs

Split core nose (may appear initially as a crack). Damage is self-evident, but cracks will only show after cleaning. Fault: pre-ignition or wrong gap-setting technique. Check: ignition timing, cooling system, fuel octane rating (too low) and fuel mixture (too weak). Discard plugs, rectify fault immediately

4 Distributor – lubrication

1   It is important that the distributor cam is lubricated with Vaseline (petroleum jelly) or grease at regular intervals (see Routine Maintenance). Also the automatic timing control weights and cam spindle are lubricated with engine oil.

2   Great care should be taken not to use too much lubricant as any excess that finds its way onto the contact breaker points could cause burning and misfiring.

3   To gain access to the cam spindle, lift away the distributor cap and rotor arm. Apply no more than two drops of engine oil onto the felt pad. This will run down the spindle when the engine is hot and lubricate the bearings.

4   To lubricate the automatic timing control, allow a few drops of oil to pass through the holes in the contact breaker baseplate through which the cam emerges. Apply not more than one drop of oil to the pivot post of the moving contact breaker point. Wipe away excess oil and refit the rotor arm and distributor cap.

5 Distributor – removal

1   To remove the distributor from the engine, mark the four spark plug leads so that they may be refitted to the correct plugs and pull off the four spark plug lead connectors.

2   Disconnect the high tension lead from the centre of the distributor cap by gripping the end cap and pulling. Also disconnect the low tension lead from the ignition coil.

3   Pull off the rubber union holding the vacuum pipe to the distributor vacuum advance housing.

4   If it is not wished to disturb the timing, turn the crankshaft until the timing marks are in line and the rotor arm is pointing to number 1 spark plug segment in the distributor cap (Fig. 4.4). This will facilitate refitting the distributor providing the crankshaft is not moved whilst the distributor is away from the engine. Mark the position of the rotor in relation to the distributor body, *after* it has been lifted clear.

5   Remove the distributor body clamp bolt which holds the distributor clamp plate to the engine and lift out the distributor (photos).

6 Distributor (Bosch) – dismantling

1   With the distributor on the bench, release the two spring clips retaining the cap and lift away the cap.

2   Pull the rotor arm off the distributor cam spindle.

3   Remove the contact breaker points, as described in Section 3.

4   Unscrew and remove the condenser securing screw and lift away the condenser and connector.

5   Next carefully remove the U-shaped clip from the pullrod of the vacuum unit.

6   Undo and remove the two screws that secure the vacuum unit to the side of the distributor body. Lift away the vacuum unit.

7   The distributor cap spring clip retainers may be removed by undoing and removing the screws and lifting away the clips and retainers. This is the limit of the dismantling which should be

attempted, since none of the parts beneath the breaker plate, including the drivegear, can be renewed. For general notes on inspection and repair, refer to Section 8.

7 Distributor (Motorcraft) – dismantling

1   Refer to Section 6, and follow the instructions given in paragraphs 1 to 3.

2   Next prise off the small circlip from the vacuum unit pivot post.

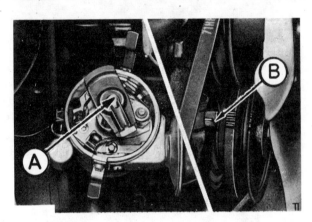

Fig. 4.4 Rotor facing No 1 contact (A) with timing mark (B) aligned – Mexico RS 2000 shown) (Sec 5)

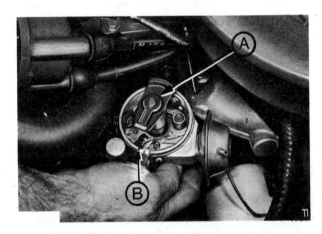

Fig. 4.5 Mark rotor arm position (A) relative to distributor body (B) on withdrawal (Mexico/RS 2000 engine shown) (Sec 5)

5.5a Distributor clamp and bolt (Mexico and RS 2000)

5.5b Removing distributor clamp bolt (RS 1800)

5.5c Distributor removal from the RS 1800 engine

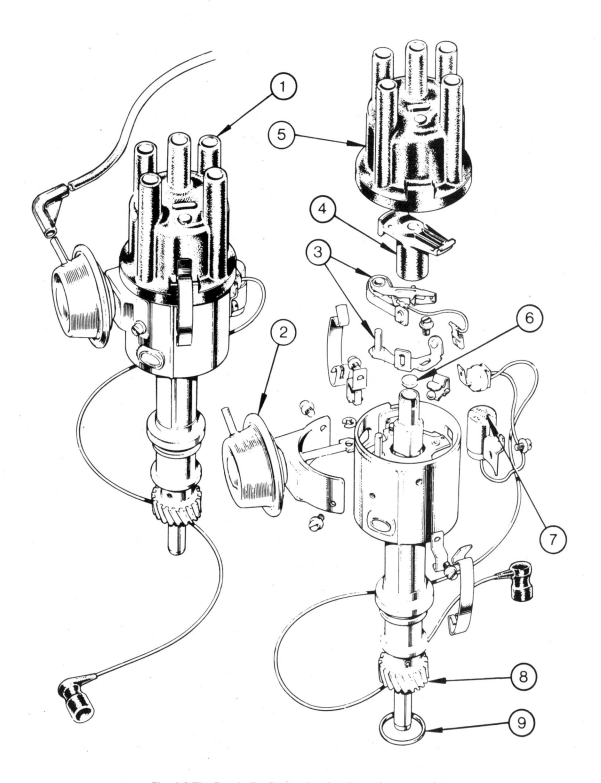

Fig. 4.6 The Bosch distributor showing the main components
(Sec 6)

1	Distributor assembly	4	Rotor arm	7	Condenser
2	Vacuum unit	5	Cap	8	Drivegear
3	Contact breaker	6	Felt wick	9	Seal

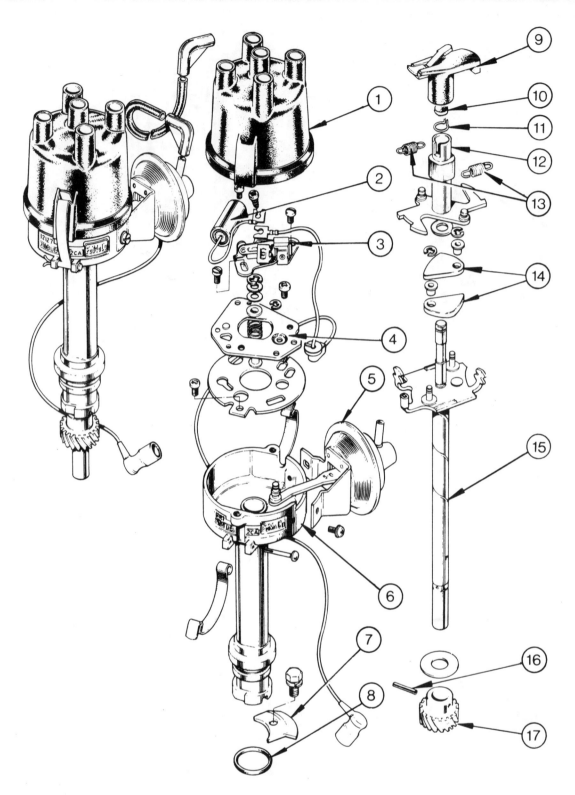

Fig. 4.7 The Motorcraft distributor showing the main components
(Sec 7)

1	Cap	7	Distributor clamp	13	Advance springs
2	Condenser	8	Seal	14	Advance weights
3	Contact breakers	9	Rotor arm	15	Shaft
4	Baseplate	10	Felt wick	16	Pin
5	Vacuum unit	11	Spring clip	17	Drivegear
6	Body	12	Cam		

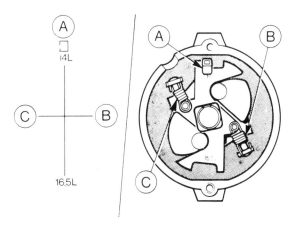

Fig. 4.8 Typical sketch only, showing location of bump stop (A), thin spring (B) and thick spring (C) (Sec 7)

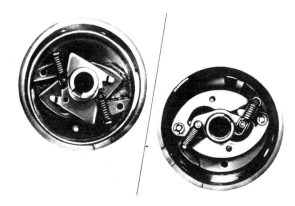

Fig. 4.9 Alternative types of centrifugal weight layouts (Sec 7)

3 Take out the two screws that hold the breaker plate to the distributor body and lift it away.

4 Undo and remove the condenser retaining screw and lift away the condenser.

5 Take off the circlip, flat washer and two wave washers from the pivot post. Separate the two plates. Be careful not to lose the spring now left on the pivot post.

6 Pull the low tension wire and grommet from the lower plate.

7 Undo the two screws holding the vacuum unit to the body. Take off the unit.

8 Make a sketch of the position of the advance springs and weights in relation to the bump stop, noting the identification letters (Fig. 4.8). Also note which spring – thick or thin – is fitted to which post.

9 Dismantle the spindle by taking out the felt pad in the top. Remove the spring clip using small pliers.

10 Prise off the bump stop and lift out the spring and weight assembly. Remove the thrust washer.

11 It is only necessary to remove the spindle and lower plate if it is excessively worn. If this is the case, with a suitable pin punch tap out the gear lockpin.

12 The gear may now be drawn off the shaft with a universal puller. If there is no means of holding the legs these must be bound together with wire to stop them springing apart during removal.

13 Finally withdraw the shaft from the distributor body.

8 Distributor – inspection and repair

1 Check the contact breaker points for wear, burning or pitting. Check the distributor cap for signs of tracking indicated by a thin black line between the segments. Renew the cap if any signs of tracking are found.

2 If the metal portion of the rotor arm is badly burned or loose, renew the arm. If only slightly burned clean the end with a fine file. Check that the contact spring has adequate pressure and the bearing surface is clean and in good condition.

3 Check that the carbon brush in the distributor cap is unbroken and stands proud of its holder.

4 Examine the centrifugal weights and pivots for wear and the advance springs for slackness. They can be checked by comparing with new parts. If they are slack they must be renewed.

5 Check the points assembly for fit on the breaker plate, and the cam follower for wear.

6 Examine the fit of the spindle in the distributor body. If there is excessive side movement it will be necessary either to fit a new bush or obtain a new body.

9 Distributor (Bosch) – reassembly

1 Place the distributor cap retaining spring clip and retainers on the outside of the distributor body and secure the retainers with the two screws.

2 Position the contact breaker assembly on the breaker plate in such a manner than the entire lower surface of the assembly contacts the plate. Refit the contact breaker assembly securing screw, but do not fully tighten yet.

3 Hook the diaphragm assembly pullrod into contact with the pivot pin.

4 Secure the diaphragm to the distributor body with the two screws. Also refit the condenser to the terminal side of the diaphragm bracket securing screw. The condenser must firmly contact its lower stop on the housing.

5 Apply a little grease or petroleum jelly to the cam and also to the heel of the breaker lever.

6 Reset the contact breaker points, as described in Section 2, and then refit the rotor arm and distributor cap.

10 Distributor (Motorcraft) – reassembly

1 Reassembly is a straightforward reversal of the dismantling process, but there are several points which must be noted.

2 Check that the drivegear is not 180° out of position, as the pin bores may be slightly misaligned. Secure it with a new pin.

3 Coat the upper shaft with a lithium based grease, ensuring that the undercut is filled.

4 When fitting the cam spindle assembly, first replace the thrust washer, then refer to the sketch made in Section 7, paragraph 8. Check that the assembly moves freely without binding.

5 Position the spring clip legs opposite the rotor arm slot.

6 Before assembling the breaker plates make sure that the nylon bearing studs are correctly located in their holes in the upper breaker plate, and the small earth spring is fitted on the pivot post.

7 When all is assembled reset the contact breaker points, as described in Section 2.

11 Distributor – installation

1 If a new shaft or gear has not been fitted (ie; the original parts are still being used) and the engine has not been moved, it will not be necessary to re-time the ignition.

2 Align the rotor arm with the mark on the distributor body (Section 5, paragraph 4). Insert the distributor into its location with the vacuum advance assembly to the rear.

3 Notice that the rotor arm rotates as the gears mesh. The rotor arm must settle in exactly the same direction that it was in before the distributor was removed. To do this lift out the assembly far enough to rotate the shaft one tooth at a time, lowering it home to check the direction with the assembly fully home. Fit the distributor clamp plate and plain washer and secure them with the retaining bolt.

4 With the distributor assembly fitted reconnect the low tension lead from the side of the distributor to the CB or negative (-) terminal on the coil. Reconnect the HT lead to the centre of the distributor cap and refit the rubber union of the vacuum pipe which runs from the

induction manifold to the side of the vacuum advance unit.

5   If the engine has been disturbed, refer to Section 14 for details on retiming.

12 Condenser – removal, testing and refitting

1   The purpose of the condenser (sometimes known as a capacitor) is to ensure that when the contact breaker points open there is no sparking across them which would waste voltage and cause wear.

2   The condenser is fitted in parallel with the contact breaker points. If it develops a short-circuit, it will cause ignition failure as the contact breaker will be prevented from correctly interrupting the low tension circuit.

3   If the engine becomes very difficult to start or begins to misfire after several miles of running and the breaker points show signs of excessive burning, then the condition of the condenser must be suspect. One further test can be made by separating the points using an insulated screwdriver with the ignition switched on. If this is accompanied by a bright flash, it is indicative that the condenser has failed.

4   Without special test equipment the only certain way to diagnose condenser trouble is to replace a suspected unit with a new one and note if there is any improvement.

5   To remove the condenser from the distributor take off the distributor cap and rotor arm.

6   *Bosch:* Disconnect the low tension leads from the coil and to the contact breaker. Release the condenser cable from the side of the distributor body and then undo and remove the screw that secures the condenser to the side of the distributor. Lift away the condenser.

7   *Ford:* Slacken the self-tapping screw holding the condenser lead and low tension lead to the contact breaker. Slide out the forked terminal on the end of the condenser low tension lead. Undo and remove the condenser retaining screw and remove the condenser from the breaker plate.

8   To refit the condenser, simply reverse the order of removal.

13 Spark plugs and HT leads

1   The correct functioning of the spark plugs is vital for the correct running and efficiency of the engine.

2   The plugs fitted as standard are listed in the Specifications. At regular intervals (see Routine Maintenance) the plugs should be removed, examined, cleaned, and if excessively worn, renewed. The condition of the spark plugs will also tell much about the overall condition of the engine.

3   Before removing the spark plugs, detach the leads and wipe any dirt or oil from around the plug seat. This is particularly important with the RS 1800 engine where the vertical plug wells are deeply recessed

13.2 Removing the plug lead and well protector on the RS 1800 engine

in the middle of the cylinder head and any oil and dirt around the plugs will fall into the combustion chamber as soon as the plugs are removed.

4   If the insulator nose of the spark plug is clean and white, with no deposits, this is indicative of a weak mixture, or too hot a plug (a hot plug transfers heat away from the electrode slowly – a cold plug transfers it away quickly).

5   If the tip and insulator nose are covered with hard black deposits, then this is indicative that the mixture is too rich. Should the plug be black and oily, then it is likely that the engine is fairly worn, as well as the mixture being too rich.

6   If the insulator nose is covered with light tan to greyish brown deposits, then the mixture is correct and it is likely that the engine is in good condition.

7   If there are any traces of long brown taperng stains on the outside of the white portion of the plug, then the plug will have to be renewed, as this shows that there is a faulty joint between the plug body and the insulator, and compression is being allowed to leak away.

8   Plugs should be cleaned by a sand blasting machine which will free them from carbon more thoroughly than cleaning by hand. The machine will also test the condition of the plugs under compression. Any plug that fails to spark at the recommended pressure should be renewed.

9   The spark plug gap is of considerable importance, as, if it is too large or too small, the size of the spark and its efficiency will be seriously impaired. The spark plug gap should be set to the figure given in the Specifications at the beginning of this Chapter.

10   To set it, measure the gap with a feeler gauge, and then bend open or close, the outer plug electrode until the correct gap is achieved. The centre electrode should never be bent as this may crack the insulation and cause plug failure, if nothing worse.

11   When refitting the plugs, remember to refit the leads from the distributor in the correct firing order, which is 1-3-4-2 (No 1 cylinder being the one nearest the radiator).

12   The plug leads require no routine attention other than being kept clean and wiped over regularly.

13   At regular intervals, however, if it is possible, disconnect the leads from the plugs and distributor one at a time and make sure no water has found its way onto the connections. Remove any corrosion from the brass ends, wipe the collars on top of the distributor, and refit the leads.

14 Ignition timing

1   One of two methods may be used to check the ignition timing. With the first method, connect a test bulb between the distributor LT terminal and earth.

2   Rotate the crankshaft by using a suitable spanner on the crankshaft pulley bolt, or rolling the car while in gear, until No 1 piston is rising on its compression stroke. On RS 2000 and Mexico models it is possible to recognise a compression stroke by the pressure felt on a finger over the spark plug hole. A more certain way is to remove the rocker cover and watch the valves – a cylinder on its compression stroke has both valves closed. On RS 1800 models No 1 piston will be on its compression stroke when the timing marks on the camshaft sprocket are nearing the reference mark on the cam cover (Fig. 4.10).

3   Continue turning the engine until the correct timing mark is aligned with the reference pointer. On Mexico and RS 2000 models the timing marks on the crankshaft pulley are measured in 2° intervals from the TDC mark (photo). On RS 1800 models the ignition mark should align with the reference pointer on the cam cover. The correct static advance value is given in the Specifications.

4   Switch on the ignition and release the distributor clamp pinchbolt. Turn the distributor in either direction until the test bulb just lights up which indicates that the contact breaker points have just opened.

5   Tighten the pinch-bolt without moving the position of the distributor.

6   Remove the test bulb and switch off the ignition.

7   With the second method, a more precise setting is obtained.

8   Mark with chalk or paint the correct timing mark on the crankshaft pulley or camshaft sprocket (as applicable) and the reference point.

9   Disconnect the vacuum pipe from the distributor and plug the pipe.

10   Connect a timing light (stroboscope) in accordance with the manufacturer's instructions. This is usually between the end of No 1 spark plug lead and the spark plug terminal.

Fig. 4.10 Ignition timing marks – RS 1800 (Sec 14)

A Ignition mark
B TDC mark
C Reference mark on the cam cover

14.3 Crankshaft pulley TDC mark (A) and timing pointer (B) – Mexico and RS 2000 engines

11 Start the engine and let it idle, making sure that the idling speed is below 1000 rev/min, otherwise the mechanical advance mechanism will start to operate and give a false indication of the engine timing.
12 Point the stroboscope at the white marks and they will appear stationary and, if the timing is correct, in alignment. If the marks do not appear to be in alignment, release the distributor clamp plate pinch-bolt and turn the distributor body fractionally in either direction until the timing marks coincide.
13 If this cannot be achieved check that the drivegear has meshed on the correct tooth by lifting out the distributor and repositioning it.
14 When the timing is correct retighten the pinch-bolt, switch off the engine and remake the original connections.

15 Fault diagnosis – ignition system

1   By far the majority of breakdown and running troubles are caused by faults in the ignition system either in the low tension or high tension circuits.
2   There are two main symptoms indicating ignition faults. Either the engine will not start or fire, or the engine is difficult to start and misfires. If it is a regular misfire, ie; the engine is running on only two or three cylinders, the fault is almost sure to be in the secondary or high tension circuit. If the misfiring is intermittent, the fault could be either the high or low tension circuits. If the car stops suddenly, or will not start at all, it is likely that the fault is in the low tension circuit. Loss of power and overheating, apart from faulty carburation settings, are normally due to faults in the distributor or to incorrect ignition timing.

Engine fails to start
3   If the engine fails to start and the car was running normally when it was last used, first check there is fuel in the petrol tank. If the engine turns over normally on the starter motor and the battery is evidently well charged, then the fault may be in either the high or low tension circuits. First check the HT circuit. If the battery is known to be fully charged, the ignition light comes on, and the starter motor fails to turn the engine, check the tightness of the leads on the battery terminals and also the secureness of the earth lead to its connection to the body. It is quite common for the leads to have worked loose, even if they look and feel secure. If one of the battery terminal posts gets very hot when trying to work the starter motor this is a sure indication of a faulty connection to that terminal.
4   One of the commonest reasons for bad starting is wet or damp spark plug leads or distributor. Remove the distributor cap. If condensation is visible internally dry the cap with a rag and also wipe over the leads. Refit the cap.
5   If the engine still fails to start, check that current is reaching the plugs, by disconnecting each plug lead in turn at the spark plug end, inserting a screw or nail into the plug cap and holding the end of the screw or nail about $\frac{3}{16}$ in (5 mm) away from the cylinder block. (Hold the lead with a dry cloth or a rubber glove to avoid electric shocks.) Spin the engine on the starter motor.
6   Sparking between the end of the cable and the block should be fairly strong with a strong regular blue spark. If current is reaching the plugs, then remove them and clean and regap them. The engine should now start.
7   If there is no spark at the plug leads take off the HT lead from the centre of the distributor cap and hold it to the block as before. Spin the engine on the starter once more. A rapid succession of blue sparks between the end of the lead and the block indicates that the coil is in order and that the distributor cap is cracked, the rotor arm faulty, or the carbon brush in the top of the distributor cap is not making good contact with the spring on the rotor arm. Possibly, the points are in bad condition. Renew them as described in this Chapter, Section 3.
8   If there are no sparks from the end of the lead from the coil check the connections at the coil end of the lead. If it is in order start checking the low tension circuit.
9   Use a 12V voltmeter or a 12V bulb and two lengths of wire. With the ignition switched on and the points open (for these tests it is sufficient to separate the points with a piece of dry paper), test between the low tension wire to the coil (it is marked SW or +) and earth. No reading indicates a break in the supply from the ignition switch. Check the connections at the switch to see if any are loose. Refit them and the engine should run. A reading shows a faulty coil or condenser, or broken lead between the coil and the distributor.
10   Take the condenser wire off the points assembly and with the points open test between the moving point and earth. If there now is a reading then the fault is in the condenser. Fit a new one as described in this Chapter, Section 12, and the fault is cleared.
11   With no reading from the moving point to earth, take a reading between earth and the CB or negative (-) terminal of the coil. A reading here shows a broken wire which will need to be replaced between the coil and distributor. No reading confirms that the coil has failed and must be renewed, after which the engine will run once more. Remember to refit the condenser wire to the points assembly.

Engine misfires
12   If the engine misfires regularly run it at a fast idling speed. Pull off each of the plug caps in turn and listen to the note of the engine. Hold the plug cap in a dry cloth or with a rubber glove as additional protection against a shock from the HT supply.
13   No difference in engine running will be noticed when the lead from the defective circuit is removed. Removing the lead from one of the good cylinders will accentuate the misfire.
14   Remove the plug lead from the end of the defective plug, insert a screw or nail into the plug cap and hold it about $\frac{3}{16}$ in (5 mm) away from the block. Re-start the engine. If the sparking is fairly strong and regular the fault must lie in the spark plug.
15   The plug may be loose, the insulation may be cracked, or the electrodes may have burnt away giving too wide a gap for the spark to

jump. Worse still, one of the electrodes may have broken off.

16 If there is no spark at the end of the plug lead, or if it is weak and intermittent, check the lead from the distributor to the plug. If the insulation is cracked or perished, renew the lead. Check the connections at the distributor cap.

17 If there is still no spark, examine the distributor cap carefully for tracking. This can be recognised by a very thin black line running between two or more electrodes, or between an electrode and some other part of the distributor. These lines are paths which now conduct electricity across the cap thus letting it run to earth. The only answer is a new distributor cap.

18 Apart from the ignition timing being incorrect, other causes of misfiring have already been dealt with under the section dealing with the failure of the engine to start. To recap – these are that:

(a) The coil may be faulty giving an intermittent misfire
(b) There may be a damaged wire or loose connection in the low tension circuit
(c) The condenser may be short-circuiting
(d) There may be a mechanical fault in the distributor (broken driving spindle or contact breaker spring)

19 If the ignition timing is too far retarded, it should be noted that the engine will tend to overheat, and there will be a quite noticeable drop in power. If the engine is overheating and the power is down, and the ignition timing is correct, then the carburettor should be checked, as it is likely that this is where the fault lies.

Chapter 5 Clutch

Contents

Specifications

General

Clutch type	Single dry plate, diaphragm spring
Actuation	Cable

Friction disc (driven plate)

Diameter	8.5 in (216 mm)
Lining material	Ferodo 2124F
Minimum lining thickness allowable	0.118 in (3.0 mm)

Adjustment data

Pedal backlift	0.87 ± 0.16 in (22 ± 4 mm)
Total pedal travel	5.9 in (150 mm)

Torque wrench settings

	lbf ft	kgf m
Clutch housing to gearbox	30 to 34	4.1 to 4.7
Clutch housing to engine	26 to 30	3.5 to 4.1
Pressure plate to flywheel	13 to 15	1.7 to 2.1

1 General description

All models have an 8.5 in (216 mm) diameter clutch of either Borg and Beck or Laycock manufacture.

The clutch assembly comprises a steel cover which is dowelled and bolted to the rear face of the flywheel and contains the pressure plate diaphragm spring and fulcrum rings.

The clutch friction disc is free to slide along the splined gearbox first motion shaft and is held in position between the flywheel and the pressure plate by the pressure of the pressure plate spring. Friction lining material is riveted to the disc and it has a spring cushioned hub to absorb transmission shocks and to help ensure a smooth take-off.

The circular diaphragm spring is mounted on shouldered pins and held in place in the cover by two fulcrum rings. The spring is also held to the pressure plate by three spring steel clips which are riveted in position.

The clutch is actuated by a cable controlled by the clutch pedal. The clutch release mechanism consists of a release fork and bearing which are in permanent contact with the release fingers on the pressure plate. There should therefore never be any free play at the release fork. Wear of the friction material in the clutch is taken up by means of a cable adjuster on the clutch bellhousing.

Depressing the clutch pedal actuates the clutch release lever by means of the cable. The release lever pushes the release bearing forward to bear against the release fingers, so moving the centre of the diaphragm spring inward. The spring is sandwiched between two annular rings which act as fulcrum points. As the centre of the spring is pushed in, the outside of the spring is pushed out, so moving the pressure plate backward and disengaging the pressure plate from the friction disc.

When the clutch pedal is released, the diaphragm spring forces the pressure plate into contact with the high friction linings on the clutch disc and at the same time pushes the disc a fraction of an inch forward

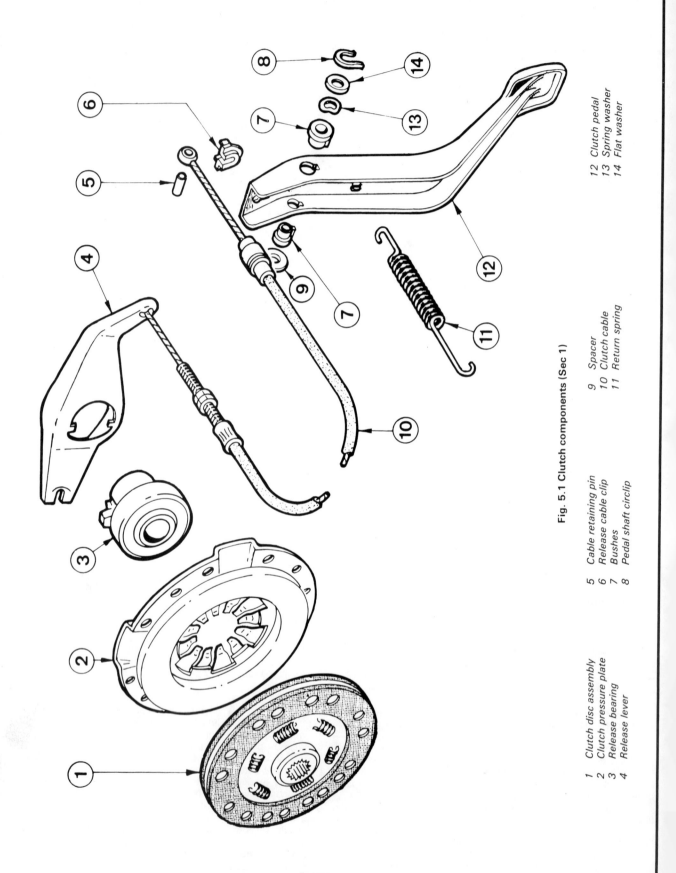

Fig. 5.1 Clutch components (Sec 1)

1 Clutch disc assembly
2 Clutch pressure plate
3 Release bearing
4 Release lever

5 Cable retaining pin
6 Release cable clip
7 Bushes
8 Pedal shaft circlip

9 Spacer
10 Clutch cable
11 Return spring

12 Clutch pedal
13 Spring washer
14 Flat washer

on its splines so engaging it with the flywheel. The clutch disc is now firmly sandwiched between the pressure plate and the flywheel so the drive is taken up.

2 Clutch – adjustment

1   At regular intervals (as specified in Routine Maintenance) the clutch pedal backlift must be checked and adjusted, if necessary, to compensate for wear in the friction linings.
2   Slacken the locknut on the threaded portion of the outer cable at the clutch bellhousing (photo).
3   Check that the cable is not kinked, or frayed, then grasp the outer case of the cable and pull the cable forward to take up any free play in the cable.
4   Turn the adjusting nut down the adjuster thread until it contacts the cable bush in the bellhousing, then press the pedal to the floor several times to ensure all components are properly seated.
5   Reset the adjusting nut until there is the specified free backlift movement at the clutch pedal pad. Before checking the backlift push the pedal slowly down to the floor and, equally slowly, allow it to return to the 'rest' position. Allowing the pedal to spring back may not necessarily cause it to reach its normal 'rest' position.
6   If the pedal backlift movement is too small *slacken* the adjusting nut, if too great *tighten* the adjusting nut.
7   When the adjustment is correct tighten the locknut without disturbing the adjusting nut, then recheck the backlift.

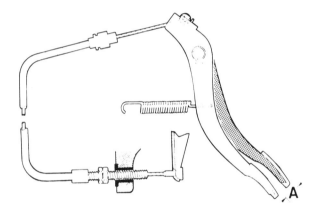

Fig. 5.2 Clutch pedal free movement (Sec 2)

A   Backlift

3 Clutch – removal

1   Remove the gearbox, as described in the next Chapter.
2   Scribe a mating line from the clutch cover to the flywheel to ensure identical positioning on refitting and then remove the clutch assembly by unscrewing the six bolts holding the cover to the rear face

of the flywheel. Unscrew the bolts diagonally half a turn at a time to prevent distortion of the cover flange.
3   The friction disc should already be marked for orientation, but if it isn't make a note, or mark it accordingly. When the clutch friction disc is removed, a certain amount of asbestos dust is likely to be present. The best method of cleaning is to use a vacuum cleaner, as *inhaling asbestos dust is injurious to health*.
4   With all the bolts and spring washers removed, lift the clutch assembly off the locating dowels. The friction disc may fall out at this stage as it is not attached to either the clutch cover assembly or the flywheel.

4 Clutch assembly – servicing

1   It is recommended that the friction disc is exchanged for a factory reconditioned unit. Do not attempt to fit new friction linings yourself. This is seldom satisfactory and the small saving in cost is not worthwhile.
2   The pressure plate assembly should also be renewed on an exchange basis as it requires the use of jigs and considerable skill to set it up when it has been dismantled.
3   If the friction disc is being renewed, always renew the release bearing at the same time to avoid later dismantling (see Section 6).
4   The friction disc should be renewed if the friction linings have worn down to, or almost down to, the minimum specified thickness. If the linings are oil stained, renew the friction disc and establish and rectify the cause which will almost certainly be the gearbox front oil seal or the crankshaft rear oil seal having failed.
5   Check the machined faces of the flywheel and the pressure plate. If either is grooved it should be machined until smooth, or renewed.
6   If the pressure plate is cracked or split it is essential that an exchange unit is fitted, also if the pressure of the diaphragm spring is suspect.
7   Check the release bearing for smoothness of operation. There should be no harshness or slackness in it. It should spin reasonably freely, bearing in mind it has been pre-packed with grease.

5 Clutch – refitting

1   It is important that no oil or grease gets onto the clutch disc friction linings, or the pressure plate and flywheel faces. It is advisable to refit the clutch with clean hands and to wipe down the pressure plate and flywheel faces with a clean, dry rag before assembly begins.
2   Position the friction disc against the flywheel, ensuring that it is facing the correct way as marked.
3   Locate the clutch cover/pressure plate assembly on the dowels with the mating marks in alignment (photo).
4   Insert the six bolts and their spring washers finger tight so that the friction disc is just gripped, but can be slid sideways.
5   The clutch friction disc must now be centralised so that when the gearbox is mated to the engine, the gearbox first motion shaft will pass smoothly through the splined hub of the disc.
6   Centralising is best carried out using an old first motion shaft, but a rod of equivalent diameter with a stepped end to engage in the spigot bush located in the centre of the flywheel will serve as a good substitute (photo).

2.2 The clutch cable adjuster and locknut

5.3 Refit the clutch cover/pressure plate assembly

5.6 Centralising the clutch friction disc (driven plate)

7   Insert the centralising tool and move it to centralise the friction disc. The tool should be easy to withdraw without any side pressure.
8   Tighten the clutch cover to flywheel bolts evenly in diagonal sequence and finally tighten them to the specified torque.
9   Refit the gearbox, as given in the next Chapter.

6   Release bearing – removal and refitting

1   The clutch release bearing is only accessible for inspection or renewal when either the engine or gearbox are removed. Therefore, whenever the gearbox is withdrawn for servicing of the clutch to be carried out, the clutch release bearing, which is located within the bellhousing on the clutch release lever, should be renewed.
2   Two types of release bearing have been fitted. The earlier models had a non-self-centering release bearing, but from October 1977 a self-centering release bearing was fitted, which gives improved operation to the original non-centering type. The bearings can be identified with reference to Fig. 5.3.
3   Wear in the non-centering type can give rise to jerky pedal action when disengaging the clutch, so it is recommended that the later type is fitted whenever work on the clutch or gearbox is undertaken.
4   The release bearing is a relatively inexpensive but important component, and unless it is nearly new it is a mistake not to replace it during an overhaul of the clutch.
5   The release bearing and lever can be withdrawn from the clutch housing.
6   To free the bearing from the release lever, simply rotate the bearing through 90° and remove. Note which way round the bearing is fitted (photo). On later models the bearing is removed by simply pulling free.
7   Before fitting the release bearing, always lubricate the hub bore and release lever contact face with a molybdenum disulphide grease.
8   Refitting is otherwise a straightforward reversal of removal.

7   Clutch cable – removal and refitting

1   Open the bonnet, and for safety reasons disconnect the battery.
2   Chock the rear wheels, jack up the front of the car and support on firmly based stands. Ease off the rubber grommet from the rear face of the clutch housing (photo).
3   Push the clutch pedal hard against the stop and with an open-ended spanner slacken the locknut and clutch adjustment nut. These are located on the clutch bellhousing.
4   It will now be possible to lift the cable ball end from the slotted end of the release lever. Whilst this is being done take great care not to accidentally disengage the release lever from the bearing hub.
5   Lever the cable eye end and pin from the cable retention bush in the pedal with a small screwdriver.

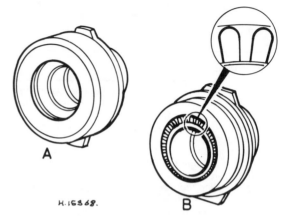

H.16368.

Fig. 5.3 Non self-centering (A), and self-centering (B) types of clutch release bearing (Sec 6)

6   Withdraw the pin from the eye and withdraw the cable assembly from the abutment tube in the dash panel.
7   Refitting is a straightforward reversal of the removal sequence. Lubricate the pivot pin. Refer to Section 2 and adjust the cable on completion. Check that it has no tight bends in it, and will not chafe against any moving parts.

8   Clutch – fault diagnosis

There are four main faults to which the clutch and release mechanism are prone. They may occur by themselves or in conjunction with any of the other faults. They are clutch squeal, slip, spin and judder.

Clutch squeal
1   If, on taking up the drive or when changing gear, the clutch squeals, this is a sure indication of a badly worn clutch release bearing.
2   As well as regular wear due to normal use, wear of the clutch release bearing is much accentuated if the clutch is ridden, or held down for long periods in gear, with the engine running. To minimise wear of this component, the car should always be taken out of gear at traffic lights and for similar hold-ups.
3   The clutch release bearing is not an expensive item, but difficult to get at for renewal.

Clutch slip
4   Clutch slip is a self-evident condition which occurs when the clutch friction disc (driven plate) is badly worn, oil or grease have got

6.6 The clutch release lever and bearing

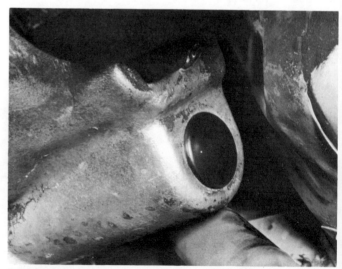

7.2 Remove the rubber plug for access in order to detach the clutch cable from the release lever

onto the flywheel or pressure plate faces, or the pressure plate itself is faulty.

5   The reason for clutch slip is that, due to one of the faults listed above, there is either insufficient pressure from the pressure plate, or insufficient friction from the friction disc to ensure solid drive.

6   If small amounts of oil get onto the clutch, they will be burnt off under the heat of the clutch engagement and in the process gradually darken the linings. Excessive oil on the clutch will burn off leaving a carbon deposit which can cause quite bad slip, or fierceness, spin and judder.

7   If clutch slip is suspected, and confirmation of this condition is required, there are several tests which can be made.

8   With the engine in second or third gear and pulling lightly up a moderate incline, sudden depression of the accelerator pedal may cause the engine to increase its speed without any increase in road speed. Easing off on the accelerator will then give a definite drop in engine speed without the car slowing.

9   In extreme cases of clutch slip the engine will race under normal acceleration conditions.

Clutch spin

10   Clutch spin is a condition which occurs when the release arm travel is excessive, there is an obstruction in the clutch, either on the primary gear splines, or in the operating lever itself, or the oil may have partially burnt off the clutch linings and have left a resinous deposit which is causing the friction disc to stick to the pressure plate or flywheel.

11   The reason for clutch spin is that due to any, or a combination, of the faults just listed, the clutch pressure plate is not completely freeing from the centre disc even with the clutch pedal fully depressed.

12   If clutch spin is suspected, the condition can be confirmed by extreme difficulty in engaging first gear from rest, difficulty in changing gear, and very sudden take-up of the clutch drive at the fully depressed end of the clutch pedal travel as the clutch is released.

13   Check that the clutch cable is correctly adjusted and if in order, then the fault lies internally in the clutch. It will then be necessary to remove the clutch for examination and to check the gearbox input shaft.

Clutch judder

14   Clutch judder is a self-evident condition which occurs when the gearbox or engine mountings are loose or too flexible, when there is oil on the faces of the clutch friction disc, or when the clutch pressure plate has been incorrectly adjusted during assembly.

15   The reason for clutch judder is that due to one of the faults just listed, the clutch pressure plate is not freeing smoothly from the friction disc, and is snatching.

16   Clutch judder normally occurs when the clutch pedal is released in first or reverse gears, and the whole car shudders as it moves backward or forward.

Chapter 6 Gearbox

Contents

Specifications

General

Designation (all models)	Ford type 'B'
Number of gears	4 forward, 1 reverse
Type of gears	Helical, constant mesh
Synchromesh	All forward gears

Gear ratios

	1600 Mexico and RS 2000	RS 1800
First	3.65:1	3.36:1
Second	1.97:1	1.81:1
Third	1.37:1	1.26:1
Fourth	1.00:1	1.00:1
Reverse	3.66:1	3.66:1

Lubrication

Lubricant type	SAE 80 EP gear oil
Lubricant capacity	2.4 Imp pints (1.35 litres)

Overhaul data

Countershaft cluster gear endfloat	0.006 to 0.018 in (0.15 to 0.45 mm)
Thrust washer thickness	0.061 to 0.063 in (1.55 to 1.60 mm)
Diameter of countershaft	0.68 in (17.3 mm)

Torque wrench settings

	lbf ft	kgf m
Transmission cover bolts	7 to 8	0.9 to 1.1
Extension housing (to gearbox)	33 to 37	4.5 to 5.0
Drivegear bearing retainer (to gearbox)	7 to 8	0.9 to 1.1
Clutch housing (to gearbox)	30 to 34	4.1 to 4.7
Clutch housing to engine	26 to 30	3.5 to 4.1
Gearbox to support crossmember	37 to 42	5.0 to 5.7
Rear engine mounting blocks	12 to 15	1.6 to 2.0
Adaptor blocks to floorpan	12 to 15	1.6 to 2.0

1 General description

The Ford type 'B' gearbox is used on all three models covered by this manual. This gearbox has four forward and one reverse gear, the forward gears being helically cut whilst the reverse gear is straight cut. Synchromesh is fitted between 1st and 2nd, 2nd and 3rd, and 3rd and 4th gears.

The bellhousing and gearbox case separate castings. The bellhousing and rear extension housing are manufactured in aluminium alloy whilst the main gearcase is of cast steel.

The selector forks are free to slide on the selector rod which also serves as the gearchange shaft. At the gearbox end of this rod lies the selector arm, which, depending on the position of the gear-lever, places the appropriate selector fork in the position necessary for the synchroniser sleeve to engage with the dog teeth on the gear selected.

It is impossible to select two gears at once because of an interlock guard plate which pivots on the right-hand side of the gearbox casing. The selector forks, when not in use, are positively held by the guard plate in their disengaged positions.

All forward gears on the mainshaft and input shaft are in constant mesh with their corresponding gears on the countershaft gear cluster and are helically cut to achieve quiet running.

The countershaft reverse gear has straight-cut spur teeth that

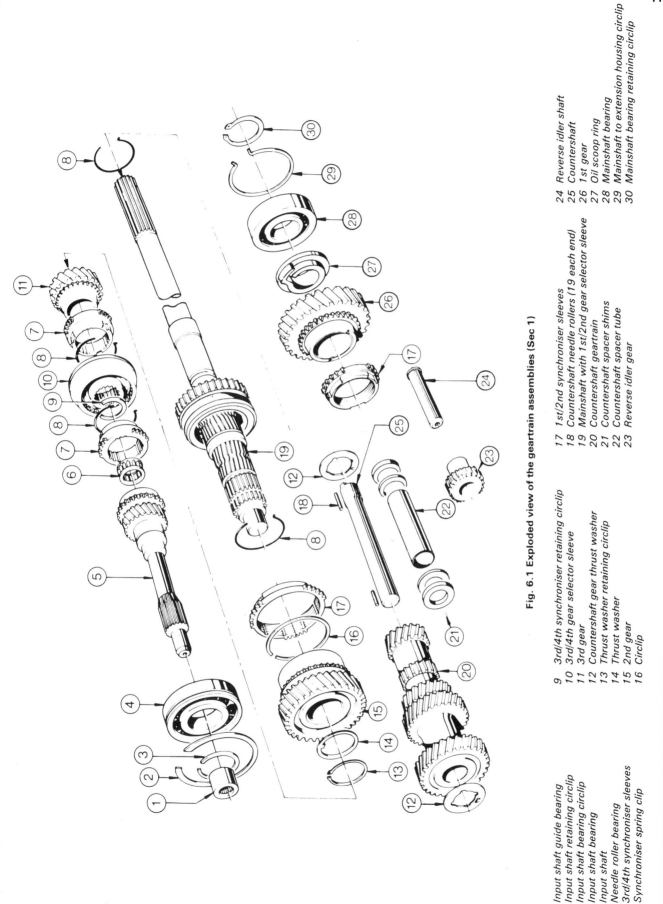

Fig. 6.1 Exploded view of the geartrain assemblies (Sec 1)

1   Input shaft guide bearing
2   Input shaft retaining circlip
3   Input shaft bearing circlip
4   Input shaft bearing
5   Input shaft
6   Needle roller bearing
7   3rd/4th synchroniser sleeves
8   Synchroniser spring clip

9   3rd/4th synchroniser retaining circlip
10 3rd/4th gear selector sleeve
11 3rd gear
12 Countershaft gear thrust washer
13 Thrust washer retaining circlip
14 Thrust washer
15 2nd gear
16 Circlip

17 1st/2nd synchroniser sleeves
18 Countershaft needle rollers (19 each end)
19 Mainshaft with 1st/2nd gear selector sleeve
20 Countershaft geartrain
21 Countershaft spacer shims
22 Countershaft spacer tube
23 Reverse idler gear

24 Reverse idler shaft
25 Countershaft
26 1st gear
27 Oil scoop ring
28 Mainshaft bearing
29 Mainshaft to extension housing circlip
30 Mainshaft bearing retaining circlip

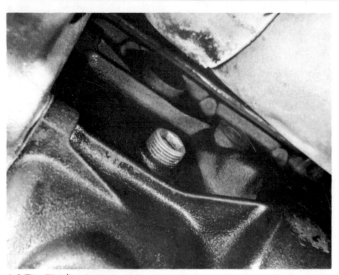

1.0 The filler/level plug location

drive the toothed 1st/2nd gear selector sleeve on the mainshaft through an interposed sliding idler gear.

The gearbox is of simple design using a minimum number of components. Where close tolerances and limits are required, manufacturing tolerances are compensated for and excessive endfloat or backlash eliminated by the fitting of selected circlips. When overhauling the gearbox always use new circlips, never refit ones that have already been used.

Very little is required in the way of maintenance. The oil level must be checked at 6000 mile (10 000 km) intervals by removing the oil level/filler plug on the left-hand side of the gearcase (photo). Access to this plug is from underneath, and you will need to have the car over an inspection pit or raised on jacks and stands (whilst keeping it level) to make this check.

2 Gearbox – removal and refitting

The gearbox can be removed as a unit with the engine through the engine compartment, as described in Chapter 1. Alternatively, the gearbox can be separated from the rear of the engine at the bellhousing and the gearbox lowered from under the car, as given below.

1   If a hoist or an inspection pit is not available then run the back of the car up a pair of ramps or jack it up and fit axle stands. Next jack up the front of the car and support it on axle stands.

2   For safety reasons, disconnect the battery earth terminal.

3   Working inside the car, push the front seats rearwards as far as possible.

4   Where fitted, remove the centre console, secured by two screws each side and detach it, together with any ancillary wire connections.

5   Pull the gear lever gaiter upwards, then remove the circlip from its

groove in the gearlever to release the tension in the spring (if necessary). The circlip is fitted adjacent to the smaller end of the spring. Bend back the lockring tabs and unscrew the plastic dome nut using a suitably cranked spanner (open jaw) or an adjustable spanner. Failing this, use a drift to drive the nut free, but take care not to damage it. With the nut unscrewed, lift the gear lever away (photos).

6   You will now need to work underneath the car. Start by detaching the exhaust system at the manifold connecting flange. Unhook and detach the system from under the car and move it out of the way.

7   Loosen the clutch cable adjuster and detach the cable from the release lever (Chapter 5). Getting an assistant to operate the clutch pedal will simplify this operation.

8   Mark the mating flanges of the propeller shaft and final drive so that they may be reconnected in their original positions and undo and remove the four securing bolts. Support the rear of the propeller shaft (by leaving one bolt in place through the flanges).

9   Unscrew and remove the centre bearing support-to-floor panel securing bolts taking note of any shims, but maintain the propeller shaft in the suspended position untill a container is positioned under the rear end of the gearbox extension. This will catch the oil which will flow out of the extension when the propeller shaft is withdrawn.

10   Lower the rear end of the propeller shaft and then pull it rearwards so detaching the front end from the rear of the gearbox and lift it away from under the car.

11   Wrap some polythene around the end of the gearbox and secure it with string or wire to stop any oil running out.

12   Make a note of the cable connections to the starter motor and detach the cables.

13   Undo and remove the three bolts that secure the starter motor to the gearbox flange, but leave the motor in position. It cannot be withdrawn without lowering the crossmember under the engine sump (as described in Chapter 1).

14   Pull free the plug connection from the reverse light switch located on the side of the remote control housing.

15   Using a pair of circlip pliers remove the circlip retaining the speedometer drive cable end to the gearbox extension housing (photo). Pull the speedometer cable away from the housing.

16   Support the weight of the gearbox by positioning a jack (trolley jack, if available) underneath it.

17   On all models you will need to lower the crossmember under the engine sump, as given in Chapter 1, Section 71.

18   Remove the lower engine-to-transmission bolts from underneath, then unscrew and remove the upper engine-to-transmission housing securing bolts, which are accessible from the engine compartment.

19   Undo and remove the four bolts, spring and plain washers that secure the gearbox support crossmember to the body (photo).

20   The assistance of a second person is now required who should be ready to help in taking the weight of the gearbox.

21   **Do not** allow the weight of the gearbox to hang on the input shaft (first motion shaft) as it is easily bent. Carefully separate the gearbox from the engine by sliding it rearwards from the clutch housing. It will be necessary to lower the jack or stand to give clearance for the gearbox from the underside of the body.

22   If major work is to be undertaken on the gearbox it is recommended that the exterior be washed with paraffin and dried with a lint-free rag. To remove the gearbox mounting, unscrew and remove the single bolt which secures it in position.

2.5a Pull the gaiter up the lever ...

2.5b ... bend back the lockring tabs using a screwdriver

2.5c ... unscrew the nut and withdraw the lever assembly

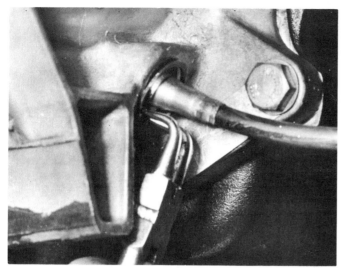

2.15 Remove the speedometer cable securing clip

2.19 Remove the gearbox support crossmember bolts from each side

3.5 Remove the clutch housing to gearbox bolts

23 When the gearbox is ready for refitting to the car, start by assembling the crossmember to the rubber mounting and securing them to the gearbox by the large central bolt and washer which should be tightened to the specified torque.

24 Check that the adaptor plate is in place on the rear of the engine and then fit the gearbox. A certain amount of movement and positioning may be necessary to get the input shaft splines fully into the splined hub in the middle of the clutch. When the gearbox is fully home, refit the two lower bellhousing bolts.

25 Refit the four crossmember bolts and spring washers.

26 Refit the engine-to-transmission securing bolts and also the starter motor bolts. Reconnect the starter motor leads.

27 Raise the engine sump crossmember and refit the original mounting bolts, then reconnect the steering column and connections, as described in Chapter 1.

28 Reconnect the propeller shaft, gearbox end first, and ensure that the mating marks across the rear axle and rear propeller shaft flanges align (refer to Chapter 7 for the full refitting procedure). Refit the speedometer cable to the extension housing and the clutch cable to the release arm. Reconnect the lead to the reversing light switch.

29 Reconnect and adjust the clutch cable, as given in Chapter 5.

30 Reconnect the exhaust system.

31 Top up the gearbox oil and refit the level/filler plug to complete the operations underneath the car, but check to make sure everything is complete before lowering it from the axle stands or ramps.

32 Refit the gear lever and bend the locktabs over to secure the nut in position when tightened. Refit the gaiter and, where applicable, the centre console.

33 Reconnect the battery.

3 Gearbox – dismantling

1 Place the complete unit on a firm bench or table and ensure that you have the following tools available, in addition to the normal range of spanners etc.

   (a) Good quality circlip pliers, 2 pairs - 1 expanding and 1 contracting
   (b) Soft-faced mallet, at least 2 lb (1 kg)
   (c) Drifts, steel and brass 0.375 inch (9.525 mm) diameter
   (d) Small containers for needle rollers
   (e) Engineer's vice mounted on firm bench
   (f) Selection of metal tubing
   (g) Vernier gauge

Any attempt to dismantle and overhaul the gearbox without the foregoing tools is not impossible, but will certainly be very difficult and inconvenient.

2 Read the whole of this Section before starting work.

3 The internal parts of the gearboxes are shown in Fig. 6.1.

4 Withdraw the release bearing from the clutch release lever by simply pulling or prising it free.

5 Undo and remove the four bolts and spring washers that secure the clutch housing to the gearbox main case (photo).

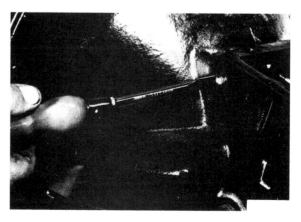

Fig. 6.2 Locking bar side plug removal (Sec 3)

3.7 Extension housing rear cover removal. Note the reversing light switch (arrowed)

3.10 Locking bar and spring removal

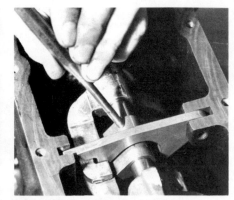

3.12a Reverse selector boss spring pin removal

3.12b Selector rail removal

3.13 Selector fork removal

3.16 Countershaft removal using a drift

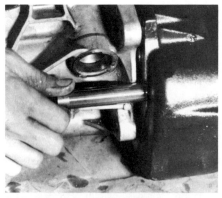

3.17 Lifting away the countershaft

3.19 Removal of extension housing and mainshaft assembly

3.22 Input bearing retainer and O-ring removal

3.23 Prise bearing outer track from main casing using a suitable screwdriver in order to remove the input shaft

3.24 Lift out the countershaft geartrain

3.28 Mainshaft being tapped through the extension housing for removal

6 Draw the clutch housing forwards away from the main case.
7 Using a suitable drift, working through the gear lever aperture, tap out the extension housing rear cover (photo).
8 Unscrew and remove the eight top cover securing bolts and then remove the cover, together with its gasket.
9 The gearbox oil can now be drained into a suitable container by inverting the box and allowing the oil to drain out of the upper inspection aperture.
10 Remove the side plug (Fig. 6.2) and remove the spring and locking bar (possibly with the aid of a bar magnet) (photo).
11 Remove the blanking plug from the rear of the gearbox casing and drive out the lockplate spring pin using a suitable pin punch.
12 Remove the spring pin from the reverse selector boss (photo). Remove the selector rail rearwards (photo).
13 Lift out both selector forks, the lockplate and the selector boss (photo).
14 Unscrew and remove the bolts and spring washers that secure the extension housing to the main casing.
15 Rotate the extension housing until the cutaway is in such a position that the countershaft can be drawn from the main casing.
16 Using a suitable diameter soft metal drift tap the countershaft rearwards until it is possible to pull it from the rear face of the main case (photo).
17 Remove the countershaft from the main case (photo).
18 Allow the countershaft geartrain to drop to the bottom of the main case.
19 Remove the gearbox extension housing and mainshaft assembly from the gearbox (photo).
20 Remove the input shaft needle roller bearing.
21 Undo and remove the bolts and spring washers that secure the spigot bearing to the front face of the main case.
22 Lift away the bearing retainer from over the input shaft. Recover the O-ring (photo).
23 Remove the input shaft assembly (forwards) after prising the bearing outer track from the main casing (photo).
24 Lift the countershaft geartrain from inside the main case. Note which way round it is fitted (photo). Recover the two countershaft thrust washers.
25 Insert a suitable bolt into the reverse gear idler shaft with a nut, washer and suitable socket. Tighten the nut and withdraw the idler shaft (Fig. 6.3).
26 Withdraw the circlip from the pin, and remove the reverse gear relay lever.
27 Prise out the speedometer drivegear cover from the extension housing, and withdraw the drivegear.
28 Remove the mainshaft bearing circlip from the extension housing

(Fig. 6.4). Drive the mainshaft assembly from the extension housing using a soft-faced mallet (photo).

4 Gearbox – inspection

1 Thoroughly clean the interior of the gearbox, and check for dropped needle rollers and spring pins.
2 Carefully clean and then examine all the component parts for general wear, distortion, slackness of fit, and damage to machined faces and threads.
3 Examine the gearwheels for excessive wear and chipping of the teeth. Renew them as necessary.
4 Examine the countershaft for signs of wear, where the needle rollers bear. If a small ridge can be felt at either end of the shaft it will be necessary to renew it. Renew the thrust washers at each end.
5 The four synchroniser rings are bound to be badly worn and it is false economy not to renew them. New rings will improve the smoothness and speed of the gearchange considerably.
6 The needle roller bearing and cage, located between the nose of the mainshaft and the annulus in the rear of the input shaft, is also liable to wear, and should be renewed as a matter of course.
7 Examine the condition of the two ball-bearing assemblies, one on the input shaft and one on the mainshaft. Check them for noisy operation, looseness between the inner and outer races, and for general wear. Normally they should be renewed on a gearbox that is being rebuilt.
8 If either of the synchroniser units is worn it will be necessary to buy a complete assembly as the parts are not sold individually. Also check the blocker bars for wear.
9 Examine the ends of the selector forks where they rub against the channels in the periphery of the synchroniser units. If possible compare the selector forks with new units to help determine the wear that has occurred. Renew them if worn.
10 If the bearing bush in the extension is badly worn it is best to take the extension to your local Ford garage to have the bearing pulled out and a new one fitted. Note that this is normally done with the mainshaft assembly still located in the extension housing.
11 The oil seals in the extension housing and main drivegear bearing retainer should be renewed as a matter of course. Drive out the old seal with the aid of a drift or broad screwdriver. it will be found that the seal comes out quite easily.
12 With a piece of wood or suitably sized tube to spread the load evenly, carefully tap a new seal into place ensuring that it enters the bore squarely.

Fig. 6.3 Reverse gear idler shaft removal method (Sec 3)

Fig. 6.4 Mainshaft bearing circlip ends (arrowed) (Sec 3)

5.1 Input shaft bearing retaining circlip

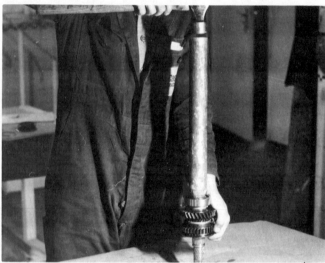

5.5 Input shaft bearing refitting

Fig. 6.5 The drivegear bearing retainer and oil seal (Sec 5)

5   Input shaft – dismantling and reassembly

1   The input shaft assembly may be dismantled by first removing the circlip using a pair of circlip pliers (photo).
2   Place the drivegear on the top of the vice with the outer track of the race resting on soft faces.
3   Using a soft-faced hammer drive the input shaft through the race inner track. The strain placed on the bearing does not matter, as the bearing would not be removed unless it was being renewed. Alternatively use a three-legged universal puller.
4   Lift away the race from the drivegear noting that the circlip groove on the outer track is offset towards the front.
5   To assemble the input shaft, place the race against soft metal (eg an old bearing shell suitably straightened) on the top of the jaws of the vice and, using a drift located in the mainshaft spigot bearing hole in the rear of the input shaft, drive the shaft into the bearing. Make quite sure the bearing is the correct way round. Alternatively use a piece of long tube of suitable diameter (photo).
6   Refit the circlip that secures the bearing.
7   It is advisable to renew the drivegear bearing retainer oil seal before reassembly. This can be prised out with a screwdriver and the new seal pressed into position with its seal lip towards the gearbox. Smear the seal lip with a multi-purpose grease prior to refitting.

6   Mainshaft – dismantling and reassembly

1   With the mainshaft on the bench, remove the synchroniser sleeve fro the front.
2   Using a pair of circlip pliers, expand the circlip that retains the third and top synchromesh hub on the mainshaft (photo).
3   Remove the third and top synchromesh assembly from the end of the mainshaft. Remove the synchroniser sleeve from the third gear. Remove the third gear.
4   Using a pair of circlip pliers expand the circlip located at the rear of the mainshaft bearing, lift it from its groove and slide it down the mainshaft (photo).
5   Place the mainshaft on soft faces placed on the jaws of a vice so that the rear end is uppermost and the face of the first gear is on the vice.
6   Using a soft-faced mallet, drive the mainshaft through the gear and bearing assembly.
7   Lift away the speedometer gear, bearing, large circlip, oil scoop ring, 1st gear and synchroniser sleeve.
8   Remove the circlip and then remove the thrust washer, 2nd gear and the synchroniser sleeve. The synchroniser hub cannot be removed from the mainshaft.
9   Mark the synchromesh sleeve, hub and blocker bars for each synchromesh unit so that they may be refitted in their original positions.
10 Slide the synchromesh sleeve from the hub and lift away the blocker bars and springs.
11 When new synchroniser assemblies are being fitted, they should be dismantled and thoroughly cleaned of all traces of preservative.
12 Lightly lubricate all parts with gearbox oil before reassembly.
13 The main reassembly procedure can now be commenced, but first note that selected circlips will be needed at some stages during reassembly. It is therefore necessary to read through the procedure before reassembly commences so that the necessary circlips can be obtained.
14 Assemble the synchronisers by sliding the sleeve onto the hub with the mating marks aligned. Fit the blocker bars and springs, with the springs staggered, and the tagged ends of the springs in the same blocker bar (Fig. 6.8).
15 Fit the 1st/2nd selector sleeve with the groove to the front (photo).
16 Slide the 2nd gear synchroniser sleeve and second gear onto the mainshaft with the cone facing the rear (photo). Fit the thrust washer and secure with a circlip.
17 Fit the 1st gear synchroniser sleeve and the 1st gear onto the mainshaft with the cone facing the front. Slide the oil scoop ring into position with the large diameter away from 1st gear (towards the bearing), as shown in Fig. 6.9.
18 It will now be necessary to select a new large circlip to eliminate endfloat of the mainshaft. To do this, first fit the original circlip in its groove in the gearbox extension and draw it outwards (ie away from

6.2 Removing the circlip from the end of the mainshaft

6.4 Mainshaft rear bearing retaining circlip removal

6.15 Synchromesh sleeve to hub assembly

6.16 2nd gear synchroniser sleeve and 2nd gear being fitted to the mainshaft

TC/16/86

Fig. 6.6 The gearbox mainshaft and the fixed 1st/2nd synchroniser hub (Sec 6)

Fig. 6.7 The synchroniser components (Sec 6)

Fig. 6.8 Synchroniser spring clip alignment (Sec 6)

Fig. 6.9 Locating the oil scoop washer (Sec 6)

Fig. 6.10 Measure the bearing-to-circlip clearance (Sec 6)

Fig. 6.11 Measure the bearing width (Sec 6)

Fig. 6.12 Speedometer drivegear location to be set at distance 'A' which is 2.02 in (51.2 mm) (Sec 6)

Fig. 6.13 Fitting the 3rd/4th gear synchroniser/retaining clip (Sec 6)

6.20 Rear bearing retaining circlip refitting

the rear of the extension). Now accurately measure the dimension from the base of the bearing housing to the outer edge of the circlip and record the figure. Also accurately measure the thickness of the bearing outer track (Figs. 6.10 and 6.11) and subtract this figure from the depth already recorded. This will give the required circlip thickness.

19 Loosely fit the selected circlip, lubricate the bearing's contact surfaces, then press it onto the shaft. To press the bearing home, close the jaws of the vice until they are not quite touching the mainshaft, and with the bearing resting squarely against the side of the vice jaws draw the bearing on by tapping the end of the shaft with a soft-faced mallet.

20 Refit the small circlip retaining the main bearing in place. This is

also a selected circlip and must be fitted so that all endfloat between the bearing inner track and the circlip edge is eliminated (photo).

21 Refit the speedometer drivegear. Drive the gear onto the shaft using a suitable diameter tube until the dimension 'A' shown in Fig. 6.12 is 2.02 in (51.2 mm).

22 Slide on the 3rd gear with the cone facing the front, the synchroniser sleeve and the synchroniser assembly (photo).

23 Using a suitable piece of tube, drive on the synchroniser assembly, with the longer hub to the front. Secure with the circlip.

---

7 Gearbox – reassembly

1 Place the extension housing on its side and carefully insert the mainshaft (photo).

2 Place the extension housing on the edge of the bench so that the mainshaft end can protrude when fully home. Using a soft-faced mallet drive the mainshaft bearing into the extension housing bore (photo).

3 Using a pair of pointed pliers and small screwdriver refit the bearing retaining circlip. This is a fiddly job and can take some time (photo).

4 Apply grease to the mating face of the extension housing and fit a new gasket (photo).

5 Refit the reverse relay arm and spring onto the pivot pin, and secure with a circlip.

6 Place the reverse idler gear into its location in the main casing and engage it with the reverse relay arm. Slide in the idler shaft, and tap it home with a mallet.

7 The countershaft geartrain needle roller bearings are next re-assembled. The countershaft has a spacer tube and 19 needle rollers at each end, the longer of the rollers being fitted at the rear. The thicker spacer rings are fitted at the outer ends. Assemble by sliding the spacer tube into position in the countershaft bore, then smear the two ends with grease and insert a thin spacer shim (photo).

8 Fit the needle rollers into the forward end of the bore (photo). Do not handle the needle rollers more than absolutely necessary as they

6.22 3rd gear, synchroniser sleeve and hub assembly

7.1 Fitting mainshaft into the extension housing (stage 1)

7.2 Drive the mainshaft bearing into the extension housing (stage 2)

7.3 Fit the bearing retaining circlip

7.4 Locate a new gasket to the greased face of the extension housing

7.7 Insert spacer shim into countershaft bore ...

7.8 ... followed by the needle rollers

7.9 Insert the second spacer shim

7.11 Fit the second set of needle rollers into the countershaft bore

7.14 Fit thrust washers to greased face of countershaft geartrain

7.15 Locate the countershaft gear assembly into the main casing

7.17 Locate the bearing retainer over the input shaft ...

7.18 ... and fit the retaining bolts with sealant on the threads

7.22 Inserting the mainshaft into the main casing

7.24 Insert the countershaft into the main casing

7.29 Fit the blanking plug to the main case rear face

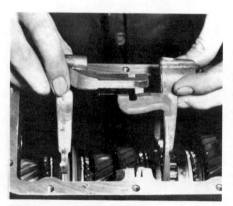

7.30a Locate the selector forks ...

7.30b ... and reverse selector boss (slide into lockplate)

will warm up and therefore not adhere to the grease.

9 With the first set needle rollers in position carefully fit the second spacer shim (photo).

10 Obtain a piece of bar or tube having approximately the same diameter as the countershaft and the same length as the countershaft geartrain. Slide this halfway into the bore of the countershaft geartrain so acting as a retainer for the needle rollers.

11 Insert a spacer shim into the rear end of the countershaft geartrain bore and fit the second set of needle rollers in the same manner as for the first set (photo).

12 Fit the last spacer shim and push the previously obtained bar or tube through the second set of needle roller bearings.

13 Smear grease on each thrust washer face of the countershaft geartrain.

14 Fit the thrust washers to the countershaft geartrain (photo) with their tabs located into the casing slots.

15 Carefully lower the countershaft geartrain into the main casing making sure that the thrust washers are not dislodged (photo).

16 Support the main casing on the bench so that it is upright and insert the input shaft from the front.

17 Smear some grease on the groove in the front face of the main casing and fit a new O-ring seal. Then locate the bearing retainer over the input shaft, ensuring that the internal recess is towards the bottom or aligns with marks made when dismantling (photo).

18 Before fitting the bearing retainer bolts (or any bolts in contact with the gearbox oil chamber), smear their threads with sealant (photo).

19 Tighten the bolts of the bearing retainer in diagonal sequence to ensure that the O-ring seals correctly.

20 Apply some grease to the caged bearing that fits into the bore in the rear of the input shaft. Fit the bearing into the bore.

21 Fit the synchroniser sleeve to the taper on the rear of the input shaft.

22 Carefully insert the mainshaft through the rear face of the main casing (photo).

23 Turn the extension housing until the cutaway is positoned such that the countershaft can be inserted through the main casing rear face.

24 Turn the input shaft and mainshaft so that the countershaft geartrain can drop into engagement. Visually line up the countershaft bore hole in the main case with the centre of the countershaft geartrain and slide the countershaft into position (photo). The milled end of the countershaft is towards the rear of the main case.

25 Turn the countershaft until it is positioned as shown in Fig. 6.15. Tap it in until the main part of the shaft is flush with the rear face.

26 Check that the idler shaft and countershaft protrusions will line up with the slots in the extension housing and push the extension housing up to the rear face of the main casing.

27 Secure the extension housing with the bolts and spring washers (apply sealant to the bolt threads).

28 Refit the speedometer driven gear and tap home the cover.

29 Fit the selector lockplate and secure with the spring pin. Fit a new blanking plug at the rear of the housing (photo).

30 Insert both selector forks (photo) and the reverse selector boss (photo).

31 Slide the selector rail, from the rear through the bosses, and lock with the spring pin (photo).

32 Refit the blocker bar, spring pin and screw plug into the side of the housing.

33 Refit the top cover and secure with eight bolts.

34 Fit the extension housing rear cover, coated with sealing compound. Secure with three blows from a pin punch, spread around the edge.

35 Wipe the mating faces of the clutch housing and main casing and offer up the clutch housing.

36 Secure the clutch housing with the bolts and spring washers (photo).

37 Fit the clutch release arm to the clutch housing and then the release bearing to the release arm.

38 The gearbox is now ready for refitting (Section 2). Do not forget to refill with the correct grade of oil (once the gearbox is in position in the car).

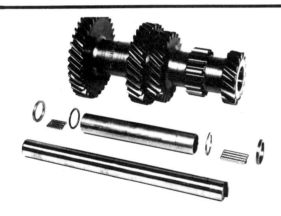

Fig. 6.14 The countershaft unit showing the bearings and spacers (Sec 7)

Fig. 6.15 Position the countershaft as shown (Sec 7)

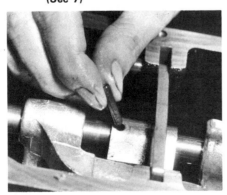

7.31 Fit spring pin to reverse selector boss and rail

7.36 Secure the clutch housing to main case bolts (fitted with spring washers)

8   Fault diagnosis – gearbox

Symptom	Reason(s)
Weak or ineffective synchromesh	Synchronising cones worn, split or damaged Baulk ring synchromesh dogs worn, or damaged
Jumps out of gear	Broken gearchange fork rod spring Gearbox coupling dogs badly worn Selector fork rod groove badly worn
Excessive noise	Incorrect grade of oil in gearbox or oil level too low Bush or needle roller bearings worn or damaged Gear teeth excessively worn or damaged Countershaft thrust washers worn allowing excessive endplay
Excessive difficulty in engaging gear	Clutch cable adjustment incorrect

Note: *It is sometimes difficult to decide whether it is worthwhile removing and dismantling the gearbox for a fault which may be nothing more than a minor irritant. Gearboxes which howl, or where the synchromesh can be 'beaten' by a quick gear change, may continue to perform for a long time in this stage. A worn gearbox usually needs a complete rebuild to eliminate noise because the various gears, if re-aligned on new bearings, will continue to howl when different wearing surfaces are presented to each other.*

The decision to overhaul, therefore, must be considered with regard to time and money available, relative to the degree of noise or malfunction that the driver can tolerate.

Chapter 7 Propeller shaft

Contents

Specifications

Type .... Two-section open shaft with two universal joints and one constant velocity joint, with central support bearing

Torque wrench settings

	lbf ft	kgf m
Driveshaft-to-pinion flange bolts	44 to 48	6.0 to 6.5
Centre bearing-to-floor bolts	13 to 17	1.8 to 2.3

1 General description

On all models the drive from the gearbox is transmitted to the rear axle by a two-piece propeller shaft. At each end of the propeller shaft assembly there is a universal joint which allows for the vertical movement of the rear axle. Each universal joint comprises a four-legged centre spider, four needle roller bearings and two yokes.

The rear end of the front shaft is fitted with a centre bearing, immediately to the rear of which is a constant velocity joint. The universal joints are of lubricant sealed type and therefore require no maintenance.

2 Propeller shaft – removal and refitting

1   Jack up the rear of the car, or position the rear of the car over a pit or on a ramp.
2   If the rear of the car is jacked up, supplement the jack with safety stands or support blocks so that danger is minimised should the jack collapse.
3   If the rear wheels are off the ground, place the car in gear or put the handbrake on to ensure that the propeller shaft does not turn when an attempt is made to loosen the four nuts securing the propeller shaft to the rear axle.

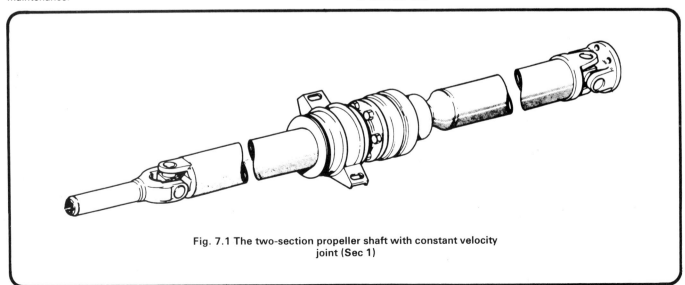

Fig. 7.1 The two-section propeller shaft with constant velocity
joint (Sec 1)

2.4 Make an alignment mark across the shaft and rear axle flange (as arrowed)

2.6 The centre bearing assembly showing the mounting bolts (arrowed)

2.8 The propeller shaft forward joint connection to the gearbox

4 The propeller shaft is carefully balanced to fine limits and it is important that it is refitted in exactly the same position it was in prior to its removal (unless a new shaft assembly is being fitted). Scratch a mark on the propeller shaft and rear axle flange edges to ensure accurate mating when the time comes for reassembly (photo).

5 Unscrew and remove the four self-locking nuts, bolts and securing washers which hold the flange on the rear axle.

6 Support the rear of the propeller shaft (leave one bolt through the flange) and then unscrew and remove the centre bearing mounting bolts (photo). As the centre bearing is lowered note any shims fitted between the bearing flanges and the floor panel. Keep these shims handy for reassembly as they must be refitted to align the front and rear driveshaft sections.

7 Place a large can or tray under the rear of the gearbox extension to catch any oil which is likely to leak through the spline lubricating holes whilst the propeller shaft is removed.

8 Supporting the two shafts, push them forwards (towards the gearbox) and detach the rear flange, then lower the assembly and withdraw the front shaft from the gearbox mainshaft splines (photo). The shafts can then be removed from underneath the car.

9 Refitting the propeller shaft is a reversal of the removal procedure. Support the rear of the car in such a manner that the rear axle hangs down freely. As the shaft at the front end is re-engaged with the gearbox mainshaft, take care not to damage the oil seal – renew it if you do.

10 Refit the U-shaped packing shims on the central bearing mounting bolts to ensure the correct angular relationship between the two shafts. Do not tighten the bolts fully at this stage.

11 Ensure that the mating marks scratched on the propeller shaft and rear axle flange line up, then tighten the flange bolts to the specified torque.

12 Pull the front shaft section towards the front of the vehicle until the constant velocity joint is felt to bear against the rear of the centre bearing.

13 With the centre bearing held in this position fully tighten the bearing bolts to the specified torque.

14 Top up the gearbox oil level and lower the car.

3 Propeller shaft – overhaul

Universal joints

1 The universal joints are of the staked type, and were not intended to be repairable. However, proprietary kits have recently become available for the overhaul of such joints.

2 Before purchasing a repair kit, make sure that you have the tools and facilities to use it. Typically a large vice, a good-sized hammer and a selection of tubes and drifts will be required.

3 Remember also that if the universal joint yokes have been damaged or distorted, any attempt at overhaul is futile.

Constant velocity joint

4 Several types of CV joint have been fitted. Only the type of joint which is screwed or bolted together can be renewed. Riveted joints are not removable.

5 If removing a CV joint, remember to maintain the angular relationship between the front and rear propeller shaft sections. Imbalance may otherwise result.

Centre bearing

6 If the CV joint is of the non-removable type, centre bearing failure necessitates the renewal of the complete shaft assembly.

7 If the CV joint can be removed, the centre bearing can be drawn off the shaft and a new bearing installed.

8 A typical centre bearing assembly is shown in Fig. 7.2.

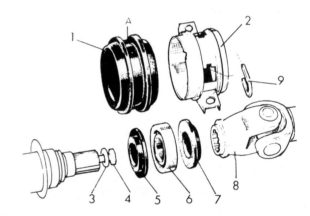

Fig. 7.2 A typical centre bearing – exploded view (Sec 3)

A	Insulator boss	5	Cap
1	Insulator	6	Bearing
2	Housing	7	Cap
3	Lockplate	8	Yoke
4	Bolt	9	U-ring

General

9 In view of the difficulties associated with partial overhaul of the shaft, and the distressing vibration produced by an out-of-balance or distorted shaft, the DIY owner is recommended to consult a Ford dealer or propeller shaft specialist to ascertain the cost of a new or reconditioned shaft before embarking on piecemeal repair.

Chapter 8 Rear axle

Contents

Specifications

General

Axle type .... Ford type 'C' (Timken), Hypoid semi-floating, detachable differential carrier
Ratio (all models) 3.54:1
Number of crownwheel teeth 39
Number of pinion teeth 11

Lubrication
Lubricant type .... SAE 90EP gear oil
Lubricant capacity .... 1.6 Imp pt (0.9 litres)

Crownwheel-to-pinion backlash .... 0.004 to 0.008 in (0.10 to 0.20 mm)

Torque wrench settings

	lbf ft	kgf m
Differential-to-axle housing carrier bolts	26 to 30	3.6 to 4.1
Half shaft-to-axle flange plate bolts	15 to 18	2.1 to 2.5
Bearing cap bolts	46 to 51	6.4 to 7.0
Crownwheel-to-differential case bolts	50 to 55	6.9 to 7.6
Plug	26 to 31	3.6 to 4.3

1 General description

The Escort Mexico and both RS models are fitted with a Ford type 'C' axle, more commonly known as the Timken type. On this type of axle the differential assembly can be removed with the axle in position on the car.

The axle casing of banjo design carries the differential assembly. This comprises a crownwheel and pinion mounted in the differential carrier which is bolted to the front of the axle casing.

The pinion is mounted on two taper roller bearings which are preloaded to partially collapse the tubular spacer which is located

between them. The crownwheel is bolted to the differential case which is also supported on two taper roller bearings.

The axleshafts (halfshafts) are splined to the differential side gears and run in ball-races in the axle casings at their outer ends. The ball-races have integral oil seals.

2 Rear axle – removal and refitting

1 Loosen the rear wheel nuts, then raise and support the rear of the vehicle body and the differential casing with axle stands or jacks so that the rear wheels are clear of the ground. This is most easily done

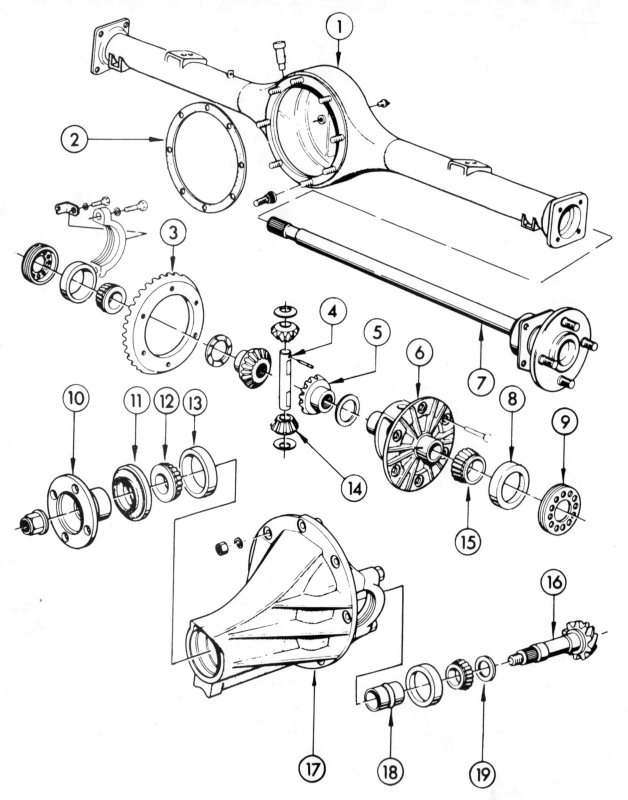

**Fig. 8.1 Exploded view of the Timken 'C' type axle assembly
(Sec 1)**

1	Rear axle housing	6	Differential case
2	Gasket	7	Halfshaft
3	Crownwheel	8	Taper roller bearing
4	Differential pinion		outer race
	gear shaft	9	Adjusting nut
5	Differential side	10	Drive pinion flange
	gear	11	Oil seal

12	Inner race with taper	15	Inner race with taper
	rollers		rollers
13	Taper roller bearing	16	Drive pinion
	outer race	17	Differential carrier
14	Differential pinion	18	Collapsible spacer,
	gear		drive pinion
		19	Drive pinion shim

by placing a jack under the centre of the differential, jacking up the axle and then fitting chocks under the mounting points at the front of the rear springs to support the body (Fig 8.2).

2 Remove both rear wheels.

3 Mark the propeller shaft and differential drive flanges to ensure refitting in the same relative positions. Undo and remove the nuts and bolts holding the two flanges together.

4 Release the handbrake inside the car, then disconnect the handbrake lever clevis from the lever of the right-hand side backplate. Withdraw the spring clip from the cable sheath at the handbrake rod bracket on the axle tube, compress the spring and pull the cable back so that the inner cable can be slid out of the slit in the bracket.

5 Unscrew the union on the brake pipe at the junction on the rear axle and have handy either a jar to catch the hydraulic fluid or a plug to block the end of the pipe. Do not allow dirt to enter the exposed brake pipes whilst they are disconnected.

6 Unscrew the radius arm bolts at the axle end on each side and detach each radius from the axle casing.

7 Undo the self-locking nuts holding the shock absorbers to the spring plates, thus freeing their lower ends. It may be necessary to slightly raise the jack under the axle casing to free the shock absorbers.

8 Unscrew the nuts from under the spring retaining plates. These nuts screw onto the ends of the inverted U-bolts which retain the axle

to the spring. Remove the U-bolts, bump stops and spring retaining plates.

9 The axle assembly will now be resting free on the centre jack and can now be removed by lifting it through the space between the road spring and the bodyframe sidemember.

10 Installation is a direct reversal of the removal procedure, but the spring U-bolts should not be finally tightened until the full weight of the car is on the suspension (refer to Chapter 11). Finally, bleed the brakes as described in Chapter 9.

3 Axleshaft (halfshaft) – removal and refitting

1 Loosen the wheel nuts on the side concerned and then raise the rear of the car and support the bodyframe and axle casing securely using suitable jacks and axle stands.

2 Remove the rear roadwheel.

3 Remove the brake drum, referring to Chapter 9 if necessary.

4 Unscrew and remove the four self-locking nuts which secure the flange plate to the axle casing end flanges.

5 A slide hammer should now be attached to the hub studs and the axleshaft withdrawn. A slide hammer can be made up using an old

Fig. 8.2 Support the rear end with axle stands (Sec 2)

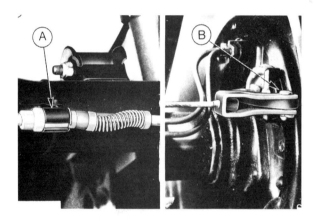

Fig. 8.3 Disconnect handbrake cable at spring clip (A) and brake backplate lever (B) (Sec 2)

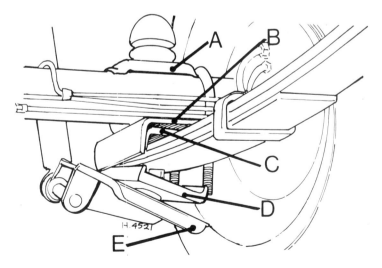

Fig. 8.4 Axle to spring location (Sec 2)

| A | Bump rubber | C | Upper insulator | D | Lower insulator | E | Attachment plate |
| | Insulator retainer | | (rubber) | | (rubber) | | |

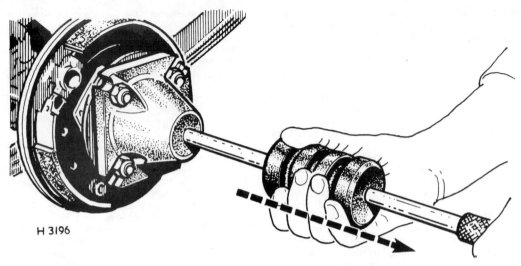

H 3196

Fig. 8.5 Withdrawing an axleshaft using a slide hammer (Sec 3)

axleshaft, but an alternative method of removing the shaft is to bolt on the roadwheel and strike it simultaneously on both inside edges of the rim at opposite ends. It must be emphasised that it is quite useless to attempt to try to pull the axleshaft from the axle casing as you will only succeed in pulling the vehicle off the jacks or stands.

6   Refitting is a reversal of removal. Pass the axleshaft into the axle casing, holding the shaft horizontally until the splines at its inner end engage with the splines in the differential gears. Tap the hub/bearing assembly fully home with a hammer and wooden block.

4   Axleshaft (halfshaft) bearing/oil seal – renewal

1   Withdraw the axleshaft as described in the preceding Section.
2   Secure the assembly in a vice, the jaws of which have been fitted with soft metal protectors.
3   Drill an 8 mm (0.3 in) hole in the bearing securing collar (Fig. 8.6) and then remove the collar by splitting it with a cold chisel. Take care not to damage the shaft during these operations.
4   Using a suitable press, draw off the combined bearing/oil seal.
5   On the axleshaft install the bearing retainer plate, the new bearing (seal side towards differential) and a new bearing collar.
6   Applying pressure to the collar only, using a press or bearing puller, seat the components against the shoulder of the axleshaft flange.
7   Install the axleshaft, as described in the preceding Section.

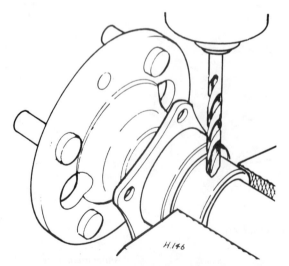

H.146

Fig. 8.6 Drilling a hole in the bearing inner ring prior to splitting it with a cold chisel (Sec 4)

5   Pinion bearing oil seal – renewal

Note: *Renewal of the drive pinion oil seal requires a great deal of care and the use of some special equipment. Without these, the collapsible spacer can be damaged which will require its renewal, and this operation is outside the scope of the do-it-yourself motorist because a special tool is required for removal of the pinion bearing. Whenever the pinion oil seal is renewed, it is essential that the self-locking pinion nut is also renewed.*

1   Jack up the rear of the vehicle and support it securely under the bodyframe.
2   Remove the rear roadwheels and brake drums.
3   Disconnect the propeller shaft from the rear axle drive pinion after marking them for correct alignment (Chapter 7).
4   Using a spring balance and length of cord wound round the drive pinion flange, determine the torque required to turn the drive pinion and record it. Alternatively, a socket wrench fitted to the pinion nut and a suitable torque wrench may be used.
5   Mark the coupling flange in relation to the pinion splines to ensure that they are refitted in the same position (photo).
6   Hold the pinion coupling flange by placing two 2-inch long bolts through two opposite holes, bolting them up tight; undo the self-locking nut whilst holding a large screwdriver or tyre lever between the two bolts for leverage. Using a standard two or three-leg puller, remove the coupling flange from the pinion shaft. Also remove the dust deflector (if fitted).
7   Using a hammer and a small chisel or screwdriver, remove the oil seal from the pinion housing. During this operation great care must be taken to ensure that the pinion shaft is not scored in any way. Note that there will be some spillage of the axle oil as the seal is removed.
8   Carefully clean the contact area inside the pinion housing, then apply a film of general purpose grease to this surface and between the lips of the new oil seal. Do not remove the existing grease from the replacement seal.
9   Using a tube of suitable diameter, press in the new seal to its full depth in the pinion housing and refit the dust deflector (if applicable).
10 Refit the coupling flange in its correct relative position to the pinion shaft.
11 Using a new self-locking nut, prevent the flange from turning, then carefully and slowly tighten the nut until the same turning torque is achieved as recorded at paragraph 4. Continue tightening until an additional 2 to 3 lbf in (2 to 4 kgf cm) is achieved, to allow for the friction of the new oil seal. After this torque has been obtained, do not further tighten the self-locking nut or the collapsible spacer will be damaged (see note at beginning of Section).
12 Remove the two bolts from the coupling flange, then refit the propeller shaft, taking note of the alignment marks made when removing.
13 Top up the rear axle with the correct grade of oil, then refit the brake drums and roadwheels.
14 Lower the car to the ground.

5.5 Mark the position of pinion flange in relation to the drive pinion

6 Differential carrier – removal and refitting

1 To remove the differential carrier assembly, jack up the rear of the vehicle, remove both roadwheels and brake drums and then partially withdraw both axleshafts as described in Section 3.

2 Disconnect the propeller shaft at the rear end, as described in Chapter 7.

3 Undo the eight self-locking nuts holding the differential carrier assembly to the axle casing. Pull the assembly slightly forward and allow the oil to drain in a suitable tray or bowl. The carrier complete with the crownwheel can now be lifted clear with the gasket.

4 Most professional garages will prefer to renew the complete differential carrier assembly as a unit if it is worn, rather than to dismantle the unit to renew any damaged or worn parts. To do the job correctly requires the use of special and expensive tools which the majority of garages do not have. Because of this, if the differential is to be overhauled rather than exchanged, the necessary repairs must be entrusted to a suitably equipped Ford garage.

5 Before refitting, carefully clean the mating faces of the carrier and axle casing.

6 Refitting is then a direct reversal of the above instructions. The eight nuts retaining the differential carrier assembly to the axle casing should be tightened to the specified torque. Refill with oil.

7 Fault diagnosis – rear axle

Symptom	Reason(s)
Oil leakage	Faulty pinion oil seal
	Faulty axleshaft oil seals
	Defective carrier-to-axle case gasket
Noise	Lack of oil
	Worn bearings
	General wear
'Clonk' on taking up drive and excessive backlash	Incorrectly tightened pinion nut
	Worn components
	Worn axleshaft splines
	Elongated roadwheel bolt holes
	Worn propeller shaft universal joints

Chapter 9 Braking system

Contents

Specifications

General

System type	Hydraulic, servo-assisted; discs front, self-adjusting drums rear. Handbrake mechanical to rear wheels

Front brakes

Disc diameter (outer)	9.7 in (247.5 mm)
Disc diameter (inner)	5.5 in (139.8 mm)
Disc thickness	0.5 in (12.7 mm)
Minimum allowable disc thickness	0.45 in (11.4 mm)
Disc run-out (including hub)	0.002 in (0.05 mm) maximum
Caliper cylinder diameter	2.125 in (54.0 mm)
Pad material	Ferodo 2445
Pad lining minimum thickness	0.06 in (1.5 mm)
Total swept brake area (2 wheels)	182 in² (1175 cm²)

Rear brakes

Drum diameter	9 in (228.6 mm)
Shoe width	1.75 in (44.5 mm)
Lining material	DON 242
Lining minimum thickness	0.06 in (1.5 mm)
Wheel cylinder diameter	0.75 in (19.05 mm)

Servo

Manufacturer	Teves or Girling
Diameter of vacuum cylinder	152.4 mm
Amplification factor	2.2 : 1

Brake pedal free height (engine running)   6.7 in (170 mm)

Torque wrench settings

	lbf ft	kgf m
Caliper to front suspension unit	35 to 50	4.8 to 6.9
Brake disc to hub	30 to 34	4.2 to 4.7
Brake backplate:		
Timken axle	15 to 18	2.1 to 2.5
Salisbury axle	20 to 23	2.8 to 3.2
Hydraulic unions	5 to 7	0.7 to 1.0
Bleed valves (maximum)	8	1.1

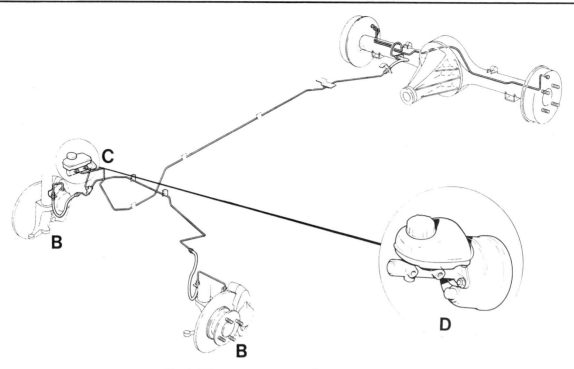

Fig. 9.1 The brake pipe layout (RHD shown) (Sec 1)

B   Disc brake units
C   Master cylinder

D   Master cylinder and
    servo unit

1   General description

Disc brakes are fitted to the front wheels and drum brakes to the rear. All are operated under servo assistance from the brake pedal, this being connected to the master cylinder and servo assembly.

The hydraulic system is of the dual line principle, whereby the front disc brake calipers have a separate hydraulic system to that of the rear drum brake wheel cylinders, so that, if failure of the hydraulic pipes to the front or rear brakes occurs, half the braking system is still operative (Fig. 9.1). Servo assistance in this condition is still available.

The front brake disc is secured to the hub flange and the caliper is mounted on the steering knuckle and wheel stub, so that the disc is able to rotate in between the two halves of the calipers. Inside each half of the caliper is a hydraulic cylinder, this being interconnected by a drilling which allows hydraulic fluid pressure to be transmitted to both halves. A piston operates in each cylinder, and is in contact with the outer face of the brake pad. By depressing the brake pedal, hydraulic fluid pressure is increased by the servo unit and transmitted to the caliper by a system of metal and flexible hoses, whereupon the pistons are moved outwards so pushing the pads onto the face of the disc and reducing the rotational speed of the disc.

The rear drum brakes have one cylinder operating two shoes. When the brake pedal is depressed, hydraulic fluid pressure, increased by the servo unit, is transmitted to the rear brake wheel cylinders by a system of metal and flexible pipes. The pressure moves the pistons outwards so pushing the shoe linings into contact with the inside circumference of the brake drum and reducing the rotational speed of the drum.

The handbrake provides an independent means of rear brake application, and is cable operated.

Attached to each of the rear brake units is an automatic adjuster which operates in conjunction with the footbrake.

Whenever it is necessary to obtain spare parts for the braking system great care must be taken to ensure that the correct parts are obtained.

Models produced from October 1978 are fitted with a brake fluid level warning indicator switch in the master cylinder reservoir cap. When the fluids drops to the predetermined minimum level in the reservoir, the switch contacts close and a warning light is illuminated on the instrument panel. A test switch is provided to check that the warning light is in an operational condition.

On models produced from August 1978, the rear brakes have inspection apertures in their backplates in line with the leading edge of the leading shoe. The inspection aperture is normally covered by a rubber blanking plug to prevent the ingress of road dirt. This can be prised free for inspection of the lining wear of the leading shoe (always subjected to the fastest wear rate) during routine maintenance and service checks.

2   Braking system – inspection and maintenance

1   Check the fluid level in the reservoir as described in the Routine Maintenance Section at the beginning of this manual. Always use the specified fluid for topping-up or refilling the system. The use of other fluid could result in brake failure caused by perishing or swelling of the seals within the master and operating cylinders.
2   If topping-up becomes frequent, then check the metal piping and flexible hoses for leaks, and check for worn brake or master cylinders which will also cause loss of fluid.
3   At the specified intervals, or if brake malfunction is suspected,

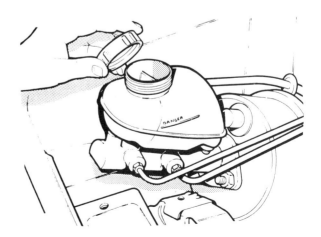

Fig. 9.2 Check the brake fluid level (Sec 2)

examine the front disc pads for wear. If any one pad is worn down to the specified minimum thickness, all four must be renewed. Refer to Section 5 for details.

4   Also at the specified intervals, inspect the rear brake shoes (Section 8) and renew as necessary.

5   Periodically it is advisable to renew the hydraulic fluid, at the same time renewing all hydraulic seals and flexible hoses, together with any sections of rigid hydraulic pipe which may have deteriorated.

3   Bleeding the hydraulic system

1   If any of the hydraulic components in the braking system have been removed or disconnected, or if the fluid level in the master cylinder has been allowed to fall appreciably, it is inevitable that air will have been introduced into the system. The removal of all this air from the hydraulic system is essential if the brakes are to function correctly, and the process of removing it is known as bleeding.

2   There are a number of one-man, do-it-yourself, brake bleeding kits currently available from motor accessory shops. It is recommended that one of these kits should be used whenever possible as they greatly simplify the bleeding operation and also reduce the risk of expelled air and fluid being drawn back into the system.

3   If one of these kits is not available then it will be necessary to gather together a clean jar and a suitable length of clear plastic tubing which is a tight fit over the bleed screw, and also to engage the help of an assistant.

4   Before commencing the bleeding operation, check that all rigid pipes and flexible hoses are in good condition and that all hydraulic unions are tight. Take great care not to allow hydraulic fluid to come into contact with the vehicle paintwork, otherwise the finish will be seriously damaged. Wash off any spilled fluid immediately with cold water.

5   If hydraulic fluid has been lost from the master cylinder, due to a leak in the system, ensure that the cause is traced and rectified before proceeding further or a serious malfunction of the braking system may occur.

6   To bleed the system, clean the area around the bleed screw at the wheel cylinder to be bled. If the hydraulic system has only been partially disconnected and suitable precautions were taken to prevent further loss of fluid, it should only be necessary to bleed that part of the system. However, if the entire system is to be bled, start at the wheel furthest away from the master cylinder. Note that there is only one bleed screw for both rear brakes.

7   Remove the master cylinder filler cap and top up the reservoir. Periodically check the fluid level during the bleeding operation and top up as necessary.

8   If a one-man brake bleeding kit is being used, connect the outlet tube to the bleed screw and then open the screw half a turn. If possible position the unit so that it can be viewed from the car, then depress the brake pedal to the floor and slowly release it. The one-way valve in the kit will prevent expelled air from returning to the system at the end of each stroke. Repeat this operation until clean hydraulic fluid, free from air bubbles, can be seen coming through the tube. Now tighten the bleed screw and remove the outlet tube.

9   If a one-man brake bleeding kit is not available, connect one end of the plastic tubing to the bleed screw and immerse the other end in the jar containing sufficient clean hydraulic fluid to keep the end of the tube submerged (photo). Open the bleed screw half a turn and have your assistant depress the brake pedal to the floor and then slowly release it. Tighten the bleed screw at the end of each downstroke to prevent expelled air and fluid from being drawn back into the system. Repeat this operation until clean hydraulic fluid, free from air bubbles, can be seen coming through the tube. Now tighten the bleed screw and remove the plastic tube.

10   If the entire system is being bled the procedures described above should now be repeated at each bleed screw, finishing at the wheel nearest to the master cylinder. Do not forget to recheck the fluid level in the master cylinder at regular intervals and top up as necessary.

11   When completed, recheck the fluid level in the master cylinder, top up if necessary and refit the cap. Check the 'feel' of the brake pedal which should be firm and free from any 'sponginess' which would indicate air still present in the system.

12   Discard any expelled hydraulic fluid as it is likely to be contaminated with moisture, air and dirt which makes it unsuitable for further use.

13   It will be noticed that during the bleeding operation the effort required to depress the pedal the full stroke will increase because of the loss of vacuum assistance as it is destroyed by repeated operation of the servo unit. Although the servo unit will be inoperable as far as assistance is concerned it does not affect the brake bleed operation.

14   On later models fitted with a fluid level warning system, check the operation of the system switch by removing the filler cap with the ignition switched on. The warning light should illuminate.

4   Hydraulic pipes and hoses – inspection, removal and refitting

1   Periodically, and certainly well in advance of the DoE Test, all brake pipes, connections and unions should be completely and carefully examined.

2   Examine first all the unions for signs of leaks. Then look at the flexible hoses for signs of fraying and chafing (as well as for leaks). This is only a preliminary inspection of the flexible hoses, as exterior condition does not necessarily indicate the interior condition which will be considered later.

3   The steel pipes must be examined equally carefully (photo). They must be thoroughly cleaned and examined for signs of dents or other percussive damage, rust and corrosion. Rust and corrosion should be scraped off, and if the depth of pitting in the pipes is significant, they will require renewal. This is most likely in those areas underneath the chassis and along the rear suspension arms and where the pipes are exposed to the full force of road and weather conditions.

4   If any section of pipe is to be removed, first take off the fluid reservoir cap, line it with a piece of polythene film to make it airtight and screw it back on. This will minimise the amount of fluid dripping out of the system when the pipes are removed.

5   Rigid pipe removal is usually quite straightforward. The unions at each end are undone and the pipe drawn out of the connection. The clips which may hold it to the car body are bent back and it is then removed. Underneath the cars the exposed union can be particularly stubborn, defying the efforts of an open-ended spanner. As few people will have the special split ring spanner required, a self-gripping wrench is the only answer. If the pipe is being renewed, new unions will be provided. If not, then one will have to put up with the possibility of burring over the flats on the unions by using a self-gripping wrench for refitting also.

6   Flexible hoses are always fitted to a rigid support bracket where they join a rigid pipe, the bracket being fixed to the chassis or suspension arm. The rigid pipe unions must first be removed from the flexible union. Then the locknut securing the flexible pipe to the bracket must be unscrewed, releasing the end of the pipe from the bracket. As these connections are usually exposed they are, more often than not, rusted up and a penetrating fluid is virtually essential to aid removal. When undoing them, both halves must be supported as the bracket is not strong enough to support the torque required to undo the nut and can be snapped off easily.

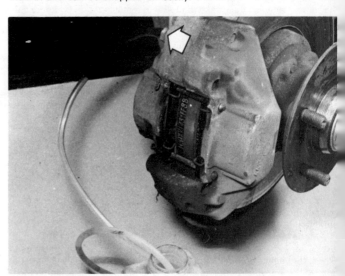

3.9 Bleeding the hydraulic circuit at a front brake caliper (bleed screw arrowed)

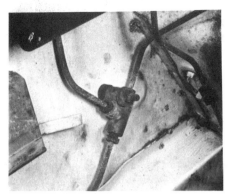

4.3 Examine the brake pipes and connections for condition and security

5.4 Front brake caliper – extract the pin securing clips (one is arrowed)

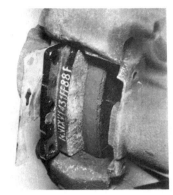

5.10a Insert new pad and shim – note: arrow on shim to face upwards

5.10b Insert the second pad and shim in the caliper ...

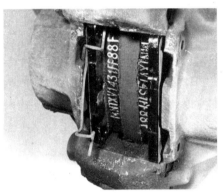

5.10c ... then locate the anti-rattle clips each side ...

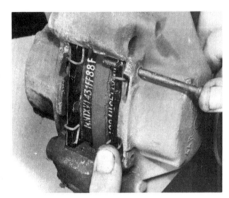

5.10d ... followed by the retaining pins

7   Once the flexible hose is removed, examine the internal bore. If clear of fluid it should be possible to see through it. Any specks of rubber which come out, or signs of restriction in the bore, mean that the inner lining is breaking up and the hose must be renewed.

8   Rigid pipes which need renewing can usually be purchased at your local garage where they have the pipe, unions and special tools to make them up. All that they need to know is the pipe length required and the type of flare used at the ends of the pipe. These may be different at each end of the same pipe. If possible, it is a good idea to take the old pipe along as a pattern.

9   Refitting of pipes is a straightforward reversal of the removal procedure. It is best to get all the sets (bends) made prior to fitting. Also, any acute bends should be put in by the garage on a bending machine, otherwise there is the possibility of kinking them and restricting the bore area and thus, fluid flow.

10 With the pipes refitted, remove the polythene from the reservoir cap and bleed the system as described in the previous Section.

5   Front brake pads – inspection, removal and refitting

1   Apply the handbrake, remove the front wheel trim, slacken the wheel nuts, jack-up the front of the car and place on firmly based axle stands. Remove the front wheel.

2   Inspect the amount of friction material left on the pads. The pads **must** be renewed when the lining thickness of any one pad has been reduced to the minimum given in the Specifications, or if it is thought that the pads will wear below the minimum thickness before the next inspection. Pads which are contaminated with grease or hydraulic fluid must also be renewed, and the source of contamination dealt with. Only renew pads in complete axle sets, ie all four, otherwise uneven braking may result.

3   If the fluid level in the master cylinder reservoir is high, when the pistons are moved into their bores to accommodate new pads the level could rise sufficiently for the fluid to overflow. Place absorbent cloth around the reservoir or syphon a little fluid out, so preventing paintwork damage caused by being in contact with the hydraulic fluid.

4   Using a pair of long-nosed pliers extract the two small spring clips

that hold the main retaining pins in place (photo).

5   Remove the main retaining pins and wire anti-rattle clips.

6   The friction pads can now be removed from the caliper. If they prove difficult to remove by hand, a pair of long nosed pliers can be used. Lift away the shims.

7   Before commencing reassembly it should be noted that cars manufactured in late 1977 are fitted with disc brakes having a PVC coating on either the outer face of the brake pad backplate or on the pad shims. *When fitting brake pads, it is important to note that the anti-squeak coating must only be incorporated on one of the components, ie it is not permissible to have the coating on both the backplate and the shims.*

8   Carefully clean the recesses in the caliper in which the friction pads and shims lie, and the exposed faces of each piston from all traces of dust or rust.

9   Using a piece of wood carefully retract the pistons.

10 Fit new friction pads and shims, with the arrow on the shim pointing upwards. Insert the anti-rattle clips and the pad retaining pins and secure with the spring clips (photos).

11 Refit the roadwheel and lower the car, then fully tighten the wheel nuts. Repeat the operation on the other front wheel.

12 To correctly seat the pistons pump the brake pedal several times and finally top up the hydraulic fluid level in the master cylinder reservoir as necessary.

6   Brake caliper – removal, servicing and refitting

1   Apply the handbrake, loose the wheel nuts, jack up the front of the car and place on firmly based axle stands. Remove the front wheel.

2   Wipe the top of the brake master cylinder reservoir and unscrew the cap. Place a piece of polythene sheet over the top of the reservoir and refit the cap. This is to reduce the flow of hydraulic fluid syphoning out during subsequent operations.

3   Remove the friction pads, as described in Section 5.

4   If it is intended to fit new caliper pistons and/or seals, depress the brake pedal to bring the pistons into contact with the disc and so assist subsequent removal of the pistons.

5   Disconnect the hydraulic fluid line either at the rear of the caliper body or at the suspension leg, and close the exposed ends with tape or a suitable plug to prevent the ingress of dirt.

6   Bend back the locking tabs on the caliper mounting bolts and unscrew and remove the bolts. The caliper unit can now be withdrawn from the disc.

7   Remove the retaining rings and detach the dust excluding covers from each of the cylinders (see Fig. 9.3).

8   Apply air pressure from a tyre pump at the fluid inlet port of the caliper and eject the pistons. Do not allow the pistons to fall to the ground during this operation. Mark them with their respective locations using a piece of masking tape.

9   Pick out the rubber seals from the cylinder bores, taking great care not to scratch the surface of the bore.

10   Clean all components in brake fluid or methylated spirit and discard the old seals. Examine the surfaces of the pistons and cylinder bores for scoring or 'bright' wear areas. If these are evident, renew the complete caliper unit.

11   Obtain a repair kit and assemble the seals into the cylinder grooves using only the fingers to manipulate them.

12   Dip the pistons in clean hydraulic fluid and insert them into the cylinder bores. Press each piston as far as it will go into the cylinder, making sure that the piston crown (solid end) enters first.

13   Engage the dust excluders into the piston recessed ends and attach them to the caliper body; then fit the retaining rings.

14   Refitting is a reversal of removal, but tighten the securing bolts to the specified torque.

15   Using a screwdriver, pliers or a suitable chisel, bend up the locking plate tabs to secure the bolts.

16   Remove the tape from the end of the hydraulic hose connection and reconnect it to the union, taking care not to cross-thread the union nut during the initial turns. Do not overtighten the nut and, if possible, use a torque wrench and special slotted end ring spanner attachment to tighten to the specified torque.

17   Take the cap off the master cylinder reservoir and push the pistons into their bores to accommodate the pads. Watch the level of hydraulic fluid in the master cylinder reservoir as it can overflow if too high whilst the pistons are being retracted. Place absorbent cloth around the reservoir or syphon a little fluid out, preventing paintwork damage caused by being in contact with the hydraulic fluid.

18   If the old pads are being re-used, refit them into their respective original positions. If new pads are being used it does not matter which side they are fitted. Refit the shims and clips (see Section 5).

19   Insert the two pad and shim retaining pins and secure in position with the spring clips.

20   Bleed the hydraulic system as described in Section 3. Refit the roadwheel and lower the car.

7   Brake disc – removal and refitting

1   The brake disc is not normally removed from the hub unless it is to be renewed.

2   Remove the hub and disc assembly complete (Chapter 11).

3   Separate the hub from the disc by knocking back the locking tabs and undoing the four bolts. Discard the disc, bolts and locking tabs.

4   Before fitting a new disc to the hub, thoroughly clean the mating surfaces of both components. If this is not done properly, and dirt is

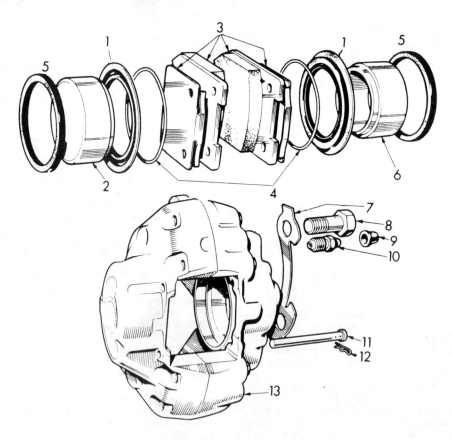

Fig. 9.3 Front brake caliper components (Sec 6)

1	Dust excluders	5	Piston seals	10	Bleed valve
2	Piston	6	Piston	11	Pad retaining pin
3	Friction pads and shims	7	Locking plate	12	Pin retaining clip
4	Dust excluder retaining rings	8	Bolt	13	Caliper body
		9	Dust cap		

allowed to get between the hub and the disc, it will seriously affect disc brake run-out when it is checked after reassembly.

5   Fit the hub and disc together using new locking tabs and bolts. Tighten the bolts to the specified torque and bend up the locking tabs.

6   Refit the disc and hub assembly.

8   Rear brake shoes – inspection, removal and refitting

1   Models produced from August 1978 have a brake shoe inspection aperture incorporated in the rear brake backplate, together with a blanking plug. The aperture is positioned over the fastest wearing section of the leading brake shoe on each rear brake. The plug is easily removed by simply prising it free.

2   On models not fitted with an inspection aperture it will be necessary to remove the brake drum for brake separation. It is recommended that the drums are removed for cleaning at the intervals quoted in *Routine Maintenance,* and a thorough inspection of the brake components can be made at that time, to ensure that they are in good condition.

3   After high mileages, it will be necessary to fit replacement shoes with new linings. Refitting new brake linings to shoes is not considered economical neither is it possible without the use of special equipment. However, if the services of a local garage or workshop having brake relining equipment are available then there is no reason why the original shoes should not be successfully relined. Ensure that the correct specification linings are fitted to the shoes.

4   Chock the front wheels, jack up the rear of the car and place on firmly based axle stands. Remove the roadwheel.

5   Carefully lift off the drum. If necessary, lever out the handbrake lever abutment stop from the rear of the backplate.

6   Remove the small holding springs from each shoe by turning the two small top washers through 90° (photo).

8.6 Removing a brake shoe holding spring and washer

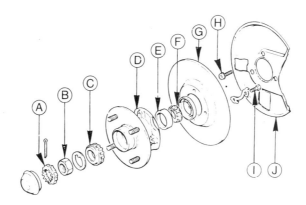

Fig. 9.4 The hub and disc assembly component parts (Sec 7)

A	Nut retainer	E	Bearing cone	H	Bolt
B	Nut	F	Inner bearing	I	Bolt
C	Outer taper bearing	G	Disc	J	Dust shield
D	Hub casting				

Fig. 9.5 Removing the hub and disc assembly from the stub axle (Sec 7)

Fig. 9.6 Remove the retaining bolts to separate the hub and disc (Sec 7)

Fig. 9.7 Note the abutment stop retaining pin hole when disconnecting (Sec 8)

A Handbrake actuating lever
B Abutment stop
C Pin
D Dust cover

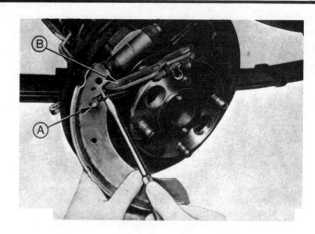

Fig. 9.8 Disengage the handbrake actuating lever (A) and the self-adjusting assembly (B) (Sec 8)

Fig. 9.9 Grease points (arrowed) on rear brake assembly (Sec 8)

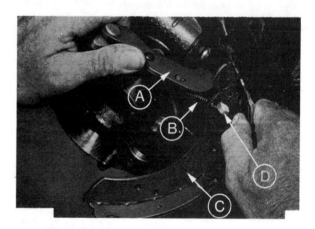

Fig. 9.10 Refitting the trailing shoe (C) showing the self-adjuster (A), the spring (B) and the handbrake actuating arm (D) connections (Sec 8)

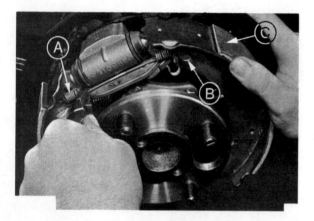

Fig. 9.11 Reconnecting the return spring (A), with leading shoe (C) and self-adjuster arm (B) located (Sec 8)

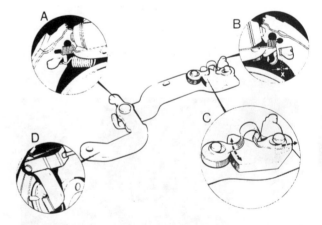

Fig. 9.12 Check the self-adjuster connections are correctly made (Sec 8)

A Shoe end of handbrake actuating lever
B Shoe to drum clearance 'X' when brakes released (non-adjustable)
C Movement of serrated adjuster to reset mechanism
D Handbrake cable end of actuating lever

7 Disengage the spring clip and remove the clevis pin and washers securing the handbrake cable to the right-hand brake assembly at the handbrake actuating arm. (On the left-hand brake assembly the handbrake rod must be disconnected from the lever) (photo).

8 The abutment stop must now be removed from the backplate. The stop is a hinged arrangement secured by a nylon pin. To remove the stop lever out the pin (Fig. 9.7).

9 Carefully lever the brake shoes from their bottom guides and detach the lower return spring (photos). Lever the leading shoe from the wheel cylinder slot and self-adjusting arm, disconnect the pull-off spring and lift the shoe off the backplate.

10 Unlock the trailing shoe from the actuating lever, disconnect the pull-off spring and lift the shoe off the backplate. Note that trailing/leading shoe identification is simplified by the fact that the lining is riveted to the trailing shoe, and bonded to the leading shoe. *They must not be fitted the other way round.*

11 The brake linings should be examined and must be renewed if they are worn down to or near the specified minimum.

12 Refitting of the brake shoes is a direct reversal of the removal procedure, but great care must be taken to ensure that the return springs are correctly fitted and that the contact points shown in Fig. 9.9 are lightly greased with brake grease.

13 Reset the self-adjusting mechanism by using a screwdriver to lever the serrated arm away from the wheel at the same time pushing the serrated end of the arm towards the backplate to the limit of the serrations.

14 Adjust the brake by applying the footbrake two or three times after the drum has been refitted.

8.7 Drum backplate, showing hydraulic line connections to the wheel cylinder and the handbrake cable actuating arm

8.9a Detach the lower return spring ...

8.9b ... followed by the upper spring and adjuster mechanism

9 Drum brake wheel operating cylinder – removal and refitting

1 Referring to the previous Section, remove the brake drum and shoes, together with the self-adjusting mechanism.

2 Free the hydraulic pipe from the wheel cylinder at the union on the brake backplate (there are two unions on the right-hand backplate). Plug the exposed end(s) of the disconnected fluid pipe(s) to prevent the ingress of dirt and fluid leakage.

3 If hydraulic fluid is leaking from the brake wheel cylinder, it will be necessary to dismantle it and renew the seals. Should brake fluid be found running down the side of the wheel, or if it is noticed that a pool of liquid forms alongside one wheel or the level in the master cylinder drops, it is also indicative of failed seals.

4 The servicing details of the wheel cylinder are given in the following Section. Although it is possible to renew the seals with the cylinder in position it is preferable to remove the unit for convenience.

5 Undo and remove the two bolts and spring washers securing the wheel cylinder to the backplate and lift the cylinder off the plate.

6 Refitting of the cylinder is a direct reversal of the removal procedure. Refer to the previous Section for details of refitting the brake shoes and the adjuster mechanism. On completion bleed the hydraulic system, as given in Section 3.

10 Drum brake wheel operating cylinder – servicing

1 The drum brake wheel operating cylinder can only be dismantled, cleaned, inspected and overhauled (new seals fitted) if either the brake drum, shoes and adjusters are removed or the wheel cylinder itself is removed (preferable). Refer to the previous two Sections for removal as necessary, then proceed as follows.

2 Clean the exterior of the unit by brushing off all dust and wiping with a piece of rag soaked in methylated spirit.

3 Pull off the rubber dust covers from each end of the cylinder.

4 Eject the pistons and coil spring from the cylinder bore by either tapping through or applying air pressure from a tyre pump at the fluid inlet union. In extreme cases it may be found that the pistons are reluctant to exit from the cylinder and this could well mean that one or both pistons are seized in position. In such instances the wheel cylinder should be renewed as a unit.

5 Once the pistons are removed their seals can be levered free from their location grooves, but note the direction of fitting and do not scratch or damage the piston surfaces in any way.

6 Thoroughly clean the cylinder bore using clean hydraulic fluid and blow or wipe it dry using a lint-free cloth.

7 Examine the surfaces of the piston and cylinder bore for scoring or

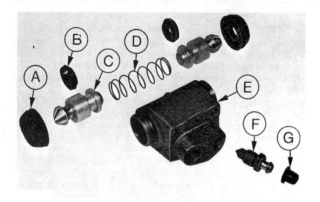

Fig. 9.13 Rear wheel cylinder components (Sec 10)

A Dust cover   E Wheel cylinder
B Piston seal   F Bleed nipple (where applicable)
C Piston   G Dust cover (where applicable)
D Centre spring

Fig. 9.14 Check for zero clearance at abutment point 'C' (Sec 11)

11.4 The handbrake cable adjuster

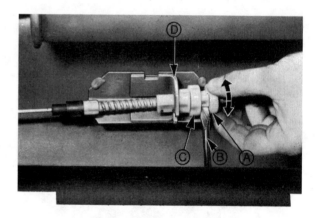

Fig. 9.15 Handbrake cable adjustment (Sec 11)

A Adjustment nut
B Screwdriver inserted to disengage tapered adjuster nut from keyed sleeve (C)
D Tunnel abutment bracket

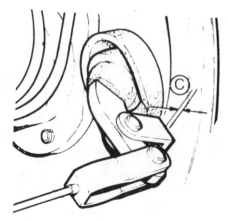

Fig. 9.16 Check that the fully adjusted clearance at C is between 0.12 and 0.18 in (3.0 and 4.5 mm) when adjustment is complete (Sec 11)

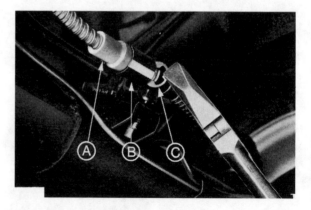

Fig. 9.17 Detach cable (A) from traverse rod bracket (B) by removing retaining clip (C) (Sec 12)

'bright' wear areas. If these are evident, renew the complete cylinder assembly.

8   Discard the old seals and purchase a repair kit which will contain all the necessary seals and renewable components.

9   Dip the new seals in clean hydraulic fluid and fit them to the pistons using only the fingers to manipulate them into position. Ensure that the orientation of the seals is correct (as noted during dismantling, and shown in Fig. 9.13).

10 Insert the pistons together with the central coil spring into position in the cylinder, having lubricated the pistons and cylinder bore with new hydraulic fluid of the specified type. Take care when fitting not to distort or damage the seals as they are compressed into the cylinder bore.

11 Locate the cylinder dust cover at each end before refitting the cylinder (if removed). For cylinder and brake shoe assembly refitting, refer to the previous Sections.

11 Handbrake – adjustment

1   The handbrake is normally adjusted by the operation of the automatic adjusting mechanism of the rear brakes. However, if the operating cable has stretched or in the event of a new cable having been fitted (Section 12) carry out the following procedure.

2   Chock the front wheels; release the handbrake fully and then jack up the rear of the car and support it on axle stands.

3   Check that the handbrake cable follows its correct run and is properly located in its guides, then ensure that both levers are fully seated by checking that there is no clearance between the backplate lever hinged abutment and the backplate (Fig. 9.14).

4   Locate the cable adjuster (photo) on the underside of the floorpan and turn the keyed sleeve (C in Fig. 9.15) so that the key engages with the slot on the tunnel bracket.

5   Insert a screwdriver blade between the adjusting nut and keyed sleeve to disengage the nut from the sleeve so that the nut can be freely turned by hand.

6   Turn the nut as necessary to remove all slack from the mechanism; this is indicated by a *total* clearance of 4.0 to 5.0 mm (0.16 to 0.20 in) existing at the handbrake actuating lever abutment points (C in Fig. 9.16). It is in order for a zero clearance to exist on one side and the maximum total clearance on the other side, as both will equalise when the handbrake is operated.

7   Fully apply the handbrake, then release it fully to settle the mechanism. Then check that the sum of the abutment clearances at each side totals between 3.0 and 4.5 mm (0.12 and 0.18 in); again it

is in order for a zero clearance to exist on one side.

8   The handbrake cable should not be tightened outside the above limits otherwise the self-adjusting mechanism will not operate correctly; with this system it is in order for the handbrake lever to travel up to 10 notches before the rear brakes are fully applied.

9   Remove the axle stands and lower the jack.

12 Handbrake cable – renewal

1   Chock the front roadwheels, jack up the rear of the vehicle and release the handbrake fully. Support the car at the rear with axle stands.

2   Disconnect the handbrake cable from the brake operating lever by removing the clip (or split pin) and the clevis pin (photo 14.2).

3   Turn to the right-hand brake drum and disconnect the cable from the actuating lever in the drum by first removing the spring clip and then pushing out the clevis pin.

4   Prise the clip retaining the cable to the traverse rod off its location and then slide the cable clear of the traverse rod bracket (Fig. 9.17).

5   Slide the caliper, complete with adjusting nut and keyed sleeve, clear of the cable adjuster bracket on the underside of the floorpan, and then off the vehicle, pulling the cable through the slots in the guide brackets as necessary to disengage the cable from the guides.

6   Fitting the new cable is a reversal of removal but grease the guides and when installed, adjust it as described in Section 11.

13 Handbake cable traverse rod – removal and refitting

1   Chock the front roadwheels, jack up the rear of the vehicle and fully release the handbrake. Support the car at the rear on axle stands.

2   Turn to the right-hand brake drum and disconnect the cable from the actuating lever in the drum by first removing the spring clip and then pushing out the clevis pin.

3   Prise the spring clip retaining the cable to the traverse rod off its location, then slide the cable clear of the rod bracket.

4   Disconnect the traverse rod from the actuating lever on the left-hand drum by removing the spring clip and pushing out the clevis pin.

5   Slide the rod through its mounting bush on the axle casing and lift it clear of the vehicle.

6   Refitting of the rod is a direct reversal of the removal procedure, but first check the condition of the axle casing bush and renew if necessary.

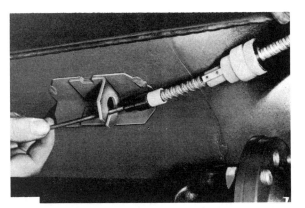

Fig. 9.18 Withdraw the cable from the abutment bracket (Sec 12)

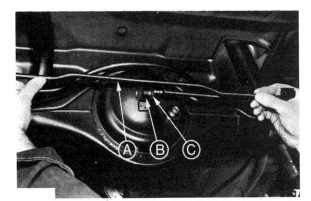

Fig. 9.19 Removing the traverse rod (A) from bracket (B) and bush (C) (Sec 13)

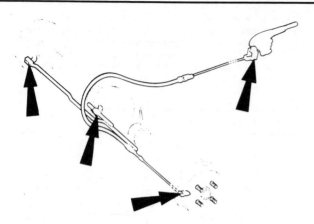

Fig. 9.20 Handbrake cable system grease points (arrowed) (Sec 13)

14.2 Handbrake cable to lever connection (clevis pin arrowed)

7   Grease the rod location at the actuating lever, casing bush, and coupling with a lithium-based grease (Fig. 9.20).

8   On completion check the handbrake for satisfactory operation and adjustment (Section 11) before lowering the car.

14 Handbrake lever – removal and refitting

1   Jack up the front of the vehicle, chock the rear wheels and fully release the handbrake. Support the front of the car with axle stands.

2   From underneath the vehicle, disconnect the cable from the handbrake lever, where the lever protrudes through the floor pan, by removing the spring clip and pushing out the clevis pin (photo).

3   Working inside the passenger compartment, carefully pull the carpet away from the base of the lever to expose the screws retaining the handbrake lever gaiter.

4   Unscrew and remove the screws then lift away the metal gaiter surround and pull the gaiter off the handbrake lever.

5   Undo and remove the bolts holding the lever to the floor pan, and remove the lever from the vehicle.

6   Refit in the reverse order to removal, but ensure that the handbrake lever is in the off position when reconnecting the handbrake cable, and lubricate the clevis pin with grease before assembling. On completion check the handbrake for satisfactory operation and adjustment (Section 11) before lowering the car.

15 Brake master cylinder – removal and refitting

1   Apply the handbrake and chock the front wheels. Drain the fluid from the master cylinder reservoir and master cylinder by attaching a plastic bleed tube to one of the brake bleed screws. Undo the screw one turn and then pump the fluid out into a clean glass container by means of the brake pedal. Hold the brake pedal against the floor at the end of each stroke and tighten the bleed screw. When the pedal has returned to its normal position loosen the bleed screw and repeat the process until the reservoir is empty.

2   On models fitted with a master cylinder fluid level warning system you will need to detach the connector on the reservoir filler cap when removing it.

3   Wipe the area around the two union nuts on the side of the master cylinder body and using an open-ended spanner undo the two union nuts. Tape over the ends of the pipes to stop dirt ingress.

4   Undo and remove the two nuts and spring washers that secure the master cylinder to the servo unit. Lift away the master cylinder, taking care that no hydraulic fluid is allowed to drip onto the paintwork.

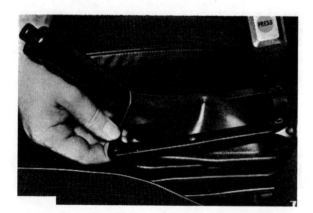

Fig. 9.21 Lift the gaiter and surround clear (Sec 14)

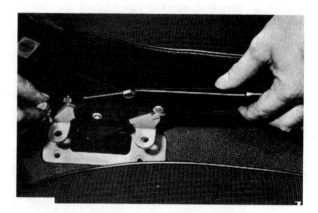

Fig. 9.22 Remove the lever (Sec 14)

5   Refitting is the reverse sequence to removal. Always start the union nuts before finally tightening the master cylinder nuts. It will be necessary to bleed the hydraulic system: full details will be found in Section 3.

16 Brake master cylinder – dismantling, examination and re-assembly

One of two types of brake master cylinder will be fitted, these being shown in Figs. 9.23 and 9.24. For identification they are referred to as Type 'A' and Type 'B' respectively. Externally the Type 'B' master cylinder is identified by the piston stop screw which is not fitted to the Type 'A' master cylinder.

If a replacement master cylinder is to be fitted, it will be necessary to lubricate the seals before fitting to the car as they have a protective coating when originally assembled. Remove the blanking plugs from the hydraulic pipe union seatings. Inject clean hydraulic fluid into the master cylinder and operate the primary piston several times so that the fluid spreads over all the internal working surfaces.

If the master cylinder is to be dismantled after removal, proceed as given below, according to master cylinder type.

Type 'A' – dismantling
1   Prise free the rubber protector boot from the end of the cylinder and then, using suitable circlip pliers, extract the pushrod retaining clip and withdraw the pushrod.
2   Unscrew and remove the screws securing the reservoir to the main body and then pull the reservoir free.
3   Extract the seal washer from the primary recuperating valve orifice, then unscrew and remove the valve retaining plug using a suitable hexagon key. The primary recuperating valve unit can then be lifted out.
4   Temporarily plug the two outlet ports and the primary recuperating valve orifice, then, using a compressed air jet or tyre pump applied very carefully into the secondary recuperating valve orifice, blow out the master cylinder components. Take care to ensure that all parts are caught as they emerge from the cylinder and lay them out in a clean working area in order and orientation of fitting. If compressed air is not available you may be able to remove the cylinder components by shaking them out.
5   Remove the seal from the primary piston, noting its orientation.
6   The secondary piston is secured to the spring retainer by a tab which is engaged under the piston front shoulder. Lift the tab to remove the piston. Compressing the spring, move the retainer to the side and detach the secondary recuperating valve stem from it. The valve spacer, washer and seal can then be slid from the valve stem.
7   Dismantling of this cylinder type is now complete and it can be cleaned and inspected as described in paragraphs 14 to 16.

Type 'B' – dismantling
8   Grip the reservoir and support the cylinder. Pull the reservoir from the cylinder and remove the rubber plugs.
9   Push the primary piston down into the cylinder to release its tension against the retaining circlip and then, using suitable circlip pliers, extract the retaining clip from the cylinder.
10 Unscrew and remove the piston stop screw from the top of the master cylinder.
11 Extract the primary piston together with its stop washer.
12 The secondary piston can now be removed from the cylinder by

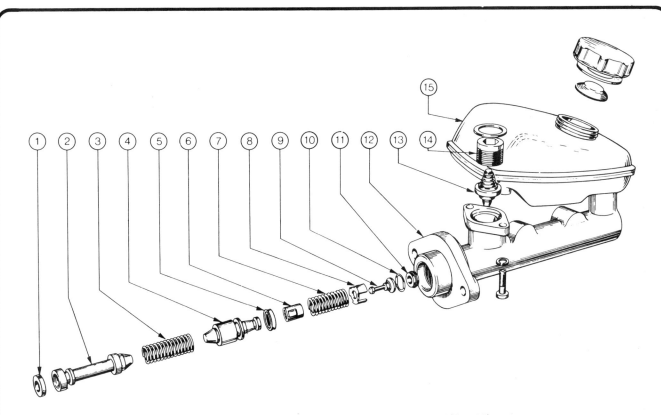

Fig. 9.23 Brake master cylinder components – type 'A' (Sec 16)

1 Seal (primary piston)	6 Spring retainer	11 Valve seal
2 Primary piston	7 Spring	12 Master cylinder body
3 Spring	8 Valve spacer	13 Recuperating valve
4 Secondary piston	9 Secondary recuperating	(primary)
5 Seal (secondary	valve	14 Retaining plug
piston)	10 Spring washer (special)	15 Reservoir

applying a controlled amount of compressed air into the front hydraulic outlet connection. Catch the piston as it emerges and note which way round it fits in the cylinder. The secondary piston spring can be shaken out of the cylinder if it has remained in place.

13 Lay out the components of the primary and secondary pistons in order of fitting for cleaning and inspection. When removing the seals note their orientation.

Cleaning and examination (Types 'A' and 'B' master cylinders)

14 Clean the components in methylated spirit or the specified brake fluid, and wipe dry with a lint-free cloth.

15 Examine the bore of the cylinder carefully for any signs of scores or ridges. If this is found to be smooth all over new seals can be fitted. If, however, there is any doubt of the condition of the bore, then a new cylinder must be fitted. If examination of the seals shows them to be apparently oversize, or swollen, or very loose on the plungers, suspect oil contamination in the system. Oil will swell these rubber seals, and if one is found to be swollen, it is reasonable to assume that all seals in the braking system will need attention.

16 All components must be assembled wet, by first dipping them into clean brake fluid of the specified type. Ensure that the master cylinder bore and the respective orifices are perfectly clean before commencing reassembly. Smear the cylinder bore with hydraulic fluid.

Type 'A' – reassembly

17 Locate the new seal onto the secondary piston.

18 Fit the spring washer onto the valve stem with the seal and seal spacer (the legs of which face the seal). The washer must be fitted concentrically onto the valve stem rear shoulder with its convex side to the shoulder flange.

19 Locate the spring over the valve stem and fit the spring retainer. The spring is then compressed to engage the valve stem boss into the retainer recess.

20 Locate the secondary piston spigot end into the spring retainer and press down the tab to secure it against the piston shoulder.

21 Lubricate the secondary piston unit in brake fluid and insert it into the master cylinder bore (valve end to the front of the cylinder).

22 Locate the new primary piston seal and then fit the piston with spring into the cylinder bore (having lubricated it with hydraulic fluid). This piston is fitted with the drilled end to the front.

23 Locate the pushrod into the end of the primary piston, fit the guide washer and make secure by fitting the retaining circlip. Check that the pushrod is able to move freely.

24 Insert the primary recuperating valve into its orifice and, if necessary, move the pushrod to allow its entry. Refit the retaining plug.

25 Operate the pushrod and check that the primary recuperating valve opens as the pushrod is fully withdrawn, and closes when fully

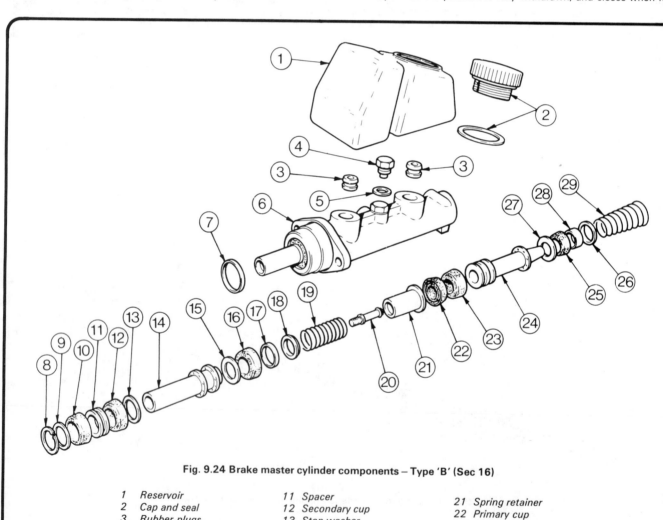

Fig. 9.24 Brake master cylinder components – Type 'B' (Sec 16)

1 Reservoir	11 Spacer	21 Spring retainer
2 Cap and seal	12 Secondary cup	22 Primary cup
3 Rubber plugs	13 Stop washer	23 Secondary cup
4 Stop screw	14 Primary piston	24 Secondary piston
5 Stop screw washer	15 Shims	25 Primary cup
6 Cylinder	16 Primary cup	26 Spring seat
7 Fluid seal	17 Thrust washer	27 Shims
8 Circlip	18 Spring seat	28 Thrust washer
9 Stop washer	19 Spring	29 Spring
10 Secondary cup	20 Special screw	

inserted, then fit the new seal washer into the top of the recuperating valve port.

26 Refit the fluid reservoir to complete. The master cylinder is now ready for refitting to the servo unit. The hydraulic lines must be reconnected and the brake hydraulic circuits bled (Section 3).

Type 'B' – reassembly

27 Lubricate and fit the new secondary piston seal into position on the piston, followed by the shims, cups, thrust washer, spring and spring seat. This assembled piston assembly can now be refitted to the master cylinder bore (having first lubricated both the piston assembly and bore with hydraulic fluid). Push the piston down the bore so that it is beyond the stop screw location. Fit the stop screw and washer, release the piston so that it recoils to contact the stop screw, then fully tighten the screw. It should be noted that since the length of the stop screw and the thickness of the seal washer are important for the efficiency of the master cylinder, they should not be modified in any way.

28 Assemble the primary piston with the primary piston shim, cup seal, thrust washer, spring and spring seat with spring retainer and the special screw (which must not be overtightened) (Fig. 9.25). Lubricate the assembled unit and fit it into the master cylinder, then insert the circlip.

29 Apart from refitting the fluid reservoir with the new seal plugs, the master cylinder is now assembled and ready for refitting to the servo unit. Do not move the pistons (the secondary in particular in case it contacts the stop screw) until each of the master cylinder chambers have been refilled with fluid.

30 After refitting the cylinder to the servo unit, connect the hydraulic pipes and then bleed the system as described in Section 3.

17 Vacuum servo unit – description

A vacuum servo unit is fitted into the brake hydraulic circuit in series with the master cylinder, to provide assistance to the driver when the brake pedal is depressed. This reduces the effort required by the driver to operate the brakes under all braking conditions.

The unit operates by vacuum obtained from the induction manifold and comprises, basically, a booster diaphragm and check valve. The servo unit and hydraulic master cylinder are connected together so that the servo unit piston rod acts as the master cylinder pushrod. The driver's effort is transmitted through another pushrod to the servo unit piston and its built-in control system. The servo unit piston does not fit tightly into the cylinder, but has a strong diaphragm to keep its edges in constant contact with the cylinder wall, so assuring an airtight seal between the two parts. The forward chamber is held under vacuum conditions created in the inlet manifold of the engine and, during periods when the brake pedal is not in use, the controls open a passage to the rear chamber so placing it under vacuum conditions as well. When the brake pedal is depressed, the vacuum passage to the rear chamber is cut off and the chamber opened to atmospheric pressure. The consequent rush of air pushes the servo piston forward in the vacuum chamber and operates the main pushrod to the master cylinder.

The controls are designed so that assistance is given under all conditions and, when the brakes are not required, vacuum in the rear chamber is established when the brake pedal is released. All air from the atmosphere entering the rear chamber is passed through a small air filter.

Under normal operating conditions the vacuum servo unit is very reliable and does not require overhaul except at very high mileages. In this case it is far better to obtain a service exchange unit, rather than repair the original unit.

18 Vacuum servo unit – removal and refitting

1 Remove the vacuum supply pipe from the servo unit (photo) and then undo the brake fluid pipes from the master cylinder (photo). Block the ends of the pipes to prevent the entry of dirt.

2 Take the master cylinder off the front of the servo unit by undoing the two retaining nuts and washers.

3 Detach the servo pushrod from the brake pedal by removing the spring clip, clevis pin and clevis pin bushes.

4 Working underneath the right-hand wing, undo and remove the

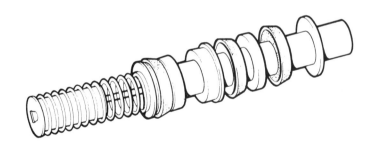

Fig. 9.25 Master cylinder primary piston assembly (Type 'B')
(Sec 16)

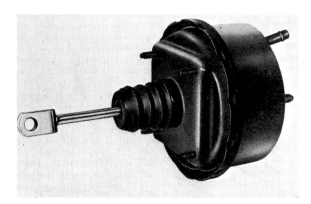

Fig. 9.26 Brake vacuum servo unit (Sec 17)

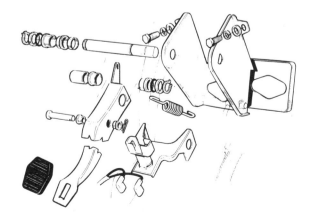

Fig. 9.27 Brake pedal and support bracket components (Sec 18)

18.1a Detach the vacuum pipe from the servo unit ...

18.1b ... then detach the hydraulic lines from the master cylinder

two nuts and one bolt which hold the servo unit mounting bracket to the side of the car.

5   From under the bonnet, undo and remove the two nuts which hold the rear of the servo mounting bracket to the bulkhead. Remove the servo unit complete with its mounting bracket from the car.

6   From halfway along the mounting bracket, separate the servo pushrod and the pedal pushrod from the pivoted relay lever by removing the spring clip, the clevis pin and clevis bush.

7   Then undo the four nuts and spring washers holding the servo unit to its mounting bracket and detach the servo.

8   Refitting of the servo unit and its mounting bracket are a direct reversal of the above procedure.

19 Brake pedal – removal and refitting

1   Remove the cross-head screw, nut, bolt and push-in clip securing the driver's side parcel shelf to its various brackets, then detach the shelf.

2   Disconnect the brake actuating pushrod from the brake pedal, by removing the securing clip and detaching the clevis (photo).

3   Remove the circlip from the end of the pedal shaft, then push the shaft into the pedal box and through the pedal bushes until the pedal can be dropped clear of the box.

4   Disconnect the pedal return spring and remove the pedal from the vehicle.

5   Inspect the pedal bushes for wear whilst the pedal and shaft are dismantled and, if necessary, press them out and renew them.

6   Refitting is a direct reversal of the removal procedure. Lubricate the pedal shaft and bushes as they are assembled. On completion check the brake pedal free height as follows.

7   Chock the front and rear wheels, and fully release the handbrake.

8   Measure the distance from the floor to the top of the pedal (Fig. 9.29), using a pointed rod pressed through the carpet and sound deadener. The engine should be idling during the check so that the servo is operational.

9   If the free height is not as given in the Specifications, first check that the floor and brake pedal are not damaged or distorted. If still not correct, the pedal linkage or bushing may be worn, or the fault may lie in the master cylinder or servo unit.

20 Pressure differential valve – description

On LHD models a brake pressure differential valve is fitted. This valve is essentially a shuttle valve, the opposing sides of which are connected to the front and rear hydraulic brake circuits (dual system). Whilst equal pressure is maintained in both circuits, the valve remains centralised (in balance) but should the pressure drop in either circuit

19.2 Brake pedal assembly, showing the stop-light switch wires (1), the operating rod clevis pin (2) and the pedal shaft (arrow indicates circlip position) (3)

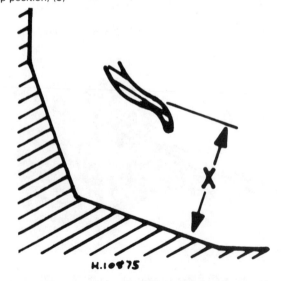

H.10975

Fig. 9.28 Brake pedal free height check dimension 'X' (see Specifications) (Sec 19)

due to a leaking pipe or cylinder seal, then the valve is displaced – blocking the affected circuit and closing an electrical contact to illuminate a warning light on the facia panel.

21 Pressure differential valve – servicing

1   Disconnect the five hydraulic pipes at the unions on the pressure differential valve and to prevent too much loss of hydraulic fluid, either place a piece of polythene under the cap of the master cylinder and screw it down tightly, or plug the ends of the two pipes leading from the master cylinder.
2   Remove the nut and washer securing the differential valve assembly to the wing apron and lift the assembly off the wing, after first disconnecting the switch multi-plug.
3   Carefully unscrew and remove the switch unit from the top of the valve body.
4   Unscrew the stop bolt from the end of the valve body and from the opposite end use a thin rod or screwdriver to push the piston, two sleeves and seals out of the valve body bore.
5   Remove the two rubber seals, together with the piston sleeves, off their respective ends of the piston.
6   Clean all components using clean hydraulic fluid and put them on a clean sheet of paper ready for inspection. Examine the piston for score marks, pitting or signs of corrosion. Similarly, check the condition of the valve body bore, where doubt exists as to the condition of the components they must be renewed.
7   Remember that new seals will only be effective if the piston, sleeves and cylinder bore are in perfect condition.
8   Check that the two circlips on the piston body are in good condition then slide the piston sleeves over the end of the piston and secure them in place with two new seals.
9   Insert the piston, sleeve and seal assembly into the valve body after first lubricating the body and assembly with clean brake fluid. Assemble a new washer to the retaining bolt and then screw the bolt into the end of the valve body. Refit the switch unit.
10 Refitting of the valve on the wing apron is a reversal of the removal procedure.

22 Brake pressure control valve (fitted from 1978) – removal and refitting

1   This device is fitted into the brake circuit between the master cylinder and the rear brakes. Its purpose is to regulate the hydraulic pressure applied to the rear brakes to prevent them locking the rear wheels before the front wheels when the car is lightly loaded. This is to reduce the vehicle's chances of skidding – increasing its stability whilst reducing the stopping distances. The valve operates after a predetermined deceleration rate is obtained.
2   Should the valve become defective it cannot be repaired and must therefore be renewed.
3   To remove the valve, disconnect the hydraulic line connections from it, having sealed the hydraulic reservoir filler neck with a sheet of polythene and screwed the cap back on to prevent excessive loss of fluid. Plug the ends of the disconnected lines to prevent the ingress of dirt.
4   The valve fastening can then be unscrewed and the pressure control valve removed.
5   Refit in the reverse order to removal and top up and bleed the hydraulic system, as given in Section 3.

23 Stop-light switch – removal, refitting and adjustment

1   Open the bonnet and for safety reasons, disconnect the battery earth lead.
2   Remove the parcel shelf under the dashboard on the driver's side (one screw, one bolt and a clip secure it in position).
3   Detach the cables from the switch (see photo 19.2), then unscrew and remove the switch locknut. The switch can then be removed from its retaining bracket.
4   Refitting of the switch is the reverse sequence to removal, but ensure that the switch is adjusted so that when the brake pedal is in the rest position, the switch is depressed by half its total travel.
5   Check for satisfactory operation before fully tightening the locknut and refitting the parcel shelf.

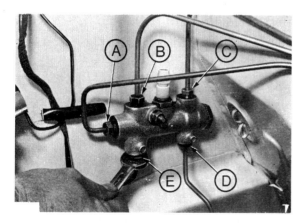

Fig. 9.29 The pressure differential valve hydraulic pipe connections (Sec 21)

A	To left-hand front brake	D	To rear brakes
B	From master cylinder	E	To right-hand front brake
C	From master cylinder		

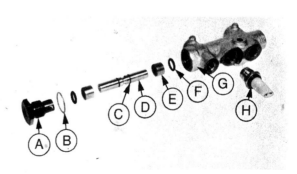

Fig. 9.30 Differential valve – exploded view (Sec 21)

A	End bolt	E	Sleeve
B	Washer	F	Seal
C	Piston circlip	G	Valve body
D	Piston	H	Switch

24 Fault diagnosis – braking system

Symptom	Reason(s)
Pedal travels almost to floor before brakes operate	Brake fluid level too low Caliper leaking Master cylinder leaking (bubbles in master cylinder fluid) Brake flexible hose leaking Brake line fractured Brake system unions loose Pad or shoe linings over 75% worn
Brake pedal feels springy	New linings not yet bedded-in Brake discs or drums badly worn or cracked Master cylinder and/or vacuum servo unit securing nuts loose
Brake pedal feels spongy and soggy	Caliper or wheel cylinder leaking Master cylinder leaking (bubbles in master cylinder reservoir) Brake pipe line or flexible hose leaking Unions in brake system loose
Excessive effort required to brake car	Pad or shoe linings badly worn New pads or shoes recently fitted – not yet bedded-in Harder linings fitted than standard, causing increase in pedal pressure Linings and brake drums contaminated with oil, grease or hydraulic fluid Vacuum servo unit not working
Brakes uneven and pulling to one side	Linings and discs or drums contaminated with oil, grease or hydraulic fluid Tyre pressures unequal Brake caliper loose Brake pads or shoes fitted incorrectly Different type of linings fitted at each wheel Anchorages for front suspension or rear suspension loose Brake disc or drums badly worn, cracked or distorted

Chapter 10 Electrical system

Contents

Specifications

General

System type	12 volt, negative earth
Battery type	Lead acid
Battery capacity (typical)	55 Ah

Alternator (Bosch)
Type .... K1-35A or K1-55A
Nominal rated output at 13.5 volts and 6000 rpm .... 355 amps (K1-35A) or 55 amps (K1-55A)
Stator winding resistance .... 0.10 to 0.14 ohms per phase
Rotor winding resistance .... 4.0 to 4.4 ohms at 20°C (68°F)
Minimum brush length (protruding from brush box) .... 5 mm (0.197 in)
Regulating voltage at 4000 rpm and 3 to 7 amp load .... 13.7 to 14.5

Alternator (Lucas)
Type .... 17 ACR or 18 ACR
Nominal rated output .... 35 amps (17 ACR) or 43 amps (18 ACR)
Stator winding resistance .... 0.10 to 0.14 ohms per phase
Rotor winding resistance .... 3.25 ohms $\pm$ 5% at 20°C (68°F)
Minimum brush length (protruding from brush box) .... 5 mm (0.197 in)
Regulating voltage at 4000 rpm and 3 to 7 amp load .... 14.2 to 14.6

Alternator (Femsa)
Type .... ALD 12-32 or ALD 12-33
Nominal rated output .... 32 amps
Stator winding resistance .... 0.16 to 0.18 ohms per phase
Rotor winding resistance .... 4.85 to 5.15 ohms at 20°C (68°F)
Minimum brush length (protruding from brush box) .... 7 mm (0.28 in)
Regulating voltage at 4000 rpm and 3 to 7 amp load .... 13.7 to 14.5
Field relay closing voltage .... 2.0 to 2.8

Starter motor (Bosch)
Type .... 0.7 PS, pre-engaged
Brush length, minimum .... 10 mm (0.39 in)
Brush spring pressure .... 0.9 to 1.3 kg (2.0 to 2.9 lb)
Commutator minimum diameter .... 32.8 mm (1.29 in)
Commutator out-of-round .... 0.3 mm (0.012 in) maximum
Armature endfloat .... 0.1 to 0.3 mm (0.004 to 0.012 in)

Starter motor (Lucas)
Type .... M35J (inertia or pre-engaged) or 5M90 (pre-engaged)
Brush length, minimum .... 8 mm (0.32 in)
Brush spring pressure .... 0.8 kg (1.8 lb)
Commutator minimum thickness .... 2 mm (0.08 in)
Armature endfloat (not inertia motor) .... 0.25 mm (0.01 in)
Light running current .... 65 amps maximum

Starter motor (Nippondenso)
Brush length, minimum .... 13 mm (0.5 in)
Commutator minimum diameter .... 30.7 mm (1.21 in)
Commutator undercut .... 0.5 to 0.8 mm (0.020 to 0.032 in)

Fuses (typical)*

Fuse No	Rating	Circuits protected
1	8 amps (later 16 amps)	Cigar lighter, interior light, hazard flashers, clock, glovebox light (if fitted)
2	8 amps	LH side and tail lights, number plate light
3	8 amps	RH side and tail lights, instrument illumination
4	8 amps	Headlamps (main beam)
5	8 amps	Headlamps (dipped beam)
6	8 amps (later 16 amps)	Direction indicators, stop-lamps, reversing lamps, heater motor
7	8 amps	Windscreen wiper and washer, instruments

The following line fuses are located on or near their respective components

–	16 amps	*Heated rear window relay*
–	2 amps	*Radio (medium slow blow)*
–	16 amps	*Auxiliary lamp relay*

Refer to fuse block lid for fuse numbers and circuit details

Bulbs (typical)

	Wattage
Headlamp	60/45 or 60/55
Auxiliary lamps	55
Direction indicators	21
Side repeater lamps (when fitted)	4
Stop/tail lamps	21/5
Parking (side) lamps	4
Reversing lamps	21
Rear foglamp (when fitted)	21
Number plate light	4
Interior light	5
Instrument panel (illumination)	2.6
Instrument panel (warning)	1.3

1 General description

The electrical system is a 12 volt negative earth system, the negative terminal of the battery going to earth via the engine block.

The battery supplies a steady amount of current for all the electrical circuits on the vehicle, and provides a reserve of current during the short periods when the current being consumed by the various vehicle circuits exceeds that being produced by the charging circuit.

The alternator fitted to the vehicle will generally be of Lucas manufacture, although Bosch, or Femsa alternators may be fitted as alternatives. All the alternators are belt-driven from the engine crankshaft pulley.

Either inertia or pre-engaged starter motors are fitted, the type used being dependent on model variant and territory. Where an inertia starter is used it will be the Lucas M35J, this motor being fitted only to vehicles produced in Britain. The alternative pre-engaged motor can be of either Lucas, Bosch or Nippondenso manufacture.

Exterior lighting consists of headlamps (with integral sidelamps), front direction indicators, and rear side/stop/direction indicators combined in one unit. A separate lamp assembly, housed in the rear bumper, illuminates the rear number plate.

The Mexico and RS 1800 variants are fitted with a pair of 7 inch circular headlamps. The RS 2000 differs in having four headlights, also circular, but only $6\frac{1}{8}$ inch diameter.

A two-speed windscreen wiper is fitted to all models. An intermittent function is also available by moving the switch stalk downwards from the off/park position.

Full instrumentation is supplied on all models and includes a tachometer (engine revolution counter) and separate oil, water temperature and fuel gauges.

2 Battery – maintenance and inspection

1 Normal weekly battery maintenance consists of checking the electrolyte level of each cell to ensure that the separators are covered by $\frac{1}{4}$ in (6 mm) of electrolyte. If the level has fallen top up the battery using distilled water only (photo). Do not overfill. If a battery is overfilled or any electrolyte spilled, immediately wipe away the excess as electrolyte attacks and corrodes any metal it comes into contact with very rapidly.

2 As well as keeping the terminals clean and covered with petroleum jelly, the top of the battery, and especially the top of the cells, should be kept clean and dry. This helps prevent corrosion and ensures that the battery does not become partially discharged by leakage through dampness and dirt.

3 Once every three months remove the battery and inspect the battery securing bolts, the battery clamp plate, tray, and battery leads for corrosion (white fluffy deposits on the metal which are brittle to touch). If any corrosion is found, clean off the deposits with ammonia and paint over the clean metal with an anti-rust/anti-acid paint.

4 At the same time inspect the battery case for cracks. If a crack is found, clean and plug it with one of the proprietary compounds manufactured for this purpose. If leakage through the crack has been excessive then it will be necessary to refill the appropriate cell with fresh electrolyte as detailed later. Cracks are frequently caused to the top of the battery case by pouring in distilled water in the middle of winter *after* instead of *before* a run. This gives the water no chance to mix with the electrolyte and so the former freezes and splits the battery case.

5 If topping up the battery becomes excessive and the case has been inspected for cracks that could cause leakage, but none are found, the battery is being overcharged and the charging circuit will have to be checked.

6 Every three months check the specific gravity with a hydrometer to determine the state of charge and the condition of the electrolyte. There should be very little variation between the different cells and if a variation in excess of 0.025 is present, it will be due to either:

(a) *Loss of electrolyte from the battery caused by spillage or a leak resulting in a drop in the specific gravity of the electrolyte. The deficiency was probably made up with distilled water instead of fresh electrolyte*

(b) *An internal short-circuit caused by buckling of the plates or a similar malady pointing to the likelihood of total battery failure in the near future*

7 The specific gravity of the electrolyte for fully charged and fully discharged conditions at the electrolyte temperature indicated, is listed below.

Fully discharged	Electrolyte temperature	Fully charged
1.098	38°C (100°F)	1.268
1.102	32°C (90°F)	1.272
1.106	27°C (80°F)	1.276
1.110	21°C (70°F)	1.280
1.114	16°C (60°F)	1.284
1.118	10°C (50°F)	1.288
1.122	4°C (40°F)	1.292
1.126	-1.5°C (30°F)	1.296

3 Battery – electrolyte replenishment

1 If the battery is in a fully charged state and one of the cells maintains a specific gravity reading which is 0.025 or more lower than the others, and a check of each cell has been made with a voltmeter to check for short-circuits (a four to seven second test should give a steady reading of between 1.2 to 1.8 volts), then it is likely that electrolyte has been lost from the cell which shows the low reading.

2.1 Topping up the battery cells

Fig. 10.1 Checking battery electrolyte specific gravity (Sec 2)

2   Top up the cell with a solution of 1 part sulphuric acid to 2.5 parts of water. If the cell is already fully topped up, draw some electrolyte out of it with a pipette.

3   When mixing the sulphuric acid and water **never add water to sulphuric acid** – always pour the acid slowly into the water in a glass container. **If water is added to sulphuric acid it will explode.**

4   Continue to top up the cell with the freshly made electrolyte and then recharge the battery and check the hydrometer readings.

4   Battery – removal and refitting

1   The battery is positioned on a tray in the front of the engine compartment forward of the nearside suspension.

2   Disconnect the earthed negative lead and then the positive lead by slackening the retaining nuts and bolts or by unscrewing the retaining screws if these are fitted.

3   Remove the battery clamp and carefully lift the battery off its tray. Hold the battery vertically to ensure that no electrolyte is spilled.

4   Refitting is a direct reversal of this procedure. Refit the positive lead and the earth (negative) lead, smearing the terminals with petroleum jelly to prevent corrosion. Never use an ordinary grease as applied to other parts of the car.

5   Battery – charging

1   In winter time when heavy demand is placed upon the battery, such as when starting from cold, and much electrical equipment is continually in use, it is a good idea to occasionally have the battery fully charged from an external source at the rate of 3.5 to 4 amps.

2   Continue to charge the battery at this rate until no further rise in specific gravity is noted over a four hour period.

3   Alternatively, a trickle charger charging at the rate of 1.5 amps can be safely used overnight.

4   Specially rapid boost charges which are claimed to restore the power of the battery in 1 to 2 hours are most dangerous as they can cause serious damage to the battery plates through over-heating.

5   While charging the battery, note that the temperature of the electrolyte should never exceed 100°F (37.8°C).

6   Alternator – general description

The main advantage of the alternator lies in its ability to provide a high charge at low revolutions. Driving slowly in heavy traffic with a dynamo invariably means no charge is reaching the battery. In similar conditions, even with the wiper, heater, lights and perhaps radio switched on, the alternator will ensure a charge reaches the battery.

The three makes of alternator generate alternating current (ac) which is changed to direct current (dc) by an internal diode system. They all have a regulator which limits the output to 14 volts maximum at all times. The regulator is mounted internally for Bosch and Lucas, and mounted on the inner wing for Femsa alternators. A warning lamp illuminates if the alternator fails to operate.

The alternator assembly basically consists of a fixed coil winding (stator) in an aluminium housing, which incorporates the mounting lugs. Inside this stator, rotates a shaft wound coil (rotor). The shaft is supported at each end by ball-race bearings which are lubricated for life.

Slip rings are used to conduct current to and from the rotor field coils via two carbon brushes which bear against them. By keeping the mean diameter of the slip rings to a minimum, relative speed between brushes and rings, and hence wear, are also minimal.

The rotor is belt-driven from the engine through a pulley keyed to the rotor shaft. A pressed steel fan adjacent to the pulley draws cooling air through the machine. This fan forms an integral part of the alternator specification. It has been designed to provide adequate air flow with a minimum of noise, and to withstand the high stresses associated with the maximum speed. Rotation is clockwise viewed on the drive end.

The brushgear is housed in a moulding, screwed to the outside of the slip ring and bracket. This moulding thus encloses the slip ring and brushgear assembly, and together with the shielded bearing, protects the assembly against the entry of dust and moisture.

The regulator is set during manufacture and requires no further attention.

Electrical connections to external circuits are brought out to spade connector blades, these being grouped to accept a moulded connector socket which ensures correct connection.

Manufacturers' design differences are shown in Figs. 10.3, 10.4 and 10.5.

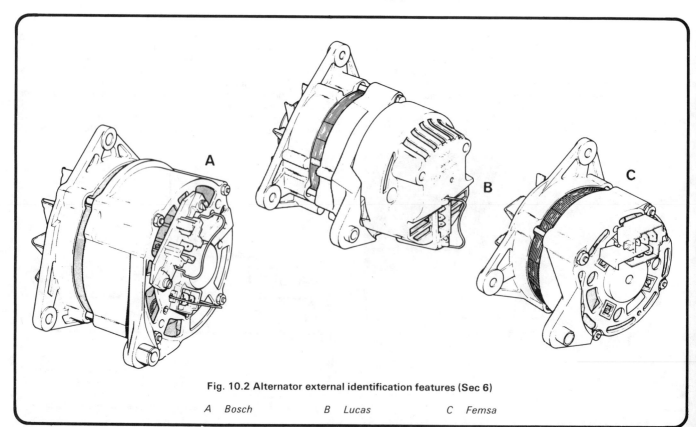

Fig. 10.2 Alternator external identification features (Sec 6)

A   Bosch   B   Lucas   C   Femsa

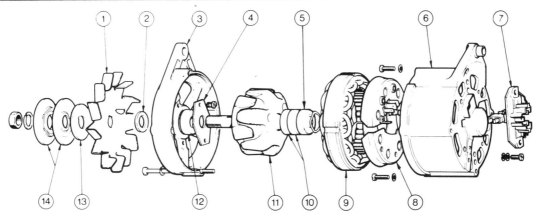

Fig. 10.3 The Bosch alternator component parts (Sec 6)

1 Fan	5 Slip ring end bearing	9 Stator	12 Drive end bearing
2 Spacer	6 Slip ring end housing	10 Slip rings	13 Spacer
3 Drive end housing	7 Brush box and regulator	11 Rotor	14 Pulley
4 Thrust plate	8 Rectifier (diode) pack		

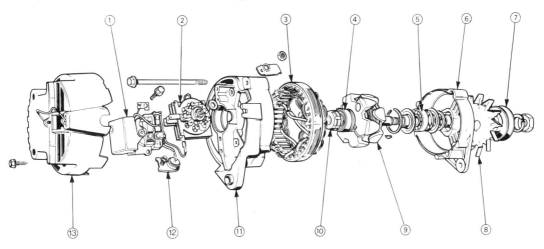

Fig. 10.4 The Lucas alternator component parts (Sec 6)

1 Regulator	5 Drive end bearing	8 Fan	11 Slip ring end housing
2 Rectifier (diode) pack	6 Drive end housing	9 Rotor	12 Surge protection diode
3 Stator	7 Pulley	10 Slip ring	13 End cover
4 Slip ring end bearing			

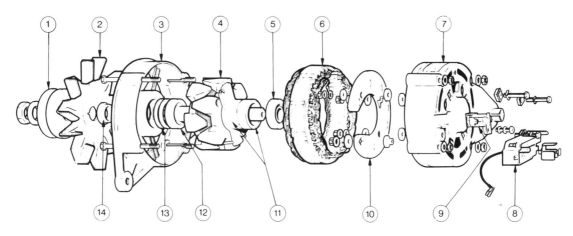

Fig. 10.5 The Femsa alternator components (Sec 6)

1 Pulley	5 Slip ring end bearing	9 Brush box	12 Drive end bearing
2 Fan	6 Stator	10 Rectifier (diode) pack	13 Thrust washer
3 Drive end housing	7 Slip ring end housing	11 Slip rings	14 Spacer
4 Rotor	8 Terminal block		

7   Alternator – maintenance

1   The equipment has been designed for minimum maintenance in service, the only items subject to wear being the brushes and bearings.
2   Brushes should be examined after about 75 000 miles (120 000 km) and renewed, if necessary. The bearings are pre-packed with grease for life, and should not require attention.
3   Check the drivebelt every 6000 miles (9600 km) for correct adjustment which should be 0.5 in (13 mm) total movement at the centre of the run between the alternator and water pump pulleys. For further details of the drivebelt adjustment refer to Chapter 2, Section 9.

8   Alternator – special precautions

Whenever the electrical system of the car is being attended to, or external means of starting the engine are used, there are certain precautions that must be taken otherwise serious and expensive damage can result.
1   Always make sure that the negative terminal of the battery is earthed. If the terminal connectors are accidentally reversed or if the battery has been reverse charged the alternator diodes will burn out.
2   The output terminal on the alternator marked 'BAT' or B+ must never be earthed, but should always be connected directly to the positive terminal of the battery.
3   Whenever the alternator is to be removed, or when disconnecting the terminals of the alternator circuit, always disconnect the battery earth terminal first.
4   The alternator must never be operated without the battery-to-alternator cable connected.
5   If the battery is to be charged by external means, always disconnect both battery cables before the external charge is connected.
6   Should it be necessary to use a booster charger or booster battery to start the engine, always double check that the negative cable is connected to negative terminal and the positive cable to positive terminal.

9   Alternator (all types) – removal and refitting

1   Disconnect the battery leads.
2   Note the terminal connections at the rear of the alternator and disconnect the plug or multi-pin connector.
3   Undo and remove the alternator adjustment arm bolt, slacken the alternator mounting bolts and push the alternator towards the engine. Lift away the drivebelt from the pulley.

4   Remove the remaining two mounting bolts and carefully lift the alternator away from the car.
5   Take care not to knock or drop the alternator as this can cause irreparable damage.
6   Refitting the alternator is the reverse sequence to removal. Adjust the drivebelt so that it has 0.5 in (13 mm) total movement at the centre of the run between the alternator and water pump pulleys (see Chapter 2, Section 9).

10   Alternator – fault diagnosis and repair

Due to the specialist knowledge and equipment required to test or service an alternator, it is recommended that if the performance is suspect, the car be taken to an automobile electrician who will have the facilities for such work. Because of this recommendation, information is limited to the inspection and renewal of the brushes. Should the alterntor not charge or the system be suspect, the following points may be checked before seeking further assistance:

(a)   *Check the drivebelt tension, as described in Section 9 of Chapter 2*
(b)   *Check the battery, as described in Section 2*
(c)   *Check all electrical cable connections for cleanliness and security*

11   Alternator brushes (Lucas) – inspection, removal and refitting

1   Undo and remove the two screws which hold on the end cover. Lift away the end cover.
2   To inspect the brushes correctly, the brush holder moulding should be removed by undoing the securing bolts (Fig. 10.6) and disconnecting the spade connector to the diode plates.
3   With the brush holder moulding removed and the brush assemblies still in position, check that they protrude from the face of the moulding by at least the specified minimum. Also check that when depressed, the spring pressure is 7 to 10 oz (198 to 283 g) when the end of the brush is flush with the face of the brush moulding. To be done with any accuracy, this requires a push type spring scale.
4   Should either of the foregoing requirements not be fulfilled, the brush/spring assemblies must be renewed. This can be done by simply removing the holding screws of each assembly and fitting the new components in position.
5   With the brush holder moulding removed, the slip rings on the face end of the rotor are exposed. These can be cleaned with a petrol soaked cloth and any signs of burning may be removed very carefully with fine glass paper. *On no account should any other abrasive be used or any attempt at machining be made.*

Fig. 10.6 Brush holder retaining bolts (arrowed) – Lucas alternator (Sec 11)

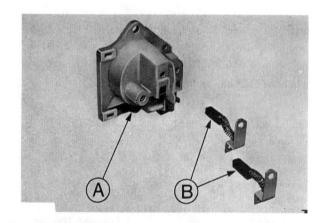

Fig. 10.7 Lucas alternator brush gear (Sec 11)

A   Brush box   *B   Brushes*

6   When the brushes are refitted they should slide smoothly in their holders. Any sticking tendency may first be rectified by wiping with a fuel soaked cloth, or if this fails, by carefully polishing with a very fine file where any binding marks may appear.

7   Reassemble in the reverse order of dismantling.

12 Alternator brushes (Bosch) – inspection, removal and refitting

1   Unscrew and remove the two screws, spring and plain washers securing the brush box to the exterior of the slip ring end housing. Detach the brush box (Fig. 10.8).

2   Check that the carbon brushes are free to slide smoothly in their guides without binding.

3   Ensure that the brush length protruding from the brush box is greater than the specified minimum. If the brushes are worn to a greater extent they must be renewed.

4   Using a pair of pliers as a heat shunt, unsolder the brush wire connections and remove the brushes and springs form the brush box moulding.

5   Check that the new brushes are free to slide in the brush box guides; if necessary lightly remove any high spots with a smooth file.

6   Insert the brushes and springs in the guides and solder the brush leads to their respective terminals.

7   Refitting the brush box is a reversal of the removal procedure.

13 Alternator brushes (Femsa) – inspection, removal and refitting

1   Disconnect the wire protruding through the slip ring end housing from its terminal on the brush box moulding.

2   Remove the single cross-head screw and withdraw the brush box moulding from its location in the slip ring end housing.

3   Check that the brushes are free to slide in their guides and that the free length of brush protruding from the brush box is greater than the specified minimum. If the brushes are worn beyond this point they must be renewed.

4   Refitting is a reversal of the removal process.

14 Starter motor (inertia type) – general description

1   The inertia starter motor (where fitted) will be the Lucas M35J. This is a series wound four pole, four brush motor, held in position by

Fig. 10.8 Brush holder retaining screws (arrowed) on the Bosch alternator (Sec 12)

A   Brushes
B   Springs

C   Brush holder

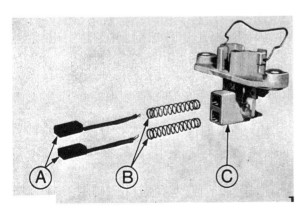

Fig. 10.9 Bosch alternator brushgear (Sec 12)

Fig. 10.10 Brush box retaining screws – Femsa (Sec 13)

A   Brush box
B   Retaining screw

C   Brush box wiring

three bolts which also serve to clamp the bellhousing flange. Refer to Fig. 10.11 for an exploded diagram of this starter motor.

2   The motor has four field coils, four pole pieces and four spring-loaded commutator brushes. Two of these brushes are earthed, and the other two are insulated and attached to the field coil ends.

3   The starter drive is a conventional pinion and spring engaging with a ring gear on the flywheel.

4   The fully insulated brushgear is housed in a plastic brush box moulding riveted to the commutator end bracket. The wedge shaped brushes have keyways to ensure their correct fitting in the brush box and are kept in contact with the face type, moulded commutator, by small coil springs.

5   The field winding on this motor is continuously wound with no interconnecting joints, one end terminating at the brush box moulding with the other end earthed to the yoke, or starter motor casing, via either a riveted eyelet, or soldered connection.

6   Unlike earlier versions of this starter motor the end brackets are held to the yoke independently of each other, each bracket being

secured to its respective location with two screws. At the drive end these screws locate into the pole shoes while at the commutator end the screws locate in tapped holes in the yoke wall.

15 Starter motor (inertia type) – testing *in situ*

1   If the starter motor fails to operate then check the condition of the battery by turning on the headlamps. If they glow brightly for several seconds and then gradually dim, the battery is in discharged condition.

2   If the headlamps glow brightly and it is obvious that the battery is in good condition, then check the tightness of the battery wiring connections (and in particular the earth lead from the battery terminal to its connection on the bodyframe). If the positive terminal on the battery becomes hot when an attempt is made to work the starter, this is a sure sign of a poor connection on the battery terminal. To rectify, remove the terminal, clean the inside of the cap and the terminal post thoroughly and reconnect. Check the tightness of the connections at

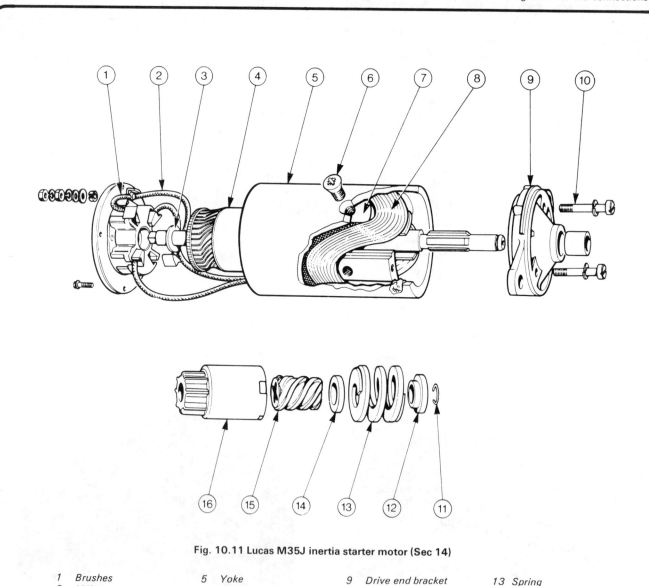

Fig. 10.11 Lucas M35J inertia starter motor (Sec 14)

1 Brushes	5 Yoke	9 Drive end bracket	13 Spring
2 Link	6 Pole screw	10 Screws	14 Washer
3 Thrust washer	7 Pole	11 Circlip	15 Sleeve
4 Armature	8 Field coil	12 Spring cup	16 Barrel and pinion

the relay (solenoid) switch and at the starter motor. Check the wiring for breaks or shorts with a suitable meter.

3   If the wiring is in order then check that the starter motor is operating. To do this, press the rubber covered button (if so equipped) in the centre of the solenoid under the bonnet. If it is working, the starter motor will be heard to click as it tries to rotate. Alternatively, check it with a voltmeter.

4   If the battery is fully charged, the wiring in order, and the solenoid working and the starter motor fails to operate, then it will have to be removed from the car for examination. Before this is done, however, ensure that the starter pinion has not jammed in mesh with the flywheel. Check by turning the square end of the armature shaft with a spanner. This will free the pinion if it is stuck in engagement with the flywheel teeth. On some models the square on the end of the shaft will be covered by a metal cap; this can be prised off.

16 Starter motor (inertia type) – removal and refitting

1   Disconnect the battery earth lead from the negative terminal.

2   Detach the starter motor cable from the terminal on the starter motor endplate.

3   To allow sufficient clearance when withdrawing the starter motor, you will need to support the engine by means of a lifting sling or positioning a suitable jack underneath the sump, so that the engine can be raised just enough to allow the starter motor to be removed. The engine mountings will have to be loosened to enable the engine to be raised the required amount, but do this after the engine is supported. When the engine is being lifted check that associated components such as the fuel line, wiring and exhaust are not distorted or damaged – disconnect where necessary.

4   Unscrew and remove the starter motor securing bolts, then pull it from its location in the clutch housing, supporting it so that the drive components are not damaged.

5   Refitting is a straightforward reversal of the removal procedure. When the starter motor is bolted back in position the engine can be lowered and the mountings retightened.

17 Starter motor (inertia type) – dismantling and reassembly

1   Mark the commutator end bracket in relation to the yoke. Remove the retaining screws and withdraw the end bracket far enough to slide the field brushes from the holder.

2   Slide the thrust washer from the armature.

3   Remove the two screws, and withdraw the drive end bracket complete with armature from the yoke and pole pieces.

4   Using a proprietary tool, compress the drive pinion cushion spring and extract the circlip from the armature.

5   Slide the spring cup, spring, washer, pinion assembly and drive end bracket from the armature.

6   Clean all the components in paraffin and wipe dry. Examine the bushes for wear, and if necessary renew them. Remove the endplate from the commutator end bracket and remove the felt bush. Drive out the bushes using a drift of suitable diameter, but before fitting the new bushes, soak them in clean engine oil at room temperature for 24 hours, or at 100°C (212°F) for 2 hours.

7   Check the length of the brushes, and renew them if they are less than the specified minimum. Note that the field brushes must be soldered to the terminal.

8   Check the continuity of the field windings by connecting a 12 volt test lamp (with 12 watt bulb) and leads between each field brush in turn and the yoke. The bulb will glow if the field windings are good.

9   If the field winding insulation is suspect, remove the rivet securing the field winding wire to the yoke and hold the wire away from the yoke. Repeat the test described in paragraph 8. If the bulb glows, the windings are faulty. If available, use an 110 volt ac supply and 15 watt bulb for this test as this will give more accurate results.

10   Check the armature shaft for distortion, and examine the commutator for excessive scoring, wear and burrs. If necessary, the commutator should be skimmed in a lathe and then polished with fine glasspaper. Make sure that it is not reduced below the specified minimum thickness, and do not undercut the mica insulation.

11   Check the armature windings for good insulation by connecting a test lamp and leads between each commutator segment in turn and the armature shaft; if the bulb glows, the insulation is faulty.

12   Temporarily insert each brush in the brush holder and check that they move freely against the springs.

13   Check the teeth of the drive pinion for wear and chipping and, if necessary, renew the pinion and barrel complete.

14   Reassembly is a reversal of dismantling, but make sure that the yoke is correctly aligned with the end brackets; a notch is provided to locate the drive end bracket. Mount the starter motor in a vice and use jump leads from a battery to test its operation.

18 Starter motor (inertia type) – servicing the drive

1   The starter motor drive is of the outboard type. When the starter motor is operated the pinion moves into engagement with the flywheel gear ring by moving in toward the starter motor.

2   If the engine kicks back, or the pinion fails to engage with the flywheel gear ring when the starter motor is actuated, no undue strain is placed on the armature shaft, as the pinion sleeve disengages from the pinion and turns independently.

3   Whenever the starter motor is removed the drive should be thoroughly washed in paraffin, shaken and a little thin oil applied. Do not over-lubricate or use thick oil, as this may cause the pinion to jam on the shaft.

19 Starter motor (inertia type) – drive removal and refitting

1   The spring is retained by a cup and circlip. The spring must be compressed by using a proprietary compressor (available from most accessory stores) so that the circlip can be extracted from the armature shaft.

2   Once removed, examine the pinion and barrel assembly and renew them if they are worn or chipped.

3   Refitting is a reversal of removal, but ensure that the pinion teeth are toward the armature windings and then lubricate the sliding surfaces with a little thin oil.

20 Starter motor (pre-engaged type) – general description

Three types of pre-engaged starter motor have been fitted to the Escort, these being of either Lucas, Bosch or Nippondenso manufacture. The Nippondenso type is similar in design to the Bosch starter motor and was only fitted between August and October of 1977.

The Bosch 0.7 PS is a four-pole, four-brush motor utilising a series field and a solenoid controlled roller clutch drive. Both the Lucas pre-engaged starter motors are similar in construction to the M35J inertia motor previously described. The drive end bracket on these motors is provided with an additional housing which serves both as a mounting point and a cover for the externally located solenoid.

The method of engagement on the pre-engaged starter is that the drive pinion is brought into mesh with the starter ring gear before the main starter current is applied.

When the ignition is switched on, current flows from the battery to the solenoid which is mounted on the top of the starter motor body. The plunger in the solenoid moves inward so causing a centrally pivoted lever to move in such a manner that the forked end pushes the drive pinion into mesh with the starter ring gear. When the solenoid plunger reaches the end of its travel, it closes an internal contact and full starting current flows to the starter field coils. The armature is then able to rotate the crankshaft so starting the engine.

A special one-way clutch is fitted to the starter drive pinion so that when the engine fires and starts to operate on its own, it does not drive the starter motor.

The brushgear is fully insulated and is made up of four brushes housed in a metal brush box riveted to the commutator end bracket. Small coil springs keep the brushes in contact with the axially moulded commutator.

The field windings are continuously wound with no interconnecting joints, the end of the windings being connected to the brushgear, while the other is connected to the battery through the solenoid contacts.

The operating position of the pivot lever is preset in manufacture and cannot be adjusted. This approach eliminates the need to set the lever to obtain correct operation of the solenoid.

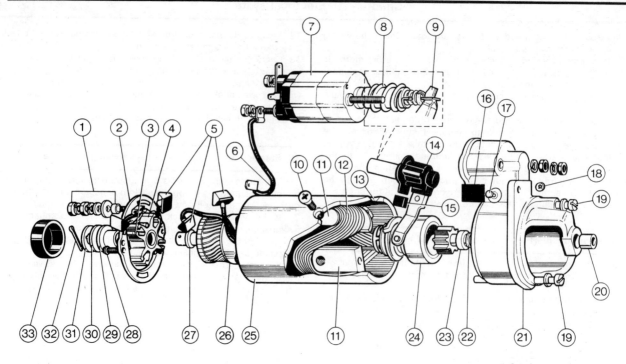

Fig. 10.12 The Lucas M35-J pre-engaged starter motor (Sec 20)

1	Terminal nuts and washers	9	Engagement lever	17	Pivot pin
2	Commutator end plate	10	Pole screw	18	Retaining clip
3	Brush housing	11	Pole shoe	19	Housing retaining screws
4	Brush springs	12	Field coils	20	Bearing bush
5	Brushes	13	Field to earth	21	Drive end housing
6	Connector link, solenoid		connection	22	Jump ring
	to starter	14	Rubber seal	23	Thrust collar
7	Solenoid unit	15	Rubber dust pad	24	Drive assembly
8	Return spring	16	Rubber dust cover	25	Yoke

26	Armature
27	Thrust washer
28	Commutator endplate retaining screws
29	Bearing bush
30	Thrust plate
31	Shim washer
32	Cotter pin
33	Dust cover

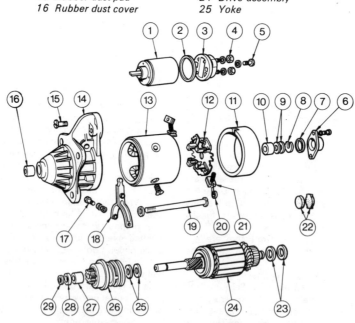

Fig. 10.13 The Bosch pre-engaged starter motor (Sec 20)

1	Solenoid	9	Thrust washer	16	Bush	23	Thrust washers
2	Ring	10	Bearing	17	Pivot pin	24	Armature
3	Terminal block	11	Commutator end housing	18	Pivot lever	25	Rings
4	Nut	12	Brush mounting plate	19	Bolt	26	Drive assembly
5	Screw	13	Yoke	20	Brush spring	27	Bush
6	Cover	14	Drive end housing	21	Brush	28	Stop ring
7	Spacer	15	Screw	22	Pads (lubricating)	29	Stop ring
8	Circlip						

21 Starter motor (pre-engaged type) – removal and refitting

Removal and refitting of this starter motor type is basically as described in Section 16 for the inertia type. The wiring connections are different, however, and these should be noted for location as they are detached from the solenoid connections.

22 Starter motor (pre-engaged type) – dismantling, inspection and reassembly

The following procedures refer to the Lucas type pre-engaged starter motor which is more commonly fitted. The overhaul procedures for the Bosch and Nippondenso starter motors are similar, but references should be made to the respective illustrations (Figs. 10.12 and 10.13) for detail differences in component design.

1   Clamp the starter motor in a vice with soft jaws and remove the plastic cap from the commutator endplate.
2   Remove the retaining clip from the end of the armature shaft and discard the clip. Remove the thrust washer. The armature shaft thrust arrangement on the Nippondenso starter motor is different, and is shown in Fig. 10.14.
3   Disconnect and remove the connecting cable from the end of the solenoid. Remove the two securing nuts and washers and guide the solenoid away from the drive end housing. Unhook the solenoid armature from the actuating lever by moving it upwards and away from the lever.
4   Remove the two drive end housing screws and guide the housing and armature assembly away from the body.
5   Remove the armature from the end housing, unhooking the actuating arm from the pinion assembly (Fig. 10.15). Remove the rubber block and sleeve from the housing.
6   Drive the pivot pin from the end housing, and remove the actuating lever. Discard the pivot pin clip, which will be distorted.
7   If it is necessary to dismantle the starter pinion drive, place the armature between soft faces in a bench vice and using a universal puller draw the jump ring from the armature.
8   Tap down the circlip retaining cover and remove the washer, circlip and cover. The pinion assembly may now be removed.
9   Draw the actuating bush towards the pinion so as to expose the circlip and remove the circlip, bush, spring and large washer. It is very important that the one-way clutch is not gripped in the vice at the point adjacent to the pinion whilst this is being carried out, otherwise the clutch will be damaged.
10   The drive pinion and one-way clutch are serviced as a complete assembly so if one part is worn or damaged a new assembly must be obtained.
11   Remove the four commutator endplate screws and carefully tap the plate free from the body. Withdraw the plate slightly, remove the two field winding brushes and remove the plate.
12   To renew the field winding brushes, their flexible connectors must be cut leaving 0.25 in (7 mm) attached to the field coils. Discard the old brushes. Solder new brushes to the flexible connector stubs. Check that the new brushes move freely in their holders.
13   The main terminal stud and its two brushes are available as a unit. To remove, take off the nut, washer and insulator and push the stud and second insulator through the end plate.
14   If cleaning the commutator with petrol fails to remove all the burnt areas and spots, then press a piece of glasspaper against the commutator and rotate the armature.
15   If the commutator is very badly worn, remove the drivegear, (if still in place on the armature), and mount the armature in a lathe. With the lathe turning at high speed take a very fine cutout of the commutator

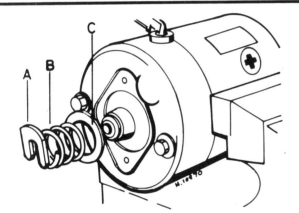

Fig. 10.14 Armature shaft thrust components on the Nippondenso starter motor (Sec 22)

A   C-washer   C   Rubber washer
B   Spring

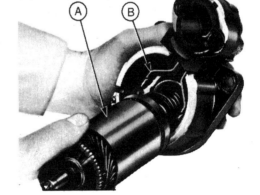

Fig. 10.15 Unhooking the pre-engaged actuating arm (B) from the armature (A) (Sec 22)

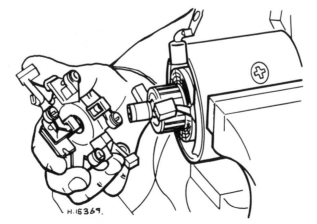

Fig. 10.16 Removing the brush gear mounting assembly on the Nippondenso starter motor (Sec 22)

and finish the surface by polishing with glasspaper. **The commutator thickness must never be less than 0.08 in (2 mm). Do not undercut the mica insulators between the commutator segments.** Only on the Nippondenso starter may the commutator be undercut, by the amount given in the Specifications (refer also to Fig. 10.17).

16 With the starter motor dismantled, test the four field coils for an open-circuit. Connect a 12 volt battery with a 12 volt bulb in one of the leads between the field terminal post and the tapping point of the field coils to which the brushes are connected. An open-circuit is proved by the bulb not lighting.

17 If the bulb lights, it does not necessarily mean that the field coils are in order, as there is a possibility that one of the coils will be earthed to the starter yoke or pole shoes. To check this, remove the lead from the brush connector and place it against a clean portion of the starter yoke. If the bulb lights, then the field coils are earthing. Renewal of the field coils calls for the use of a wheel operated screwdriver, a soldering iron, caulking and riveting operations and is beyond the scope of the majority of owners. The starter yoke should be taken to a reputable electrical engineering works for new field coils to be fitted. Alternatively, purchase an exchange starter motor.

18 If the armature is damaged this will be evident after visual inspection. Look for signs of burning, discoloration, and for conductors that have lifted away from the commutator.

19 With the starter motor stripped down, check the condition of the bushes. They should be renewed when they are sufficiently worn to allow visible side movement of the armature shaft.

20 The old bushes are simply driven out with a suitable drift and the new bushes inserted by the same method. As the bushes are of the phosphor bronze type it is essential that they are allowed to stand in engine oil for at least 24 hours before fitment. If time does not allow, place the bushes in oil at 100°C (212°F) for 2 hours. If the bush in the drive end housing is worn on the Nippondenso starter motor, the complete housing must be renewed.

21 Reassembly is the reverse sequence to dismantling, but the following points should be noted:

(a) When refitting the drive end housing, the peg on the housing should align with the notch in the casing

(b) On the Nippondenso starter motor, align the cut-outs in the brush plate with the field winding loops. When engaging the hook onto the actuating lever in the drive end housing, smear the solenoid armature hook with a lithium-based grease. Check that the armature shaft thrust arrangement is as shown in Fig. 10.14

(c) **New** retaining clips should be fitted to the actuating arm pivot pin and the armature shaft

(d) When fitting the clip to the armature shaft end it should be pressed home firmly to eliminate any endfloat in the shaft

23 Fuses – general

1 The fuse block unit is mounted on the engine compartment bulkhead and access to the fuses is gained after removing the plastic covers (photos). The circuits covered by each fuse are indicated on the plastic cover.

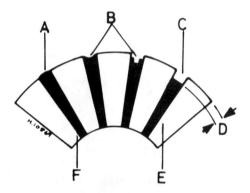

Fig. 10.17 Commutator undercutting diagram for the Nippondenso starter motor (Sec 22)

A *Protruding segment*	D *Depth of undercut*
B *Incorrect profile*	E *Segment*
C *Correct profile*	F *Mica insulation*

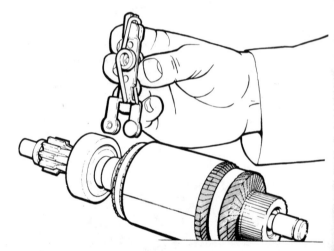

Fig. 10.18 Actuating lever orientation on the Nippondenso starter motor (Sec 22)

23.1a Remove fuse outer plastic cover ...

23.1b ... followed by the inner cover

2 Whenever a fuse has blown the reason for its failure should be established, since it indicates a defect in the circuit it protects.
3 Always renew a fuse with one of an equivalent rating, as given in the Specifications.
4 Apart from those fuses housed in the main fuse block on the bulkhead, the radio has its own in-line fuse which is located between the radio and the ignition switch. To remove this fuse for inspection or renewal simply press the two halves of the fuse holder together whilst simultaneously twisting one half in an anti-clockwise direction. Remove the fuse and refit using the reverse procedure, with the correct value fuse.
5 The heated rear window fuse is located in its operating relay unit which can be found on the underside of the dashboard to the right of the steering column. To inspect or renew this fuse pull free the plastic cover from the back face of the relay unit.
6 Do not be tempted to bypass a persistently blowing fuse with silver foil or wire. Serious damage or fire may result.

24 Direction indicator (flasher) circuit – fault tracing and rectification

1 The flasher unit is in a small metal container located in a spring clip under the dashboard on the cowl side panel. The unit is actuated by the direction indicator switch.
2 If the flasher unit fails to operate, or works very slowly or rapidly, check out the flasher indicator circuit, as detailed below, before assuming there is a fault in the unit itself.

(a) Examine the direction indicator bulbs, front and rear, for broken filaments
(b) If the external flashers are working, but the internal flasher warning light has ceased to function, check the filament in the warning light bulb and fit a new bulb if necessary
(c) If a flasher bulb is sound but does not work, check all the flasher circuit connections with the aid of the wiring diagram
(d) In the event of total indicator failure, check fuse No 6 on the fusebox. It will be fairly obvious if this fuse has blown as it also protects the stop lamps, heater motor and reversing lights
(e) With the ignition switched on, check that the current is reaching the flasher unit by connecting a voltmeter between the positive terminal and earth. If it is found that current is reaching the unit, connect the two flasher unit terminals together and operate the flasher switch. If the flasher warning light comes on, this proves that the flasher unit itself is at fault and must be renewed, as it is not possible to dismantle and repair it

25 Windscreen wiper blades – removal and refitting

1 The wiper blades should be renewed every year or whenever they fail to wipe the screen cleanly.
2 Lift the wiper arm away from the windscreen and remove the old blade by turning it in towards the arm and then disengage the arm from the slot in the blade.
3 To fit a new blade, slide the end of the wiper arm into the slotted spring fastening in the centre of the blade. Push the blade firmly onto the arm until the raised portion of the arm is fully home in the hole in the blade.
4 Some models use a different method of blade attachment. With this type simply lift the small tang at the end of the arm and then withdraw the blade from the arm (photo).

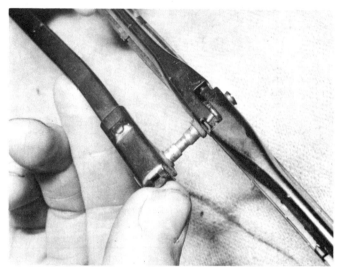

25.4 Alternative wiper blade attachment. Lift tang and remove blade from arm

26 Windscreen wiper arms – removal and refitting

1 Before removing a wiper arm, turn the windscreen wiper switch on and off to ensure the arms are in their normal parked position parallel with the bottom of the windscreen.

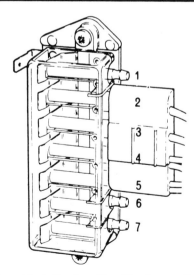

Fig. 10.19 Fuse block. For fuse identification see Specifications (Sec 23)

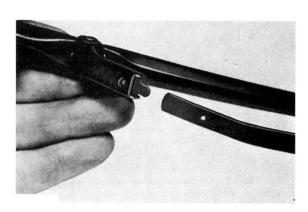

Fig. 10.20 Wiper blade-to-arm connection (Sec 25)

2   To remove an arm lift up the wiper spindle cover to expose the arm retaining nut (photo). Unscrew this nut and detach the washer, then pull the arm off the splined pivot shaft. If the arm proves difficult to remove, a screwdriver with a large blade can be used to lever the wiper arm head off the splines. Care must be taken not to damage the splines.

3   When refitting an arm, position it so it is in the correct relative parked position and then press the arm head onto the splined drive until it is fully home on the splines.

4   Refit the washer and nut and then the spindle cover.

26.2 Lift cover, unscrew nut and withdraw the wiper arm from the splined shaft

27 Windscreen wiper mechanism – fault diagnosis and rectification

1   Should the windscreen wipers fail, or work very slowly, then check the terminals on the motor for loose connections, and make sure that the insulation of the wiring is not cracked or broken – possibly causing a short-circuit. If this is in order, then check the current the motor is taking by connecting an ammeter in the circuit and turning on the wiper switch. Consumption should be between 2.3 and 3.1 amps.

2   If no current is passing through the motor, check that the switch is operating correctly.

3   If the wiper motor takes a very high current, check the wiper blades for freedom of movement. If this is satisfactory, check the gearbox cover and gear assembly for damage.

4   If the motor takes a very low current ensure that the battery is fully charged. Check the brush gear and ensure that the brushes are bearing on the commutator. If not, check the brushes for freedom of movement and, if necessary, renew the brush springs. If the brushes are very worn, they should be replaced with new ones. Check the armature by substitution if this unit is suspect.

28 Windscreen wiper motor – removal and refitting

1   Disconnect the battery by removing the negative earth lead.

2   The wiper motor is accessible from under the facia on the passenger side of the vehicle. Before the wiper motor can be removed the glovebox assembly must first be removed. This is secured by two cross-head screws at the front and a bolt at the rear.

3   Locate the face level vent hose and pull this off the rear of the face level vent stub.

4   Pull the two moulded multi-plug connectors off their respective terminals on the wiper motor end housing.

5   Remove the three bolts and spring washers securing the wiper motor end housing to the wiper motor bracket. **Do not confuse these screws with the bracket retaining screws.**

6   Slightly lower the motor then unscrew the nut securing the linkage to the motor drive link and detach the motor.

7   Refitting is a reversal of the removal procedure.

29 Windscreen wiper linkage – removal and refitting

1   Refer to Section 26 and remove the windscreen wiper arms.

2   With the arms removed carefully prise the plastic covers off the wiper linkage pivot shafts, then remove the nut, washer, spacer and nylon washer from each shaft.

3   Working inside the vehicle, remove the glovebox from the passenger side of the vehicle, then pull the face level vent hose off the face level unit stub.

4   Remove the nut securing the wiper motor linkage assembly to the wiper motor driveshaft.

5   Remove the instrument panel unit, as described in Section 44.

Fig. 10.21 Windscreen wiper motor (Sec 28)

A   Fixing holes
B   Linkage nut
      Speed control terminals

D   Power feed

Fig. 10.22 Withdrawing the wiper motor linkage (Sec 29)

6   Accessible through the instrument cluster aperture, remove the two bolts securing the demister nozzle to the body (photo). Remove the duct, via the instrument cluster aperture, after first pulling the hose off the duct stub.

7   Remove the single bolt supporting the driven side of the wiper linkage and withdraw the linkage through the instrument cluster aperture.

8   Refitting the windscreen wiper linkage is a reversal of the removal sequence. When connecting the linkage to the motor make sure that the tang on the linkage engages with the keyway on the motor driveshaft.

30 Windscreen wiper linkage pivot shaft – removal and refitting

1   Remove the windscreen wiper motor linkage, as described in Section 29.

2   Lever the pivot shaft out of its plastic balljoint. Note that for the pivot shaft at the motor end of the linkage the motor link balljoint must also be disconnected.

3   Using suitable circlip pliers remove the pivot shaft circlip and withdraw the pivot shaft assembly from the linkage.

4   Prise the clip from the end of the pivot shaft and withdraw the shaft from the bush.

5   Assemble the shaft to the bush as shown in Fig. 10.24, then refit the assembly in the reverse sequence to that described above.

31 Windscreen washer pump – removal and refitting

1   The windscreen washer pump is a push-fit on a lug located in a recess in the washer bottle (photo).

2   To remove the pump first pull the loom connector off the plug terminals then pull the washer tube off the pump outlet.

3   Before removing the pump, either remove and drain the washer bottle, or have a drain tray handy to catch the contents of the bottle when the pump is pulled off its location.

4   Refitting of the pump is a reversal of the removal process.

29.6 The demister duct retaining bolts (arrowed)

31.1 The windscreen washer reservoir showing the pump unit and connections

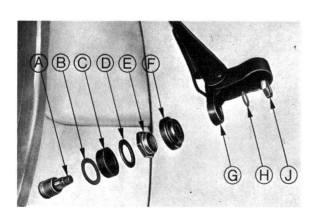

Fig. 10.23 Wiper arm assembly (Sec 29)

A	Spindle	F	Plastic cover
B	Nylon washer	G	Wiper arm
C	Distance piece	H	Washer
D	Washer	J	Nut
E	Nut		

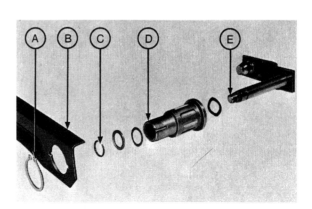

Fig. 10.24 Pivot shaft components (Sec 30)

A	Circlip	D	Bush
B	Linkage	E	Pivot shaft
C	Spring clip		

32 Windscreen washer jets – removal and refitting

1 Working under the bonnet, undo and remove the self-tapping screw securing each jet to the cowl.
2 Pull off the washer hose and lift away the jet.
3 Refitting the jet is a reverse sequence to removal. Adjust the position of the jet before finally tightening the retaining screw (Fig. 10.25).

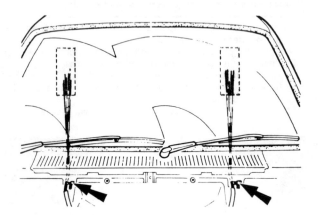

Fig. 10.25 Adjust the windscreen washer jets (Sec 32)

33 Horn – fault diagnosis and rectification

1 If the horn operates weakly or fails to sound at all, check the wiring leading to the horn plug which is located on the body panel next to the horn itself. Also check that the plug is properly pushed home and is in a clean condition, free from corrosion etc.
2 Check that the horn is secure on its mounting (photo) and that there is nothing lying on the horn body.
3 If the fault is not an external one, remove the horn cover and check the leads inside the horn. If these are sound, check the contact breaker contacts. If these are burnt or dirty, clean them with a fine file and wipe all traces of dirt and dust away with a fuel-moistened rag.

34 Headlamp – removal and refitting

Mexico and RS 1800
1 Disconnect the battery by removing the negative earth lead.
2 Remove the radiator grille by removing the twelve retaining screws.
3 Unscrew the cross-headed screws which retain the lamp to the body (photo).
4 From inside the engine compartment disconnect the parking lamp and the multi-plug, then carefully detach the lamp assembly from its location.
5 Refitting is a straightforward reversal of the above procedure. After reassembly, check that the headlamps are correctly aligned, before refitting the radiator grille.

RS 2000
6 Unscrew and remove the two cross-head screws securing the twin headlight unit surround in position (photo) and withdraw the surround (photo).
7 Carefully remove the rubber seal from the headlight unit concerned (photo).
8 Release the headlight unit retaining clips (photos), then withdraw the unit so that the rubber cover can be detached from the rear of the reflector and the headlight and (where applicable) sidelight wires can be disconnected (photo).
9 Refitting is a reversal of the removal procedure. After assembly is complete, check the headlight beam alignment as given in Section 37.

33.2 Horn location

34.3 Remove cross-head screws which secure the headlamp to the body

34.6a Remove the two unit surround screws (arrowed) ...

34.6b ... and remove the surround (RS 2000)

34.7 Remove the rubber seal (RS 2000)

34.8a Detach the lower and ...

34.8b ... upper retaining clips to withdraw the headlight unit (RS 2000)

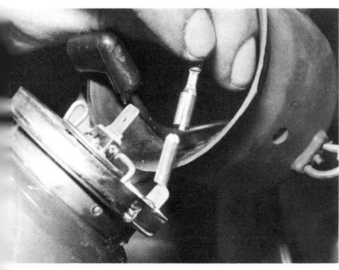

34.8c Disconnect the wires from their connectors (RS 2000)

35 Headlamp lens and reflector (Mexico and RS 1800) – removal and refitting

1   Disconnect the battery by removing the negative earth lead.
2   Remove the radiator grille by removing the twelve retaining screws.
3   Remove the single cross-head screw located at the lower inboard edge of the lens rim. Take care not to confuse this screw with either of the headlamp adjusting screws.
4   Carefully turn the lens and reflector body in an anti-clockwise direction to disengage the lens retaining slots from the headlamp adjusting screws. Do not attempt to turn these screws as this will alter the adjustment of the headlamp.
5   Lift the unit clear of the body, then remove the parking lamp bulb from its location adjacent to the headlamp bulb holder. To remove the bulb holder prise the retaining clip off its location on the holder and carefully detach the holder complete with bulb.
6   Refitting is a straightforward reversal of the above procedure. After reassembly check that the headlamps are correctly aligned and refit the radiator grille.

36 Headlamp – bulb renewal

1   Remove the headlamp lens and reflector assembly, as described in Section 34 (RS 2000) or Section 35 for the Mexico and RS 1800.
2   On Mexico and RS 1800 models, release the bulb holder retaining

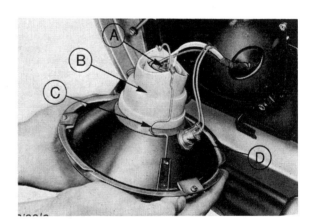

Fig. 10.26 Headlamp lens and reflector removal (Mexico/RS 1800) (Sec 35)

A   Multi-plug   C   Spring clip
B   Plastic cap   D   Parking lamp

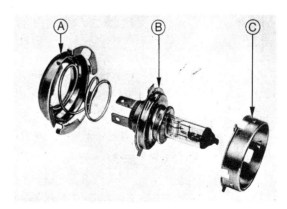

Fig. 10.27 Halogen bulb assembly – Mexico and RS 1800 (Sec 36)

A   Bulb retaining plate   C   Location plate
B   Bulb

36.3a Unhook the bulb retaining clip (arrowed) ...

36.3b ... and withdraw the bulb (RS 2000)

clip and push the plastic bulb holder cover up the loom wires to give access to the rubber multi-plug connection. Disconnect this plug from the bulb terminals, then turn the bulb retaining plate in an anticlockwise direction to disengage the lugs. Lift the retaining plate and spring clear of the bulb, then lift the bulb from the reflector.

3   On the RS 2000 model, release the bulb retaining clip (photo) and then simply pull the bulb straight out of its holder (photo).

4   When handling halogen bulbs it is important that the glass of the bulb is not touched. If the glass is inadvertently handled it **must** be wiped clean with methylated spirits **before** the lamps are switched on. Failure to observe this precaution will result in a blown bulb.

5   Refitting is a straightforward reversal of the above procedure. After reassembly check that the headlamps are correctly aligned (before refitting the radiator grille on the Mexico and RS 1800).

37 Headlights – beam alignment

The correct headlight beam alignment is of utmost importance both for your safety and that of other motorists. Accurate alignment checks and adjustments can only be carried out using specialised optical alignment equipment such as that used by garages.

A basic check and, if necessary, adjustment can be carried out using the following method, but bear in mind that this is for a normal Escort, equipped with standard suspension and tyres (set at the specified pressures). Any modifications to the standard suspension heights which affect the free standing height of the bodywork must therefore be taken into consideration.

Mexico and RS 1800

1   Position the car on level ground 33 ft (10 m) in front of a dark wall or board marked off as shown in Fig. 10.28. The wall or board must be at right-angles to the car centre-line.

2   Switch the headlamps to *dipped* beam.

3   Cover the right-hand headlamp and, by carefully adjusting the horizontal adjusting screws, align the lamp so that the intersection of the horizontal and angled light pattern coincides with the vertical line on the aiming board.

4   Similarly adjust the vertical screw (photo) so that the light/dark intersection of the beam pattern coincides with the 15° dotted line on the aiming board (see line 'B', inset of Fig. 10.28).

5   Cover the left-hand headlamp and adjust the right-hand lamp horizontal and vertical alignment in the same way as for the left-hand lamp. Switch off the headlamps.

RS 2000

6   This model has four headlamp units, the outer units functioning on both main and dipped beam, the inner units on main beam only.

7   Alignment of the outer units is achieved in the same way as described above for the Mexico and RS 1800 models, except that only one adjusting screw is fitted.

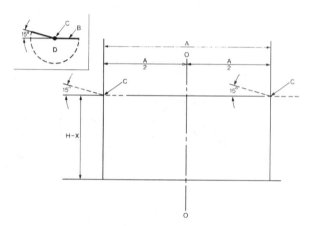

Fig. 10.28 Headlamp alignment (Sec 37)

A	=	distance between headlamp centres	
B	=	light/dark boundary	
C	=	dipped beam centre	
D	=	dipped beam pattern	

H = height from ground to lamp centres (X = 8.0 in, 200 mm)

0-0 = vehicle centre line

37.4 Headlamp vertical adjusting screw (Mexico and RS 1800)

37.8 Headlamp adjusting screw (RS 2000)

38.2 Pull sidelight bulb from headlamp reflector

39.4 Removing the indicator lamp unit retaining screws

8   Alignment of the inner units may be carried out in a similar fashion, but remember to make additional aiming marks at the appropriate positons for the new headlamp centres. With main beam switched on aim the headlights, using the adjusting screw (photo), so that the beam is approximately horizontal.

38 Front sidelight bulb – removal and refitting

1   Remove the headlamp lens and reflector assembly as described in Section 34 or 35, as applicable.
2   Pull the sidelight bulb assembly from its location in the headlight body (photo).
3   Remove the bulb by depressing, twisting and withdrawing from the holder.
4   Refitting the sidelight bulb and holder is the reverse sequence to removal. Make sure the holder fits tightly against the reflector body to prevent water ingress.

39 Front indicator – bulb and unit removal and refitting

Bulb renewal
1   Undo and remove the two cross-head screws securing the lens to the lamp body and lift away the lens (Fig. 10.29).
2   Remove the bulb by depressing, twisting and withdrawing from the holder.

3   Refitting the bulb and lens is the reverse sequence to removal. Make sure that the lens gasket is correctly seated to prevent dirt or water ingress.

Unit removal
4   Unscrew and remove the two screws securing the light unit to the bumper (photo).
5   From inside the engine compartment disconnect the lamp wires from the engine compartment loom multi-plug and detach the lamp assembly, complete with wire, from the front bumper.
6   Refitting the front direction indicator lamp assembly is the reverse sequence to removal. Check the light for satisfactory operation on completion.

40 Auxiliary lamps – general

Bulb renewal
1   Undo and remove the cross-head screw on the lens rim and draw the lens assembly forward off the lamp body.
2   Disconnect the bulb wire from the loom snap connector.
3   Release the spring clip and withdraw the bulb from the reflector body (Fig. 10.30).
4   Refitting the bulb and lens assembly is the reverse sequence to removal. Make sure that the cut-out at the top of the reflector body engages with the lug on the lamp body.

Fig. 10.29 Indicator lamp lens removed (front) for bulb renewal (Sec 39)

Fig. 10.30 Auxiliary lamp bulb renewal (Sec 40)

A   Bulb   C   Earth wire
B   Spring clip   D   Feed wire

Lamp unit removal

5 Disconnect the battery, for safety reasons.

6 Remove the nut and washer assembly securing the lamp to its mounting bracket and lift the lamp off the bracket.

7 Detach the lamp lead from the main wiring loom and completely remove the lamp assembly.

8 Refitting the auxiliary lamp is the reverse sequence to its removal. Realign the beam as described below.

Auxiliary lamp beam alignment

9 It is always advisable to have the auxiliary lamps aligned using special optical beam setting equipment, but if this is not available the following procedure may be used.

10 Check the tyre pressures and adjust as necessary. Remove any luggage from the boot or load space and place the car on level ground, then bounce the front of the vehicle to ensure that the suspension has settled.

11 Locate a white board marked as shown in Fig. 10.31 10 ft (3 m) from the front of the vehicle at 90° to the car axis.

12 Cover the headlamps and the second auxiliary lamp to prevent glare whilst carrying out the adjustment.

13 Adjust the beam so that the centre of brightest illumination lies at the intersection of the horizontal and vertical dividing lines on the board.

14 Adjust the second auxiliary lamp in a similar manner to the first one.

---

41 Rear combination lights – bulb and unit removal and refitting

Bulb renewal

1 The rear lamp assembly incorporates the following bulbs: reverse, rear/stop and direction indicator.

2 Undo and remove the cross-head screws securing the lens to the lamp body, and lift away the lens (photo).

3 The relevant bulb is removed by depressing, turning anti-clockwise and withdrawing from the holder.

4 Refitting a bulb and lens is a reversal of the removal process. Ensure that the small nylon washers are correctly located under the screw heads and that the screws are not overtightened, or cracking of the lens may result.

Light unit removal

5 Working inside the boot compartment remove the spare wheel and the plastic caps from the lamp securing stud threads (photo).

Left-hand lamp

6 Undo and remove the two nuts and washers, pull the lamp assembly off the body and remove the lamp leads after first noting the terminal connection.

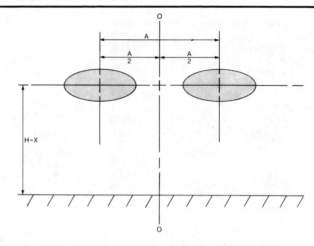

Fig. 10.31 Auxiliary lamp alignment (Sec 40)

A   Distance between lamp centres

H   Height from ground to lamp centres

OO   Vehicle centre-line

Fig. 10.32 Rear combination light outer retaining screw (arrowed) on the right-hand unit (Sec 41)

Right-hand lamp

7 Undo and remove the cross-head screws securing the lamp lens to the lamp body and detach the lens.

8 Remove the single cross-head screw exposed by the removal of the lamp lens, from its location in the reflector body (Fig. 10.32) and the washer securing the lamp to the vehicle body.

41.2 Remove rear combination light lens for access to bulbs

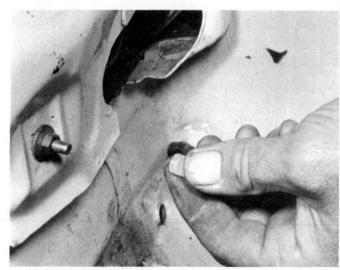

41.5 Detach plastic cap from thread of rear combinaton light securing stud in boot

9   Pull the lamp assembly rearwards, off the body and disconnect the lamp leads, after first making a note of their respective positions.

Light unit refitting
10   Refitting either lamp is a reversal of the removal procedure. Ensure that the leads are correctly and securely connected (Fig. 10.33). Check all lights on completion for satisfactory operation.

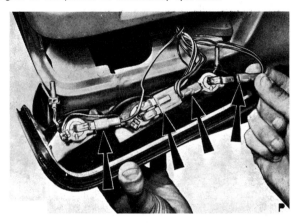

Fig. 10.33 Check that the lead connections (arrowed) are secure before refitting the combination light unit (Sec 41)

42 Rear number plate light bulb – removal and refitting

1   Depress the spring clips on each end of the lamp and carefully prise the lamp out of the bumper (photo).
2   From inside the boot disconnect the lamp wires.
3   Remove the bulb cover and lens from the lamp body by disengaging the cover from the lugs on the lamp body (photo).
4   Remove the bulb by depressing, turning it anti-clockwise and withdrawing from the body.
5   Refitting the bulb is the reverse sequence to removal.
6   Reassemble the lens to the body and press it back into position in the bumper, then check that the light operates.

43 Interior bulbs – removal and refitting

Interior light bulb
1   Carefully prise the lamp assembly from its location in the roof panel (photo).
2   Disconnect the leads to the lamp and remove the bulb from its holder.
3   Refitting the bulb and lamp is a reversal of removal.

Heated rear window warning light bulb
4   Place a wad of padding below the switch and, using a thin bladed screwdriver, carefully prise the switch from its location in the heater cover panel.
5   The bulb holder is attached to the lower of the two sets of leads entering the rear of the switch. Pull the holder out of its location and remove the bulb (Fig. 10.34).

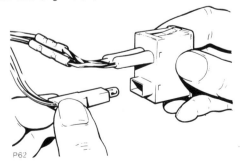

Fig. 10.34 Heated rear window warning light bulb renewal (Sec 43)

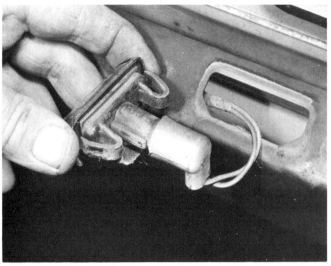

42.1 Remove number plate lamp unit from the rear bumper

42.3 Remove lens for bulb inspection/renewal

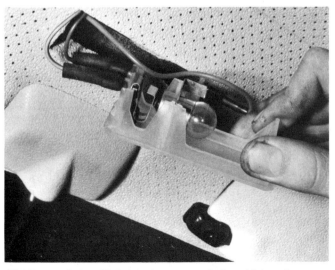

43.1 Removal of roof light lens for access to bulb and light unit

6   Refitting the bulb and switch is the reverse of the removal procedure.

Hazard warning light bulb

7   The removal procedure for this bulb is identical to that described above for the heated rear window bulb.

Boot light

8   Grip and pull the lens from the rubber holder (photo). The bulb can then be removed for renewal. Refit the lens ensuring that it is fully located.

---

44   Instrument panel unit – removal and refitting

---

1   Disconnect the battery earth lead.
2   Remove the two screws holding the edge of the insulator pad to the lower edge of the instrument panel and reach up behind the cluster to disengage the speedometer cable, by depressing the cable-to-speedometer connector on its serrated edge (Fig. 10.36).
3   Remove the upper half of the steering column shroud.
4   Remove the four instrument panel retaining screws (photo), pull the cluster away from the dash location and disconnect the wiring

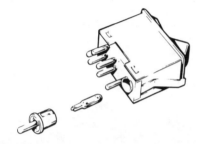

Fig. 10.35 Hazard flasher warning light bulb and holder removed from rear of switch (Sec 43)

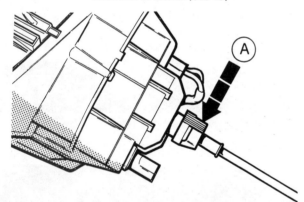

Fig. 10.36 Depress speedometer cable connector at point indicated (A) (Sec 44)

loom connectors and the oil pressure line connection. **Note:** *On removal of the instrument cluster take care not to damage the printed circuits.*
5   Refitting the instrument cluster is a reversal of the removal sequence. Check the gauges, warning lights and instruments at the earliest opportunity.

---

45   Instrument panel glass – removal and refitting

---

1   Remove the instrument panel assembly, as described in Section 44.
2   Undo and remove the screws securing the instrument cluster bezel to the panel body, detach the bezel and lift away the panel glass.
3   Refitting the instrument panel glass is the reverse of its removal. Do not forget to wipe off all traces of dust before refitting.

---

46   Instrument voltage regulator – removal and refitting

---

1   Refer to Section 44 and remove the instrument panel.
2   Undo and remove the screw that secures the voltage regulator to the rear of the instrument panel (photo) and detach the regulator and, where fitted, the radio suppressor filter.
3   Refitting the regulator is a reversal of the removal sequence.

---

47   Instrument panel bulbs – removal and refitting

---

1   Refer to Section 44 and remove the instrument panel.
2   Carefully pull the relevant bulb holder from its location on the rear of the cluster (photo) and remove the bulb.
3   Refitting the bulb and instrument panel is the reverse sequence to removal.

---

48   Speedometer head – removal and refitting

---

1   Remove the instrument panel assembly, as described in Section 44.
2   Pull the two head illuminating bulb holders from their location, locally remove the loom and set the loom and holders to one side, clear of the working area.
3   Undo and remove the four screws securing the speedometer head housing to the instrument panel body and lift away the housing complete with the head (Fig. 10.37).
4   Undo and remove the two screws securing the head to the head housing and detach the head.
5   Refitting the speedometer head is the reverse of its removal.

---

49   Speedometer inner and outer cables – removal and refitting

---

1   Chock the rear wheels, jack up the front end of the vehicle and support it on firmly based stands.
2   Locate the cable entry in the side of the gearbox, and, using a pair

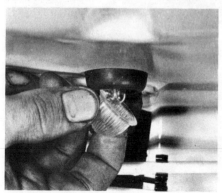

43.8 Removal of the boot light lens for bulb inspection/renewal

44.4 Instrument panel retaining screw locations (arrowed)

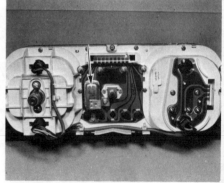

46.2 Rear view of the instrument panel. Voltage regulator is arrowed

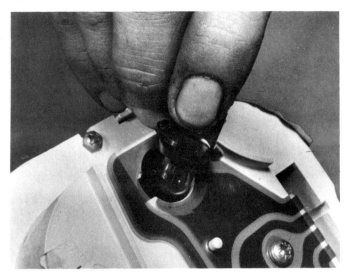

47.2 Instrument panel light removal

Fig. 10.37 Speedometer removal from instrument panel (Sec 48)

of circlip pliers, remove the retaining circlip and pull the cable from the gearbox.
3   Unclip the cable from its clips along the side-members and underbody.
4   From inside the vehicle removal the sound insulating cover sufficiently to gain access to the rear of the instrument panel. Press down the grooved section of the cable clip to disengage the locking catch; the cable can then be pulled from the speedometer head.
5   The cable can then be pulled through the engine compartment rear bulkhead and into the engine compartment.
6   Refitting the cable is a reversal of the removal procedure. Avoid making sharp bends or kinks in the cable.

50 Tachometer – removal and refitting

1   Remove the instrument panel assembly, as described in Section 44.
2   Remove the illuminating bulb holder and locally remove the bulb holder wiring loom.
3   Undo and remove the four screws securing the tachometer housing to the instrument panel body and lift the housing, complete with tachometer off the body.
4   Undo and remove the two screws and three terminal nuts retaining the tachometer to the housing and detach the tachometer.
5   Refitting of the tachometer is a reversal of the removal procedure.

51 Fuel gauge – removal and refitting

1   Remove the instrument panel and then remove the speedometer head and tachometer, as described in Sections 48 and 50 respectively.

2   Remove the single screw securing the voltage regulator and lift the regulator off the cluster body.
3   Undo and remove the four screws securing the gauge housing to the panel body and lift the housing complete with gauges off the body.
4   Remove the two nuts securing the gauge studs to the housing and withdraw the gauge from the housing.
5   Refitting is a reversal of the removal procedure.

52 Temperature gauge – removal and refitting

The procedure for removing and refitting the temperature gauge is identical to that described in Section 51 for the fuel gauge.

53 Oil pressure gauge – removal and refitting

The procedure for removing and refitting the oil pressure gauge is similar to that given in Section 51 for the removal/refitting of the fuel gauge.

54 Instrument panel printed circuit – removal and refitting

1   Refer to Section 44 and remove the instrument panel.
2   With the cluster removed and working on the rear face of the panel, unclip the loom from the lower edge of the panel and pull the speedometer and tachometer bulb holders from their locations in the rear of these instruments.
3   Undo and remove the terminal nuts from their locations on the rear of the tachometer, then undo the single retaining screw and unclip and detach the printed circuit from the rear of the tachometer.
4   Remove the tachometer, as detailed in Section 50.
5   Remove the speedometer head, as detailed in Section 48.
6   Remove the single screw securing the instrument voltage regulator and lift the regulator off the panel. Pull the five remaining bulb holders from their locations then unscrew and remove the remaining four terminal nuts and detach the printed circuit.
7   Refitting of the printed circuit is a reversal of the removal procedure.

55 Clock – removal and refitting

1   Disconnect the battery earth lead.
2   Remove the two glovebox/clock housing securing screws (one each side – photo) and partially withdraw the glovebox to enable the wiring connection to the clock rear face to be detached. The clock can then be detached from the panel and withdrawn.
3   Refit in the reverse order to removal and reset the clock.

55.2 Clock and glovebox right-hand retaining screw

56 Cigarette lighter – removal and refitting

1   Disconnect the battery earth lead.
2   The cigarette lighter is housed in the central switch panel and to gain access for its removal the panel must first be removed. On the RS 1800 and RS 2000 models this will entail the removal of the radio and/or centre console, in which case refer also to Chapter 12 for further details.
3   Undo and remove the four screws securing the upper edge of the switch cover panel (photo) and the two screws securing the lower edge and pull the cover rearwards off the dash panel.
4   Pull the element out of the cigarette lighter body and the wiring loom off the rear of the body.
5   Push the locking collar and integral bulb holder in against spring tension and then turn anti-clockwise to disengage the locking tangs. Withdraw the body and plastic collar from the aperture in the panel.
6   Refitting of the cigarette lighter and cover panel is a reversal of the removal procedure.

57 Ignition switch – removal and refitting

1   For safety reasons, disconnect the battery.
2   Remove the steering column shrouds then insert the ignition key and turn it to the accessory position 'I'.
3   Locate the small hole in the switch perimeter and insert a suitable small diameter tool to depress the lock spring, at the same time pulling the key and cylinder away from the housing. It may be necessary to turn the key slightly in both directions while removing the cylinder.
4   The cylinder can be removed from the barrel by first ensuring that the key is fully entered. Then carefully remove the retaining circlip and

withdraw the key 5 mm (0.2 in); the barrel can now be separated from the cylinder.
5   Reassembling and refitting the switch is a reversal of the removal procedure, but make sure that the barrel is refitted to the cylinder in its original position. Turn the key to the accessory position '1' in order to fit the retaining circlip. When the assembly is refitted, check its operation in all the positions before finally reconnecting the battery negative lead.

56.3 Switch panel upper securing screw locations (arrowed)

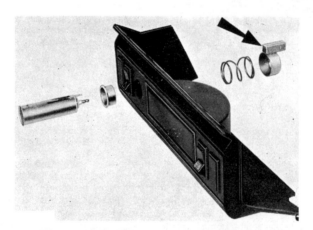

Fig. 10.38 Cigarette lighter components – the lock collar is arrowed (Sec 56)

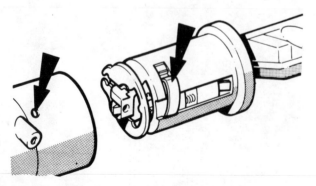

Fig. 10.39 Location of the ignition switch cylinder retaining spring (Sec 57)

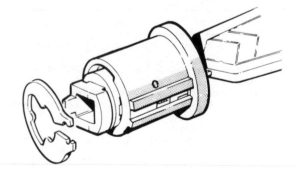

Fig. 10.40 Fitting the ignition switch barrel retaining circlip (Sec 57)

58 Light switch – removal and refitting

1   Disconnect the battery earth lead.
2   Unscrew and remove the three lower column shroud retaining screws and then detach the lower and upper shrouds.
3   Pull the two multi-plugs off the switch then undo and remove the two bolts securing the switch (photo) and lift the switch off the column.
4   Refitting of the light switch is a reversal of the removal procedure. Check the operation of the lights on completion.

59 Direction indicator switch – removal and refitting

The removal and installation of the direction indicator switch is identical to that described in Section 58 for the light switch.

60 Switches (general) – removal and refitting

Whenever removing any of the switches named below, first detach the battery earth lead for safety reasons.

Courtesy light switch
1   Ease the switch from the door pillar and detach the wiring loom.
2   Refitting the switch is the reverse sequence to removal.

Heated rear window (HRW) switch
3   Place a wad of padding below the switch and using a thin bladed screwdriver, carefully prise the switch from its location in the heater cover panel. The bulb at the rear of the switch can then be renewed, if necessary.
4   Disconnect the leads from the rear of the switch.
5   Refitting the HRW switch is a reversal of the removal procedure.

Hazard (emergency) flasher switch
6   The removal and refitting of this switch is identical to that given above for the heated rear window switch.

Heater motor switch
7   Remove the heater control assembly, as described in Chapter 12.
8   From the rear of the control assembly undo and remove the two screws securing the switch and lift the switch off the control panel.
9   Refitting the switch is the reverse sequence to removal.

58.3 Column switches showing the two securing bolts (arrowed)

Reversing light switch
10   Jack up the front of the car and support it on axle stands. Disconnect the battery earth lead.
11   Locate the switch on the gearbox extension housing and disconnect the wiring plug.
12   Unscrew and remove the switch.
13   Refitting is a reversal of removal, but make sure that the wire is well clear of the exhaust and the gearbox.

61 Auxiliary lamp relay – removal and refitting

1   The auxiliary lamp relay is located on the wing apron adjacent to the battery. To remove the relay pull off the multi-plug, then undo and remove the two cross-head screws securing the relay to the body.
2   Refitting is a reversal of removal.

62 Heated rear window relay – removal and refitting

1   The heated rear window relay is located on the underside of the instrument panel adjacent to the steering column. To remove the relay

Fig. 10.41 The heater motor switch (Sec 60)

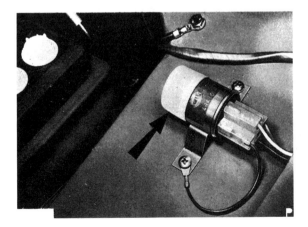

Fig. 10.42 Auxiliary lamp relay unit (arrowed) (Sec 61)

pull off the multi-plug, then undo and remove the two cross-head screws securing the relay to the body.
2   Refitting is a reversal of removal.

63 Direction indicator relay – removal and refitting

1   Disconnect the battery, and remove the instrument panel assembly, as detailed in Section 44.
2   Through the instrument panel aperture in the instrument panel, unclip the direction indicator relay from its location on the steering column bracket. Disconnect the multi-plug from the relay and remove the relay from the vehicle.
3   Refitting the relay is a reversal of the removal procedure.

64 Radio – removal and refitting

Without centre console
1   Open the bonnet and disconnect the battery.
2   Remove the four screws and flat washers, two each side, securing the radio receiver surround to the radio bracket and detach the surround.
3   Pull the radio control knobs off the switch stalks and remove the nut and washer assemblies securing each stalk to the radio bracket.
4   Undo and remove the single screw securing the rear of the receiver to the bracket, then lower the receiver off the bracket before disconnecting the aerial, earth, speaker, and supply leads. Remove the receiver from the vehicle.
5   Refitting of the radio receiver is a reversal of the removal process. However, when finally installed the receiver must be tuned to the aerial. To do this first select a weak medium wave station, turn the volume to maximum and, using a small electrical screwdriver turn the aerial screw (located in the top RH corner of the front face of the receiver) a half turn in either direction until maximum volume is obtained.

With centre console
6   Follow the procedure given in paragraphs 1 and 3.
7   The radio mounting plate is held in the radio aperture by two pop rivets. These must now be drilled out and the mounting plate removed.
8   Once the mounting plate has been removed, the radio can be withdrawn from the radio aperture and the speaker, aerial, earth and power supply leads disconnected from the receiver.
9   Refitting is the reversal of the removal procedure, not forgetting to tune the aerial, as described in paragraph 5.

65 Radio loudspeaker – removal and refitting

1   Open the bonnet and disconnect the battery.
2   Remove the instrument panel as described in Section 44.

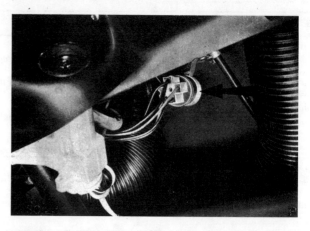

Fig. 10.43 The heated rear window relay unit (arrowed) (Sec 62)

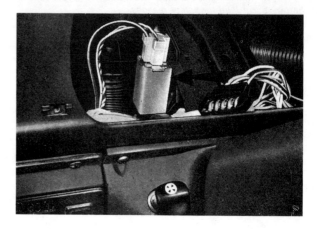

Fig. 10.44 The direction indicator relay unit (arrowed) (Sec 63)

3   Working through the instrument panel aperture, disconnect the loudspeaker leads from the rear of the receiver.
4   Using a suitable cranked screwdriver, remove the two loudspeaker securing screws, then remove the loudspeaker via the instrument panel aperture.
5   If necessary, detach the loudspeaker mounting plate.
6   Refitting the loudspeaker is a reversal of the removal procedure.

66 Fault diagnosis – electrical system

Symptom	Reason(s)
Starter motor fails to turn engine	Battery discharged Battery defective internally Battery terminal leads loose or earth lead not securely attached to body Loose or broken connections in starter motor circuit Starter motor switch or solenoid faulty Starter motor pinion jammed in mesh with flywheel gear ring Starter brushes badly worn, sticking, or brush wires loose Commutator dirty, worn, or burnt Starter motor armature faulty Field coils earthed
Starter motor turns engine very slowly	Battery in discharged condition Starter brushes badly worn, sticking, or brush wires loose Loose wires in starter motor circuit
Starter motor operates without turning engine	Starter motor pinion sticking on the screwed sleeve Dirt or oil on drivegear Pinion or flywheel gear teeth broken or worn
Starter motor noisy or excessively rough engagement	Lack of attention or mechanical damage Pinion or flywheel gear teeth broken or worn Starter drive main spring broken Starter motor retaining bolts loose
Battery will not hold charge for more than a few days	Wear or damage Battery defective internally Electrolyte level too low or electrolyte too weak due to leakage Plate separators no longer fully effective Battery plates severely sulphated
Insufficient current flow to keep battery charged	Fan/alternator belt slipping Battery terminal connections loose or corroded Alternator not charging properly Short in lighting circuit causing continual battery drain Regulator unit not working correctly
Ignition light fails to go out, battery runs flat in a few days	Alternator not charging Fanbelt loose and slipping, or broken Brushes worn, sticking, broken, or dirty Brush springs weak or broken
Regulator or cut-out fails to work correctly	Regulator incorrectly set Cut-out incorrectly set Open circuit in wiring of cut-out and regulator unit
Fuel gauge gives no reading	Fuel tank empty Electric cable between tank sender unit and gauge earthed or loose Fuel gauge case not earthed Fuel gauge supply cable interrupted Fuel gauge unit broken
Fuel gauge registers full all the time	Electric cable between tank unit and gauge broken or disconnected
Horn operates all the time	Horn push either earthed or stuck down Horn cable to horn push earthed
Horn fails to operate	Blown fuse Cable or cable connection loose, broken or disconnected Horn has an internal fault
Horn emits intermittent or unsatisfactory noise	Cable connections loose Horn incorrectly adjusted
Lights do not come on	If engine not running, battery discharged Light bulb filament burnt out or bulbs broken Wire connections loose, disconnected or broken Light switch shorting or otherwise faulty
Lights come on but fade out	If engine not running battery discharged

Symptom	Reason(s)
Lights give very poor illumination	Lamp glasses dirty Reflector tarnished or dirty Lamps badly out of adjustment Incorrect bulb with too low wattage fitted Existing bulbs old and badly discoloured Electrical wiring too thin not allowing full current to pass
Lights work erratically - flashing on and off, especially over bumps	Battery terminals or earth connection loose Lights not earthing properly Contacts in light switch faulty
Wiper motor fails to work	Blown fuse Wire connections loose, disconnected, or broken Brushes badly worn Armature worn or faulty Field coils faulty
Wiper motor works very slowly and takes excessive current	Commutator dirty, greasy, or burnt Drive to wheelboxes too bent or unlubricated Wheelbox spindle binding or damaged Armature bearings dry or unaligned

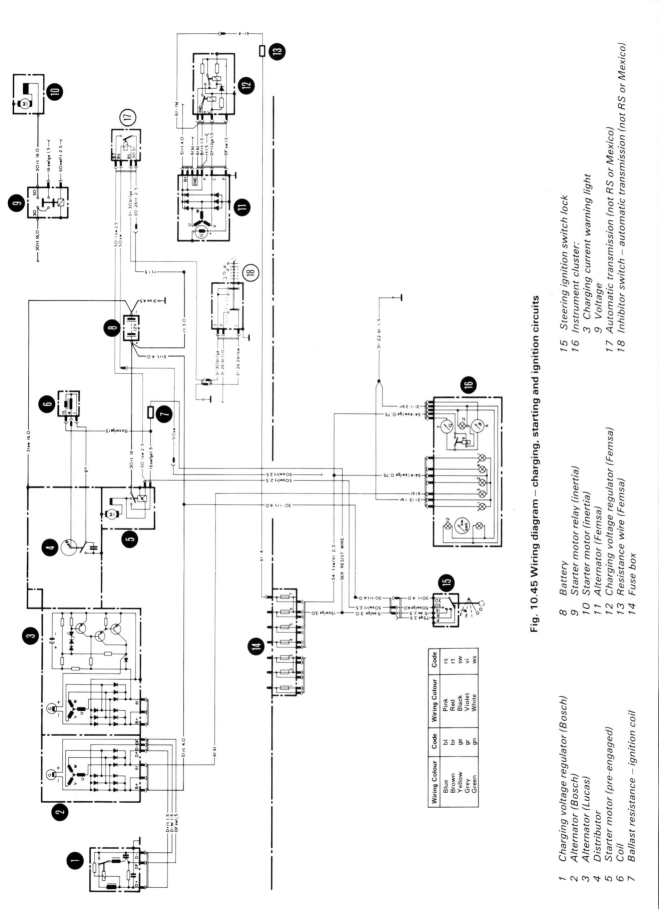

Fig. 10.45 Wiring diagram – charging, starting and ignition circuits

Wiring Colour	Code	Wiring Colour	Code
Blue	bl	Pink	rs
Brown	br	Red	rt
Yellow	ge	Black	sw
Grey	gr	Violet	vi
Green	gn	White	ws

1   Charging voltage regulator (Bosch)
2   Alternator (Bosch)
3   Alternator (Lucas)
4   Distributor
5   Starter motor (pre-engaged)
6   Coil
7   Ballast resistance – ignition coil

8   Battery
9   Starter motor relay (inertia)
10   Starter motor (inertia)
11   Alternator (Femsa)
12   Charging voltage regulator (Femsa)
13   Resistance wire (Femsa)
14   Fuse box

15   Steering ignition switch lock
16   Instrument cluster:
  3   Charging current warning light
  9   Voltage
17   Automatic transmission (not RS or Mexico)
18   Inhibitor switch – automatic transmission (not RS or Mexico)

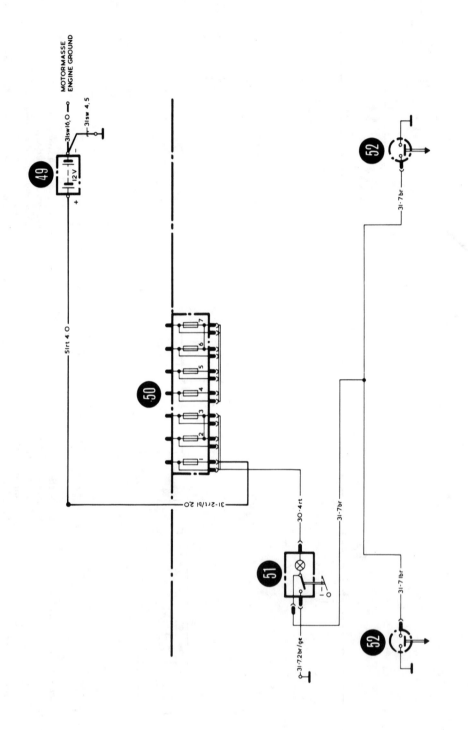

Fig. 10.46 Wiring diagram – interior lights

49 Battery

50 Fuse box

51 Interior lamp

52 Courtesy light switch

For wiring colour code refer to Fig. 10.45

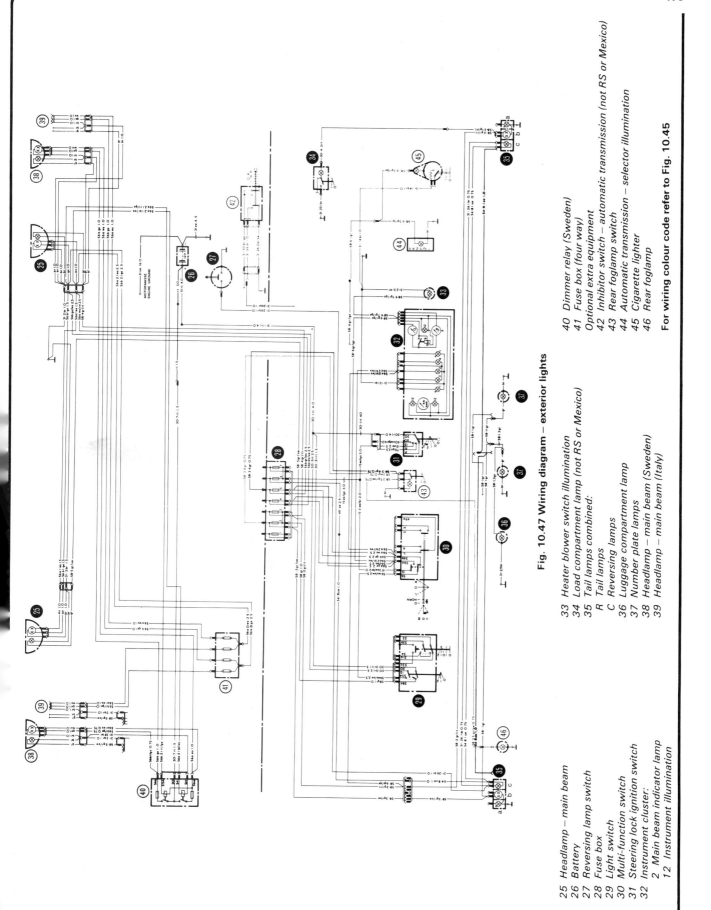

Fig. 10.47 Wiring diagram – exterior lights

25 Headlamp – main beam
26 Battery
27 Reversing lamp switch
28 Fuse box
29 Light switch
30 Multi-function switch
31 Steering lock ignition switch
32 Instrument cluster:
  2 Main beam indicator lamp
  12 Instrument illumination
33 Heater blower switch illumination
34 Load compartment lamp (not RS or Mexico)
35 Tail lamps combined:
  R Tail lamps
  C Reversing lamps
36 Luggage compartment lamp
37 Number plate lamps
38 Headlamp – main beam (Sweden)
39 Headlamp – main beam (Italy)
40 Dimmer relay (Sweden)
41 Fuse box (four way)
Optional extra equipment
42 Inhibitor switch – automatic transmission (not RS or Mexico)
43 Rear foglamp switch
44 Automatic transmission – selector illumination
45 Cigarette lighter
46 Rear foglamp

For wiring colour code refer to Fig. 10.45

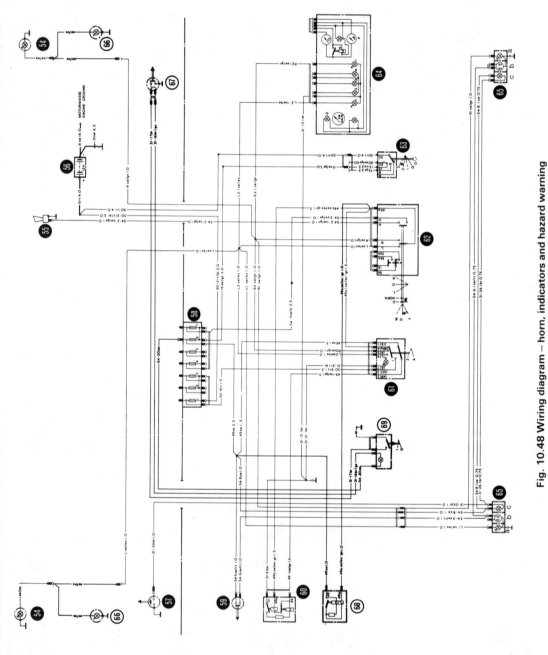

Fig. 10.48 Wiring diagram – horn, indicators and hazard warning lights

54 Flasher lamps (front)
55 Horn
56 Battery
57 Reversing lamp switch
58 Fuse box

59 Stop-light switch
60 Flasher unit
61 Hazard flasher switch
62 Multi-function switch
63 Steering lock ignition switch

64 Instrument cluster:
    1 Flasher warning light (green)
65 Combined tail lamp:
    a Flasher lamps
    b Stop-lights
    c Reversing lamps

66 Side repeater flashers lamps
67 Dual circuit brake warning system switch
68 Flasher unit (without hazard flasher system)
69 Dual circuit brake warning system control switch

For wiring colour code refer to Fig. 10.45

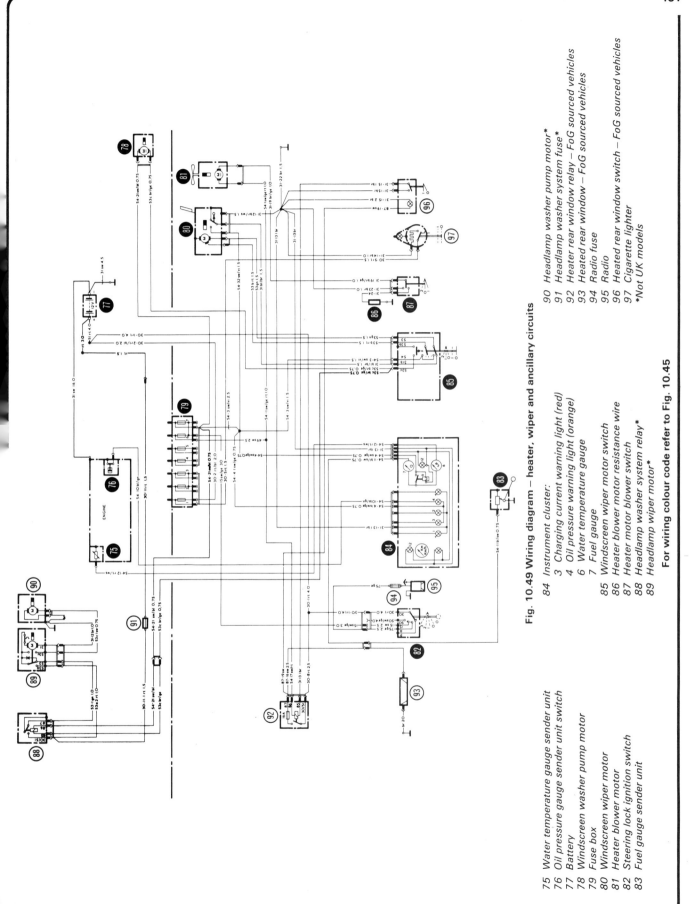

Fig. 10.49 Wiring diagram — heater, wiper and ancillary circuits

75 Water temperature gauge sender unit
76 Oil pressure gauge sender unit switch
77 Battery
78 Windscreen washer pump motor
79 Fuse box
80 Windscreen wiper motor
81 Heater blower motor
82 Steering lock ignition switch
83 Fuel gauge sender unit

84 Instrument cluster:
  3 Charging current warning light (red)
  4 Oil pressure warning light (orange)
  6 Water temperature gauge
  7 Fuel gauge
85 Windscreen wiper motor switch
86 Heater blower motor resistance wire
87 Heater motor blower switch
88 Headlamp washer system relay*
89 Headlamp wiper motor*

90 Headlamp washer pump motor*
91 Headlamp washer system fuse*
92 Heater rear window relay – FoG sourced vehicles
93 Heated rear window – FoG sourced vehicles
94 Radio fuse
95 Radio
96 Heated rear window switch – FoG sourced vehicles
97 Cigarette lighter
*Not UK models

For wiring colour code refer to Fig. 10.45

Chapter 11 Suspension and steering

Contents

Specifications

Front suspension
Type .... Independent MacPherson strut

Control
Lateral .... Track control arms
Longitudinal .... Stabiliser bar

Shock absorbers .... Telescopic, hydraulic, double-acting

Wheel alignment
Castor angle:
    Nominal .... 1° 45'
    Tolerance range .... 1° 15' to 2° 30'
Camber angle:
    Nominal .... 0° 40'
    Tolerance range .... 0° 5' to 1° 25'
Toe-in .... 0.08 to 0.15 in (2 to 4 mm)

Wheel bearing grease (lithium based) .... Ford specification S-MIC-4515A

Front springs
Colour code (standard) .... Brown/grey
Free length .... 10.35 in (263 mm)
Total coils 5.98

Steering gear
General
Type .... Rack-and-pinion
Rack travel (lock to lock) .... 129 mm (5.08 in)
Turns (lock to lock)* 3.5
Teeth on pinion (helical) 5

Lubrication
Lubricant capacity .... 0.15 litre (0.25 Imp pt, 0.30 US pt)
Lubricant type .... SAE 90 EP

Steering gear adjustment .... Shims

Pinion bearing preload shim and gasket details
71EB-3K544-AA	Steel (0.127 mm; 0.005 in)
71EB-3K544-BA	Steel (0.178 mm; 0.007 in)
71EB-3K544-CA	Steel (0.254 mm; 0.010 in)
71EB-3K544-DA (must always be used)	Steel (2.286 mm; 0.090 in)
3024E-3581-B	Gasket (0.127 mm; 0.005 in)

Rack slipper bearing shim details
3024E-3K544-J	Steel 0.051 mm (0.002 in)
3024E-3K544-K	Steel 0.127 mm (0.005 in)
3024E-3K544-L	Steel 0.254 mm (0.010 in)
3024E-3K544-M	Steel 0.381 mm (0.015 in)
3024E-3K544-N	Steel 0.508 mm (0.020 in)

*Standard steering rack. A high ratio rack may be fitted, giving 2.5 turns lock to lock

Rear suspension
Type .... Semi-elliptical longitudinal leaf spring stabilised by two forward facing radius arms

Shock absorbers ....
Double-acting, telescopic, hydraulic

Springs
Type	Semi-elliptical
Number of leaves	3
Leaf length	47 in (1194 mm)
Leaf thickness	0.24 in (6.1 mm)

Tyres
Size .... 175/70 x 13

Pressures (normal loading*)
Front	24 lbf/in^2 (1.7 kgf/cm^2)
Rear	22 lbf/in^2 (1.5 kgf/cm^2)

*Up to three persons. For heavier loads, increase rear tyre pressure to 24 lbf/in^2 (1.7 kgf/cm^2)

For sustained high speeds increase as follows:
Non 'S' tyres	3 lbf/in^2 (0.21 kgf/cm^2)
'S' tyres	Nil
'SR' tyres	1.5 lbf/in^2 (0.11 kgf/cm^2) for every 6 mph above 100 mph

Tightening torques
	lbf ft	kgf m
Front suspension crossmember to body side-member	29 to 37	4.1 to 5.1
Steering rack clamp to crossmember	15 to 18	2.1 to 2.5
Wheel bearing nuts	27	3.7
Brake caliper mounting bolts	35 to 50	4.8 to 5.9
Brake disc to hub assembly	30 to 34	4.2 to 4.7
Lower arm to suspension unit	30 to 35	4.2 to 4.9
Lower arm-to-crossmember pivot bolts	18 to 22	2.5 to 3.1
Stabiliser to lower arm	15 to 45	2.1 to 6.2
Stabiliser bar-to-body mounting brackets	21 to 24	2.9 to 3.4
Suspension unit upper mounting bolts	15 to 18	2.0 to 2.4
Track rod to steering arm	18 to 22	2.5 to 3.1
Suspension unit piston rod nut*	29 to 33	4.1 to 4.6
Shock absorber to rear axle bolts	25 to 31	3.4 to 4.2
Shock absorber to floorpan nut	15 to 21	2.1 to 2.8
Lock nut	12 to 15	1.6 to 2.1
Rear spring front end-to-floorpan bolts	52 to 66	7.0 to 9.0
Rear spring rear end-to-floorpan bolts	19 to 23	2.6 to 3.1
U-bolt	18 to 27	2.5 to 3.7
Radius arm-to-floor side member bolts	44 to 52	6.0 to 7.0
Radius arm-to-axle bolts	26 to 31	3.5 to 4.2
Steering gear to crossmember	15 to 18	2.1 to 2.5
Track rod end to steering arm	18 to 22	2.5 to 3.0
Coupling to pinion spline	11 to 13	1.4 to 1.7
Coupling to steering shaft spline	11 to 13	1.4 to 1.7
Steering wheel to steering shaft	20 to 25	2.8 to 3.5
Steering pinion cover plate bolts	6 to 8	0.8 to 1.1
Wheels nuts		
Steel wheels	50 to 65	7.0 to 9.0
Aluminium wheels	90 to 105	12.0 to 14.0

*These to be tightened with the wheels in the straight-ahead position and the weight of the car resting on its wheels. They should be locked by punching a slot using a 2.5 mm (0.1 in) diameter ball ended punch.

1 General description

Each of the independent front suspension MacPherson strut units consists of a vertical strut enclosing a double-acting shock absorber surrounded by a coil spring. The upper end of each strut is secured to the top of the wing valance under the bonnet by rubber mountings.

The wheel spindle (stub axle) carrying the brake assembly and wheel hub is forged integrally with the suspension unit foot.

The steering arms are connected to each unit which are in turn connected to track rods and thence to the rack-and-pinion steering gear.

The lower end of each suspension unit is located by a track control arm.

A stabilising torsion bar (anti-roll bar) is fitted between the outer ends of each track control arm and secured at the front to mountings on the body front member.

On all models a rubber rebound stop is fitted inside the suspension unit. This prevents the spring becoming over-extended and jumping out of its mounting plates.

Whenever repairs have been carried out on a suspension unit it is essential to check the wheel alignment as the linkage could be altered which would affect the correct front wheel settings.

Every time the car goes over a bump, vertical movement of a front wheel pushes the damper body upward against the combined resistance of the coil spring and the shock absorber piston. Hydraulic fluid in the shock absorber is displaced and it is then forced through the compression valve into the space between the inner and outer cylinder. On the downward movement of the suspension, the road spring forces the shock absorber body downward against the pressure of the hydraulic fluid which is forced back again through the rebound valve. In this way the natural oscillations of the spring are damped out and a comfortable ride is obtained.

On the front uprights there is a shroud inside the coil spring which protects the machined surface of the piston rod from road dirt.

The upper mounting assembly consists of a steel sleeve with a rubber bush bonded to it.

The steering gear on the Escort is rack-and-pinion and is located on the front crossmember by two U-shaped clamps. The pinion is connected to the steering column by a flexible coupling. Turning the steering wheel causes the rack to move in a lateral direction and the track rods attached to either end of the rack pass this movement to the steering arms on the suspension/axle units thereby moving the roadwheels.

Two adjustments are possible on the steering gear, namely rack damper adjustment and pinion bearing pre-load adjustment, but the steering gear must be removed from the car to carry out these adjustments. Both adjustments are made by varying the thickness of shim packs.

The rear axle is located by two inverted U-bolts at each end of the casing to underslung semi-elliptical leaf springs which provide both lateral and longtitudinal location.

To prevent axle 'wind up', twin radius arms are fitted. These are located between the axle case and the floor mounting side-members near the rear spring forward mountings. The radius arm mounting/pivot bolts are located in rubber bushes, as are the springs and shock absorbers.

The double-acting telescopic shock absorbers are fitted between the axle and reinforced mountings in the floorpan. These shock absorbers work on the same principle as the front shock absorbers.

Note: *The suspension and steering component details dealt with in this Chapter apply only to standard factory produced models — not those that have been modified with RS optional equipment and fittings.*

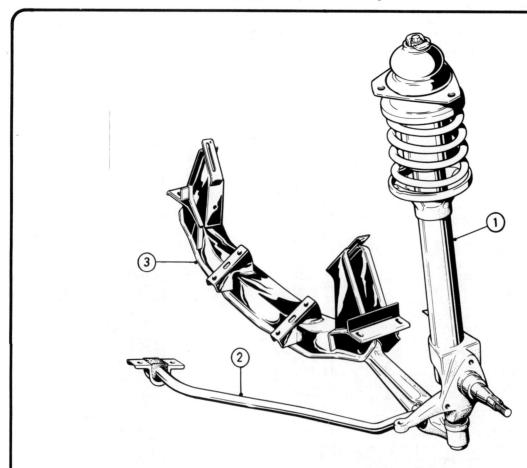

Fig. 11.1 The front suspension assembly (Sec 1)

| 1 | MacPherson strut | 2 | Anti-roll bar | 3 | The engine and steering box crossmounting |

2.3 Front suspension/steering check points showing rubber bushes (1), rubber gaiters (2) and steering rack rubber bellows (3)

2 Suspension and steering – maintenance and inspection

At the intervals specified in Routine Maintenance:

1   Brush the rear roadsprings free from dirt and apply either penetrating oil or engine oil to the leaves with a spray or brush. Do not allow oil to come into contact with the rubber bushes at the spring eyes.

2   Check the torque setting of the U-bolts and shackle bolts (rear suspension).

3   Inspect the rubber bushes (photo) for deterioration or wear and renew if necessary, as described later in this Chapter.

4   At a similar mileage interval, check the condition of the rubber bellows at both ends of the steering rack. Renew them if they are split or perished.

5   Check the condition of the rubber gaiters on all the steering balljoints and renew them if they are split or perished. It is unlikely that the gaiters themselves can be obtained without purchasing a complete balljoint.

6   Check all suspension securing bolts and nuts for correct tightening torque in accordance with the figures given in the Specifications.

7   Examine the front suspension strut for signs of oil leakage ('B' Fig. 11.2), or score marks on the piston rod ('A' Fig. 11.2). Then check the shock absorber movement and determine whether the action feels stiff, or, alternatively, notchy or spongy.

8   If any of the above checks reveal wear or some malfunction the relevant components should be renewed.

3 Front hub/disc assembly – removal, maintenance and refitting

1   Raise the front of the vehicle and support it on suitable axle stands. Remove the appropriate roadwheel.

2   Loosen the 17 mm nut securing the brake line to the suspension leg bracket at the junction of the flexible and metal pipes (Fig. 11.3).

3   Knock back the locking tabs on the two caliper unit securing bolts. Unscrew and remove the bolts.

4   Very carefully, taking care not to twist or damage the brake pipes, guide the caliper unit away from the disc at the same time disengaging the brake line from the suspension strut bracket. Using a suitable length of wire, suspend the caliper from the vehicle body away from the work area, making sure that the caliper is securely held and that the brake lines are not twisted (Fig. 11.4). A piece of soft packing between the disc pads will effectively prevent these components closing up.

5   Knock the dust cap from the end of the hub and then withdraw the split pin, nut, thrust washer and outer bearing.

6   Pull the hub/disc assembly from the stub axle.

7   From the back of the hub assembly, carefully prise out the grease seal and remove the inner tapered bearing. Then bend up the locktabs

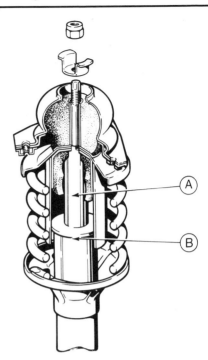

Fig. 11.2 Check the front suspension strut for score marks on the piston rod (A) and for oil leaks at (B) (Sec 2)

Fig. 11.3 Removing the 17 mm locknut before sliding the pipe/hose assembly from the suspension leg bracket (Sec 3)

Fig. 11.4 Suspend caliper unit with cord (A) from underbody to prevent distortion or possible fracture of brake line (Sec 3)

on the four bolts securing the disc to the hub, remove the bolts and separate the disc and hub assembly.

8   If the hub and disc are being removed for maintenance of, or access to, the hub bearings this can be carried out with the disc in place. For details on bearing removal refer to Section 4.

9   Carefully clean out the hub and wash the bearings with petrol, making sure that no grease or oil is allowed to get onto the brake disc.

10 Working the grease well into the bearings, fully pack the bearing cages and rollers with grease. Leave the hub and grease seal empty to allow for subsequent expansion of the grease.

11 To reassemble the hub, first fit the inner bearing and then gently tap the grease seal back into the hub. If the seal was at all damaged during removal, a new one must be fitted.

12 Reposition the disc on the hub assembly and secure the two components using the four bolts and new tab washers. Tighten the bolts to the specified torque setting.

13 Refit the hub and disc assembly on the stub axle and slide on the outer bearing and thrust washer.

14 Tighten the centre adjusting nut to a torque of 27 lbf ft (3.73 kgf m) whilst rotating the hub and disc to ensure free movement, then slacken the nut off 120° (two nut flats) and fit the nut retainer and new split pin, but do not bend back the split pin.

15 At this stage it is advisable, if a dial gauge is available, to check the disc for run-out. The measurement should be taken as near to the edge of the worn, smooth part of the disc as possible and must not exceed 0.002 in (0.05 mm). If it is more, check the mating surfaces of the disc

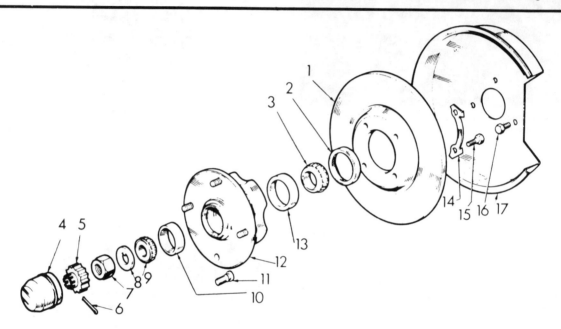

Fig. 11.5 Front wheel hub/disc assembly components (Sec 3)

1 Disc	7 Nut	13 Inner bearing track
2 Grease seal	8 Thrust washer	14 Lockplate
3 Inner roller bearing	9 Outer bearing	15 Bolt
4 Dust cap	10 Outer bearing track	16 Bolt
5 Nut retainer	11 Roadwheel stud	17 Splash shield
6 Split pin	12 Hub	

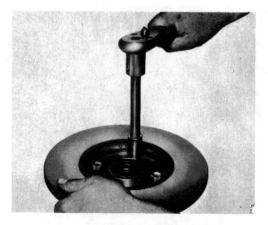

Fig. 11.6 Remove the disc-to-hub securing bolts (Sec 3)

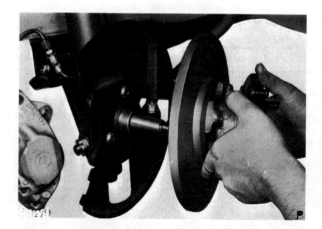

Fig. 11.7 Refitting the disc/hub assembly (Sec 3)

3.16 Refit the hub dust cap

and hub for dirt or damage and check the bearings and cups for excessive wear or damage. Renew the disc if the run-out is excessive or it appears deeply scored.

16 Bend the ends of the spit pin and refit the dust cap (photo).

17 Carefully push the disc pads apart sufficiently to allow the caliper to align around the disc. Secure the caliper in position, tighten the retaining bolts to the specified torque and retain with new tab washers. Carefully guide the brake pipes into the suspension strut bracket and tighten the 17 mm nut. Refit the roadwheel(s).

18 On completion lower the car from the axle stands and tighten the roadwheel nuts to the specified torque.

4 Front hub bearings – checking for wear and renewal

1 To check the condition of the hub bearings, jack up the front end of the car and grasp the roadwheel at two opposite points to check for any rocking movement in the wheel hub. Watch carefully for any movement in the steering gear, which can easily be mistaken for hub movement. If movement is observed in the balljoints, they must be renewed.

2 If a front wheel hub has excessive movement, first try adjusting the bearing play, by removing the hub cap and then levering off the small dust cap. Remove the split pin through the stub axle and take off the adjusting nut retainer.

3 Tighten the centre adjusting nut to a torque of 27 lbf ft (3.73 kgf m) and then slacken it off 120° (two nut flats). Refit the nut retainer and fit a new split pin.

4 Where this action does not remove the rocking, or if a grinding or grating sound can be heard when the hub is rotated, then the bearings must be renewed.

5 Remove the hub/disc assembly as previously described. Remove the outer bearing.

6 Prise out the grease seal from the back of the hub and remove the inner bearing.

7 Drive out the bearing outer tracks from each end of the hub and then thoroughly clean the grease from the hub interior.

8 It is essential to keep the new bearings in their individual packs until required for fitting. Do not open them and mix the roller races and tracks, but keep them as matched pairs.

9 Drive in the new bearing outer tracks using a suitable piece of tubing. Ensure that they are fully home in their recesses. Fit a new grease seal.

10 Grease the bearings as described in Section 3, paragraph 10.

11 Refitting is a reversal of removal. Adjust the bearings as described in paragraph 3.

Fig. 11.8 Driving out a hub bearing track (Sec 4)

5 Front coil spring – removal and refitting

1 If a front coil spring is to be removed for any reason you will have to remove the front suspension unit on the side concerned, before the spring itself can be detached from the suspension strut. Unlike earlier Escort models, it is not possible to remove the spring from the strut when *in situ*.

2 The details of the suspension unit removal, and spring detachment, are given in Section 6.

3 If a new spring is to be fitted, take care that the replacement is of the same rating as the spring it replaces (and matches the opposing side spring). This is particularly important with the Mexico and RS Series Escort models since they may well have been modified at some time for competition purposes. Springs with alternative compression pressures are available through Ford Rallye Sport dealers.

6 Front suspension unit – removal and refitting

1 Raise the car at the front end and support it on axle stands. Remove the roadwheel on the side to be worked on.

2 Unbolt and remove the brake caliper, but to avoid disconnecting the hydraulic line, suspend the caliper with a suitable piece of cord from an upper body part. Refer to Chapter 9 (Section 6) for details.

3 Remove the split pin and castellated nut and detach the track rod end from the steering arm using a balljoint separator.

4 Now remove the split pin and castellated nut securing the track control arm to the base of the suspension unit and disengage the taper

.4 The front suspension strut upper securing bolts

joint using a separator (Fig. 11.9). Once the taper joint is released, use a suitable length of bar and lever downwards on the anti-roll bar to fully separate the control arm from the stabiliser. The inner end of the lever should be located under the track control arm pivot bolt/crossmember when levering.

5   Working under the bonnet, unscrew and remove the three bolts on the side apron holding the top of the suspension unit in place (photo) and then lower the unit away from the car.

6   With the unit securely mounted in a bench vice unscrew the three Allen screws retaining the brake disc splash shield to the unit and detach the shield.

7   Before removing the coil spring fit a suitable spring compressor (Fig. 11.10), around the spring and tighten each compressor a little, in turn, until the load, or action, of the spring on the top mount is released. Use a proper spring compressor, **do not** improvise.

8   Unscrew the piston nut from the piston spindle and remove the cranked retainer, top mount, upper spring retainer, bump roller and spring from the unit. **While unscrewing the piston nut do not grip the piston shaft in order to stop the piston turning with the nut.** A flat section is provided at the top of the piston shaft for this purpose.

9   Refitting is a direct reversal of the removal procedure, but remember to use a split pin on the track control arm-to-suspension unit castellated nut.

10   The lower control arm-to-crossmember pivot bolt, the control arm-to-suspension unit nut and the top mounting bolts must be tightened to their specified torque wrench settings. The piston nut must be locked by staking.

7 Front suspension unit – overhaul

*The following overhaul procedures are for the normal oil-filled damper units (shock absorbers). If gas-filled dampers have been fitted at any time they should not be dismantled. If on inspection you find excessive wear or damage has occurred with a standard oil-filled damper strut and renewal is necessary, you may consider renewing it with a gas-filled type, in which case you will need to renew **both** front strut assemblies. Your Ford Rallye Sport dealer will advise you.*

For standard oil-filled damper struts proceed as follows:

1   Remove the suspension unit from the vehicle and remove the bump rubber, top mount and spring (Section 6).

2   The bump stop platform nut normally requires a special tool for removal. However, the nut can be removed using a round-nosed punch in the two slots cut in the upper surface of the nut.

3   With the platform nut removed withdraw the O-ring seal, gland and the piston rod and cylinder assembly from the suspension unit.

4   At the base of the piston rod cylinder there is a castellated valve assembly which is a push fit into the cylinder bore. The valve can be pulled from the cylinder after first imparting a twisting action with a suitable lever.

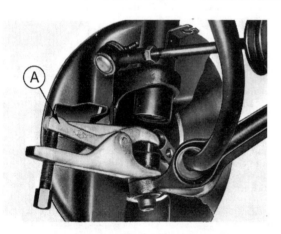

Fig. 11.9 Taper joint separator (A) being used to detach the track control arm (Sec 6)

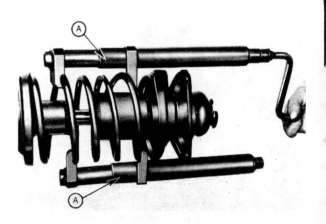

Fig. 11.10 Coil spring compressor (A) in position – in this instance Ford tool No. P-5045 (Sec 6)

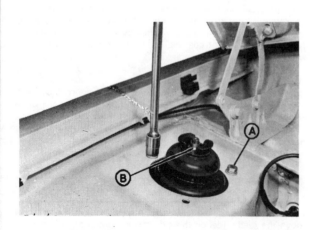

Fig. 11.11 Tighten suspension by location bolts (A) to specified torque, followed by piston rod nut (B). Peen nut shoulder into piston slot to secure (Sec 6)

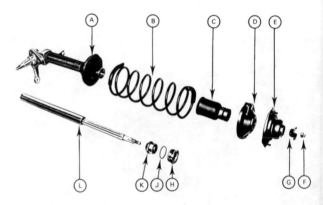

Fig. 11.12 Front suspension unit components (standard, with oil-filled damper) (Sec 7)

A	Unit	G Cranked retainer
B	Front spring	H Bump stop platform
C	Bump rubber	J Seal
D	Upper spring retainer	K Gland
E	Top mount assembly	L Piston and cylinder
F	Piston rod nut	assembly

5   Remove the piston rod and piston from the cylinder and examine for signs of damage or wear, in particular look for signs of scoring on the piston rod round the area of the gland and seal. The piston must not be removed from the rod.

6   Drain the oil from the unit and clean the cylinder piston and unit with a suitable solvent using a lint-free cloth. An old chamois leather is useful for finally wiping the components dry.

7   Reassembly is a direct reversal of the dismantling procedure. However, when filling the unit with oil prior to refitting the piston rod and cylinder assembly use **exactly** 326 cc of Ford shock absorber fluid M100502E. To avoid damaging the new unit seals, cover the threads of the piston rod with adhesive tape before fitting the seal or gland.

8   Anti-roll bar and track control arm bushes – removal and refitting

1   Jack up the front of the vehicle, support the vehicle on suitable stands and remove both front roadwheels.

2   Working under the car at the front, knock back the locking tabs on the four bolts securing the two front clamps which hold the anti-roll bar to the frame and then undo the four bolts and remove the clamps and rubber insulators.

3   Remove the split pins from the castellated nuts retaining the anti-roll bar to the track control arms (photo) then undo the nuts and pull off the large washers, carefully noting the way in which they are fitted.

4   Pull the anti-roll bar forward out of the two track control arms and remove it from the vehicle.

5   Clean the road dirt and rust from the car, then slide the rubber mounting bushes around the bar and off the ends. Use rubber lubricant on the bar to assist in the removal of the bushes.

6   Whilst the anti-roll bar is removed, check the condition of the track control arm bushes in the crossmember mounting. If in need of renewal they are best attended to now.

7   Unscrew the control arm-to-mounting pivot bolt nut and remove it, together with its washer. Before renewing the pivot bolt position the steering to full lock so that the rack bellows will not be damaged during the bolt removal (and refitting). Withdraw the bolt, noting that its head is towards the front end of the car.

8   Lower the control arm from the mounting and extract the old bush.

9   Press the new bush into the control arm location eye. A suitable rubber lubricant will ease fitting. Relocate the arm into the mounting. Reinsert the pivot bolt (with its head to the front) and then locate the washer and nut, but do not tighten fully until the car is free standing.

10 Refitting of the anti-roll bar is a direct reversal of the removal

8.3 Remove split pins and nut at each end of the anti-roll bar at its connection to the track control arm (arrowed)

procedure, but new locking tabs must be used on the front clamp bolts and new split pins on the castellated nuts. The nuts on the clamps and the castellated nuts on each end of the anti-roll bar must not be fully tightened until the vehicle is resting on its wheels.

11 With the car free standing on its wheels, the anti-roll bar nuts and control arm pivot nuts can be fully tightened to their respective torque wrench settings. New split pins must be fitted to the castellated nuts to secure them.

9   Steering gear – removal and refitting

1   Before starting this job set the front wheels in a straight-ahead position. Then jack up the front of the vehicle and place blocks under the wheels; lower the vehicle slightly on the jack so that the track rods are in a near horizontal position.

2   Remove the nut and bolt from the clamp at the front of the flexible coupling on the steering column. This clamp holds the coupling to the pinion splines.

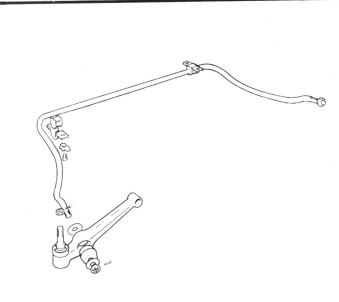

Fig. 11.13 Anti-roll bar and bushes (Sec 8)

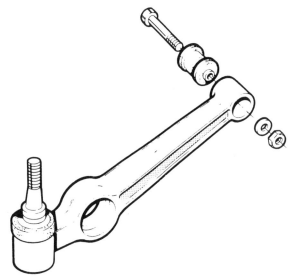

Fig. 11.14 Track control arm to front crossmember mounting bush assembly (Sec 8)

9.3 Steering rack-to-crossmember securing bolts and locktabs (arrowed)

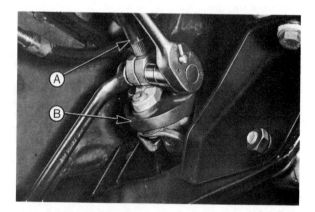

Fig. 11.15 Steering column (A) and coupling (B) – removing clamp bolt using a ring spanner and socket (Sec 9)

Fig. 11.16 Reconnecting a track rod to its steering arm (A) (Sec 9)

3   Working on the front crossmember, knock back the locking tabs on the two nuts on each U-clamp, undo the nut and remove the locking tabs and clamps (photo).
4   Remove the split pins and castellated nuts from the ends of each track rod where they join the steering arms. Separate the track rods from the steering arms using a balljoint extractor or wedges and lower the steering gear downwards out of the car.
5   Before refitting the steering gear, make sure that the wheels have remained in the straight-ahead position. Also check the condition of the mounting rubbers round the housing and if they appear worn or damaged, renew them.
6   Check that the steering gear is also in the straight-ahead position. This can be done by ensuring that the distances between the ends of both track rods and the steering gear housing on both sides are the same.
7   Place the steering gear in its location on the crossmember and at the same time mate up the splines on the pinion with the splines in the clamp on the steering column flexible coupling.
8   Locate the two steering gear retaining clamps. Using new locktabs under the securing bolts, tighten the bolts to the specified torque wrench setting, then bend up the locktabs to secure.
9   Reconnect the track rods to the steering arms (Fig. 11.6), fit the castellated nuts, tighten them to the specified torque and then fit new split pins to secure.
10   Tighten the clamp bolt on the steering column flexible coupling to the specified torque having first made sure that the pinion is correctly located in the splines.
11   Jack up the car, remove the blocks from under the wheels and lower the car to the ground. It is advisable at this stage to take your car to your local Ford dealer and have the toe-in checked. A basic check and, if necessary, adjustment can be made, as described in Section 15.

10 Steering gear – dismantling and reassembly

1   Remove the steering gear from the car (Section 9).
2   Unscrew the balljoints and locknuts from the end of each track rod, having previously marked the threads to ensure correct positioning on reassembly. Alternatively, the number of turns required to undo the balljoint can be counted and noted.
3   Slacken off the clips securing the rubber bellows to each track rod and the steering gear housing then pull off the bellows. Have a quantity of rags handy to catch the oil which will escape when the bellows are removed.
4   To dismantle the steering gear, it is only necessary to remove the track rod which is furthest away from the pinion on either right or left-hand drive cars.
5   To remove the track rod place the steering gear in a soft jawed vice. Working on the track rod balljoint, carefully drill out the pin which locks the ballhousing to the locknut. Great care must be taken not to

Fig. 11.17 Track rod housing lock pin is drilled out (Sec 10)

drill too deeply or you will drill into the threads on the rack, thus causing irreparable damage. The hole should be 3 mm (0.12 in) dia and a maximum of 9.5 mm (0.38 in) deep.

6 Using two pairs of mole wrenches firmly grip the locknut and undo the ballhousing from the end of the rack.

7 Take out the spring and ball seat from the recess in the end of the rack and then unscrew the locknut from the threads on the rack. The spring and ball seal must be replaced by new components on reassembly. Repeat for the other track rod assembly.

8 Now remove the two bolts securing the rack slipper cover plate. This plate is the one on the front face of the rack casting, adjacent to the pinion shaft. With the cover removed, detach the shims and withdraw the spring O-ring and slipper from the rack.

9 Remove the two bolts from the remaining cover plate immediately below the pinion shaft and detach the shim pack and gasket, together with the pinion shaft lower bearing (Fig. 11.19).

10 Remove the pinion oil seal from the cover plate. The pinion shaft and upper bearing assembly can now be withdrawn from the rack casting. Examine the upper bearing for signs of wear, or damage; if

necessary the bearing can be pulled from the shaft after first removing all traces of paint from the splined end.

11 The toothed rack can now be withdrawn from the casting.

12 Carefully examine all parts for signs of wear or damage. Check the condition of the rack support bush at the opposite end of the casing from the pinion. If this is worn, renew it. If the rack or pinion teeth are in any way damaged, a completely new steering gear will have to be fitted.

13 To commence reassembly, fit the lower pinion bearing and thrust washer into their recess in the casing.

14 Insert the rack into the casing from the pinion end and position it in the straight-ahead position by equalising the amount it protrudes at either end of the casing.

15 Locate the remaining pinion bearing and thrust washer onto the pinion and fit the pinion into the casing so that the larger master spline on the pinion shaft is parallel to the rack and on the right-hand side of the pinion. This applies to both right and left-hand drive cars.

16 Refit the pinion bearing cover plate and adjust the shim pack to give the necessary clearance; similarly assemble the rack slipper,

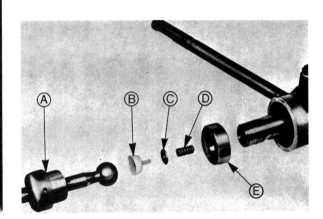

Fig. 11.18 Track rod-to-steering rack assembly components (Sec 10)

A   Track rod housing   D   Spring
B   Nylon seat   E   Locknut
C   Washer

Fig. 11.19 Remove the pinion bearing (lower) for inspection (Sec 10)

Fig. 11.20 Locating the pinion, with upper bearing fitted (Sec 10)

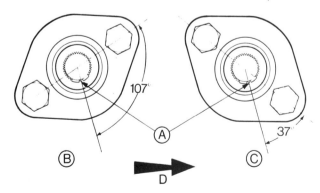

Fig. 11.21 Location of pinion master spline with the steering rack at the mid-point of its travel (Sec 10)

A   Master spline   D   Right-hand side of
B   Pinion, LHD vehicles   vehicle
C   Pinion, RHD vehicles

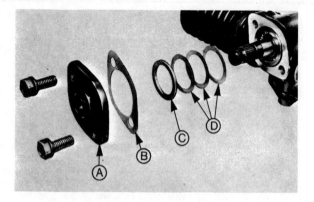

Fig. 11.22 Pinion bearing adjustment (Sec 10)

A   Cover plate   C   Thick shim
B   Gasket   D   Shim pack

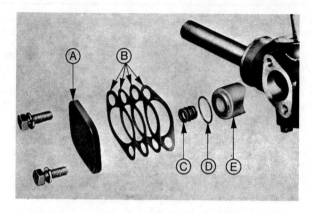

Fig. 11.23 Steering rack adjustment (Sec 10)

A   Cover plate   D   Seal
B   Shim pack   E   Slipper (or yoke)
C   Spring

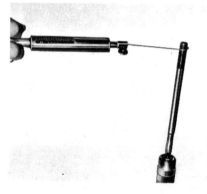

Fig. 11.24 Measuring track rod articulation using a spring balance
(Sec 10)

Fig. 11.25 Using feeler gauges adjacent to the bolt location to
measure pinion bearing preload. The gasket is not in place when
this measurement is taken (Sec 11)

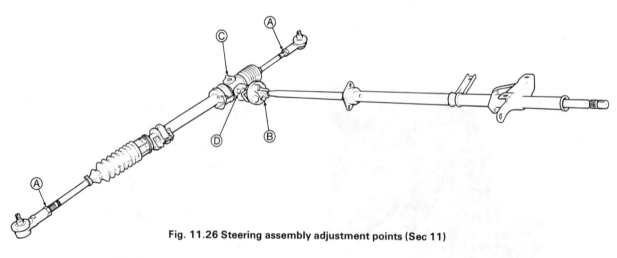

Fig. 11.26 Steering assembly adjustment points (Sec 11)

A   Toe-in adjustment at   C   Rack adjustment via shim
    track rod end   pack and slipper
B   Coupling shaft adjustment   D   Pinion bearing adjustment
    on steering column splines

spring shims and cover plate, again adjusting the shim pack to give the required clearance (Figs. 11.22 and 11.23).

17 To refit each track rod, in turn first fit a new spring and ball seat to the recess in the end of the rack shaft and refit the locknut onto the threads of the rack.

18 Lubricate the ball, ball seat and ballhousing with a small amount of SAE 90EP oil. Then slide the ballhousing over the track rod and screw the housing onto the rack threads, keeping the track rod in the horizontal position until the track rod starts to become stiff to move.

19 Using a normal spring balance hook it round the track rod a quarter of an inch (6 mm) from the end and check the effort required to move it from the horizontal position (Fig. 11.24).

20 By adjusting the tightness of the ballhousing on the rack threads the effort required to move the track rod must be set at 5 lb (2.3 kg).

21 Tighten the locknut up to the housing and then re-check that the effort required to move the track rod is still correct at 5 lb (2.3 kg).

22 On the line where the locknut and ballhousing meet, drill a 0.12 inch (3 mm) diameter hole which must be 0.38 inch (9.5 mm) deep. Even if the two halves of the old hole previously drilled out align, a new hole must still be drilled.

23 Tap a new retaining pin into the hole and peen the end over to secure it.

24 Refit the rubber bellows and the track rod ends ensuring that the rod ends are fitted in exactly the same position from which they were removed.

25 Do not attempt to re-use the wire type clips used in production to retain the ends of the bellows. Special worm drive type clips are available for use in service and these **must** be used. The inside surface of the bellows should be lightly smeared with grease at the point where it contacts the groove in the track rod. The track rod clips should not be fully tightened until the toe-in setting has been adjusted; when the clips are finally tightened the clip bolt heads must face the front of the vehicle and the gaiter must not be twisted.

26 Remove the cover plate and pour in the specified quantity of EP 90 grade oil. Alternatively, the oil can be poured into the casing via the pinion end with the bellows removed.

27 Carry out both the adjustments described in Section 11.

28 Refit the steering gear (Section 9) and then have the toe-in checked at your Ford dealer, or refer to Section 15.

11 Steering gear – adjustments

For the steering gear to function correctly, two adjustments must be carried out whenever the unit is dismantled or reassembled and the settings must be maintained when wear calls for further adjustment.

To carry out these adjustments, remove the steering gear from the car (Section 9), then mount the steering gear in a soft jawed vice so that the pinion is in a horizontal position and the rack damper cover plate at the top.

Remove the rack damper cover plate by undoing the two retaining bolts, then take off the gasket and shims from under the plate. Also remove the two small springs and the recessed yoke which bears on the rack.

Remove the pinion bearing cover plate, gasket and shim pack.

Pinion bearing adjustment

Select three shims, one of which must be 2.286 mm (0.090 in) thick and placed immediately against the cover plate. Tighten the cover plate bolts to compress the shim pack then slacken the bolts so that the cover plate just touches the shim pack.

Using feeler gauges measure the gap between the underside of the cover plate and the machined surface of the housing adjacent to each cover plate bolt. This gap should be 0.18 to 0.23 mm (0.007 to 0.009 in), if necessary adjust the shim pack by adding or deleting shims from the selection listed in the Specifications.

Remove the cover plate and refit using a new gasket, smear a suitable sealer around the bolt threads and finally tighten the cover bolts to the specified torque.

Rack slipper adjustment

To set the rack damper adjustment, replace the slipper in its location on the rack and make sure it is fully home. Then measure the distance between the uppermost part of the slipper and the top of the steering gear casing.

Assemble a shim pack, including gaskets, to give a dimension

0.050 to 0.125 mm (0.002 to 0.005 in) greater than the dimension recorded in paragraph 8 above.

10 An alternative and more accurate method of establishing this dimension is to use a dial gauge zeroed on the rack slipper housing with the stylus of the gauge on the slipper housing. Traverse the rack until the highest slipper position is obtained and use the reading recorded, (ie; the maximum dial gauge deflection), as the base dimension.

11 Select shims from the list in the Specifications to give a dimension 0.050 to 0.125 mm (0.002 to 0.005 in) greater than the dimension recorded on the gauge.

12 It is important that the slipper adjustment is correctly set if heavy, stiff steering and 'knocking' from the rack are to be avoided.

13 Refit the spring into its recess in the yoke and position the new shim pack so that the gasket is next to the cover plate. Replace the cover plate having first applied a sealing compound to the bolt threads. Then tighten down the bolts to the specified torque.

12 Steering wheel and column – removal and refitting

1 Place the vehicle with the wheels in the straight-ahead position, disconnect the battery by removing the negative earth lead, then disconnect the lower end of the steering shaft from the flexible coupling by removing the nut and bolt on the top clamp of the coupling. Removal of the flexible coupling clamp bolts can be assisted if the front of the vehicle is raised on stands.

2 Locate the small rubber screw cap on the surface of the upper half of the steering column shroud. Remove the cap, unscrew the screw exposed by the cap removal, and detach the upper half of the shroud.

3 Remove the screws securing the lower half of the shroud to the steering column bracket and the edge of the facia.

4 Disconnect the multi-plug connections joining the column switch wiring and the ignition switch wiring to the main wiring looms.

5 Remove the bolt securing the underside of the driver's side package tray to the steering column support bracket.

6 Fold back the carpet from around the area where the steering column passes through the floor, then unbolt the plate from the floor.

7 Undo the two nuts and bolts holding the upper steering column bracket to the underside of the facia panel, then lift the complete steering column assembly into the car, and thence from the vehicle.

8 To refit the steering column, pass it through the hole in the floor and mate up the splines on the shaft with the clamp on the flexible coupling. Tighten the nut to the specified torque, ensuring that the rubber disc is not distorted (see Fig. 11.27).

9 Secure the top bracket on the column to the underside of the facia panel with the nuts and bolts, but do not tighten them down at this stage.

10 Secure the column lower support bracket to the floor and tighten down the nuts. Now return to the upper bracket and tighten down the nuts and bolts. This order of procedure ensures correct alignment of the steering column.

11 The remainder of the refitting procedure is a direct reversal of the removal sequence.

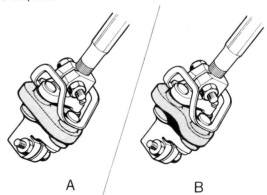

Fig. 11.27 Rubber disc in steering column-to-pinion shaft coupling. This disc must be assembled without distortion (A) and not as at (B). To relieve the condition shown at (B) slide the coupling up the column splines before tightening the clamp bolts (Sec 12)

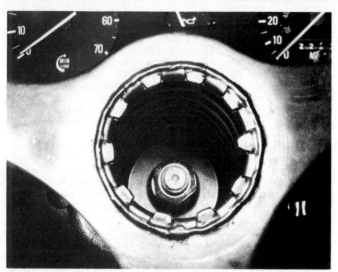

13.1 Steering wheel with central emblem removed showing the wheel to column securing nut and collapsible can. A long box spanner or socket and extension is required to remove this nut

13 Steering column – servicing

1   Prise out the centre emblem on the steering wheel bar, undo the nut retaining the wheel to the steering shaft and detach the wheel, together with the indicator actuating cam, spring and spacer. Take care not to damage or distort the steering wheel collapsible can section (photo). This can section is designed to progressively collapse under excessive pressure, as may occur during front end impact. If the collapsible can is damaged or distorted, it will not function correctly in an emergency; therefore, it is particularly important to check the can after impact. Where damage or distortion is found, the steering wheel must be renewed. If the can has been partially collapsed or stretched, *no attempt should be made to return it to its original position.*
2   Remove the two bolts clamping the combined indicator and horn switch to the steering column upper bracket and detach the switch.
3   Similarly unscrew the two cross-head screws holding the combined wash-wipe/light switch and bracket assembly to the column and carefully detach the assembly.
4   Remove the lower half of the steering column shroud.

Fig. 11.28 Steering wheel collapsible can (A) and column (B) (Sec 13)

5   Remove the combined ignition switch steering column lock, as described in Chapter 10, Section 57.
6   Tap the roll pin from its location in the lower end of the shaft and withdraw the lower bearing washer.
7   The steering shaft can now be withdrawn from the upper end of the steering column.
8   Remove the upper bearing from its location at the top of the steering column by driving it out from below using a long rod.
9   Similarly remove the lower bearing from the lower end of the column, then pull the plate and insulator rubber off the end of the column.
10 Check that the splines at both ends of the steering shaft are in good order.
11 Reassembly is a reversal of dismantling. Tighten the steering wheel nut to the specified torque.

14 Steering column lock – removal and refitting

1   Refer to Chapter 10, Section 57.

15 Front wheel alignment

1   Accurate front wheel alignment is essential to provide good steering and slow tyre wear. Before considering the steering angles,

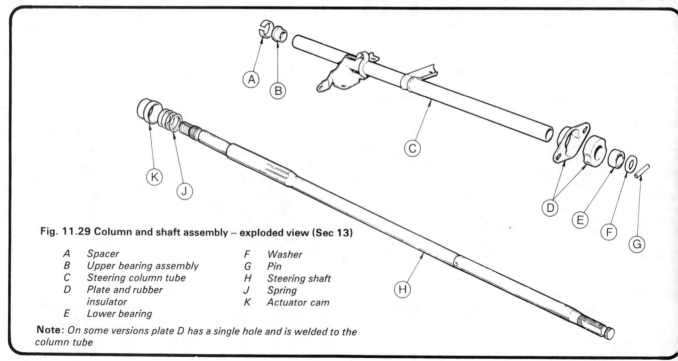

Fig. 11.29 Column and shaft assembly – exploded view (Sec 13)

A   Spacer
B   Upper bearing assembly
C   Steering column tube
D   Plate and rubber
      insulator
E   Lower bearing
F   Washer
G   Pin
H   Steering shaft
J   Spring
K   Actuator cam

Note: *On some versions plate D has a single hole and is welded to the column tube*

check that the tyres are correctly inflated, that the roadwheels are not buckled, that the hub bearings are not worn or incorrectly adjusted and that the steering gear and linkage is in good order without slackness or wear at the joints.

2   Wheel alignment consists of four factors:

Camber – the angle at which the front wheels are set from the vertical when viewed from the front of the car. Positive camber is the angle that the wheels are tilted outwards at the top of their vertical centre line.

Castor – the angle between the steering axis and a vertical line when viewed from each side of the vehicle. Positive castor is when the steering axis is inclined rearwards at the top.

Steering axis inclination – the angle, when viewed from the front of the vehicle, between the vertical and an imaginary line drawn between the upper and lower suspension/steering pivots.

Toe-in – the amount by which the distance between the front inside edges of the front wheels (measured at hub height) is less than that measured between the rear inside edges of the wheels.

3   The only steering adjustment which can be made by the home mechanic is for toe-in (tracking) the rest of the geometry having been set in production. It is recommended that the toe-in of the front wheels should be checked and adjusted by a service station having modern wheel alignment gauges but where this is not possible carry out the following procedure.

4   Place the vehicle on level ground with the wheels in the straight-ahead position.

5   Obtain one of the proprietary tracking gauges or make one from a length of tubing, suitably cranked to clear the engine sump and bellhousing and having an adjustment nut and setscrew at one end.

6   With the gauge, measure the distance between the two inner wheel rims at hub height at the front of the roadwheel.

7   Roll the vehicle forward or backward so that a chalk mark made on the tyre wall will move through 180° ($\frac{1}{2}$ a turn). Now (without altering the setting previously obtained on the gauge) place the gauge between the inner wheel rims at hub height at the rear of the roadwheel. This measurement should be greater by the specified toe-in for the front wheels.

8   Where the toe-in is found to be incorrect, slacken both track rod end locknuts and the outer clips on the steering rack rubber gaiters and ensure that the gaiters are not sticking to the track rods.

9   Rotate both track rods equally until the correct toe-in is obtained. Do not rotate the track rods more than $\frac{1}{4}$ of a turn at a time before re-checking with the gauge.

10   Tighten the track rod end locknuts ensuring that the track rod end balljoints are held in the centre of their arc of travel during tightening. Tighten the gaiter clips.

16 Rear shock absorbers – inspection and refitting

1   Chock the front wheels and jack-up the front of the vehicle. The roadwheels need not be removed but it will be more convenient to do so.

2   Open the boot to gain access to the shock absorber top mountings. These are located beneath the domed covers at the front corners of the boot floor (photo). Remove the covers, unscrew the nut and locknut assemblies and detach the flat washer and bush.

3   From underneath the vehicle remove the nut securing the shock absorber lower mounting to the stud on the spring shackle plate (photo).

4   Pull the shock absorber off the stud and then from its location in the floorpan, compressing the shock absorber as necessary to enable its removal.

5   Once removed, the shock absorber should be secured vertically in a vice, the jaws of which grip the lower mounting eye.

6   Fully extend and contract the shock absorber ten or twelve times and observe if there is strong resistance in both directions. If this is so, then the unit is operating satisfactorily and can be refitted. If there is no resistance, or the unit jumps erratically during its movement, it must be renewed as it is not repairable.

7   Examine the shock absorber body for fluid leakage, also the rubber mounting bushes for wear or deterioration. If there is evidence of these, renew the unit.

8   Refitting of the shock absorbers is a reversal of the removal procedure.

17 Radius arm – removal and refitting

1   Chock the front wheels, jack up the rear of the vehicle and support it on axle stands. The rear roadwheels need not be removed, but it will be more convenient to do so.

2   Unscrew and remove the radius arm-to-axle casing retaining bolt.

3   Straighten the tab washer securing the floor side-member-to-radius arm bolt (photo), then unscrew and remove the bolt. The radius arm can then be withdrawn.

4   To renew the radius arm bush, support the arm and press the old

Fig. 11.30 Radius cam-to-body bolt showing the tab washer (arrowed) (Sec 17)

6.2 Rear shock absorber upper mounting with cover removed

16.3 Rear shock absorber lower mounting securing nut (arrowed)

17.3 Radius arm forward mounting bolt (arrowed)

bush out, using a suitable tube or Ford special tool number 15-003. Clean out the bush eye and before fitting the new bush, lubricate it with glycerine to ease fitting. Press the new bush into position.

5   Refitting a radius arm is a reversal of the removal procedure. Loosely locate the floor mounting bolt initially then insert the axle bolt at the other end. You may have to raise or lower the axle to insert the bolt without forcing it.

6   With the floor mounting and axle mounting bolts loosely located, lower the car to the ground so that it is free standing and then tighten the bolts to their specified torque wrench settings. Bend over the tab on the washer under the floor mounting bolt head to secure the bolt in position.

18 Rear roadsprings – removal and refitting

1   Chock the front wheels to prevent the car moving, then jack up the rear of the car and support it on axle stands. To make the springs more accessible, remove the roadwheels.

2   Position a trolley jack underneath the differential housing to support the rear axle assembly when the springs are removed. Do not raise the jack under the differential housing so that the springs are flattened, but raise it just enough to take the full weight of the axle with the springs fully extended.

3   Undo the rear shackle nuts (photo) and remove the combined shackle bolt and plate assemblies. Then, if fitted, remove the small rubber bushes from the body aperture.

4   Undo the nut from the front mounting and take out the bolt running through the mounting (photo).

5   Undo the nuts on the ends of the four U-bolts (photo) and remove the U-bolts together with the attachment plate and rubber spring insulators. Also remove the bump stops from the top of the U-bolts.

6   The rubber bushes can be pressed or driven out and the new bushes installed as described for the radius arm in the previous Section. A little glycerine or brake fluid will allow the bushes to be pressed in more easily.

7   Refitting is a direct reversal of the above procedure. The nuts on the U-bolts, spring front mounting and rear shackles must be tightened to the specified torque but only **after** the car has been lowered onto its wheels.

19 Wheels and tyres

1   Check the tyre pressures weekly (when they are cold).

2   Frequently inspect the tyre walls and treads for damage and pick out any large stones which have become trapped in the tread pattern.

3   If the wheels and tyres have been balanced on the car then they should not be moved to a different axle position. If they have been balanced off the car then, in the interests of extending tread life, they can be moved between front and rear on the same side of the car and the spare incorporated in the rotational pattern.

4   Never mix tyres of different construction or very dissimilar tread patterns.

5   Always keep the wheel nuts tightened to the specified torque and if the bolt holes become elongated or flattened, renew the wheel.

6   Occasionally, clean the inner faces of the roadwheels and if there is any sign of rust or corrosion, paint them with metal preservative paint. **Note**: *Corrosion on aluminium alloy wheels may be evidence of a more serious problem which could lead to wheel failure. If corrosion is evident, consult your Ford dealer for advice.*

7   Before removing a roadwheel which has been balanced on the car, always mark one wheel stud and bolt hole so that the roadwheel may be refitted in the same relative position to maintain the balance.

18.3 Rear spring-to-rear shackle securing bolt

18.4 Rear spring forward mounting

18.5 Rear spring-to-axle U-bolt mountings and insulators

20 Fault diagnosis – suspension and steering

Symptom	Reason(s)
Steering feels vague, car wanders and floats at speed	General wear or damage Tyre pressures uneven Shock absorbers worn Spring clips broken Steering gear balljoints badly worn Suspension geometry incorrect Steering mechanism free play excessive Front suspension and rear axle pick-up points out of alignment
Stiff and heavy steering	Lack of maintenance or accident damage Tyre pressures too low Front wheel toe-in incorrect Suspension geometry incorrect Steering gear incorrectly adjusted too tightly Steering column badly misaligned

Symptom	Reason(s)
Wheel wobble and vibration	General wear or damage
	Wheel nuts loose
	Front wheels and tyres out of balance
	Steering balljoints badly worn
	Hub bearings badly worn
	Steering gear free play excessive
	Front springs loose, weak or broken

Chapter 12 Bodywork and fittings

Contents

1 General description

The combined body and underframe are of welded all-steel unit construction, similar to that of the standard Escort, but having added reinforcement points built into the bodyshell during manufacture. These points are shown in Fig. 12.1, together with the soundproofing panel locations.

The Mexico, RS 1800 and RS2000 models all have a two-door bodyshell, but the RS 2000 differs from the other two variants in having a single unit front section panel which incorporates the front grille and an airdam (spoiler). This panel is manufactured in polyurethane, as is the rear spoiler (fitted to all models). This is an important point to remember when using a welding torch in the close proximity of these items.

The heating and ventilation system introduces separate fresh air ventilation through adjustable face level vents; these vents can be used for side window demisting during damp weather.

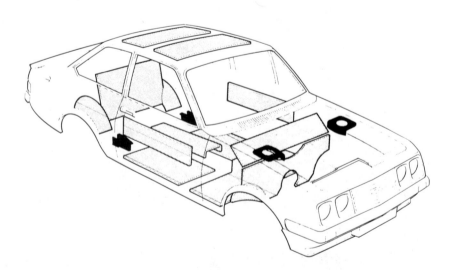

Fig. 12.1 The RS Series Escort models have added reinforcement at the points shown. The sound insulating panels are also shown in this cutaway view of the bodyshell (Sec 1)

All models are fitted with bucket seats at the front, and a bench seat at the rear. The rake of the front seat is infinitely adjustable via a wheel controlled mechanism on the seat side.

2   Maintenance – bodywork and underframe

1   The general condition of a vehicle's bodywork is the one thing that significantly affects its value. Maintenance is easy but needs to be regular. Neglect, particularly after minor damage, can lead quickly to further deterioration and costly repair bills. It is important also to keep watch on those parts of the vehicle not immediately visible, for instance the underside, inside all the wheel arches, the lower part of the engine compartment and the drain channels (photos).

2.1a Probe the body drain channels with a piece of stiff wire to clean them ...

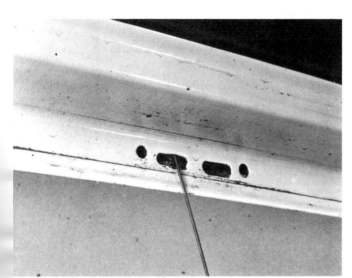

2.1b ... and also keep the door underside drain channels clear

2   The basic maintenance routine for the bodywork is washing – preferably with a lot of water, from a hose. This will remove all the loose solids which may have stuck to the vehicle. It is important to flush these off in such a way as to prevent grit from scratching the finish. The wheel arches and underframe need washing in the same way to remove any accumulated mud which will retain moisture and tend to encourage rust. Paradoxically enough, the best time to clean the underframe and wheel arches is in wet weather when the mud is thoroughly wet and soft. In very wet weather the underframe is usually

cleaned of large accumulations automatically and this is a good time for inspection.
3   Periodically, it is a good idea to have the whole of the underframe of the vehicle steam cleaned, engine compartment included, so that a thorough inspection can be carried out to see what minor repairs and renovations are necessary. Steam cleaning is available at many garages and is necessary for removal of the accumulation of oily grime which sometimes is allowed to become thick in certain areas. If steam cleaning facilities are not available, there are one or two excellent grease solvents available which can be brush applied. The dirt can then be simply hosed off.
4   After washing paintwork, wipe off with a chamois leather to give an unspotted clear finish. A coat of clear protective wax polish will give added protection against chemical pollutants in the air. If the paintwork sheen has dulled or oxidised, use a cleaner/polisher combination to restore the brilliance of the shine. This requires a little effort, but such dulling is usually caused because regular washing has been neglected. Always check that the door and ventilator opening drain holes and pipes are completely clear so that water can be drained out. Brightwork should be treated in the same way as paintwork. Windscreens and windows can be kept clear of the smeary film which often appears, by adding a little ammonia to the water. If they are scratched, a good rub with a proprietary metal polish will often clear them. Never use any form of wax or other body or chromium polish on the windscreen.

3   Maintenance – upholstery and carpets

1   Mats and carpets should be brushed or vacuum cleaned regularly to keep them free of grit. If they are badly stained remove them from the vehicle for scrubbing or sponging and make quite sure they are dry before refitting. Seats and interior trim panels can be kept clean by wiping with a damp cloth. If they do become stained (which can be more apparent on light coloured upholstery) use a little liquid detergent and a soft nail brush to scour the grime out of the grain of the material. Do not forget to keep the headlining clean in the same way as the upholstery. When using liquid cleaners inside the vehicle do not over-wet the surfaces being cleaned. Excessive damp could get into the seams and padded interior causing stains, offensive odours or even rot. If the inside of the vehicle gets wet accidentally it is worthwhile taking some trouble to dry it out properly, particularly where carpets are involved. *Do not leave oil or electric heaters inside the vehicle for this purpose.*

4   Minor body damage – repair

The photographic sequences on pages 214 and 215 illustrate the operations detailed in the following sub-sections.

Repair of minor scratches in bodywork
If the scratch is very superficial, and does not penetrate to the metal of the bodywork, repair is very simple. Lightly rub the area of the scratch with a paintwork renovator, or a very fine cutting paste, to remove loose paint from the scratch and to clear the surrounding bodywork of wax polish. Rinse the area with clean water.
    Apply touch-up paint to the scratch using a fine paint brush; continue to apply fine layers of paint until the surface of the paint in the scratch is level with the surrounding paintwork. Allow the new paint at least two weeks to harden: then blend it into the surrounding paintwork by rubbing the scratch area with a paintwork renovator or a very fine cutting paste. Finally, apply wax polish.
    Where the scratch has penetrated right through to the metal of the bodywork, causing the metal to rust, a different repair technique is required. Remove any loose rust from the bottom of the scratch with a penknife, then apply rust inhibiting paint to prevent the formation of rust in the future. Using a rubber or nylon applicator fill the scratch with bodystopper paste. If required, this paste can be mixed with cellulose thinners to provide a very thin paste which is ideal for filling narrow scratches. Before the stopper-paste in the scratch hardens, wrap a piece of smooth cotton rag around the top of a finger. Dip the finger in cellulose thinners and then quickly sweep it across the surface of the stopper-paste in the scratch; this will ensure that the surface of the stopper-paste is slightly hollowed. The scratch can now be painted over as described earlier in this Section.

Repair of dents in bodywork

When deep denting of the vehicle's bodywork has taken place, the first task is to pull the dent out, until the affected bodywork almost attains its original shape. There is little point in trying to restore the original shape completely, as the metal in the damaged area will have stretched on impact and cannot be reshaped fully to its original contour. It is better to bring the level of the dent up to a point which is about $\frac{1}{8}$ in (3 mm) below the level of the surrounding bodywork. In cases where the dent is very shallow anyway, it is not worth trying to pull it out at all. If the underside of the dent is accessible, it can be hammered out gently from behind, using a mallet with a wooden or plastic head. Whilst doing this, hold a suitable block of wood firmly against the outside of the panel to absorb the impact from the hammer blows and thus prevent a large area of the bodywork from being 'belled-out'.

Should the dent be in a section of the bodywork which has a double skin or some other factor making it inaccessible from behind, a different technique is called for. Drill several small holes through the metal inside the area – particularly in the deeper section. Then screw long self-tapping screws into the holes just sufficiently for them to gain a good purchase in the metal. Now the dent can be pulled out by pulling on the protruding heads of the screws with a pair of pliers.

The next stage of the repair is the removal of the paint from the damaged area, and from an inch or so of the surrounding 'sound' bodywork. This is accomplished most easily by using a wire brush or abrasive pad on a power drill, although it can be done just as effectively by hand using sheets of abrasive paper. To complete the preparation for filling, score the surface of the bare metal with a screwdriver or the tang of a file, or alternatively, drill small holes in the affected area. This will provide a really good 'key' for the filler paste.

To complete the repair see the Section on filling and re-spraying.

Repair of rust holes or gashes in bodywork

Remove all paint from the affected area and from an inch or so of the surrounding 'sound' bodywork, using an abrasive pad or a wire brush on a power drill. If these are not available a few sheets of abrasive paper will do the job just as effectively. With the paint removed you will be able to gauge the severity of the corrosion and therefore decide whether to renew the whole panel (if this is possible) or to repair the affected area. New body panels are not as expensive as most people think and it is often quicker and more satisfactory to fit a new panel than to attempt to repair large areas of corrosion.

Remove all fittings from the affected area except those which will act as a guide to the original shape of the damaged bodywork (eg headlamp shells etc). Then, using tin snips or a hacksaw blade, remove all loose metal and any other metal badly affected by corrosion. Hammer the edges of the hole inwards in order to create a slight depression for the filler paste.

Wire brush the affected area to remove the powdery rust from the surface of the remaining metal. Paint the affected area with rust inhibiting paint; if the back of the rusted area is accessible treat this also.

Before filling can take place it will be necessary to block the hole in some way. This can be achieved by the use of zinc gauze or aluminium tape.

Zinc gauze is probably the best material to use for a large hole. Cut a piece to the approximate size and shape of the hole to be filled, then position it in the hole so that its edges are below the level of the surrounding bodywork. It can be retained in position by several blobs of filler paste around its periphery.

Aluminium tape should be used for small or very narrow holes. Pull a piece off the roll and trim it to the approximate size and shape required, then pull off the backing paper (if used) and stick the tape over the hole; it can be overlapped if the thickness of one piece is insufficient. Burnish down the edges of the tape with the handle of a screwdriver or similar, to ensure that the tape is securely attached to the metal underneath.

Bodywork repairs – filling and re-spraying

Before using this Section, see the Sections on dent, deep scratch, rust holes and gash repairs.

Many types of bodyfiller are available, but generally speaking those proprietary kits which contain a tin of filler paste and a tube of resin hardener are best for this type of repair. A wide, flexible plastic or nylon applicator will be found invaluable for imparting a smooth and well contoured finish to the surface of the filler.

Mix up a little filler on a clean piece of card or board – measure the hardener carefully (follow the maker's instructions on the pack) otherwise the filler will set too rapidly or too slowly.

Using the applicator apply the filler paste to the prepared area; draw the applicator across the surface of the filler to achieve the correct contour and to level the filler surface. As soon as a contour that approximates to the correct one is achieved, stop working the paste – if you carry on too long the paste will become sticky and begin to 'pick up' on the applicator. Continue to add thin layers of filler paste at twenty-minute intervals until the level of the filler is just proud of the surrounding bodywork.

Once the filler has hardened, excess can be removed using a metal plane or file. From then on, progressively finer grades of abrasive paper should be used, starting with a 40 grade production paper and finishing with 400 grade wet-and-dry paper. Always wrap the abrasive paper around a flat rubber, cork, or wooden block – otherwise the surface of the filler will not be completely flat. During the smoothing of the filler surface the wet-and-dry paper should be periodically rinsed in water. This will ensure that a very smooth finish is imparted to the filler at the final stage.

At this stage the 'dent' should be surrounded by a ring of bare metal, which in turn should be encircled by the finely 'feathered' edge of the good paintwork. Rinse the repair area with clean water, until all of the dust produced by the rubbing-down operation has gone.

Spray the whole repair area with a light coat of primer – this will show up any imperfections in the surface of the filler. Repair these imperfections with fresh filler paste or bodystopper, and once more smooth the surface with abrasive paper. If bodystopper is used, it can be mixed with cellulose thinners to form a really thin paste which is ideal for filling small holes. Repeat this spray and repair procedure until you are satisfied that the surface of the filler, and the feathered edge of the paintwork are perfect. Clean the repair area with clean water and allow to dry fully.

The repair area is now ready for final spraying. Paint spraying must be carried out in a warm, dry, windless and dust free atmosphere. This condition can be created artificially if you have access to a large indoor working area, but if you are forced to work in the open, you will have to pick your day very carefully. If you are working indoors, dousing the floor in the work area with water will help to settle the dust which would otherwise be in the atmosphere. If the repair area is confined to one body panel, mask off the surrounding panels; this will help to minimise the effects of a slight mis-match in paint colours. Bodywork fittings (eg chrome strips, door handles etc) will also need to be masked off. Use genuine masking tape and several thicknesses of newspaper for the masking operations.

Before commencing to spray, agitate the aerosol can thoroughly, then spray a test area (an old tin, or similar) until the technique is mastered. Cover the repair area with a thick coat of primer; the thickness should be built up using several thin layers of paint rather than one thick one. Using 400 grade wet-and-dry paper, rub down the surface of the primer until it is really smooth. While doing this, the work area should be thoroughly doused with water, and the wet-and-dry paper periodically rinsed in water. Allow to dry before spraying on more paint.

Spray on the top coat, again building up the thickness by using several thin layers of paint. Start spraying in the centre of the repair area and then, using a circular motion, work outwards until the whole repair area and about 2 inches of the surrounding original paintwork is covered. Remove all masking material 10 to 15 minutes after spraying on the final coat of paint.

Allow the new paint at least two weeks to harden, then, using a paintwork renovator or a very fine cutting paste, blend the edges of the paint into the existing paintwork. Finally, apply wax polish.

---

5 Major body damage – repair

1   Because the body is built on the unitary principle and is integral with the underframe, major damage must be repaired by competent mechanics with the necessary welding and hydraulic straightening equipment.
2   If the damage has been serious, it is vital that the body is checked for correct alignment, as otherwise the handling of the car will suffer and many other faults such as excessive wear in the tyres, transmission and steering may occur.

6 Maintenance – hinges and locks

Once every six months, or 6000 miles (9600 km), the door, bonnet and boot hinges should be oiled with a few drops of engine oil from an oil can.

1   To oil a hinge, check that the plastic plugs in the ends of the hollow hinge pin are in place, then prise the top plug out of its location in the pin.

2   Fill the hollow pin with oil and refit the top plug, carefully wiping away any overspill.

3   Open and close the door several times to disperse the oil then repeat the process for the remaining hinges. The door striker plates can be given a thin smear of grease to reduce wear and ensure free-movement.

7 Front bumper – removal and refitting

1   Disconnect the battery earth lead, then the leads to the indicator lights.

2   From within the wheel arch unscrew and remove the bumper-to-corner bracket retaining nut.

3   Unscrew and remove the retaining nut for the bumper support bracket on the underside at the front. The bumper can now be removed, complete with indicator light unit.

4   Refitting is a reversal of the above procedure, but before finally tightening the retaining nuts ensure that the bumper is set straight relative to the ground and adjacent body components.

5   Check that the indicator operates on reconnecting the battery lead.

8 Front surround unit (RS 2000) – removal and refitting

1   Disconnect the battery earth lead.

2   Raise and support the front of the car on axle stands.

3   Remove the headlight surround from each side. These are each secured by two cross-head screws.

4   With the bonnet raised, unscrew and remove the four cross-head screws securing the front grille at its top edge. Access to the screws is through the grille and inner headlight apertures (see Fig. 12.2).

5   Unscrew and remove the three cross-head screws from underneath the front bumper (photo).

6   Working under the car, unscrew the two bolts through the bumper bar and the four nuts from the panel lower edge (photo).

7   Unscrew and remove the wheel arch flange bolt and the four nuts securing the panel to the front wing on each side. Should the bolts or

8.5 Remove the cross-head screws beneath the bumper (RS 2000)

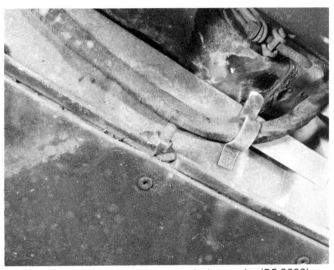

8.6 Front surround panel securing nut on its lower edge (RS 2000)

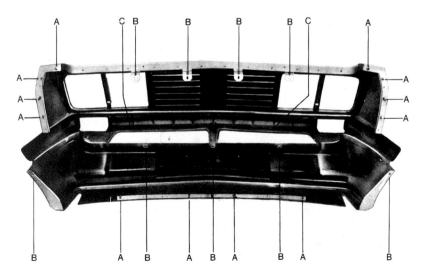

Fig. 12.2 The RS 2000 front surround panel fastening positions (Sec 8)

A   Studs and nuts   B   Cross-head screw   C   Bolts

nuts be badly corroded, clean them and then soak them in penetrating oil before trying to move them. Do not apply heat to them, since the surround panel assembly is manufactured in polyurethane and must not be exposed to temperatures above 180°F (80°C).

8   When the respective fastenings have been removed the front panel unit can be pulled forwards and away from the car.

9   Refitting is a reversal of the removal procedure, but do not fully tighten the fastening nuts and bolts until all are in position and the panel aligned. All fastenings are tightened to the same torque wrench setting of between 17 and 23 lbf in (19.5 and 26.5 kgf cm).

9   Front spoiler – removal and refitting

1   Jack up the front end of the car and support it with axle stands.
2   Working underneath the front end, unscrew and remove the spoiler-to-radiator grille panel securing nuts. There are four nuts in all.
3   Now unscrew and remove the single bolt from each wheel arch flange and withdraw the spoiler.
4   Refitting is a reversal of the removal process, but check the spoiler alignment before fully tightening the fastenings.

10   Rear spoiler – removal and refitting

1   Raise and support the boot lid, then unscrew and remove the four spoiler securing bolts on the inside and lift the spoiler clear.
2   Refit in the reverse order to removal, but check the spoiler alignment before fully tightening the retaining bolts.

11   Rear bumper – removal and refitting

1   Disconnect the battery earth lead, then detach the leads to the rear number plate light.
2   Remove the spare wheel from its location in the boot, then unscrew and remove the nuts or bolts (as applicable), which are accessible from inside the boot (photo), together with their washers from each end of the bumper.
3   The RS 2000 differs in that the rear bumper extends further down the body side at each corner and is secured on the side panels by two cross-head screws per side. These screws are recessed and covered by plastic plugs. Prise free the plugs and remove the screws (photo).
4   Remove the bumper-to-support brackets each side at the rear, working underneath, and withdraw the bumper. These fastenings may well require a soaking in penetrating oil to loosen them.
5   Refit in the reverse order to removal, aligning the bumper correctly before fully tightening the fastenings. On completion check that the number plate light is operational.

12   Door rattles – tracing and rectification

1   The most common cause of door rattle is a misaligned, loose or worn striker plate, but other causes may be:

   (a) *Loose door handles or window winder handles*
   (b) *Loose, or misaligned door lock components*
   (c) *Loose or worn remote control mechanism*

2   It is quite possible for door rattles to be the result of a combination of the above faults so a careful examination must be made to determine the cause of the fault.
3   If the nose of the striker plate is worn and as a result the door rattles, renew and then adjust the plate, as described in Section 13 (photo).
4   Should the inner door handle rattle, this is easily cured by fitting a rubber washer between the escutcheon and the handle.
5   If the door lock is found to be worn and rattles as a consequence, then fit a new lock (Section 15).

13   Door striker plate – removal, refitting and adjustment

1   Mark the position of the striker plate on the door pillar using a soft pencil.

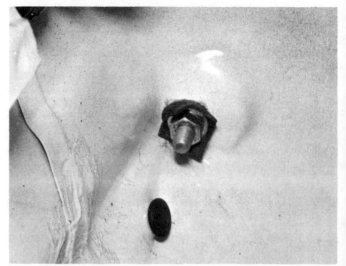

11.2 Rear bumper corner securing nut inside the boot

11.3 Remove the plastic plugs from the RS 2000 bumper for access to the securing screws

12.3 Door lock striker plate – check for wear

2   Unscrew and remove the cross-head securing screws and lift the striker plate away.

3   Refit the striker plate by positioning the plate on the door pillar within the lines previously described, and loosely securing with the screws.

4   To adjust the plate, close the door to the first of the two locking positions and visually check the alignment of the outside edge of the striker plate relative to the edge of the lock support plate. This check is best carried out by looking at the lock/striker plate from either the top, or bottom, edges of the door, while shining a light on the lock/striker plate location. The edges of the striker and lockplates should be parallel.

5   Measure the distance the door edge stands proud of the adjacent body panel; for a correctly set door this distance should be 6.00 mm (0.25 in).

6   If necessary the striker plate securing screws must be slackened and the striker plate moved until both the parallel condition and the proud condition described above are achieved (Fig. 12.3).

7   The lock claw to lock striker clearance must now be measured and, if necessary, adjusted. The lock claw is the U-shaped portion of the lock (protruding through the door) which responds to the action of the door handle. Before this measurement can be taken the lock must be in the 'open' position (ie the 'U' of the claw must be facing the striker). The correct setting is best obtained by placing a small ball of Plasticine on the top of the striker post and then gently closing and opening the door. The top of the Plasticine ball will be flattened by the lock claw and the distance between this flat edge and the striker post is the lock claw to striker clearance. This should be 2.0 mm (0.08 in). If necessary, **and without disturbing the previously obtained settings,** vertically reposition the striker plate until the correct dimension is obtained. When adjustment is correct, fully tighten the securing screws (Fig. 12.4).

14 Door trim pad – removal and refitting

1   Carefully slide the window regulator handle plastic trim upwards (ie away from the tapered end), to disengage the trim from its retaining slots. With the trim free of the slots it can be lifted clear out of the handle recess to expose the handle retaining screws.

2   Wind the window glass into the closed position. Note the position of the handle then unscrew the cross-head screw retaining the handle to the shaft, and detach the handle and bezel from the shaft (photo).

3   Undo and remove the two cross-head screws securing the door armrest (photos) and lift the armrest off the trim pad. Unscrew the private lock button (located in the top corner of the pad) off the private lock rod.

4   Press the trim panel away from the remote control door handle bezel at the same time pushing the bezel towards the hinge end of the door. This will disengage the bezel retaining lugs from their locations

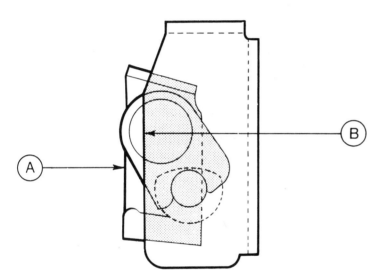

Fig. 12.3 Parallel condition between the lock striker (A) and the lock support plate (B) (Sec 13)

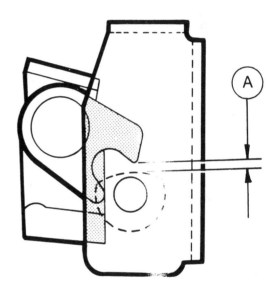

Fig. 12.4 Lock claw-to-striker clearance (Sec 13)

$A = 2.0$ mm

14.2 Unscrew the cross-head retaining screw to remove the window regulator handle

14.3a Unscrew the two screws securing the armrest to the door panel

14.3b Alternative armrest fitted to some models – also secured by two screws

14.4 Push the trim panel inwards, then slide the bezel towards the hinge end of the door

14.6 The door trim panel removed. Note the weatherproof sheet attached to the door skin

whereupon the bezel can be lifted out of its location (photo). **Do not attempt to lever the bezel out of its location as this will almost certainly result in broken retaining lugs.**

5   Where fitted, unscrew and remove the remote control adjuster stalk retaining bezel.

6   Insert a thin strip of metal with all the sharp edges removed between the recessed trim panel and the door. This will release one or two of the trim panel clips without damaging the trim and the panel can then be gently eased off by hand (photo). A short metal ruler is ideal for this job.

7   If necessary the alkathene waterproof sheeting can now be removed.

8   Refitting is generally a reversal of the removal procedure. However, the following points should be noted. If the alkathene sheet is torn, or badly distorted, it must be renewed to ensure a weatherproof seal. When the defective sheet has been removed, all traces of old adhesive, or tape, must be removed before the new double-sided tape is applied. Apply the new tape so that the edge of the tape is 6 mm (0.25 in) from the edge of the door inner panel and so that the trim clip holes are covered. If a new sheet is being made up, the door trim pad can be used as a template, with the edges of the sheet cut 5.0 mm (0.2 in) inside the periphery of the pad. Start fixing the sheet to the door at the top edge, progressing down the sides and finally pushing the lower edge of the sheet into the slot at the bottom of the door. Working upwards from the bottom, smooth the sheet down making sure that there are no air bubbles in the sheet, particularly along the bottom and sides. When the sheet has been satisfactorily smoothed down, cover the slot with tape.

15 Door lock – removal and refitting

1   Refer to Section 14, and remove the door trim pad.

2   Carefully slide the remote control door handle assembly towards the hinge end of the door to disengage it from the cut-out in the door inner panel. Turn the assembly, as necessary, to unhook the lock control rod and place the assembly to one side.

3   Locate the window frame lower retaining screw on the door inner panel; remove this screw and push the frame to one side to improve access to the lock assembly.

4   Unclip the two rods connecting the lock to the exterior handle linkage; these rods are located in the white bushes on the lock mechanism.

5   From outside the vehicle, unscrew and remove the three screws securing the lock to the door. Turn the lock claw to the 'closed' position (ie with the 'U' of the claw facing the floor), and push the lock into the door shell.

6   Lower the lock assembly into the shell sufficiently for the private lock rod to clear its housing then manoeuvre the lock through the lower cut-out and thence from the shell.

Fig. 12.5 The lock unit showing the position of the white bushes (B) and the black bush (A) (Sec 15)

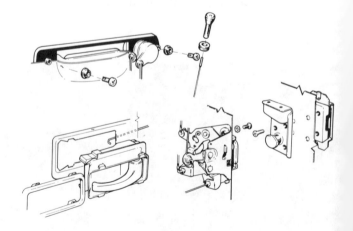

Fig. 12.6 Door lock assembly and associate components (Sec 15)

7   Refitting the door lock assembly is the reverse of the removal sequence. Check its operation before refitting the door panel trim.

16   Door lock barrel – removal and refitting

1   Remove the door trim pad, as described in Section 14.
2   Locally remove the alkathene sheet in the rear top corner of the door, to expose the exterior handle retaining screws and the door lock assembly.
3   Disconnect the exterior handle connecting rods from their locations in the door lock mechanism (the lock rods are connected to the links with white bushes).
4   Unscrew the two cross-head screws retaining the exterior handle to the door shell and carefully detach the handle, together with the lock rods, from the door.
5   Remove the lock barrel by tapping the roll pin from the end cap, and separating the end cap, U-washer, return spring and seals. Withdraw the barrel and seal from the exterior handle casting.
6   Refitting the lock barrel and exterior handle is a reversal of the removal process.

17   Door window regulator knob – renewal

1   On models produced from September 1977 a revised design of window regulator knob is fitted to comply with EEC legislation. If the knob breaks as a result of accidental impact, it can be renewed by following this procedure.
2   Remove the regulator handle as described in Section 14.
3   Using a screwdriver, rotate the remaining plastic retainer one-eighth of a turn anti-clockwise and remove it from under the handle.
4   Press out the plastic retainer and cap from the knob using a suitable drift with the knob located over a tube of internal diameter 1.125 in (28 mm). Do not prise the cap from the front of the knob.
5   Assemble the knob in reverse order, but note that the diameter of the retainer ('X' in Fig. 12.8) was increased in late 1978. It is possible to fit the larger diameter retainer to cars manufactured before 1978, but not vice versa.

18   Door window regulator – removal and refitting

1   Wind the window down and remove the door remote control handle, the window regulator handle, the armrest/door pull and trim panel (Section 14).
2   Undo the screws and washers which secure the window regulator assembly (photo). This is best achieved after lowering the window as the regulator and bracket can be seen through the lower cut-out in the door shell. Remove the screw securing the pivot plate to the door inner

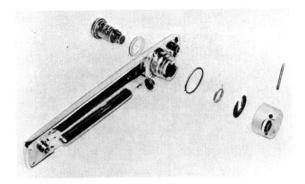

Fig. 12.7 Door handle and lock barrel components (Sec 16)

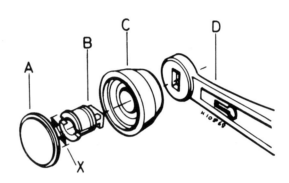

Fig. 12.8 Exploded view of modified window regulator handle (Sec 17)

A   Cap
B   Retainer
C   Knob
D   Arm
X   Retainer diameter

panel and then push the plate into the door shell so that the regulator handle shaft no longer protrudes through the inner panel.
3   Slide the regulator arm along the door glass bracket and into the enlarged area at the end of the bracket (photo). The arm can be disengaged from the bracket at this point. With the arm free, push the glass up into the closed position and withdraw the regulator assembly

18.2 Window regulator retaining screws

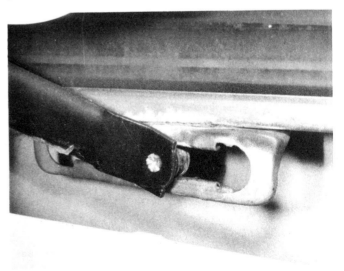

18.3 Move the regulator arm into the enlarged section of the door glass bracket

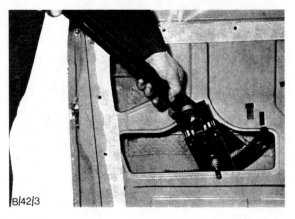

Fig. 12.9 Withdrawing the door window regulator mechanism (Sec 18)

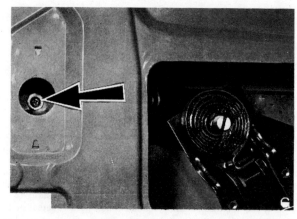

Fig. 12.10 Quarter-light dividing channel lower securing screw (arrowed) (Sec 19)

Fig. 12.11 Door glass removal (from passenger side) (Sec 19)

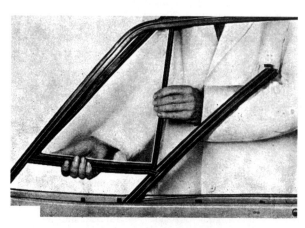

Fig. 12.12 Remove the quarter-light glass from the outer side of the door (Sec 20)

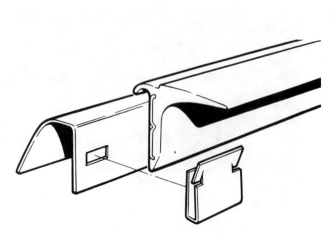

Fig. 12.13 Door weatherstrip and moulding assembly (Sec 21)

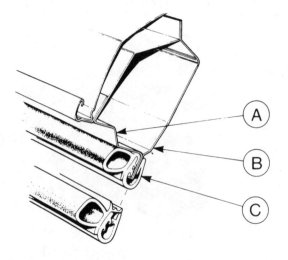

Fig. 12.14 Door aperture weatherstrip (Sec 21)

A   Roof
B   Roof rail
C   Weatherstrip

through the lower door cut-out. If necessary, remove the screw securing the lower end of the frame and push the frame to one side to gain access for removing the regulator.

4   Refitting the regulator is the reverse of the removal sequence.

19 Door glass – removal and refitting

1   Remove the door trim pad, as described in Section 14.
2   Prise the inner and outer door belt weatherstrips from their retaining clips in the upper gap between the door inner and outer panels.
3   Remove the screw securing the upper end of the quarter-light dividing channel to the frame, and the single screw securing the lower end to the door inner panel. Tilt the dividing channel, as necessary, to enable its removal from the door shell.
4   Remove the door window glass by sliding the glass along the regulator arm until the arm can be disengaged from the glass retaining bracket.
5   Push the regulator arm clear of the glass and withdraw the glass from the shell, passing the window frame on the passenger compartment side (Fig. 12.11).
6   Refitting the door glass is the reverse sequence to removal.

20 Door fixed quarter-lights – removal and refitting

1   Commence removal of these components from the front door by first removing the inner and outer weatherstrips and their clips (Section 21).
2   Remove the screw which secures the top of the quarter-light dividing channel to the door frame.
3   Remove the door interior trim pad as previously described (Section 14) and then remove the screw and washer securing the bottom of the dividing channel.
4   Pull the sliding channel down and then incline it toward the rear of the vehicle. The ventilator or fixed quarter-light may now be lifted from the door frame (Fig. 12.12).
5   Refitting is a reversal of removal.

21 Door belt weatherstrip (outer) – removal and refitting

1   Wind the window down to its fullest extent. Carefully prise the weatherstrips and moulding assembly out of the retaining clips along the top edge of the door shell.
2   With the weatherstrip and moulding assembly clear of the door belt, carefully prise the U-clips securing the moulding and weatherstrip together off the assembly, and separate the moulding and weatherstrip.
3   Refit the weatherstrip by first aligning it along the moulding and securing with the U-clips then locate the combined moulding and weatherstrip in the door shell clips.

22 Door – removal and refitting

1   Using a soft pencil accurately mark the outline of the door hinge on the body. Disconnect the door check arm by removing the check arm pin, then remove the hinge nuts and detach the door complete with hinges (Figs. 12.15 and 12.16).
2   For storage it is best to stand the door on an old blanket and allow it to rest against a wall, with the contact point between window frame and wall also well padded.
3   Refitting is a reversal of removal, but before finally tightening the hinge nuts check the door set in the door aperture as follows.
4   Remove the door scuff plate and pull the door aperture weatherstrip off the door aperture flange.
5   Undo the four screws and remove the door striker plate, close the door and check the gap between the door and aperture flange; this should be 0.5 to 0.65 in, (12 to 16 mm). If necessary work the flange to achieve the correct clearance.
6   Ensure that the door is correctly aligned in the aperture relative to the contours of the aperture and the body side breaklines; then finally tighten the hinge bolts.
7   Adjust the door striker plate, as described in Section 13.

23 Bonnet – removal and refitting

1   Open the hood and support it open using the bonnet stay. To act as a datum for refitting, mark round the position of the hinge brackets on the underside of the bonnet with a soft pencil.
2   With the assistance of a second person hold the bonnet in the open position and release the stay.
3   Undo and remove the two bolts, spring and plain washers that secure each hinge to the bonnet (photo), and lift the bonnet off the

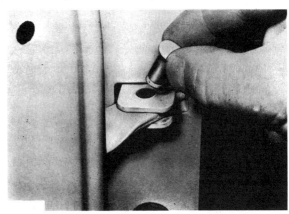

Fig. 12.15 Extract the door check arm pin (Sec 22)

Fig. 12.16 Door hinge retaining nuts (lower) (arrowed) (Sec 22)

| A | Bump stops | C | Hinges |
| B | Bonnet lock spring | D | Striker |

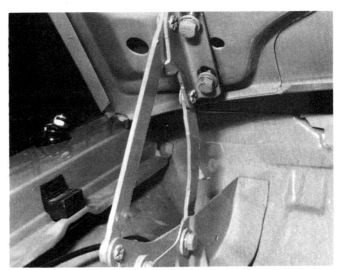

23.3 Release the bolts securing the bonnet to the hinges and carefully lift the bonnet away. Do not forget to mark around the hinges before slackening the bolts

Fig. 12.17 Bonnet adjustment points (Sec 23)

Fig. 12.18 Refit the bonnet striker. When it is properly adjusted fully tighten the locknut (A) (Sec 23)

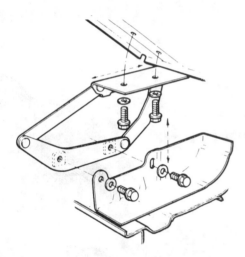

Fig. 12.19 Bonnet hinge assembly (Sec 23)

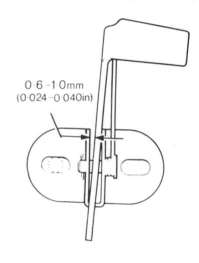

0·6 – 1·0mm
(0·024 – 0·040in)

Fig. 12.20 Check that the bonnet safety catch has the necessary clearance for satisfactory operation (Sec 23)

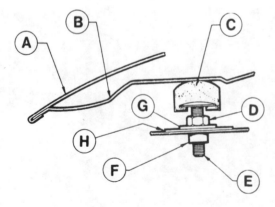

Fig. 12.21 Bonnet bump stop assembly (Sec 23)

A	Bonnet panel	E	Bump stop thread
B	Bonnet inner panel	F	Weld nut
C	Bump rubber	G	Front crossmember
D	Locknut	H	Front crossmember

Fig. 12.22 Bonnet cable clamp (arrowed) (Sec 24)

vehicle, taking care not to damage the top of the wings.
4   Lean the bonnet against a wall with the contact points suitably padded to protect the paintwork against damage.
5   Refitting the bonnet is the reverse sequence to removal. If the hinge brackets are correctly aligned to the previously marked lines the bonnet should be correctly positioned in its aperture. However, if the adjustment has been disturbed the bonnet can be readjusted as follows. Remove the bonnet lock striker after first slackening the locknut.
6   Slacken the locknuts on the rubber bump stops at either end of the front crossmember and screw the bump stops fully into their locations.

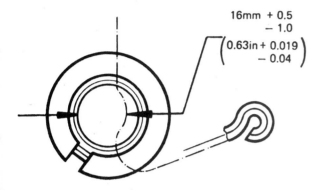

16mm + 0.5
        − 1.0

$$\left(0.63\text{in} + 0.019 \atop - 0.04 \right)$$

Fig. 12.23 Bonnet release spring setting dimension (Sec 24)

7   Close the bonnet and check the gaps on either side of the bonnet between the wings and the gap between the rear edge of the bonnet and the cowl panel. These must be equal along this length and, in the case of the bonnet to wing gap, equal on either side of the bonnet. If necessary, move the bonnet on the hinges to achieve the necessary alignment, then fully tighten the hinge bolts (Fig. 12.19).
8   Check the height of the front of the bonnet relative to the adjacent wings. Progressively screw the bump stops out of their locations until the bonnet is flush with the tops of the wings. Tighten the locknuts on the rubbers when this stage of the bonnet adjustment is correct.
9   Check that the bonnet release spring is correctly adjusted (Section 24).
10 Refit the striker in its location on the underside of the bonnet and screw the striker in, or out, to achieve the following conditions:

   (a) When released from a height of 300 mm (11.8 in) above the 'pop-up' position the bonnet must fully engage
   (b) When released from a height of up to 75 mm (3 in) above the 'pop-up' position only the safety catch must engage

When these conditions are fulfilled tighten the striker locknut.

24 Bonnet release cable – adjustment

1   The bonnet release cable is adjusted by applying tension to the cable until the bonnet release spring is pulled into a set position relative to the spring aperture. The cable is then clamped in position.
2   The cable clamp screw is located on the rear of the front body panel adjacent to the radiator. To gain access to the screw head first remove the radiator grille. Alternatively, if a suitably sized socket set is available the screw can be slackened by inserting the socket attachment through the bars of the grille.
3   Unclip the cable from its retaining clips around the side of the engine compartment and pull the cable through the clamp until the bonnet lock spring setting is as shown in Fig. 12.23.
4   Hold the cable in this position and retighten the clamp bolt. Close the bonnet and operate the release lever; the bonnet should 'pop-up' freely. If it does not, recheck the spring setting, if this is correct readjust the bonnet lock striker.

25 Bonnet release spring – removal and refitting

1   Slacken the bonnet release cable clamp screw.
2   Unscrew the screw retaining the bonnet release spring clamp plate. Withdraw the spring arm from the aperture in the lock support plate and manoeuvre the spring until the release cable loop can be disengaged from the release spring arm.
3   When the cable has been disconnected manoeuvre the spring around in the lock support plate and out of its location via the aperture in the rear of the crossmember.
4   Refitting is a reversal of the removal procedure. Before finally tightening the cable clamp screw adjust the release spring, as described in Section 24.

26 Boot lid and lock – removal and refitting

1   Open the boot lid and mark the position of the hinge plates using a soft pencil.
2   Release the cranked end of the torsion bar (used to counterbalance the lid) from its retaining bracket. Disconnect the double cranked end from the hinge and withdraw the torsion bar.
3   Remove the hinge securing bolts and their washers, and lift the lid away.
4   The boot lock can be removed without removing the boot lid.
5   To remove the lock assembly remove the spring clip from the end of the lock spindle and remove the three bolts which secure the lock to the boot lid.
6   To remove the lock barrel from two door models, insert a pair of long nosed pliers through the aperture left after withdrawal of the lock mechanism, and compress the legs of the lock barrel retaining clip.
7   Refitting of all components is a reversal of removal, but if necessary adjust the lock striker by slightly loosening its retaining bolts to provide positive closure of the boot lid without any rattling.

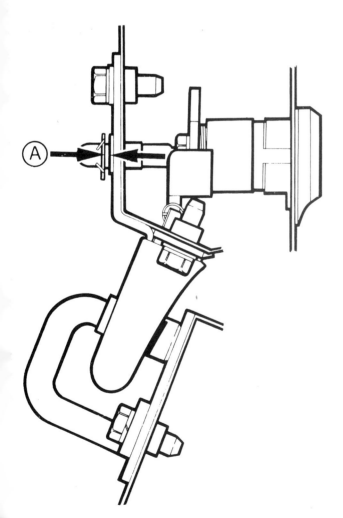

Fig. 12.24 Position of clip on boot lid lock barrel spindle (Sec 26)

A = 2.0 ± 1.0 mm

27 Windscreen – removal and refitting

1   If you are unfortunate enough to have a windscreen shatter or should you wish to renew your present windscreen, fitting a replacement is one of the few jobs which the average owner is advised to leave to a professional. For the owner who wishes to do the job himself the following instructions are given.

2   If the screen has shattered, cover the bonnet with a blanket or cloth to prevent accidental damage and remove the windscreen wiper blades and arms (Chapter 10).

3   Cover the facia demister slots and then knock the crystals out of the rubber frame. Withdraw the rubber surround and clean the glass channel free from mastic or glass crystals. If it is cut or hardened, renew it.

4   If the screen is intact, first check the type of screen fitted to the vehicle, this can be either 'laminated' or 'toughened'. To identify whether the screen is toughened or laminated, locate the manufacturer's trademark which will include either the word 'toughened' or 'laminated' or the letters 'T' or 'L'.

5   Before commencing windscreen removal, remove the windscreen wiper arms and blades, as described in Chapter 10, then cover the windscreen cowl and bonnet to prevent accidental damage to the paintwork.

6   Sitting inside the vehicle, and starting at one corner of the screen, use a blunt ended lever to push the weatherstrip lip under the weatherstrip aperture flange, at the same time pushing the glass forwards to fully disengage the glass and rubber from the flange. Continue the process, working in small lengths at a time, around the periphery of the screen until the glass and weatherstrip assembly is completely out of the screen aperture.

7   An alternative method **not** to be used on laminated screens: put on a pair of soft shoes and sit in one of the front seats. With a piece of soft cloth between the soles of your shoes and the windscreen glass, place both feet in one top corner of the windscreen and push firmly.

8   When the rubber surround has freed itself from the body flange in that area, repeat the process at frequent intervals along the top edge of the windscreen until, from outside the car, the glass and rubber surround can be removed together.

9   Gently prise out the clip which covers the joint of the finisher strip and pull the finisher strip out of the rubber surround. Then remove the rubber surround from the glass.

10   Check the weatherstrip for signs of perishing, cuts, or distortion; if there is any doubt about the condition of a weatherstrip it should be renewed. If the rubber is deemed suitable for further service it must be completely cleaned of all traces of hardened sealer before it is fitted to the new glass.

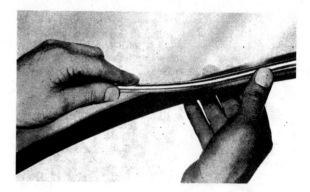

Fig. 12.25 Mylar finisher strip removal from weatherstrip (Sec 27)

11   Check the windscreen aperture in the vehicle to ensure that the flange is free from buckles and distortion and that all traces of hardened sealer are removed from both sides of the flange.

12   Apply a suitable sealer to the rubber-to-body groove. In this groove fit a fine but strong piece of cord right the way round allowing an overlap of about 6 inches (150 mm) at the joint.

13   From outside the car, place the windscreen in its correct position, making sure the loose end of the cord is inside the car.

14   With an assistant pressing firmly on the outside of the windscreen get into the car and pull out the cord, thus drawing the lip of the rubber surround over the body flange (Fig. 12.27).

15   Apply a further layer of sealer to the underside of the rubber glass groove from outside the car.

16   Refit the finisher strip into its groove in the rubber surround and refit the clip which covers its joint.

17   Carefully clean off any surplus sealer from the windscreen glass before it has a chance to harden, and then refit the windscreen wiper arms and blades.

28 Rear window – removal and refitting

The procedure for removing the rear window is identical to that described for the windscreen.

Fig. 12.26 Inserting cord into weatherstrip-to-body groove. If the cord is first passed through to thin metal tube and the tube then inserted into the weatherstrip groove, positioning the cord is simply a matter of drawing the tube around the periphery of the weatherstrip (Sec 27)

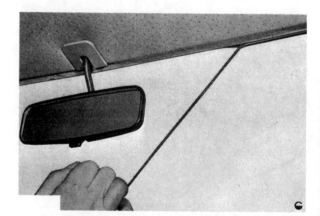

Fig. 12.27 Refitting the windscreen (Sec 27)
Note that the cord is being pulled at right-angles to the aperture flange

29 Fixed rear quarter glass – removal and refitting

1 Have an assistant ready to catch the glass as it is released from the body aperture. Working from inside the vehicle use a blunt screwdriver to carefully ease the weatherstrip rubber off the aperture flange, at the same time pushing on the glass to release the glass and rubber from the aperture.

2 Remove the weatherstrip from the glass and remove all traces of old sealer from the glass-to-weatherstrip groove. Inspect the weatherstrip for signs of splitting, or deterioration. If there is any doubt about the condition of the weatherstrip it must be renewed.

3 Check that the window aperture moulding is correctly positioned on the aperture flange and that the double sided sponge sealing strip is in good condition.

4 Fit a length of cord in the weatherstrip to body groove, so that the ends of the cord have a crossover of approximately 150 mm (6.0 in) at the bottom centre of the glass.

5 Offer the glass and weatherstrip assembly to the aperture with the ends of the cord inside the vehicle. Engage the weatherstrip with the flange along the top of the window aperture and push the lower edge firmly into contact with the bottom flange. With an assistant working inside the vehicle, and pulling one end of the cord, **at right-angles to the glass,** push, or tap the glass very firmly adjacent to the cord, to assist in pulling the weatherstrip over the flange.

6 Seal the weatherstrip to glass location with a suitable glass sealer.

30 Radiator grille – removal and refitting (Mexico and RS 1800)

Open the bonnet and support in the open position. Undo and remove the screws that secure the radiator grille to the front body crossmembers, and lift the grille away from the body. Refitting is a reversal of removal, but first check to ensure that the special grille nuts are in place in their locations on the crossmembers.

31 Heater unit – removal and refitting

1 Disconnect the battery by removing the negative earth lead and drain the cooling system, referring to Chapter 2.

2 Remove the centre console, as described in Section 37, and also detach and remove the glove compartment.

3 Working under the bonnet, slacken off the two cable clips on the heater water hoses and then pull the hoses off the bulkhead.

4 Remove the heater pipe sealing plate and gasket from the bulkhead by undoing the two retaining screws.

5 Unscrew the four screws retaining the top edge of the heater

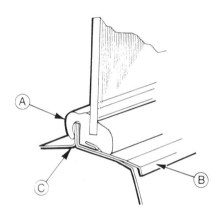

Fig. 12.28 Fixed rear quarter glass assembly (Sec 29)

A   Weatherstrip rubber   C   Flange
B   Moulding

Fig. 12.29 Offering fixed rear quarter window into body aperture. Note cord crossover at centre of lower edge of glass (Sec 29)

Fig. 12.30 Radiator grille special nut locations on front crossmembers. Note that only one half of grille is shown as nut locations are symmetrical about the centre-line (Sec 30)

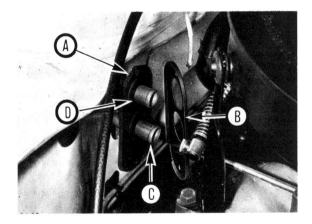

Fig. 12.31 Detach the heater hoses at their bulkhead connection (engine side) (Sec 31)

A   Foam gasket   C   Hot water intake
B   Cover plate   D   Hot water outlet

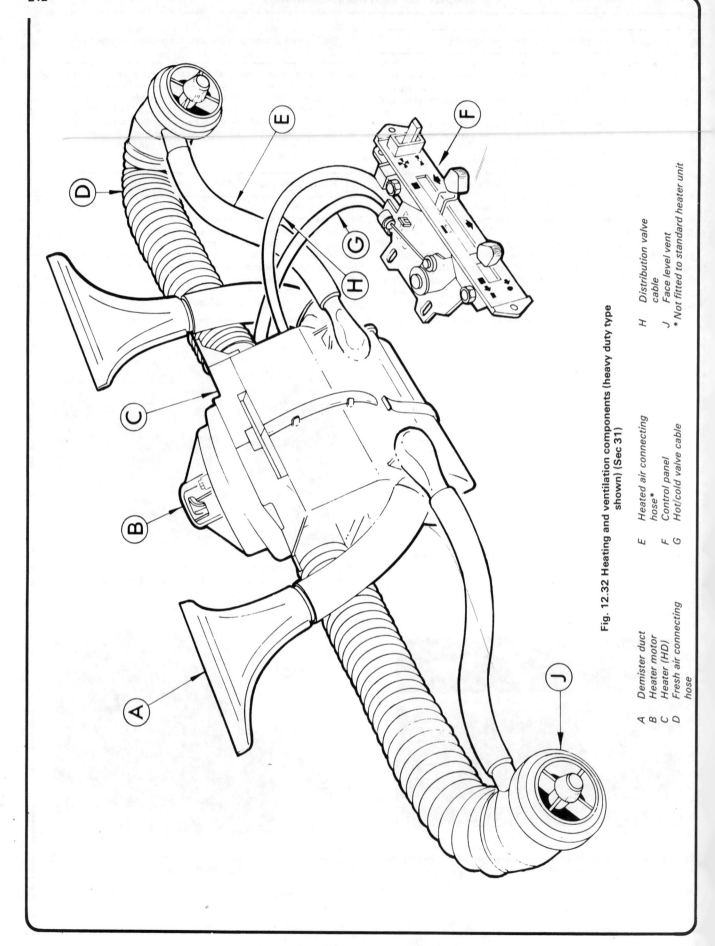

Fig. 12.32 Heating and ventilation components (heavy duty type shown) (Sec 31)

A   Demister duct
B   Heater motor
C   Heater (HD)
D   Fresh air connecting hose

E   Heated air connecting hose*
F   Control panel
G   Hot/cold valve cable

H   Distribution valve cable
J   Face level vent
* Not fitted to standard heater unit

cover panel and the two screws securing the lower edge (Fig. 12.33). Lower the panel sufficiently to gain access to the rear of the switch assemblies and disconnect the multiplugs. Continue lowering the panel clear of the working area.

6   Remove the trim clips securing the front passenger side parcel shelf to its support bracket on the cowl side trim panel, then undo the two bolts holding the shelf to the heater and lift the shelf away.

7   Unscrew the single screw securing the heater cover panel bracket and detach the bracket (Fig. 12.34).

8   Carefully pull the demister hoses and the face level vent hoses off their respective heater outlets.

9   Unscrew the two nuts securing the side demister duct to the cowl panel and detach the duct. **Note**: *Removing the duct provides access for the subsequent removal of the heater unit.*

10 Disconnect the leads to the heater, at their snap connectors.

11 Carefully disconnect the inner heater control cables from their slots on the two arms on the heater, then remove the clips on the heater body which hold the cables in place (Fig. 12.35). Tuck the cables out of harm's way.

12 Undo the four bolts holding the heater mechanism to the cowl top panel and remove the heater from its location via the passenger side of the vehicle, taking care not to spill any remaining coolant from the heater unit as it is withdrawn.

13 Refitting of the complete mechanism is a direct reversal of the above procedure. Set the heater controls as shown in Fig. 12.37

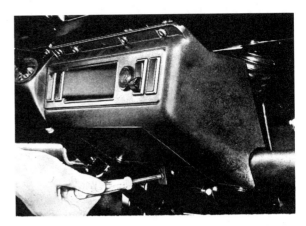

Fig. 12.33 Removing heater unit cover (Sec 31)

before connecting the control cables to the heater unit; the valves should be in the end position.

14 Remember to refill the cooling system with the heater control lever set to full on. Check for coolant leaks on completion.

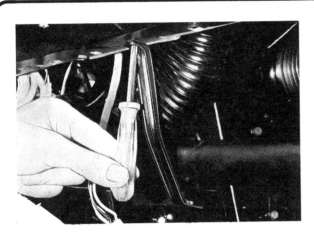

Fig. 12.34 Detach the cover bracket (Sec 31)

Fig. 12.35 Detach the leads and cables from the heater unit (cable clips arrowed) (Sec 31)

Fig. 12.36 Heater unit-to-cowl top panel bolts (Sec 31)

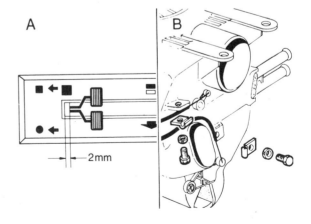

Fig. 12.37 Heater unit control cables – refitting (Sec 31)

A   *Position of control panel levers*

B   *Temperature and distribution valves in their end position*

This sequence of photographs deals with the repair of the dent and paintwork damage shown in this photo. The procedure will be similar for the repair of a hole. It should be noted that the procedures given here are simplified — more explicit instructions will be found in the text

In the case of a dent the first job — after removing surrounding trim — is to hammer out the dent where access is possible. This will minimise filling. Here, the large dent having been hammered out, the damaged area is being made slightly concave

Now all paint must be removed from the damaged area, by rubbing with coarse abrasive paper. Alternatively, a wire brush or abrasive pad can be used in a power drill. Where the repair area meets good paintwork, the edge of the paintwork should be 'feathered', using a finer grade of abrasive paper

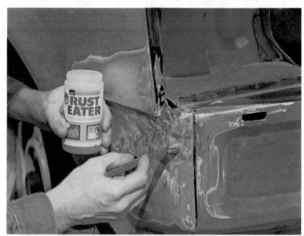

In the case of a hole caused by rusting, all damaged sheet-metal should be cut away before proceeding to this stage. Here, the damaged area is being treated with rust remover and inhibitor before being filled

Mix the body filler according to its manufacturer's instructions. In the case of corrosion damage, it will be necessary to block off any large holes before filling — this can be done with zinc gauze or aluminium tape. Make sure the area is absolutely clean before...

...applying the filler. Filler should be applied with a flexible applicator, as shown, for best results; the wooden spatula being used for confined areas. Apply thin layers of filler at 20-minute intervals, until the surface of the filler is slightly proud of the surrounding bodywork

Initial shaping can be done with a Surform plane or Dreadnought file. Then, using progressively finer grades of wet-and-dry paper, wrapped around a sanding block, and copious amounts of clean water, rub down the filler until really smooth and flat. Again, feather the edges of adjoining paintwork

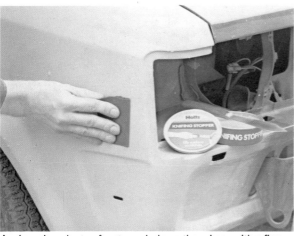

Again, using plenty of water, rub down the primer with a fine grade of wet-and-dry paper (400 grade is probably best) until it is really smooth and well blended into the surrounding paintwork. Any remaining imperfections can now be filled by carefully applied knifing stopper paste

The top coat can now be applied. When working out of doors, pick a dry, warm and wind-free day. Ensure surrounding areas are protected from over-spray. Agitate the aerosol thoroughly, then spray the centre of the repair area, working outwards with a circular motion. Apply the paint as several thin coats

The whole repair area can now be sprayed or brush-painted with primer. If spraying, ensure adjoining areas are protected from over-spray. Note that at least one inch of the surrounding sound paintwork should be coated with primer. Primer has a 'thick' consistency, so will fill small imperfections

When the stopper has hardened, rub down the repair area again before applying the final coat of primer. Before rubbing down this last coat of primer, ensure the repair area is blemish-free – use more stopper if necessary. To ensure that the surface of the primer is really smooth use some finishing compound

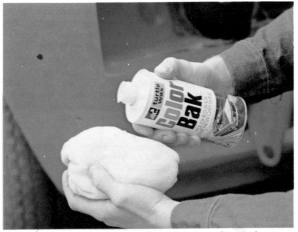

After a period of about two weeks, which the paint needs to harden fully, the surface of the repaired area can be 'cut' with a mild cutting compound prior to wax polishing. When carrying out bodywork repairs, remember that the quality of the finished job is proportional to the time and effort expended

Fig. 12.38 Bracket retaining clamp removal using circlip pliers
(Sec 32)

Fig. 12.39 Remove the heater motor resistance plug (Sec 32)

32 Heater unit – dismantling and reassembling

1   Remove the heater unit from the car, as given in Section 31.
2   Carefully pull free the foam ring, disconnect the plug and withdraw
the supply cables from the bracket mountings.
3   From within the motor housing, remove the two retaining clamps
using a pair of circlip pliers (Fig. 12.38).
4   The two halves of the heater housing can now be separated by
depressing the lugs and prising the assembly apart.
5   Carefully remove the heater motor blower and withdraw the
resistance plug from the casing (Fig. 12.39).
6   Slide the centre housing partition panel away and then carefully
withdraw the heater radiator matrix (Fig. 12.40).
7   Reassembly is a reversal of the dismantling procedure, but make
sure that the blower motor is correctly fitted to the locating lug (Fig.
12.41) and that the regulating flaps are free to move. After the first
dismantling, it is advisable to secure the two halves together with
additional spring clamps.

Fig. 12.40 Removing the partition panel (Sec 32)

33 Heater matrix – servicing

1   Having removed the heater matrix from the heat unit, (as
described in Section 32), flush the unit through with cold water. If it
is clogged, try reverse flushing it with a hose. If this fails to clear it, or
the matrix is damaged or badly corroded, exchange it for a
reconditioned unit. Do not be tempted to use chemical cleansers as
they will only loosen deposits which will in turn cause further clogging
of the fine cooling tubes. If the matrix leaks, do not attempt to solder
it as this work seldom proves satisfactory.
2   Reassembly is a reversal of removal, but when refitting the matrix
into the heater unit ensure that the gasket is fitted to the left-hand
housing side, locate the centre housing partition panel and fit the
blower motor resistance plug (see Fig. 12.39).

34 Heater controls – removal and refitting

1   Disconnect the battery and remove the heater cover panel (for
fuller details, refer to Section 31).
2   Carefully prise the heater control bezel out of its location in the
control aperture (Fig. 12.42).
3   Unscrew and remove the two screws securing the sides of the
control panel to the facia and the single screw securing the upper edge
(Fig. 12.43).
4   Pull the controls out of the control aperture and disconnect the
blower switch multi-plugs. Prise the cable clips off their locations and
disengage the cable loops from their respective levers (Fig. 12.44).
5   Reassembly is a reversal of the removal procedure, but refer to Fig.
12.37 and position the controls as shown before reconnecting the
control cables.

Fig. 12.41 Fit the blower motor with the bracket lug positioned a
shown (Sec 32)

35 Face level vent – removal and refitting

1   Using two suitably sized rods in the holes in the vent fixing rin
unscrew and remove the ring (Figs. 12.45 and 12.46).
2   From the rear of the facia, pull the face level vent stub from i
location and disconnect the vent hose(s).
3   Assemble the stub into its facia location, ensuring that the groo

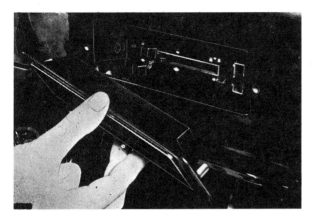

Fig. 12.42 Removing the heater control panel bezel (Sec 34)

Fig. 12.43 Location of screw securing upper edge of heater control panel (Sec 34)

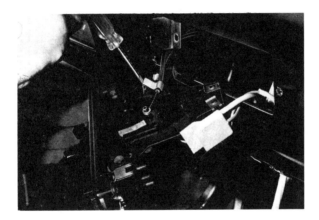

Fig. 12.44 Detach the cable clips from the control unit (Sec 34)

Fig. 12.45 Use suitable rods, as shown, to loosen the vent retaining ring (Sec 35)

Fig. 12.46 Removing the fixing ring (Sec 35)

in the stub aligns with the key in the facia cut-out. Secure the vent
with the fixing ring and reconnect the hose.

36 Demister nozzle (driver's side) – removal and refitting

1   Disconnect the battery earth lead.
2   Referring to the appropriate Sections in Chapter 10, detach and
withdraw the instrument panel cluster.
3   The demister nozzle can now be removed after unscrewing the
two nuts attaching it to the dash panel.
4   Refit in the reverse order to removal.

37 Centre console – removal and refitting

1   Remove the radio, as described in Chapter 10.
2   Remove the clock, as described in Chapter 10.
3   Unscrew the gear lever knob and knob locknut from the gearlever,
then unscrew the two screws from each side of the centre console and
lift the console off its tunnel mounting bracket.
4   Refitting the centre console is a direct reversal of the removal
procedure.

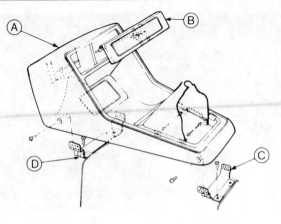

Fig. 12.47 Centre console assembly (Sec 37)

A   Centre console
B   Radio aperture cover
      plate

C   Tunnel mounted fixing
      brackets
D   Tunnel mounted fixing
      brackets

Conversion factors

Length (distance)
Inches (in)	X	25.4	= Millimetres (mm)	X	0.0394	= Inches (in)
Feet (ft)	X	0.305	= Metres (m)	X	3.281	= Feet (ft)
Miles	X	1.609	= Kilometres (km)	X	0.621	= Miles

Volume (capacity)
Cubic inches (cu in; in^3)	X	16.387	= Cubic centimetres (cc; cm^3)	X	0.061	= Cubic inches (cu in; in^3)
Imperial pints (Imp pt)	X	0.568	= Litres (l)	X	1.76	= Imperial pints (Imp pt)
Imperial quarts (Imp qt)	X	1.137	= Litres (l)	X	0.88	= Imperial quarts (Imp qt)
Imperial quarts (Imp qt)	X	1.201	= US quarts (US qt)	X	0.833	= Imperial quarts (Imp qt)
US quarts (US qt)	X	0.946	= Litres (l)	X	1.057	= US quarts (US qt)
Imperial gallons (Imp gal)	X	4.546	= Litres (l)	X	0.22	= Imperial gallons (Imp gal)
Imperial gallons (Imp gal)	X	1.201	= US gallons (US gal)	X	0.833	= Imperial gallons (Imp gal)
US gallons (US gal)	X	3.785	= Litres (l)	X	0.264	= US gallons (US gal)

Mass (weight)
Ounces (oz)	X	28.35	= Grams (g)	X	0.035	= Ounces (oz)
Pounds (lb)	X	0.454	= Kilograms (kg)	X	2.205	= Pounds (lb)

Force
Ounces-force (ozf; oz)	X	0.278	= Newtons (N)	X	3.6	= Ounces-force (ozf; oz)
Pounds-force (lbf; lb)	X	4.448	= Newtons (N)	X	0.225	= Pounds-force (lbf; lb)
Newtons (N)	X	0.1	= Kilograms-force (kgf; kg)	X	9.81	= Newtons (N)

Pressure
Pounds-force per square inch (psi; lbf/in^2; lb/in^2)	X	0.070	= Kilograms-force per square centimetre (kgf/cm^2; kg/cm^2)	X	14.223	= Pounds-force per square inch (psi; lbf/in^2; lb/in^2)
Pounds-force per square inch (psi; lbf/in^2; lb/in^2)	X	0.068	= Atmospheres (atm)	X	14.696	= Pounds-force per square inch (psi; lbf/in^2; lb/in^2)
Pounds-force per square inch (psi; lbf/in^2; lb/in^2)	X	0.069	= Bars	X	14.5	= Pounds-force per square inch (psi; lbf/in^2; lb/in^2)
Pounds-force per square inch (psi; lbf/in^2; lb/in^2)	X	6.895	= Kilopascals (kPa)	X	0.145	= Pounds-force per square inch (psi; lbf/in^2; lb/in^2)
Kilopascals (kPa)	X	0.01	= Kilograms-force per square centimetre (kgf/cm^2; kg/cm^2)	X	98.1	= Kilopascals (kPa)

Torque (moment of force)
Pounds-force inches (lbf in; lb in)	X	1.152	= Kilograms-force centimetre (kgf cm; kg cm)	X	0.868	= Pounds-force inches (lbf in; lb in)
Pounds-force inches (lbf in; lb in)	X	0.113	= Newton metres (Nm)	X	8.85	= Pounds-force inches (lbf in; lb in)
Pounds-force inches (lbf in; lb in)	X	0.083	= Pounds-force feet (lbf ft; lb ft)	X	12	= Pounds-force inches (lbf in; lb in)
Pounds-force feet (lbf ft; lb ft)	X	0.138	= Kilograms-force metres (kgf m; kg m)	X	7.233	= Pounds-force feet (lbf ft; lb ft)
Pounds-force feet (lbf ft; lb ft)	X	1.356	= Newton metres (Nm)	X	0.738	= Pounds-force feet (lbf ft; lb ft)
Newton metres (Nm)	X	0.102	= Kilograms-force metres (kgf m; kg m)	X	9.804	= Newton metres (Nm)

Power
Horsepower (hp)	X	745.7	= Watts (W)	X	0.0013	= Horsepower (hp)

Velocity (speed)
Miles per hour (miles/hr; mph)	X	1.609	= Kilometres per hour (km/hr; kph)	X	0.621	= Miles per hour (miles/hr; mph)

Fuel consumption*
Miles per gallon, Imperial (mpg)	X	0.354	= Kilometres per litre (km/l)	X	2.825	= Miles per gallon, Imperial (mpg)
Miles per gallon, US (mpg)	X	0.425	= Kilometres per litre (km/l)	X	2.352	= Miles per gallon, US (mpg)

Temperature
Degrees Fahrenheit = (°C x 1.8) + 32

Degrees Celsius (Degrees Centigrade; °C) = (°F - 32) x 0.56

*It is common practice to convert from miles per gallon (mpg) to litres/100 kilometres (l/100km), where mpg (Imperial) x l/100 km = 282 and mpg (US) x l/100 km = 235

Index

**Printed by
Haynes Publishing Group
Sparkford Yeovil Somerset
England**